INSIDE
HOLLYWOOD

60 YEARS OF GLOBE PHOTOS

PAUL NEWMAN AND JOANNE WOODWARD IN ISRAEL, *Leo Fuchs* 1959

INSIDE
HOLLYWOOD

60 YEARS OF GLOBE PHOTOS

COMPILED AND EDITED BY
RICHARD DeNEUT

KÖNEMANN

CONTENTS

INHALT

SOMMAIRE

PREFACE

I was raised just a block north of Hollywood Boulevard way back when there were clear blue skies and you felt that you could almost touch the mountains. I rode the streetcar to school and on weekends my best friend, Ilomay, and I would climb the Hollywood sign (the O's were my favorite).

My grandmother and I averaged about 8 movies a week – second-run double features – making sure we'd get in before the prices changed. My fantasy life centered around Betty Grable, Judy Garland and Mickey Rooney, Tyrone Power, Rita Hayworth and Jimmy Stewart.

CAROL BURNETT, *Sylvia Norris* 1965

When I got older, my very first summer job was ushering at Warner Brothers Theater at Hollywood and Wilcox. It was there I came in contact with real live movie stars when I showed Gregory Peck and Debbie Reynolds to their seats for the premiere of CAPTAIN HORATIO HORNBLOWER. It was also there that I got fired because I didn't want to seat a couple during the last five minutes of STRANGERS ON A TRAIN.

I loved the movies. I loved the movie magazines. My first serious crush was Peter Lawford. I cut out pictures of him and pasted them in a scrapbook. Leafing through PHOTOPLAY, for example, I could always count on tons of pictures of beautiful people doing all sorts of glamorous things: dining and dancing at the Trocadero and Ciro's, attending premieres at the Egyptian and Pantages theaters, frolicking on the beaches at Santa Monica and Malibu, even having hot dogs at a local drive-in. All the articles were positive. It was a beautiful and innocent time and I'm grateful to have grown up in it.

My dear friend Dick DeNeut (we went to UCLA together) has put together a magnificent picture book that brings back so many memories. The pictures are priceless and so are the stories behind the scenes. It's such fun to look at – time and time again.

EINLEITUNG

Ich wurde nur einen Block nördlich des Hollywood Boulevards groß, in einer Zeit, in der es noch klaren, blauen Himmel gab und du glaubtest, die Berge fast berühren zu können. Ich fuhr mit der Straßenbahn zur Schule und die Wochenenden verbrachten meine beste Freundin, Ilomay, und ich damit, auf den Hollywood-Buchstaben herumzuklettern (die Os waren meine Lieblingsbuchstaben).

Meine Großmutter und ich sahen uns im Durchschnitt acht Filme in der Woche an – Filme, die schon seit längerer Zeit liefen und von denen wir zwei für den Preis von einem sehen konnten. Meine Fantasie drehte sich um Betty Grable, Judy Garland, Mickey Rooney, Tyrone Power, Rita Hayworth und Jimmy Stewart.

Als ich älter wurde, hatte ich meinen ersten Sommerferienjob als Platzanweiserin im Warner-Brothers-Kino an der Ecke Hollywood und Wilcox. Dort kam ich mit realen Schauspielern in Berührung, als ich Gregory Peck und Debbie Reynolds bei der Premiere von DES KÖNIGS ADMIRAL (CAPTAIN HORATIO HORNBLOWER) zu ihren Sitzplätzen führte. Dort wurde ich allerdings auch gefeuert, weil ich ein Pärchen, für die letzten fünf Minuten von VERSCHWÖRUNG IM NORDEXPRESS (STRANGERS ON A TRAIN), nicht zu seinem Sitzplatz führen wollte.

Ich liebte die Filme. Ich liebte die Kinozeitschriften. Mein erster ernst zu nehmender Schwarm war Peter Lawford. Ich schnitt Bilder von ihm aus und klebte sie in ein Album. Beim Durchblättern von PHOTOPLAY konnte ich zum Beispiel immer damit rechnen, massenhaft Fotos von schönen Menschen in mondänen Situationen zu entdecken. Beim Dinieren und Tanzen im Trocadero oder im Ciro's, beim Besuch von Theaterpremieren im Egyptian und Pantages, beim Herumtollen an den Stränden von Santa Monica und Malibu und sogar beim Verzehr von Hotdogs in einem Imbiss in der Nachbarschaft. Alle Zeitschriftenartikel waren positiv. Es war eine schöne und unbeschwerte Zeit und ich bin dankbar dafür, in dieser Zeit groß geworden zu sein.

Mein lieber Freund Dick DeNeut (wir sind zusammen zur UCLA gegangen) hat ein hervorragendes Buch herausgebracht, das so viele Erinnerungen weckt. Die Fotos sind unbezahlbar, genauso wie die Geschichten, die sich hinter jedem dieser Fotos abgespielt haben. Es macht Spaß, sich das Buch wieder und wieder anzusehen.

PRÉFACE

J'ai grandi à un bloc au nord de Hollywood Boulevard, à l'époque lointaine où le ciel était bleu et où on avait presque l'impression de pouvoir toucher les montagnes. J'ai pris le tramway pour aller à l'école et me promener le week-end avec ma meilleure amie Ilomay, et j'ai escaladé le grand panneau Hollywood (dont je préférais la lettre O).

Ma grand-mère et moi allions voir près de 8 films par semaine – les séances de deux grands films en reprise – en veillant bien à entrer avant que le tarif ne change. Mon imaginaire tournait autour de Betty Grable, Judy Garland et Mickey Rooney, Tyrone Power, Rita Hayworth et Jimmy Stewart.

Plus tard, mon tout premier job d'été a été celui d'ouvreuse au Warner Brothers Theater à Hollywood et Wilcox. J'ai alors rencontré en chair et en os des vedettes du cinéma, comme cette fois où j'ai indiqué leurs places à Gregory Peck et Debbie Reynolds venus assister à la première de CAPITAINE SANS PEUR (CAPTAIN HORATIO HORNBLOWER). J'ai aussi été renvoyée parce que j'avais refusé de placer un couple pendant les cinq dernières minutes de L'INCONNU DU NORD-EXPRESS (STRANGERS ON A TRAIN).

J'aimais les films. J'adorais les magazines de cinéma.

Mon premier béguin sérieux fut pour Peter Lawford, dont je découpais les photos pour les coller dans un cahier. En feuilletant PHOTOPLAY, par exemple, je découvrais toujours des centaines de photos de gens superbes dans des occupations à mes yeux toutes plus prestigieuses les unes que les autres : dîner et danser au Trocadero et au Ciro's, assister à des premières aux cinémas Egyptian et Pantages, se promener sur les plages de Santa Monica et de Malibu, voire manger un hot-dog dans le drive-in local. Tous ces articles étaient positifs. C'était une époque innocente et heureuse, et je suis ravie de l'avoir vécue.

Mon cher ami Dick DeNeut (nous sommes allés ensemble à l'UCLA) a réalisé un magnifique recueil de photographies qui rappelle bien des souvenirs. Ces images sont aussi inestimables que les histoires qu'elles évoquent. C'est finalement très amusant de les voir et de les revoir.

The honorable CAROL BURNETT holds the award presented by her Alma Mater Hollywood High School.

CAROL BURNETT zeigt den Preis, den sie von ihrer Alma Mater Hollywood High School erhielt.

CAROL BURNETT tient dans les mains le prix qu'elle a obtenu à l'école Alma Mater d'Hollywood.

Carol Burnett

FOREWORD

Like a thousand and one others, when I was a teen I couldn't wait to get to Hollywood, inspired by the images I'd seen of the fabulous movie colony there – photographs of Humphrey Bogart and Lauren Bacall at Romanoffs, Clark Gable and Robert Stack out skeet shooting with their pals, Tony Curtis feeding wedding cake to Janet Leigh, Lana Turner dancing cheek to cheek with Turhan Bey, Barbara Stanwyck and Robert Taylor on the town and laughing uproariously at something Jack Benny had said. They all seemed to be having a lot more fun than I was having in Colfax, Washington (population then, as now: 2500). What I didn't know is that this wasn't just playtime for the Hollywood folks. They may have been dining, marrying, skeet shooting and laughing uproariously but they were also working, the helpful and willing subjects of a huge machine which helped supply their images, and those of their peers, to the hundreds of newspapers, magazines, and

ROBERT OSBORNE AND OLIVIA DeHAVILLAND, *Ralph Dominguez* 1974

other venues with an almost insatiable appetite for images of the glamour set. Everywhere the stars went, photographers went, many of them helping Globe Photos do what I don't think anyone has ever done so well or so successfully, before or since.

For nearly 60 years, Globe Photos has had photographers snapping photos of important Hollywood celebrities at work and play, all of them then available to publications around the world who might want, perhaps, a photo of Rita Hayworth in the 1940s or Marilyn Monroe in the 1950s or Paul Newman and Joanne Woodward in the 1960s, and on into the new millennium. Globe has always supplied an important service, becoming an indispensable one-stop station able to supply almost any photographic image that some editor might need.

Throughout most of those years, it was a pleasant two-way street. The stars and their publicists loved organizations like Globe Photos because through them they could get maximum coverage. It used to be a given that part of a star's year would include photos at home or at the studio for Globe. And Globe took great care of the stars, making sure they were posed in their best light, keeping only the photos which showed the star's best angles. That's the way magazine editors wanted them. That's the way the public preferred them. That's the way Globe delivered them.

VORWORT

Genau wie tausend andere konnte ich es als Teenager kaum erwarten, nach Hollywood zu fahren. Ich war inspiriert durch die Bilder, die ich von der berühmten Filmmetropole dort gesehen hatte - Fotos von Humphrey Bogart und Lauren Bacall bei Romanoffs, Clark Gable und Robert Stack beim Tontaubenschießen mit ihren Kumpeln, Tony Curtis wie er Janet Leigh mit Hochzeitskuchen füttert, Lana Turner eng umschlungen mit Turhan Bey, Barbara Stanwyck und Robert Taylor in der Stadt, lauthals über das lachend, was Jack Benny gerade gesagt hatte. Sie alle schienen viel mehr Spaß zu haben als ich in Colfax, Washington (Einwohner damals wie heute: 2500). Was ich nicht wusste, war, dass sich bei den Stars in Hollywood nicht immer nur alles um Spiel und Spaß drehte. Es mag schon sein, dass sie dinierten, heirateten, Tontauben schossen und lauthals lachten, aber sie arbeiteten auch hart. Sie waren die hilfreichen und willigen Objekte einer hiesigen Maschinerie, die ihnen wiederum dazu verhalf, ihr eigenes Image und das ihrer Kollegen an Hunderte von Zeitungen, Zeitschriften und andere Medien zu verkaufen, angetrieben durch einen fast unersättlichen Appetit auf Ruhm und Glanz. Wo Stars unterwegs waren, hielten sich auch Fotografen auf. Diese wiederum verhalfen Globe Photos dazu, das zu tun, was meiner Meinung nach bis heute noch niemand so gut oder erfolgreich getan hat, weder davor noch danach.

Seit fast 60 Jahren haben Fotografen für Globe Photos Bilder von wichtigen Hollywoodstars bei der Arbeit und in der Freizeit gemacht. Alle diese Fotos waren damit für Publikationen in der ganzen Welt verfügbar, die eventuell ein Foto von Rita Hayworth in den 40ern, von Marilyn Monroe in den 50ern oder von Paul Newman und Joanne Woodward in den 60ern und so weiter bis ins neue Jahrtausend, haben wollten. Globe hat schon immer einen wichtigen Dienst geleistet und ist zu einer unentbehrlichen Quelle geworden, die dazu in der Lage ist, je nach Bedarf nahezu jedes nur denkbare Foto an den Herausgeber zu liefern.

In den meisten dieser Jahre lebten die Stars und Publizisten friedlich miteinander. Sie mochten Organisationen wie Globe Photos, denn durch diese war eine maximale Berichterstattung garantiert. Es war selbstverständlich, dass die Stars für Fotos im Eigenheim oder im Filmstudio während des Jahres zur Verfügung standen. Und Globe kümmerte sich hervorragend um die Stars. Man war sehr darum bemüht, die Stars immer in ihrem besten Licht zu zeigen und nur die Fotos zu behalten, die sie von der besten Seite zeigten. So wollten die Herausgeber die Stars haben. So bevorzugte das Publikum sie. So lieferte Globe die Fotos.

Leider haben sich die Zeiten drastisch geändert. Das freundschaftliche Verhältnis zwischen den Stars und den Medien liegt Jahre zurück. Organisationen wie Globe Photos sind versehentlich in dieses Kreuzfeuer geraten. In der Regel sind Stars für keine Fotoreportage mehr zu haben, egal für welche Organisation. Zu viele von ihnen sind zu häufig Sensationsfotografen und Revolverblättern in die Falle gelaufen. Die einizgen Fotos, die Sie von einem aktuellen Star wie Tom Cruise oder Michelle Pfeiffer sehen können, werden entweder direkt bei den Dreharbeiten von einem Agenturfotografen oder von den Paparazzi bei der Premiere gemacht.

Man kann die Gründe dafür gut verstehen. Heutzutage kämpfen so viele Medien untereinander um die

AVANT-PROPOS

Lorsque j'étais adolescent, comme des milliers d'autres garçons ou filles de mon âge, je ne rêvais que d'aller à Hollywood découvrir la réalité des photographies de ce fabuleux monde du cinéma que je découvrais avec enthousiasme dans les magazines – Humphrey Bogart et Lauren Bacall au Romanoff's, Clark Gable et Robert Stack tirant du ball-trap avec leurs amis, Tony Curtis partageant son gâteau de mariage avec Janet Leigh, Lana Turner dansant joue contre joue avec Turhan Bey, Barbara Stanwyck et Robert Taylor se promenant en ville et riant à gorge déployée d'une plaisanterie lancée par Jack Benny … Ils avaient tous l'air de prendre du bon temps et de beaucoup plus s'amuser que moi, qui vivais à Colfax (État de Washington), une petite ville de 2 500 habitants. Ce que j'ignorais, c'est que tout n'était pas rose pour les locataires de Hollywood. Certes, ils allaient au restaurant, se mariaient, jouaient au ball-trap et riaient à gorge déployée ; mais, ouvriers efficaces et volontaires d'une énorme machine, ils devaient aussi travailler et offrir leur image, et celle de leurs pairs, à des centaines de journaux, de magazines et autres revues dont l'appétit pour les images de la « glamour-set » se révélait presque insatiable. Où qu'elles aillent, les stars retrouvaient des photographes.

Nombre de ces photographes ont permis à Globe Photos d'accomplir, en près de soixante ans, ce qu'aucune autre agence n'a sans doute jamais réalisé d'aussi belle manière ou avec autant de réussite. Leur magnifique travail – ces photos des grandes vedettes de Hollywood prises pendant leur travail ou au cours de leurs loisirs, qu'il s'agisse de Rita Hayworth en 1940, de Marilyn Monroe dans les années 1950, de Paul Newman et Joanne Woodward vers 1960, ou de n'importe quelle vedette plus contemporaine – était alors mis à disposition par Globe Photos à l'attention des publications du monde entier. Offrant un service essentiel, Globe est devenue au fil des ans une source documentaire quasi indispensable, capable de fournir pratiquement toute photographie dont aurait eu besoin un rédacteur.

L'entente était parfaitement cordiale pendant presque toutes ces années, chacun se renvoyant l'ascenseur lorsque nécessaire. Les stars et leurs agents aimaient les agences comme Globe Photos car c'est grâce à elles qu'elles pouvaient bénéficier d'une couverture médiatique maximum. Il était tacitement convenu avec Globe qu'une star devait se consacrer au moins une fois par an à des séances de photos chez elles ou dans les studios. Et Globe s'efforçait de prendre grand soin des stars, s'assurant notamment qu'elles posaient avec le meilleur éclairage et ne conservant que les photos où elles se présentaient sous leur meilleur angle. C'est ce que voulaient les rédacteurs des magazines ; c'est comme ça que le public les préférait ; c'est ce que Globe fournissait.

Hélas, les temps ont changé du tout au tout. Il y a bien des années maintenant que les relations sont rien moins qu'amicales entre les stars et les médias, quels qu'ils soient, et que des agences comme Globe Photos se trouvent prises entre deux feux. Les vedettes, trop souvent piégées par des photographes francs-tireurs et des publications en quête de sensationnel, n'acceptent plus de poser pour les agences. Les seules photos que vous pourrez voir de stars comme Tom Cruise ou Michelle Pfeiffer ont été soit prises lors d'un tournage par un photographe de plateau soit volées par un paparazzi lors d'un événement mondain quelconque.

Alas, times have changed – drastically. It's been years since relations have been friendly between stars and any of the media, and organizations like Globe Photos inadvertently got caught in some of that crossfire. Celebrities, as a rule, no longer do general photo layouts for any one organization. Too many have been stung too often by maverick photographers and sensation-seeking publications. The only photos you'll see of a current star like a Tom Cruise or a Michelle Pfeiffer are either taken on a film set by a company photographer or grabbed by the paparazzi as they pass by at a premiere.

Their reasons are understandable. Nowadays, with so much media competing for the public's eye and attention, even editors of quality magazines often plaster photos on their covers and across their pages which show a celeb at the worst possible advantage. That's reason enough to have had war declared.

It's also a reason Richard DeNeut has done us such an enormous favor by creating this book on the history of Globe Photos. It covers Globe as Globe covered Hollywood from 1942 to 2000, letting us have another and lasting look at some of those great photo sessions of the past when the stars and the press were friendly co-conspirators – the photographic visits to the star's homes, the weddings, the first shots of brand new babies and the visits to studio sets – all in a day's work at one time for the stars and for Globe.

For those of us watching on the sidelines, staring at those images on the pages of LIFE, LOOK, PHOTOPLAY, MODERN SCREEN, PARADE and the myriad of other outlets, it became an awesome magic carpet ride into another world. Soon that world would become more cynical with the media overstepping lines of privacy. All the rules of the publicity game would be drastically redefined.

The majority of the 1500 remarkable photographs in this treasury were taken in that earlier Hollywood era – when different rules of behavior were the norm. There was a time, unbelievable as it may seem now, when the entire Hollywood press corps knew that Spencer Tracy and Katharine Hepburn were not only pals but paramours, living side by side in cottages on the grounds of George Cukor's estate off the Sunset Strip. But no one said a word, no one sneaked a photo or even hinted at the possibility because Tracy was a married man, everyone liked him and his wife and Hepburn and, bottom line, there was a gentleman's agreement to not divulge the situation. Can you imagine today's press behaving in such a civilized manner?

I guarantee you're going to have a grand time traveling in this time machine. DeNeut takes us back to a world gone with the wind – full of remarkable, unforgettable images. It's a trip I suspect you'll want to take through the pages of this book many, many times.

ROBERT OSBORNE
Columnist-critic for The Hollywood Reporter
and host of Turner Classic Movies

Aufmerksamkeit der Öffentlichkeit, dass sogar Herausgeber qualitativ guter Zeitschriften häufig ihre Titelblätter und Seiten mit Fotos zupflastern, die die Stars von ihrer schlechtesten Seite zeigen. Das war Grund genug, um einen Krieg zu erklären.

Das ist auch ein Grund dafür, dass Richard DeNeut uns mit dem Verfassen dieses Buches über die Geschichte von Globe Photos einen großen Gefallen getan hat. Es umfasst Globe in dem Stil, in dem Globe Hollywood von 1942 bis 2000 dargestellt hat. Es erlaubt uns, einen erneuten und dauerhaften Blick auf manche dieser Fotoshootings in der Vergangenheit zu werfen, als Stars und Presse noch Verschworene waren. Für beide Gruppen waren Fotos im Eigenheim, von Hochzeiten oder von Neugeborenen genauso selbstverständlich wie Besuche im Filmstudio.

Diejenigen von uns, die alles vom Rand aus beobachteten, die sich die Fotos auf den Seiten von LIFE, LOOK, PHOTOPLAY, MODERN SCREEN, PARADE und der Myriade von anderen Zeitschriften anschauten, wurde es ein Flug auf dem fliegenden Teppich in eine andere Welt. Diese Welt wurde durch das Eindringen der Medien in Privatsphären immer zynischer. Alle Regeln des Spiels mit der Öffentlichkeit mussten drastisch neu definiert werden.

Die Mehrheit der 1500 bemerkenswerten Fotos in dieser Schatzkiste wurden in der früheren Hollywood-Ära gemacht, als noch andere Verhaltensregeln die Norm waren. So unglaublich es klingt, es gab eine Zeit, in der die gesamte Hollywood-Presse wusste, dass Spencer Tracy und Katharine Hepburn nicht nur Kameraden sondern Liebhaber waren, die Seite an Seite in Hütten lebten, welche sich auf George Cukors Grundbesitz unweit des Sunset Strip befanden. Allerdings verlor niemand ein Wort darüber, niemand versuchte, heimlich ein Foto zu ergattern oder setzte ein Gerücht in die Welt, da Tracy ein verheirateter Mann war, und jeder ihn, seine Frau und Hepburn mochten. Das Entscheidende war, dass es ein Gentleman's Agreement gab, die Wahrheit nicht preiszugeben. Können Sie sich vorstellen, dass die Presse sich heutzutage so zivilisiert benehmen könnte?

Ich garantiere Ihnen, dass Sie die Reise mit dieser Zeitmaschine genießen werden. DeNeut führt uns zurück in eine Zeit, die vom Winde verweht ist – voll von nennenswerten und unvergesslichen Bildern. Es ist eine Reise, von der ich annehme, dass Sie sie viele, viele Male durch die Seiten dieses Buches führen wird.

ROBERT OSBORNE
Kritiker für The Hollywood Reporter und Gastgeber der Turner Classic Movies

LANA TURNER AND TURHAN BEY, *Nate Cutler* 1945

On peut comprendre les stars lorsqu'on s'aperçoit que, à une époque où les médias se battent pour attirer l'attention et l'œil du public, même les rédactions des magazines de qualité utilisent pour leurs couvertures ou dans leurs articles des photos qui montrent les vedettes à leur pire avantage. Cette simple raison paraît suffisante pour leur déclarer la guerre.

C'est peut-être pour cette même raison – mais en cherchant à en annuler les effets négatifs – que Richard DeNeut a voulu créer ce livre et, tout comme Globe a couvert Hollywood de 1942 à 2000, nous faire la faveur d'un reportage sur son histoire. Il nous permet ainsi d'avoir un autre regard, durable, sur quelques-unes de ces grandes séances de photos du passé, celles d'une époque où les stars et la presse étaient encore d'amicaux conspirateurs et où il n'y avait rien d'extraordinaire, ni pour les stars ni pour les photographes de Globe, à faire un reportage photographique sur les demeures des vedettes, leurs mariages, leurs nouveau-nés ou les décors des studios.

Pour nous qui surveillons les coulisses en regardant les images diffusées dans les pages de LIFE, LOOK, PHOTOPLAY, MODERN SCREEN, PARADE et une myriade d'autres revues, ce retour en arrière est un superbe voyage dans un autre univers, très éloigné déjà de notre monde chaque jour davantage cynique où, les médias ayant reculé les limites de l'intimité et de la vie privée, toutes les règles de la publicité ont dû être dramatiquement redéfinies.

La majeure partie des 1500 remarquables photographies de cet ouvrage date en effet de ces années paisibles où régnaient à Hollywood d'autres comportements. Il y eut une époque où l'ensemble de la presse de Hollywood savait que Spencer Tracy et Katharine Hepburn n'étaient pas simplement amis mais amants, vivant l'un près de l'autre dans deux cottages sur la propriété de George Cukor, près de Sunset Strip. Parce que Tracy était un homme marié, que tout le monde l'aimait et appréciait sa femme et Katherine, personne ne vendit la mèche, personne ne tenta de voler une photo (ou ne l'envisagea) de leur intimité en raison d'une sorte de « gentleman's agreement » tacite. Pensez-vous que la presse actuelle puisse avoir un comportement aussi civilisé ?

Vous allez passer un moment fantastique dans cette machine à remonter le temps que nous propose Richard DeNeut. Toutes ces remarquables et inoubliables photographies nous renvoient dans un monde aujourd'hui englouti où vous replongerez, j'en suis persuadé, de nombreuses fois encore.

ROBERT OSBORNE
Éditorialiste et critique à The Hollywood Reporter
et animateur de Turner Classic Movies

NATE CUTLER WITH TROY DONAHUE AND SUZANNE PLESHETTE, 1962

DON ORNITZ WITH INGER STEVENS, MAY BRITT AND INGRID GOUDE, 1959

THE GLOBE STORY

On September 15, 1982, at the end of their work day, the staff of Globe Photos in New York was almost out of the building when news of the death of Princess Grace of Monaco reached them. To the man, they stepped back into the elevator and returned to the office. Phones were already ringing. Picture editors representing publications from all over the world needed material on the former movie queen and they knew that the Globe files would yield what they sought. Pulling photos from the files ran on into the night. By morning most of the requests had been filled. Within 24 hours, Globe Photos' pictures highlighting the life of Grace Kelly were being "put to bed" in magazines in the United States and many foreign countries.

The history of Globe Photos, one of the world's largest photo agencies, covers six decades, a period of time during which the use of editorial photography in magazines and newspapers and books and on television has grown and changed dramatically. These changes have been reflected in Globe's development as the agency changed its structure and its arena of specialty in order to meet new marketing conditions – in the words of one of its former owners, Charles Bloch, "to be where the action is."

When Globe was founded at the end of the 1930s, the agency represented only European photographers (Globe's roots were in a small "mom and pop" agency in Germany which crossed the Atlantic in the early days of the war in Europe) and the primary markets in the United States were Sunday rotogravure sections of newspapers. THE NEW YORK TIMES published such a picture magazine every Wednesday titled MID WEEK PICTORIAL. Although short-lived, it was the forerunner of the great picture magazines such as LIFE and LOOK.

DIE GLOBE STORY

Am Abend des 15. September 1982 hatte die Belegschaft von Globe Photos in New York die Agentur schon fast verlassen, als die Nachricht vom Tod der Prinzessin Grace von Monaco eintraf. Ausnahmslos nahmen alle gleich wieder den Aufzug und kehrten ins Büro zurück. Die Telefone klingelten bereits. Bildredakteure aus der ganzen Welt benötigten Material über die frühere Film-diva und wussten, dass sie in den Archiven von Globe fündig werden würden. Die Suche nach Fotos zog sich bis in die Nacht hinein. Am nächsten Morgen waren die meisten Anfragen schon beantwortet. Innerhalb von 24 Stunden wurden die Globe-Fotos, die das Leben von Grace Kelly porträtierten, in amerikanischen Zeitschriften und im Ausland veröffentlicht.

Die Geschichte von Globe Photos, einer der größten Fotoagenturen der Welt, umfasst sechs Jahrzehnte, einen Zeitraum, in dem die Anzahl der Fotos in Zeitschriften, Zeitungen, Büchern und Fernsehen stark zunahm und sich deren Verwendung drastisch verändert hat. Diese Veränderungen spiegeln sich in der Entwicklung von Globe wider, da sich die Agentur in ihrer Struktur und in ihren Schwerpunkten den neuen Bedingungen des Marktes angepasst hat, um – wie es einer der früheren Globe-Inhaber, Charles Bloch, ausdrückte – direkt „am Ball zu bleiben".

Als Globe Ende der 30er Jahre gegründet wurde, bestand die Agentur lediglich aus einer kleinen Anzahl von europäischen Fotografen (Globes Wurzeln liegen in einem Familienbetrieb in Deutschland, der in den ersten Tagen des Kriegs den Atlantik überquerte), und die ersten Märkte in den Vereinigten Staaten waren Rotationstief-druck-Beilagen der Sonntagszeitungen. THE NEW YORK TIMES veröffentlichte eine solche Beilage jeden

L'HISTOIRE DE GLOBE

Le soir du 15 septembre 1982, le personnel de Globe Photos à New York a déjà pratiquement quitté les bureaux lorsque tombe la nouvelle de la mort de la princesse Grace de Monaco. Tout le monde est aussitôt mobilisé. Les téléphones sonnent déjà dans tous les coins. Les directeurs photo de publications du monde entier ont besoin rapidement de documents sur cette ancienne reine du cinéma et savent que Globe possède évidemment ce qu'ils recherchent dans sa photothèque. On travaille toute la nuit pour sortir les photos demandées et, au matin, la plupart des demandes ont été satisfaites. Au bout de 24 heures, les photographies du fonds de Globe Photos retraçant la vie de Grace Kelly sont publiées dans les magazines des États-Unis et de plusieurs pays étrangers.

L'histoire de Globe Photos, l'une des plus importantes agences photographiques du monde, s'étale sur près de soixante ans, une période au cours de laquelle l'utilisation de la photographie rédactionnelle par les magazines, les journaux, les livres et la télévision a connu une évolution et une transformation radicales. Ces changements se sont traduits dans le développement de Globe par une modification des structures et du champ d'activité de l'agence afin de satisfaire à ces nouvelles conditions du marché et toujours « être là où il se passe quelque chose », comme aimait à le dire Charles Bloch, l'un de ses précédents directeurs.

Lors de sa fondation, à la fin des années 1930, Globe – à l'origine une petite agence « familiale » allemande qui franchit l'Atlantique dès les premiers jours de la Seconde Guerre mondiale – ne représentait que des photographes européens et n'eût pour principal marché aux États-Unis que la fourniture des illustrations pour les suppléments hebdomadaires des journaux. THE NEW YORK TIMES

When LIFE and LOOK started publication, a new era opened up for editorial photography. Photographs dominated the pages that had once been the exclusive turf of text. To help fill their pages LIFE put Globe Photos under contract for first refusal on its uncommitted pictures. The initial two-man staff of LOOK worked out of the Globe office until that magazine moved its Des Moines headquarters to New York City.

Throughout the 1940s human interest features were regularly published in both LIFE and LOOK and Globe became a prime supplier of this kind of story. Globe was represented in the very first issue of LIFE with a layout of a man-eating tiger devouring an Indian. Is it any wonder that Globe's specialty would soon be Hollywood?

During this period, the general interest magazines really came into vogue. These were the days of COLLIERS, THE AMERICAN MAGAZINE, CORONET, CLICK, PIC, FOCUS, EYE and SEE. The market for picture stories of all kinds reached a peak and no features were more in demand than those focusing on movie personalities and pretty young actresses (usually in bathing suits which was called "cheesecake" then; now, with no clothes at all, it's called "glamour".)

Immediately after the war – "to be where the action is" – Globe opened an office in Hollywood which was then the unquestioned movie capital of the world. Its small band of photographers (the first being Nate Cutler, a freelancer for a Los Angeles newspaper, who remained with the agency through five of its six decades) equipped with lighter cameras and faster film challenged the old-fashioned and slow Speed Graphic methods of the established Hollywood photographers. The agency soon became the quickest route for the studios to get features on their productions and stars into the national magazines, and into newspapers via the GLOBE HOLLYWOOD SYNDICATE, THE METROPOLITAN SUNDAY NEWSPAPER GROUP, which ran Globe's pictures on a regular basis, and THE TIMES-MIRROR SYNDICATE, which put out a

PAUL HENREID AND BETTE DAVIS, 1946

Mittwoch unter dem Titel MID WEEK PICTORIAL. Wenn auch nur von kurzer Lebensdauer, so war sie doch Vorreiter solch bedeutender Magazine wie LIFE und LOOK.

Als LIFE und LOOK mit ihren Veröffentlichungen begannen, fing eine neue Ära der Bildberichterstattung an. Fotografien dominierten nun die Seiten, die zuvor ausschließlich für Text bestimmt waren. Um seine Seiten zu füllen, schloss LIFE mit Globe Photos einen Vertrag ab, der LIFE ein Verkaufsrecht auf alle vertragsfrei entstandenen Globe-Fotos einräumte. Das anfängliche Zwei-Mann-Team von LOOK arbeitete in den Räumen der Globe-Agentur, bis die Zeitschrift ihre Niederlassung von Des Moines nach New York verlegte.

Während der 40er Jahre wurden regelmäßig publikumswirksame Artikel in LIFE und LOOK abgedruckt. Globe wurde der Hauptlieferant für diese Art von Reportagen. Im allerersten Heft von LIFE war Globe mit einer Geschichte über einen Menschen fressenden Tiger, der einen Inder verschlang, vertreten. Ist es da ein Wunder, dass Hollywood bald zur Spezialität von Globe wurde?

Während dieser Zeit waren illustrierte Zeitschriften, mit breiter Themenpalette, groß in Mode. Es war die Glanzzeit von COLLIERS, THE AMERICAN MAGAZINE, CORONET, CLICK, PIC, FOCUS, EYE und SEE. Der Markt für illustrierte Reportagen aller Art erreichte einen Höhepunkt. Artikel über Filmpersönlichkeiten und junge, schöne Filmschauspielerinnen (meistens in Badeanzügen, was man zu dieser Zeit als „Cheesecake" bezeichnete, heutzutage, ohne jegliche Bekleidung, heißt dies „Glamour") waren am beliebtesten. Unmittelbar nach dem Krieg eröffnete Globe eine Niederlassung in Hollywood, um weiter „am Ball zu bleiben". Hollywood war damals ohne Zweifel die Welt-Ïhauptstadt des Films. Die kleine Anzahl von Globe-Fotografen (der erste war Nate Cutler, ein Freiberufler, der bei einer Zeitung in Los Angeles arbeitete und der der Agentur für fünf der sechs Jahrzehnte ihres Bestehens erhalten blieb), ausgerüstet mit leichten Kameras und schnellem Film, forderte die alteingesessenen Hollywood-Fotografen mit deren langsamen und altmodischen „Speed-Graphic"-Methoden heraus. Die Agentur lieferte auf dem schnellsten Weg Material, mit dem die Studios Schlagzeilen über ihre Produktionen und Stars in die nationalen Zeitschriften und Zeitungen bringen konnten. Dies geschah über das GLOBE HOLLYWOOD SYNDICATE, die METROPOLITAN SUNDAY NEWSPAPER GROUP, die die Fotos von Globe regelmäßig veröffentlichte und das THE TIMES-MIRROR SYNDICATE, welches festvertraglich allein in den USA 178 Publikationen belieferte.

Die Zeit des Aufschwungs hatte begonnen.

Der Aufschwung von Globe fiel in die Zeit, in der Filmzeitschriften aufkamen. Es war die Glanzzeit von Publikationen wie PHOTOPLAY, MODERN SCREEN, MOVIELAND, SCREENLAND und der wichtigsten von allen, MOTION PICTURE, die 1910 zum ersten Mal erschien. Für Millionen von Amerikanern wurden diese so genannten „fan mags" zu einer wichtigen Beigabe zu den Filmen. Ihre Artikel verstärkten den Eindruck, den die Studios übermitteln wollten, wie himmlisch unser aller Leben doch sein könnte, wenn wir alle reich, berühmt, schön und beliebt wären.

Die Filmzeitschriften waren damals Liebeserklärungen an die Filmwelt und keine Sensationsblätter und

publiait ainsi tous les mercredis ce genre de magazine, le MID WEEK PICTORIAL, qui préfigurait, malgré sa brève existence, les grands magazines comme LIFE et LOOK.

La naissance de LIFE et LOOK inaugure la nouvelle ère de la photographie éditoriale, où l'image occupe l'espace autrefois exclusivement réservé au texte. Pour remplir ces pages, LIFE signe avec Globe Photos un contrat de préemption sur les images libres de droit. Deux membres du personnel de LOOK sont alors affectés en permanence dans les bureaux new-yorkais de Globe jusqu'à ce que le magazine transfère son siège social de Des Moines à New York.

Pendant les années 1940, LIFE et LOOK publient

WILLIAM CLAXTON WITH BOB BROOKMISYIER, 1957

régulièrement des articles généralistes et de faits divers, dont Globe devient naturellement le principal fournisseur des illustrations. Le tout premier exemplaire de LIFE présente ainsi un reportage photographique de l'agence montrant un tigre dévorant un Indien. Comment s'étonner ensuite que Hollywood devienne bientôt la spécialité de Globe ?

Cette période d'avant-guerre est marquée par la grande vogue des magazines d'informations générales : COLLIERS, THE AMERICAN MAGAZINE, CORONET, CLICK, PIC, FOCUS, EYE et SEE. Si le marché des histoires illustrées de tous genres atteint des sommets, rien n'est plus demandé que les reportages sur les personnalités du cinéma et les jeunes actrices, généralement photographiées en maillots de bain (un type de photographie de charme dit alors « cheesecake » par les Américains et qu'on qualifierait aujourd'hui de « glamour »).

Immédiatement après la guerre – toujours pour « être là où il se passe quelque chose » – Globe ouvre un bureau à Hollywood, alors la capitale incontestée du cinéma mondial. Équipés d'appareils photo plus légers et de pellicules plus sensibles, les photographes de la petite équipe de Globe – Nate Cutler en tête, un photographe freelance d'un journal de Los Angeles qui travailla cinquante ans pour l'agence – remettent en question les méthodes lentes

contracted weekly candid package of Globe photos to 178 newspapers in the U.S. alone.

The honeymoon was on.

Globe's move coincided with the rise of the movie magazines. It was the heyday of publications like PHOTOPLAY, MODERN SCREEN, MOVIELAND, SCREENLAND and the mother of them all, MOTION PICTURE, which began publishing in 1910. For millions of Americans the "fan mags," as they were called, were an important appendix to the movies. Their features enhanced the studio image of what heaven our lives could be if we were rich, famous, beautiful and loved.

Movie magazines then were love letters not expose sheets and they were wooed by the studios. Movie magazine readers were considered the opinion leaders among moviegoers and thus deemed able to make or break a film at the box office. And they could make stars – of a very durable kind. They were unparalleled in that particular area. They also dispensed Hollywood news of a sort, although on a monthly not daily basis. Shirley MacLaine once said, "Don't knock the fan magazines. They're what I read when I want to find out what's happening." Indeed, the fan books were becoming so much a part of the Hollywood scene that no one

ORLANDO WITH BRIGITTE BARDOT, 1964

blinked when PHOTOPLAY picked up the tab for the honeymoon of Tony Curtis and Janet Leigh which they ran as an exclusive feature.

On occasion, the studios, in essence, went into business with Globe. Layouts and portrait sittings that were produced within the studio system were often turned over (the trade term is "hand-out") to the agency because publicity departments were well aware, as odd as it may sound, that magazine editors preferred to buy photographs than run free hand-out material. Material

GENE TRINDL WITH NICK ADAMS, 1959

wurden von den Studios umworben. Ihre Leser wurden unter den Kinobesuchern als meinungsbildend angesehen; sie waren in der Lage, an den Kinokassen über den Erfolg oder Misserfolg des Films zu bestimmen. Zudem konnten diese Zeitschriften den Schauspielern zu dauerhaftem Ruhm verhelfen. Auf diesem Gebiet waren sie ohne Konkurrenz und dies, obwohl sie nicht täglich, sondern nur monatlich erschienen. Shirley MacLaine sagte einmal: „Macht euch nicht über Fanzeitschriften lustig. Aus ihnen erfahre ich alles, was passiert." Tatsächlich wurden die Fanmagazine ein Teil der Hollywoodszene, so dass es niemanden verwunderte, als PHOTOPLAY die Flitterwochen von Tony Curtis und Janet Leigh bezahlte, über die man dann in einer exklusiven Serie berichtete.

Manchmal benutzten die Studios in erster Linie Globe, um auf dem Markt präsent zu sein. Berichte und Porträtaufnahmen, die innerhalb der Studios produziert worden waren, wurden der Agentur übergeben (der Fachbegriff dafür ist „hand-out"). So seltsam es auch klingt, bevorzugten es die Zeitschriftenverleger für Fotografien zu bezahlen als kostenloses Material aus unzuverlässigen Quellen zu benutzen. Agentur-Material war exklusiv und der Verleger brauchte sich keine Sorgen zu machen, dass dieselben Fotos in einem Konkurrenzblatt erschienen. Die Studios waren am Gewinn nicht beteiligt. Sie profitierten aber davon, den begehrten Platz in den Zeitschriften zu besetzen und das war mehr wert als eine Beteiligung an den Erlösen.

Als das Fernsehen den Film in den USA als hauptsächliches Massenunterhaltungsmittel ersetzte, erweiterte dies das Aufgabengebiet von Globe. Landesweit erscheinende Zeitschriften und Fanmagazine ergriffen die Chance, über die endlose Reihe neuer Stars, die dieser neue „Riese" erschuf, zu berichten. So zwangen sie die Studios, mit den Fernsehgesellschaften in einen Wettbewerb um die Spalten in den Zeitschriften zu treten. Zu dieser Zeit hatten Filmstudios und Fernsehgesellschaften eine große Anzahl von Vertragsschauspielern. Den Stars und Starlets wurde vorgeschrieben, wo und wann sie fotografiert werden konnten. Man hoffte, dass diese Fotos in solch bekannten Publikationen wie SATURDAY EVENING POST, COSMOPOLITAN oder LADIES HOME JOURNAL erscheinen würden, aber falls nicht, waren die Fanmagazine auch noch gut genug.

Dies war eine zu leidenschaftliche Beziehung, als dass sie für immer hätte fortbestehen können.

1953 erschien dann CONFIDENTIAL.

Nichts war CONFIDENTIAL heilig. Es bewies der der Öffentlichkeit, dass man auch über Hollywoodstars

BILL KOBRIN WITH NATALIE WOOD, 1970

et démodées de Speed Graphic adoptées par les photographes « officiels » de Hollywood. Les Studios s'aperçoivent vite qu'il est plus rapide de passer par Globe pour voir publier des articles de reportage sur leurs productions et leurs stars dans les magazines nationaux mais aussi dans les journaux par l'intermédiaire du GLOBE HOLLYWOOD SYNDICATE, du METROPOLITAN SUNDAY NEWSPAPER GROUP, qui publie régulièrement les photos de Globe, et du TIMES-MIRROR SYNDICATE, qui diffuse chaque semaine les photos des reportages « sur le vif » de Globe à plus d'une centaine de journaux.

La lune de miel avec Hollywood s'annonce sous les meilleurs auspices.

L'évolution de Globe coïncide avec l'augmentation du nombre des magazines de cinéma et de leur public. C'est la grande époque de publications comme PHOTOPLAY, MODERN SCREEN, MOVIELAND, SCREENLAND, sans oublier leur modèle à tous, MOTION PICTURE, dont la première publication date de 1910. Ces « fan magazines » – ou fanzines – sont un complément essentiel aux films pour des millions

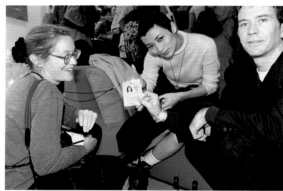

ANDREA RENAULT WITH BAI LING AND TIMOTHY HUTTON, 1999

d'Américains qui découvrent alors, dans ces images des Studios, que leur vie pourrait être un paradis s'ils étaient riches, célèbres, beaux et aimés.

Courtisées par les studios, les ciné-revues sont alors des lettres d'amour et non des chroniques à sensation. Les magazines de cinéma, dont les lecteurs sont considérés comme les leaders d'opinion du monde cinéphile, peuvent non seulement faire ou défaire un film au box office mais également – art dans lequel ils sont passés maîtres – faire d'un acteur une star. Dans une certaine mesure, ils donnent également des nouvelles de Hollywood à Hollywood, même si ce n'est que sur un rythme mensuel et non quotidien. Shirley MacLaine disait : « Ne

acquired from an agency was exclusive; the editors didn't have to worry that the same photos might appear in a rival magazine. The studios did not share in the sales; their profit was the coveted editorial space worth many times more than the actual rates.

Television's replacement of the movies as the dominant form of mass entertainment in the United States only added to Globe's arena. Nationals and fan mags embraced the forming giant's endless parade of new stars and forced the studios to compete with the networks for magazine space. It was a time when both had large stables of contract players and the stars and starlets were told when and where they would be photographed. Hopefully, what was shot would appear in one of the prestigious nationals, say SATURDAY EVENING POST or COSMOPLITAN or LADIES HOME JOURNAL but, if not, there were no objections to space in the fan mags.

It was a love affair too hot not to cool down.

STEVE PARKER WITH SHIRLEY MACLAINE, 1959

In 1953 along came CONFIDENTIAL

Nothing was sacred to CONFIDENTIAL. It gave lie to the belief that you couldn't get out a publication dealing with Hollywood personalities unless you played ball with the studios. Not only did they get a magazine out, they climbed to the biggest circulation in the country month after month, until 1957 when CONFIDENTIAL was hauled into court by the Attorney General's office in California on charges of publishing obscene and criminally libelous material.

Soon afterward, the magazine folded, but not without leaving its lasting imprint especially on the movie magazine trade. Actually, CONFIDENTIAL changed

berichten konnte, ohne dass man dem Studio gefällig war. Dieses Magazin wurde nicht nur veröffentlicht, sondern erreichte in den USA Monat für Monat immer höhere Auflagen, bis CONFIDENTIAL dann im Jahre 1957 vom Generalstaatsanwalt in Kalifornien angeklagt wurde, obszönes und verleumderisches Material zu publizieren.

Bald danach hörte die Zeitschrift auf zu existieren, nicht aber ohne einen bleibenden Einfluss hinterlassen zu haben. CONFIDENTIAL veränderte für immer den Inhalt aller amerikanischen Zeitschriften, einschließlich dem von READER'S DIGEST. Die Studios und die persönlichen PR-Agenten hielten jetzt jedoch die Fanmagazine auf Distanz.

Globe hatte nicht mit CONFIDENTIAL zusammengearbeitet. Einige wichtige Kolumnisten und Journalisten, denen nachgewiesen werden konnte, dass sie heimlich mit dem Skandalblatt Geschäfte gemacht hatten, wurden von einem auf den anderen Tag zu unerwünsch-

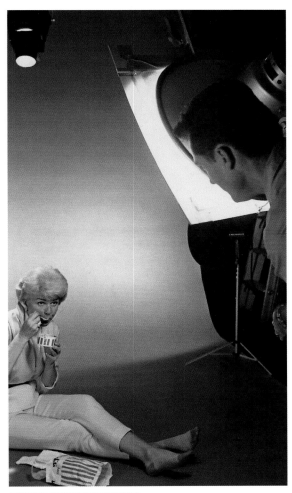
FRANK BEZ WITH DORIS DAY, 1961

ten Personen. Da Globe Angst hatte, seinen guten Ruf bei den Studios zu verlieren, wurden deren Fotos nicht mehr veröffentlicht. Trotzdem blieben die Fanmagazine ein wichtiger Markt für Globe. Auf der einen Seite war es der Agentur möglich, ihren Ruf als professionelle und faire Agentur aufrechtzuerhalten (hier war es natürlich hilfreich, dass sie die einzige ihrer Art war, die „celebrity agency" gab es damals noch nicht), auf der anderen Seite hatte der CONFIDENTIAL-Skandal bis zu einem gewissen Grad auch Auswirkungen auf Globe. Mit dem durch das Fernsehen beschleunigten Verfall der Studiomonopole verlor eine große Anzahl von Schauspielern den Schutz, den sie bis dahin durch die Studioverträge

WILLIAM READ WOODFIELD WITH JANE RUSSELL, 1957

critiquez pas les fanzines. C'est eux que je lis lorsque je veux savoir ce qui se passe ». Ces publications spécialisées font à ce point partie du décor de Hollywood que personne ne sourcille lorsque PHOTOPLAY assume les frais de la lune de miel de Tony Curtis et Janet Leigh, dont il assure le reportage exclusif.

Il est arrivé que les studios travaillent avec Globe. Les photos et les portraits qui pouvaient être réalisés dans le cadre des studios étaient ensuite souvent transmis (le terme commercial étant « distribué ») à l'agence car le département de publicité savait parfaitement, aussi étrange que cela paraisse, que les rédactions des magazines préféraient acheter ces photographies qu'en disposer gratuitement. En effet, le matériel acheté à une agence devenait une exclusivité et les rédacteurs n'avaient donc pas à craindre qu'une même photo soit publiée par un magazine concurrent. Les studios, quant à eux, ne touchaient rien sur la transaction ; en fait, l'espace éditorial dont ils bénéficiaient alors valait plusieurs fois ce qu'ils auraient dû autrement débourser en publicité.

Le remplacement du cinéma par la télévision comme principal mode de distraction de masse aux États-Unis ne fait qu'élargir le champ d'action de Globe. En élargissant leur emprise aux nouvelles stars du géant émergent, les journaux et les fanzines forcent les studios à entrer en compétition avec les chaînes de télévision pour occuper l'espace rédactionnel. À cette époque, ces deux médias disposent chacun d'une importante écurie d'acteurs sous contrat, auxquels les responsables de la communication disent quand et où ils peuvent être photographiés. Par chance, ces photographies sont généralement publiées dans l'un des prestigieux magazines nationaux, par exemple le SATURDAY EVENING POST, COSMOPOLITAN ou le LADIES HOME JOURNAL, voire, à défaut, dans les fanzines.

Mais cette passion était trop brûlante pour ne pas refroidir. Et en 1953 arrive CONFIDENTIAL

Rien n'est plus sacré pour CONFIDENTIAL. Ce magazine tabloïd réfute la croyance selon laquelle il est impossible de publier des articles concernant des personnalités de Hollywood si l'on ne s'est pas comporté honnêtement avec les Studios. CONFIDENTIAL est non seulement publié mais bat mois après mois des records de diffusion aux États-Unis. Ce succès prodigieux se prolonge jusqu'en 1957, l'année où CONFIDENTIAL est traîné en justice par le bureau du procureur de Californie pour publication d'obscénités et diffamation.

Le magazine disparaît peu de temps après non sans laisser une empreinte durable sur la forme et le contenu éditorial de tous les magazines de cinéma américains, y compris le READER'S DIGEST. En revanche, les Studios

forever the editorial content of all American magazines including THE READER'S DIGEST. But studios and personal press agents now held the fan mags at a distance.

CONFIDENTIAL had not been an outlet for Globe Photos. Several major columnists and writers who were found to have secretly contributed to the scandal rag were overnight deemed persona non grata and fearful of losing status with the studios, Globe did not lease their pictures to that publication. However, the fan mags were an important market for Globe and while the agency managed to keep its reputation for professionalism and fairness to the personalities intact (it helped, of course, that in those days the agency was the only game in town; the rise of the "celebrity agency" was still many years off), some of the movie mag curse rubbed off. With television hastening the demise of the studio monopolies, stables of players were cut loose from the protection of the majors and independent press agents sprang up to shield celebrities from scandal and innuendo. It became more difficult to set up shoots even for the nationals.

Magazines began to depend on a new tribe of photographer to fill their pages with the hot names that were not as available as they had been. It was the dawn of the paparazzi, so named for the packs of photographers that roamed the Via Veneto in Rome in search of catching celebrities off guard.

genossen hatten. Nach und nach übernahmen es jetzt unabhängige PR-Agenten, die Stars vor Skandalen und übler Nachrede zu schützen. Es wurde daher immer schwieriger, Fototermine selbst für landesweite Publikationen zu arrangieren.

Die Zeitschriften begannen, sich auf eine neue Art von Fotoreportern zu stützen, um ihre Seiten mit den berühmten Namen zu füllen, die nicht mehr so verfügbar wie bisher waren. Dies war die Geburtsstunde der „Paparazzi", benannt nach einer Horde von Fotografen, die auf der Via Veneto in Rom den Prominenten auflauerten, um diese in einem unbewachten Moment abzulichten.

Globe Photos wurde weiterhin so viel Zusammenarbeit gewährt, wie es überhaupt erlaubt war, da die Agentur schon seit langem ihren Wert als Königsweg zu den wichtigen Publikationen bewiesen hatte. Ihre Fotografen hatten traditionell einen guten Draht nicht nur zum Establishment von Hollywood, sondern auch zu den Stars. Aber um „am Ball zu bleiben", beschäftigte Globe nun neben den Hausfotografen auch noch so genannte „Straßenfotografen", die enthüllende Fotos machten. Deren Arbeit wurde ein regulärer Teil von Globes weit verbreitetem „Enthüllungs"-Dienst.

In den frühen 60er Jahren machten die Fanmagazine Platz für Jugendzeitschriften, die speziell für die neue Jugendkultur, die als Marketingobjekt entdeckt wurde,

et les attachés de presse tiennent désormais les fanzines à distance.

Globe Photos n'a pas travaillé avec CONFIDENTIAL, au contraire ! De peur de perdre la clientèle des Studios, l'agence refuse même de vendre leurs photos à ce magazine à scandales lorsqu'elle apprend que les éditorialistes et écrivains qui ont secrètement contribué au tabloïd ont été déclarés du jour au lendemain persona non grata à Hollywood. Les fanzines restent toutefois un important débouché pour Globe, qui parvient malgré tout à conserver intacte sa réputation de professionnalisme et d'honnêteté auprès des personnalités ; sa position était naturellement facilitée par le fait que l'agence était à l'époque encore la seule sur place (l'essor des « agences » pour célébrités est encore loin). Pendant que la télévision précipite la fin du monopole des studios, les acteurs larguent les amarres protectrices des grandes compagnies et se retrouvent liés aux attachés de presse indépendants qui se sont précipités pour leur éviter scandales et malveillances.

Puisqu'il devient de plus en plus difficile d'organiser des séances de photos, quand bien même elles seraient destinées à la grande presse, et que les stars ne sont plus aussi disponibles, les magazines se tournent alors vers une nouvelle race de photographes pour alimenter leurs articles : le paparazzi, nom désignant les nombreux reporters qui hantent la Via Veneto de Rome pour y surprendre les célébrités.

Globe Photos, agence désormais reconnue comme un

JOHNNIE RAY, 1954

JEANNE MOREAU, 1964

LARRY BARBIER JR. WITH AVA GARDNER, 1952

JOHN BARRETT WITH ROSIE O'DONNELL, 1996

BOB NOBLE WITH WILLIAM HOLDEN, 1952

Globe Photos continued to be accorded as much cooperation as was permitted because the agency had long since established its worth as a major route to the important publications and its photographers enjoyed a long-standing rapport not only with the Hollywood establishment but with its royalty. But – "to be where the action is" – candid street photographers were added to the stable of photographers Globe represented and their coverage became a regular part of Globe's weekly syndicated candid service.

In the early sixties the fan mags moved over and made room for the teeny bopper publications, magazines specifically designed for the bubble gum set, the new autonomous youth culture that had come into marketing power. With names like TEEN, TIGER BEAT and SEVENTEEN they focused on younger players, mostly rock and roll performers, who defined adolescence. Wildly popular for a few years, these magazines went into a slight decline in the 80s only to rise to even greater prominence in the 90s. There are now over 200 publications on the market aimed at 12-to-17-year-olds, adding names like YM, TWIST and JUMP. Established magazines such as PEOPLE and COSMOPOLITAN have spawned TEEN PEOPLE and COSMO GIRL. Teen publications may be the only other group of magazines able to make stars – only for a shorter duration than the movie magazines. Adolescence is nothing if not fickle.

Not that the fan mags disappeared. The general public's new interest in the inner workings of the entertainment industry that began in the seventies ballooned over the decade of the eighties and resulted in dozens of entertainment publications being founded on that interest (some have even lasted). PEOPLE, ROLLING STONE, TV GUIDE, PREMIERE, the cheeky ENTERTAINMENT WEEKLY, MOVIELINE, and US, which rose from the ashes of PHOTOPLAY, became the new fan magazines. And, with roots firmly planted in CONFIDENTIAL dirt, the supermarket tabloids became and have remained the circulation

geschaffen wurden. Mit Namen wie TEEN, TIGER BEAT und SEVENTEEN konzentrierten sich diese auf jüngere Künstler wie Rock-and-Roll-Musiker, die die Jugend prägten. Für ein paar Jahre waren diese Zeitschriften äußerst populär, sie verloren in den 80er Jahren dann etwas an Bedeutung, um in den 90er Jahren noch größere Popularität zu erlangen. Es gibt heute über 200 Publikationen auf dem Markt, die sich an die Gruppe der 12 bis 17 Jahre alten Jugendlichen wenden. Neu auf dem Markt sind Namen wie YM, TWIST und JUMP. Aus etablierten Magazinen wie PEOPLE und COSMOPOLITAN sind Ableger wie TEEN PEOPLE und COSMO GIRL hervorgegangen. Jugendmagazine sind vermutlich die einzige Zeitschriftenart, die ebenfalls Stars

RUSS MEYER WITH PAM GRIER, 1970

erschaffen kann, wenn auch für eine kürzere Zeitspanne als die Filmmagazine, was der Unbeständigkeit der Jugend zuzuschreiben ist.

Die Fanmagazine sind dennoch nicht verschwunden. Das Interesse der Leserschaft an den Interna der Unterhaltungsindustrie, das in den 70ern begann, wuchs sehr stark in den 80ern und fand seinen Ausdruck in der Gründung von Dutzenden von Unterhaltungszeitschriften, von denen sich einige sogar gehalten

intermédiaire essentiel avec les grandes publications et dont les photographes ont établi des rapports de longue date avec l'establishment d'Hollywood et ses commensaux, continue de bénéficier de toute la coopération possible de la part des Studios et des agents de Hollywood. Toutefois, afin de continuer à «être là où il se passe quelque chose», elle étend son écurie de photographes «en chambre» pour représenter également des photographes «de rue» et proposer leurs reportages dans son service hebdomadaire de diffusion.

Au début des années 1960, les fanzines périclitent et sont remplacés par les «teeny bopper books», des revues spécifiquement conçues à l'intention des adolescents de la génération du «bubble gum set», dont la nouvelle culture

IRV STEINBERG WITH LANA TURNER, 1968

est devenue une grande puissance commerciale. Portant des titres comme TEEN, TIGER BEAT et SEVENTEEN, ces magazines s'intéressent aux plus jeunes acteurs, et souvent à des artistes du rock-and-roll, auxquels peuvent s'identifier les adolescents. Furieusement populaires pendant plusieurs années, ces revues connaissent un léger déclin dans les années 1980 avant de retrouver une audience plus importante encore dans les années 1990. Aux États-Unis, il existe aujourd'hui plus de 200 publica-

champs. Even publications that once expressed only a passing interest in Hollywood goings-on, like THE NEW YORKER and VANITY FAIR, now feature regular coverage of not only the stars, but the moviemakers and studio bosses as well. And they all still need pictures.

These pictures now come from an increasing variety of sources. Most are still produced in-house and hand-outs continue to be planted from studio and network publicity departments. Some come from public relations companies and some from the stars themselves. And, as the vistas expand, some from foreign agencies who form partnerships with domestic agencies and exchange material.

The two main forces behind Globe Photos for sixty years have been the magazine editors that assigned and bought the pictures and the Hollywood press agents Globe had to work through to shoot those pictures. The two forces, in the early days such close collaborators, grew more at odds with one another as their goals changed, never more so than in the 80s and 90s. As magazines went from puff pieces to exposes, so did the Hollywood press agent change his stripes from pussycat to tiger. Over the years, the publicity men hired to spread the word went from being "flacks", those good ol' boys whose primary objective was to publicize their product and who could be counted upon to come up with wonderfully outrageous gimmicks to "get space", to publicists to PRs – public relations representatives (in HUSH, HUSH, SWEET CHARLOTTE, Bette Davis speaks a memorable line: "Public relations? Sounds dirty to

ADAM SCULL WITH MITZI GAYNOR, 1980

me!") – to Communication Counselors. Today some refer to themselves – with a straight face – as "Exposure Maintainance Experts" who strive and sometimes succeed to control every photograph as well as every word that appears on their clients.

But whatever they have been called, press agents, in the course of their quest to canonize the superficial, have always been small history makers.

As have the photographers represented by Globe

RON THAL WITH LYNN REDGRAVE, 1967

haben. Die neuen Fanmagazine trugen jetzt Namen wie PEOPLE, ROLLING STONE, TV GUIDE, PREMIERE, die freche ENTERTAINMENT WEEKLY, MOVIELINE und US, das aus PHOTOPLAY hervorging. Die amerikanische Regenbogenpresse, deren Wurzeln im CONFIDENTIAL-Skandalsumpf fest verankert sind, wurden und sind bis heute die „Auflagen-weltmeister". Sogar Magazine, wie THE NEW YORKER und VANITY FAIR, die sich früher nur vorübergehend für Hollywood interessiert hatten, publizieren regelmäßig Artikel nicht nur über die Stars, sondern auch über die Filmemacher und Studiobosse. Und dafür brauchen sie natürlich Fotos.

Diese Fotos kommen mittlerweile aus einer Vielzahl verschiedener Quellen. Die meisten werden immer noch selbst in Auftrag gegeben und "Hand-Outs" werden weiterhin vom Filmstudio und Publicity-Netzwerk geliefert. Einige werden von Public-Relations-Agenturen geliefert, andere von den Stars selbst. Mit der zunehmenden internationalen Vernetzung kommen Fotos auch von nicht-amerikanischen Agenturen, die Kooperationen mit amerikanischen Agenturen eingegangen sind und Material tauschen.

Die zwei Hauptantriebskräfte, die Globe Photos seit 60 Jahren angetrieben haben, sind auf der einen Seite die Magazinredakteure, die die Fotos in Auftrag gaben und kauften und auf der anderen Seite die PR-Agenten von Hollywood, mit denen Globe zusammenarbeiten musste, um diese Fotos machen zu können. Diese zwei Kräfte, die früher so eng miteinander verbunden waren, entfernten sich mehr und mehr voneinander in dem Maße, in dem sich ihre Ziele veränderten. Dies trifft besonders auf die 80er und 90er Jahre zu. In dem Maße, wie sich die Magazine von „Trivialblättern" zu „Sensationsblättern" entwickelten, wandelte sich auch der PR-Agent in Hollywood: Aus einem „Schmusekätzchen" wurde ein „Tiger". Über die Jahre hin veränderte sich die Rolle dieser Agenten, die angestellt waren, um Nachrichten zu verbreiten: von „Publicity-Leuten", die mit wunderbar verrückten Einfällen versuchten, ihr „Produkt" zu verkaufen, zunächst zu „Publizisten", dann zu

tions s'adressant aux 12-17 ans ; certaines sont nouvelles, comme YM, TWIST et JUMP, d'autres (TEEN PEOPLE et COSMO GIRL) sont des émanations de magazines reconnus tel que PEOPLE et COSMOPOLITAN. Ces revues sont peut-être les seuls magazines encore capables de promouvoir des stars même si, l'adolescence étant naturellement frivole, la gloire qu'elles en retirent est souvent plus éphémère.

Les fanzines n'ont pas disparu pour autant. Ravivé dans les années soixante-dix, l'intérêt du public pour le fonctionnement interne de l'industrie du divertissement déborde sur la décennie suivante et provoque la création de dizaines de nouveaux magazines (dont certains existent encore) : PEOPLE, ROLLING STONE, TV GUIDE, PREMIERE, les insolents ENTERTAINMENT WEEKLY et MOVIELINE, ainsi que US, né des cendres de PHOTOPLAY. À ceux-là s'ajoutent nombre de tabloïds distribués en supermarché qui suivent l'ornière de CONFIDENTIAL et deviennent rapidement les champions du tirage. Enfin, profitant du mouvement, des publications qui ne montraient autrefois qu'un intérêt de circonstance à l'égard d'Hollywood, comme THE NEW YORKER et VANITY FAIR, publient désormais régulièrement des reportages non seulement sur les stars mais également sur les réalisateurs et les patrons des Studios. Tous ont besoin d'images !

Ces photographies peuvent provenir d'un grand nombre de sources très différentes. La plupart sont réalisées par les correspondants de Globe ou reprennent les éléments transmis par les départements de publicité des studios et des chaînes de télévision. Certaines sont fournies par les agences de relations publiques des artistes, d'autres par les vedettes elles-mêmes. Et, avec l'élargissement de l'horizon médiatique, quelques-unes enfin sont l'œuvre de photographes d'agences étrangères associées à des agences américaines et avec lesquelles elles procèdent à des échanges.

Au cours de ses soixante années d'existence, Globe Photos s'est trouvé soumis à deux principaux pouvoirs, d'une part les rédactions des magazines, qui définissent les

JAY THOMPSON WITH PEGGY LEE, 1982

reportages et achètent les photographies, d'autre part les attachés de presse de Hollywood avec lesquels Globe doit traiter pour pouvoir exécuter son travail. Si elles ont étroitement collaboré dans les premiers temps, ces deux puissances se trouvent de plus en plus souvent dans des positions conflictuelles dues à l'antagonisme de leurs intérêts, notamment dans les années 1980-1990 lorsque les articles des magazines passent du ton publi-rédactionnel à celui du potin et de la révélation scandaleuse. En réaction,

ROBERT WAGNER, 1953

RICHARD HEWETT WITH DEBBIE REYNOLDS, 1967

LORENZO LAMAS, 1980

Photos. These men and women have made a record of movie and television personalities as they want to be seen, as the public wants to see them and even perhaps as they really are.

Here then is a body of work that at the time of its creation represented Hollywood as the editors of mass magazines believed their readers wanted to see it, photographs that represent Hollywood as it wanted to be seen by the world, photographs that represent Hollywood as less than objective photographers saw it. It is a remarkable body of work that seen after six decades transcends its original reason for being. Seen today, the photos make a deadly accurate record of the follies of the famous and an affectionately wicked comment on the Hollywood culture itself.

„Public Relations Vertretern", bis schließlich hin zu durchgestylten „Kommunikationsberatern". (Bette Davies sagt in HUSH, HUSH SWEET CHARLOTTE einen denkwürdigen Satz: „Public Relations? Das klingt ziemlich unanständig!"). Einige streben danach, jedes Foto und jedes Wort, dass über ihren Klienten veröffentlicht wird, zu kontrollieren. Manchmal gelingt ihnen dies sogar.

Wie auch immer sie genannt werden, so haben PR-Agenten in ihrer Bemühung, das Triviale zum Evangelium zu erheben, dennoch Geschichte im Kleinen geschrieben.

Das gilt auch für die Fotografen, die von Globe vertreten wurden. Diese Männer und Frauen haben Dokumente geschaffen, die die Film- und Fernsehpersönlichkeiten so zeigen, wie sie gesehen werden möchten, wie die Öffentlichkeit sie sehen möchte und wie sie vielleicht sogar wirklich sind.

In diesem Buch werden Fotos präsentiert, die Hollywood so darstellen, wie Magazinredakteure dachten, dass es die Leser sehen und erfahren wollten. Fotografien, die Hollywood so zeigen, wie es selbst von der Welt gesehen werden wollte und weniger wie objektive Fotografen es sahen. Es ist eine erstaunliche Kollektion, die, nachdem 60 Jahre vergangen sind, über ihre ursprüngliche Bedeutung herausgewachsen ist. Diese Fotos stellen ein peinlich genaues Dokument der Torheiten der Berühmtheiten dar und geben einen liebevollfrechen Kommentar zur Kultur von Hollywood ab.

d'animal de compagnie l'attaché de presse de Hollywood devient bête fauve. Tous ces publicitaires engagés autrefois pour répandre la bonne parole passent alors du statut « d'agent de presse » – de braves garçons proposant des combines magnifiquement extravagantes pour faire parler de leur produit (film ou acteur) – à celui d'agent de publicité puis de « public relations » – Bette Davis prononce à leur sujet cette phrase mémorable : « Relations publiques ? Cela fait sale ! » dans CHUT … CHUT … CHÈRE CHARLOTTE – et enfin de Conseillers en Communication. Aujourd'hui, certains se qualifient eux-mêmes, d'un ton très sérieux, d' « Experts en Conservation de l'Image » dont la mission est d'essayer de contrôler toutes les photographies et les légendes qui concernent leurs clients. Ils y réussissent parfois.

Il n'en demeure pas moins que, dans leur quête pour sanctifier le superficiel, les attachés de presse (ou quel que soit le titre qu'on leur a attribué) ont toujours été des inventeurs d'histoires … Tout comme d'ailleurs les photographes travaillant pour Globe Photos.

Ils ont tous, et chacun à leur manière, réalisé un portrait des personnalités du cinéma et de la télévision tel qu'elles voulaient être présentées, tel que le public voulait les voir et, peut-être même, tel qu'elles sont parfois en réalité.

Vous trouverez donc dans cet ouvrage un travail qui correspond à l'image d'Hollywood : les rédactions de la presse populaire pensaient satisfaire le désir de leurs lecteurs, des photographies qui montrent Hollywood telle qu'elle voulait être perçue par le monde, mais aussi des instantanés d'un Hollywood tel que le voyaient assez subjectivement les photographes. La raison d'être originale de ces photographies, qui couvrent soixante ans de l'histoire de Hollywood et, avec une précision terrible et affectueusement cruelle, témoignent des extravagances des stars et de la culture hollywoodienne, se trouve ici transcendée par le fait même de leur réunion.

AUDREY HEPBURN AND MEL FERRER, *Don Ornitz* 1958

THE HOME SITTING

In the 1920s and early 1930s Hollywood publicity mills emphasized disparities between stars and audience. Photographs released by the studios to magazines tended to distance the readership from the celebrity to preserve an aura of mystery and awe. By the 1940s, due in part to the rise in the number of general interest and fan magazines, studios and press began to emphasize quite a different publicity convention: Hollywood as just another American town, its citizens espousing the American virtues.

How better to perpetuate this conceit than showing the stars in their homes, with their families, miming normalcy? Elaborate at-home charades to depict the stars as just real folks. Editors and fans alike ate it up. Here were the icons of the movies doing everyday things everyone did – diapering a baby, frying an egg (though more often than not, this was simplified to boiling water for coffee), cleaning the pool, mending the roof, going to church.

Since most of these layouts were designed to appeal to the ladies under the hair dryers, married film couples were particular pets. Mr. and Mrs. Hollywood – how they live and what they do. There was, of course, the constant threat that by the time the layout hit the stands the pair might be giving interviews that began with "It was all a mistake." For this reason at least one Globe photographer always asked his married subjects to pose back to back in one setup – "for the split-up shot" – which was invariably run as a photograph torn in half.

Top photojournalists like Gene Trindl, Don Ornitz, Orlando, William Claxton, Larry Barbier Jr., John R. Hamilton, Dick Miller, Jack Stager, Tom Caffrey, Bill Kobrin, Dick Hewett, Bob Noble, Bill Greenslade, Rick Strauss, Bill Crespinel, Robert Landau and Jay Thompson recorded the real not reel life of the stars. But keep in mind it was a kind of improved reality, lit, framed and edited, and influenced by the photographer's own interpretation of a particular personality's image.

Photographer and celebrity alike were under pressure to produce an interesting layout, one that would hold the attention of the reader, so the rapport between them was of the utmost importance. The photographer was invading the inner sanctum of the home and, given the performer's natural distrust of the still camera, they had to learn to do what they could to curb anxieties. They made the subject comfortable. They gained his confidence by arranging each setup with the consideration that goes into preparing a movie scene and by keeping the poses within the star's own sense of image. Contrary to belief, performers like to be told what to do and the most successful sittings were the ones in which the photographer rather than the subject was the director.

But if all else failed, they weren't above making a bit of a fuss over the subject.

DAS PRIVATE HEIM

In den 20ern und frühen 30ern betonten die Publicity-mühlen Hollywoods die Unterschiede zwischen Stars und Publikum. Fotos, die von den Filmstudios an Zeitschriften herausgegeben wurden, tendierten dazu, die Leserschaft von den Stars zu distanzieren, um eine Aura von Geheimnis und Bewunderung zu bewahren. Zu Beginn der 40er Jahre begannen die Studios und Zeitschriften, eine einfache Form von Publicity zu betonen: Hollywood als eine einfache amerikanische Stadt mit Bürgern, die für amerikanische Tugenden stehen.

Wie hätte man dieses Image besser unterstreichen können als dadurch, dass man die Stars in ihrem eigenem Zuhause zeigte, wo sie mit ihren Familien ein normales Leben imitieren konnten? Gekünstelte Friede-Freude-Eierkuchen-Scharaden, um die Stars als ganz normale Leute darzustellen. Für Redakteure und Fans ein gefundenes Fressen! Hier waren also die Spielfilmikonen, und sie taten ganz alltägliche Dinge, die jeder tat – ein Baby wickeln, ein Spiegelei braten (auch wenn das häufiger durch Kaffeekochen vereinfacht wurde), den Swimming-pool säubern, das Dach ausbessern und in die Kirche gehen.

Da die meisten dieser Zeitschrift-Aufmacher die Damen unter den Trockenhauben ansprechen sollten, waren verheiratete Filmschauspieler ganz besonders interessant. Mr. und Mrs. Hollywood – wie sie leben und was sie tun. Natürlich war da immer die Gefahr, dass das Paar bis zur Herausgabe der Zeitschrift Interviews geben konnte, die mit „Es war alles ein Fehler" begannen. Aus diesem Grund verlangte beispielsweise ein Globe-Fotograf gleich immer noch ein „Trennungsfoto" seiner verheirateten Modelle – Rücken an Rücken, das dann ausnahmslos als ein in zwei Hälften zerrissenes Bild präsentiert wurde.

Top-Fotografen porträtierten das wirkliche und nicht das fiktive Leben der Stars. Aber man sollte bedenken, dass es eine Art verbesserte Realität war, beleuchtet, eingerahmt und editiert; beeinflusst durch die eigene Interpretation des Images einer bestimmten Persönlichkeit durch den Fotografen.

Fotograf und Stars standen gleicherweise unter dem Druck, ein interessantes Layout zu erstellen, eines, das die Aufmerksamkeit der Leser fesselte. Deshalb war ihre Beziehung zueinander sehr wichtig. Der Fotograf drang in die innerste Sphäre des Schauspielers ein und musste lernen, mit dessen natürlicher Angst vor dem Festbild umzugehen, um diese dann unter Kontrolle bringen zu können. Es wurde ein angenehmes Gesprächsthema gewählt. Das Vertrauen des Schauspielers wurde gewonnen, indem jede Kameraeinstellung an die Vorbereitung einer Filmszene angeglichen wurde, dadurch hatte der Schauspieler die Gelegenheit, die vorgeschlagenen Posen seinem eigenen Imageempfinden anzupassen. Im Gegensatz zu dem, was die allgemeine Öffentlichkeit glaubt, mögen Schauspieler es, Anweisungen zu bekommen, und die besten Sitzungen waren diejenigen, in denen anstelle des Modells der Fotograf als Regisseur fungierte.

Und wenn alles nichts nützte, waren sie sich nicht zu schade, etwas Wirbel um die Person zu machen.

DANS L'INTIMITÉ

Dès les années 1920 et le début des années 1930, les publicitaires de Hollywood ont cherché à accentuer la disparité entre les vedettes et le public. Les photographies fournies par les studios aux magazines s'efforçaient ainsi de distancier le lecteur de la star pour lui conserver une certaine aura de mystère et de respect. Dans les années 1940, en revanche, avec la multiplication des magazines et des revues cinéphiles, les studios et la presse s'engagèrent sur une voie totalement différente en présentant Hollywood comme une ville américaine ordinaire, dont les citoyens épousaient les idéaux et reflétaient les vertus de l'Amérique.

Comment mieux perpétuer cette image autrement qu'en montrant les stars chez elles, singeant une vie de famille normale dans une suite de charades compliquées où le public découvrait ces vedettes iconiques du cinéma accomplir comme n'importe qui leurs tâches quotidiennes : langer le bébé, cuire un œuf (on se contentait plus souvent de les voir faire chauffer de l'eau pour le café), nettoyer la piscine, réparer le toit ou aller à l'église. Les rédacteurs des publications et les admirateurs acceptaient en bloc la légende.

Afin de mieux séduire et enflammer l'imagination de Mme Toutlemonde lorsqu'elle lisait ces revues chez le coiffeur, les couples d'acteurs mariés — comment vivent et que font de leurs journées M. et Mme Hollywood — devinrent la cible privilégiée de ce genre de reportage angélique. Comme il subsistait toutefois le risque que le même couple ait déjà accordé un interview commençant par quelque chose comme « C'était une erreur ! » au moment où le magazine sortait en kiosque, un des photographes de Globe demandait toujours à ses sujets mariés de poser dos à dos – « la prise du divorce », invariablement publiée ensuite, le cas échéant, sous l'apparence d'une photographie déchirée.

Les meilleurs photographes de Globe deviennent les témoins de la vie réelle – et non plus fictive – des stars, il ne s'agit encore toutefois que de refléter une réalité améliorée, mise en scène et construite, influencée en outre par l'interprétation personnelle qu'a le photographe de l'image de la vedette dont il fait le portrait.

Le photographe et la star étant tous deux contraints de fournir une composition susceptible d'intéresser le lecteur, et de maintenir son attention, la qualité de leurs rapports était de la plus grande importance. Invité à pénétrer dans le sanctuaire intime de l'acteur, le photographe devait tout d'abord s'efforcer de maîtriser l'anxiété de la vedette, par nature méfiante envers la photographie. Il lui fallait mettre son sujet à l'aise et gagner sa confiance en préparant chaque scène avec le même soin que pour un plan de cinéma et lui proposer des poses en correspondance avec l'image que voulait offrir la star. Contrairement à ce que l'on pourrait croire, les acteurs aiment généralement qu'on leur dise quoi faire, et les poses les plus réussies furent celles pour lesquelles c'est le photographe et non son sujet qui en dirigeait la mise en scène.

Mais si rien ne se passait comme prévu, ni le photographe ni la star ne dédaignaient en faire toute une autre histoire.

CARY GRANT, *Eschave* 1968

JACK BENNY AND MARY LIVINGSTON, *Gerald Smith* 1958

HUMPHREY BOGART AND LAUREN BACALL, *Paul Bailey* 1956

GARY AND ROCKY COOPER, *Nate Cutler* 1958

ROCK HUDSON, *Dick Miller* 1958

PAUL NEWMAN AND JOANNE WOODWARD, *Larry Barbier Jr.* 1959

RITA MORENO, *Russ Meyer* 1957

JANE FONDA, *Jack Stager* 1960

INGER STEVENS, *Don Ornitz* 1959

ANDY WILLIAMS, *Bill Kobrin* 1963

CLORIS LEACHMAN, *Lynn McAfee* 1987

RICKY MARTIN, *Cesar Villoria* 1999

DIANE KEATON, *Bernard Nagler* 1968

PENNY MARSHALL AND ROB REINER, *Bob Noble* 1978

LOUIS JOURDAN, *Larry Barbier Jr.* 1958

TIMOTHY HUTTON, *J. Parti* 1979

GLORIA SWANSON, *Nelson Tiffany* 1953

JUDY GARLAND, *Jay Thompson* 1976

<< NATALIE WOOD AND ROBERT WAGNER, *Larry Barbier Jr.* 1958

LESLIE CARON, *Beauchamp* 1953

JOAN COLLINS, *Larry Barbier Jr.* 1959

RITA HAYWORTH, *Eric Skipsey* 1965

EARTHA KITT, *Don Ornitz* 1957

BUSTER KEATON, *John R. Hamilton* 1965

GEORGE BURNS AND GRACIE ALLEN, *Herb Ball* 1958

DANNY KAYE AND SYLVIA FINE, *Curt Gunther* 1961

JAMES FOX, *Orlando* 1966

VALERIE HARPER, *Gene Trindl* 1972

VINCENT PRICE, *Bill Kobrin* 1970

ANN SOTHERN, *Larry Barbier Jr.* 1950

MERLE OBERON, *Larry Barbier Jr.* 1950

JACQUELINE BISSET, *Omnia* 1976

LIZA MINNELLI, *Tom Caffrey* 1968

GENE AND JEANNE KELLY, *Richard Hewett* 1967

ALICE FAYE, *Roy Cummings* 1948

HARRISON FORD, *Jim Evans* 1992

HARRISON FORD, *Jay Thompson* 1967

Two portraits of an actor: HARRISON FORD, when he was just starting out, in his one-room Hollywood apartment. It would be several years of small TV roles and almost a change of career to carpentry before Ford would hit it big with the STAR WARS and INDIANA JONES blockbusters. And Harrison Ford, top box-office star, on his land in Jackson Hole, Wyoming.

THE WAY THEY WERE: TOM CRUISE was sharing digs at the beach with another fledgling actor, Emilio Estevez, when this was shot. • Looking more like Gidget than Gilda, RITA HAYWORTH in the backyard of her bachelor girl quarters in Santa Monica. • Heiress to a legendary theatrical name, DREW BARRYMORE celebrates her famous relatives (John, Ethel and Lionel Barrymore) being honored with their likenesses on a US postage stamp. • LEONARDO DI CAPRIO advertises the TV series he debuted on a few years before he skyrocketed to stardom.

Zwei Porträts eines Schauspielers: HARRISON FORD, am Beginn seiner Karriere in seinem Einzimmer-Apartment in Hollywood. Es dauerte noch einige Jahre, bevor Ford durch die Kinohits STAR WARS und INDIANA JONES ganz groß raus kam; Jahre, in denen er kleinere Fernsehrollen annahm und beinahe von Schauspieler zum Schreiner geworden wäre. Und Harrison Ford, oberster Kassen-schlager-Star, auf seinem Grundbesitz in Jackson Hole, Wyoming.

SO WIE SIE WAREN: TOM CRUISE und Emilio Estevez, einem Neuling in der Filmbranche, waren zu der Zeit damit beschäftigt, untereinander Seitenhiebe auszuteilen, als dieses Foto gemacht wurde. • Mehr Gidget als Gilda ähnelnd, RITA HAYWORTH im Hinterhof ihrer Junggesellinnenwohnung in Santa Monica. • Als Erbin eines theatralischen Namens feiert DREW BARRYMORE ihre berühmte Verwandtschaft (John, Ethel und Lionel Barrymore), die mit der Abbildung auf einer amerikanischen Briefmarke geehrt wurden. • LEONARDO DI CAPRIO wirbt für die Fernsehserie, in der er, ein paar Jahre bevor er mit einem Schlag berühmt wurde, debütierte.

TOM CRUISE, *Bob Villard* 1982

RITA HAYWORTH, *Nate Cutler* 1944

DREW BARRYMORE, *Ralph Dominguez*

LEONARDO DI CAPRIO, *Bob Villard* 1988

Deux portraits d'un acteur : HARRISON FORD, à ses tout débuts, dans son studio de Hollywood. Ce n'est qu'après plusieurs années de petits rôles à la télévision et une reconversion momentanée dans la menuiserie que Ford obtiendra finalement la popularité grâce au succès de STAR WARS et d'INDIANA JONES. Et Harrison Ford, devenu vedette au box-office, sur ses terres à Jackson Hole (Wyoming).

SOUVENIRS : TOM CRUISE partageait un appartement, sur la plage, avec Emilio Estevez, un autre acteur débutant. • Évoquant plus Gidget que Gilda, RITA HAYWORTH dans la salle de jeux de la résidence de jeunes filles où elle vivait à Santa Monica. • Descendante d'une légendaire lignée de comédiens, DREW BARRYMORE admire ses illustres parents (John, Ethel et Lionel Barrymore), qu'honore un timbre américain à leur effigie. • LEONARDO DI CAPRIO fait la publicité de la série télé dans laquelle il débuta quelques années avant de devenir une star.

SHARON GLESS, *Bob Noble* 1979

ALAN AND ARLENE ALDA, *John R. Hamilton* 1974

JIM NABORS WITH MOTHER MAVIS, *Gene Trindl* 1968

ALEXIS SMITH AND CRAIG STEVENS, *Globe Archive* 1957

KIM NOVAK AND PYEWACKET, *Larry Barbier Jr.* 1958

BARBARA RUSH AND HER PET LORIS, *Larry Barbier Jr.* 1958

CLARK AND SYLVIA GABLE, *Nate Cutle* 1955

RICKY SCHRODER, *Dennis Barna* 1979

JANE RUSSELL, *Dick Miller* 1954

SIDNEY POITIER, *Ron Thal* 1964

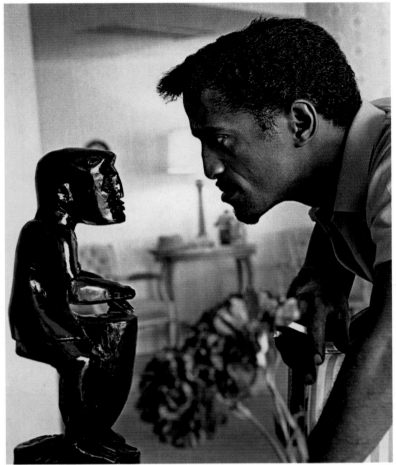

SAMMY DAVIS JR., *Bob East* 1959

JOHNNY MATHIS, *Larry Barbier Jr.* 1959

SIDNEY POITIER in his office the morning after he won the Oscar for LILIES OF THE FIELD. • SAMMY DAVIS JR. studies familiar features of an ebony head carved by a friend. • JOHNNY MATHIS welcomes the photographer to his manager's house which was his home.

SIDNEY POITIER in seinem Büro am Morgen, nachdem er den Oscar für LILIEN AUF DEM FELDE (LILIES OF THE FIELD) gewonnen hatte. • SAMMY DAVIS JR. untersucht familiäre Züge an einer Skulptur, die ein Freund aus Ebenholz geschnitzt hatte. • JOHNNY MATHIS heißt den Fotografen im Hause seines Managers willkommen, wo er gleichzeitig wohnte.

SIDNEY POITIER le lendemain de la soirée où il remporta l'Oscar pour LE LYS DES CHAMPS (LILIES OF THE FIELD). • SAMMY DAVIS JR. reconnaît des traits familiers sur une tête d'ébène sculptée par un de ses amis. • JOHNNY MATHIS accueille le photographe dans la maison de son agent où il réside alors.

ED WYNN, *Dick Miller* 1958

SAL MINEO, *Irv Steinberg* 1956

ED WYNN collected his reviews from vaudeville and burlesque through movies and television in 54 scrapbooks. • SAL MINEO kept his reviews and clippings on a bulletin board in the kitchen of his family home in New York. • Singing idol of the Roaring 20s, RUDY VALLEE collected autographs and Christmas cards from celebrity friends.

ED WYNN sammelte seine Kritiken zu Varietés, Filmen und Fernsehen in 54 Alben. • SAL MINEO hängte seine Kritiken und Zeitungsausschnitte auf einem schwarzen Brett in der Küche seines Familienhauses in New York auf. • Sängeridol der Goldenen Zwanziger, RUDY VALLEE, sammelte die Autogramme und Weihnachstkarten von berühmten Freunden.

ED WYNN conservait dans 54 albums les critiques des comédies dans lesquelles il avait joué au cinéma et à la télévision. • SAL MINEO affichait les critiques et les coupures de presse le concernant sur un mur de la cuisine de sa maison familiale à New York. • Idole de la chanson des années 1920, RUDY VALLEE a collectionné tous les autographes et les cartes de Noël de ses amis vedettes.

RUDY VALLEE, *Orlando* 1967

<< BETTE DAVIS, *Jay Thompson* 1963

GLENN FORD AND ELEANOR POWELL, *Nate Cutler* 1952

DAVID AND ELLIE JANSSEN, *Larry Barbier Jr.* 1958

GLENN FORD and wife ELEANOR POWELL were actually packing for a trip to South America when Eleanor jokingly asked Glenn to find room for a few books. • DAVID and ELLIE JANSSEN had just returned from their honeymoon when this was shot. Ellie is burning David's "little black book." • JESSICA TANDY and HUME CRONYN shared a personal and professional union for half a century. A few minutes late for the photo session, Cronyn brought his bride a bouquet. • IDA LUPINO and HOWARD DUFF, costars on and off the screen, share morning coffee on their sun porch. After a long career as a dramatic actress, Ida became one of Hollywood's first women directors. Duff came to films from radio where he was the voice of detective Sam Spade. • SUSAN HAYWARD and her husband Floyd Eaton Chalkey map out plans for a pool house on their estate in Carrolltown, Georgia – the pool being a man-made lake. The Oscar-winning actress moved to her husband's native Georgia after their marriage in 1957. • PIER ANGELI helps twin sister MARISA PAVAN prepare her wedding trousseau.

GLENN FORD und Frau ELEANOR POWELL waren wirklich dabei, für eine Reise nach Südamerika zu packen, als Eleanor Glenn zum Spaß darum bat, Platz für ein paar Bücher zu machen. • DAVID und ELLIE JANSSEN waren gerade aus ihren Flitterwochen zurückgekehrt, als dieses Foto von den beiden gemacht wurde. Ellie ist damit beschäftigt, Davids „kleines schwarzes Buch" zu verbrennen. • JESSICA TANDY und HUME CRONYN verband ein halbes Jahrhundert lang eine private und berufliche Beziehung. Cronyn, der ein paar Minuten zu spät zum Fotoshooting kam, brachte seiner Braut einen Strauß Blumen. • IDA LUPINO und HOWARD DUFF waren sowohl auf als auch hinter der Leinwand Hauptdarsteller. Hier genißen sie gemeinsam auf ihrer sonnigen Terrasse einen Kaffee. Nach einer langen Karriere als Theaterschauspielerin wurde Ida zu einer von Hollywoods ersten weiblichen Film-regisseurinnen. Duff lieh lange Zeit dem Detektiv Sam Spade seine Stimme im Radio, bevor er zum Fernsehen kam. • SUSAN HAYWARD und ihr Ehemann Floyd Eaton Chalkey arbeiten die Pläne für einen Pool auf ihrem Anwesen in Carrolltown, Georgia, aus. Der Pool war ein künstlich angelegter See. Die Schauspielerin, die einen Oscar gewonnen hatte, zog nach ihrer Hochzeit im Jahre 1957 nach Georgia, in den Heimatstaat ihres Ehemannes. • PIER ANGELI hilft ihrer Zwillingsschwester MARISA PAVAN bei der Vorbereitung ihrer Aussteuer.

GLENN FORD avait presque terminé sa valise pour partir en Amérique du Sud lorsque son épouse ELEANOR POWELL lui a demandé de trouver un peu de place dans sa valise pour y mettre quelques livres. • Tout juste de retour de leur lune de miel, ELLIE JANSSEN fait brûler le « petit carnet » de son mari DAVID. • JESSICA TANDY et HUME CRONYN vécurent et jouèrent ensemble pendant près d'un demi-siècle. Hume offre un bouquet à son épouse pour excuser son retard de quelques minutes lors de cette séance photos. • IDA LUPINO et HOWARD DUFF, partenaires à la ville et à l'écran, prennent le petit-déjeuner sur leur véranda. Ida devint l'une des premières réalisatrices de Hollywood après avoir mené une longue carrière d'actrice dramatique. Duff fut la voix du détective Sam Spade à la radio avant de faire du cinéma. • SUSAN HAYWARD et son mari Floyd Eaton Chalkey surveillent de près la construction de la « pool-house » près du lac artificiel de leur propriété de Carrolltown (Georgie). L'actrice, primée aux Oscars, s'installa dans la Georgie natale de son mari après leur mariage en 1957. • PIER ANGELI participe à la préparation du trousseau de mariage de sa sœur jumelle MARISA PAVAN.

JESSICA TANDY AND HUME CRONYN, *John Barrett* 1990

IDA LUPINO AND HOWARD DUFF, *Gene Trindl* 1967

SUSAN HAYWARD AND FLOYD EATON CHALKEY, *Bill Wilson* 1958

PIER ANGELI AND MARISA PAVAN, *Rick Strauss* 1959

MAUREEN O'HARA AND BRONWYN FITZSIMMONS, *Don Ornitz* 1963

ELIZABETH MONTGOMERY AND GIG YOUNG, *Larry Barbier Jr.* 1958

MARTHA HYER, *Larry Barbier Jr.* 1956

ANNE ARCHER AND TERRY JASTROW, *Steve Fritz* 1982

ANGIE DICKINSON, *Bill Kobrin* 1964

RICHARD BROOKS AND JEAN SIMMONS, *Don Ornitz* 1962

JACK NICHOLSON, *Vera Anderson* 1982

RICHARD BROOKS and JEAN SIMMONS shared a 17-year marriage during which time he directed her in two of her most successful films, ELMER GANTRY and THE HAPPY ENDING. • JACK NICHOLSON lights up in his Hollywood hills home. • ROBERT BLAKE dreamed of portraying John Garfield on film. • PETER O'TOOLE plays the schwam, a medieval flute. • JACK ALBERTSON and the hats he wore during his 45 years in show business. • THE CARPENTERS' two million-selling record hits bought this Downey home. • In her Rome apartment, SOPHIA LOREN displays her various awards including the Oscar on the top shelf. • LEVAR BURTON'S favorite form of relaxation is playing percussion instruments.

RICHARD BROOKS und JEAN SIMMONS waren 17 Jahre verheiratet, in denen er die Regie zu zwei ihrer erfolgreichsten Filme führte, ELMER GANTRY und HAPPY-END FÜR EINE EHE. • JACK NICHOLSON zündet sich in seinem Haus in Hollywood eine Zigarette an. • ROBERT BLAKE träumte davon, John Garfield in einem Film zu porträtieren. • PETER O'TOOLE spielt eine mittelalterliche Flöte. • JACK ALBERTSON und die Hüte, die er während seiner 45 Jahre im Showgeschäft trug. • Die zwei millionenfach verkauften Hits der CARPENTERS trugen zum Erwerb dieses Hauses in Downey, Kalifornien, bei. • In ihrem Apartment in Rom stellt SOPHIA LOREN ihre zahlreichen Auszeichnungen zur Schau, inklusive des Oscars auf dem obersten Regal. • LEVAR BURTONS entspannt sich am liebsten beim Spielen von Schlaginstrumenten.

RICHARD BROOKS et JEAN SIMMONS sont restés mariés 17 années, au cours desquelles il l'a dirigée dans deux de ses films les plus réussis, ELMER GANTRY et THE HAPPY ENDING. • JACK NICHOLSON dans sa maison, située dans les collines de Hollywood. • ROBERT BLAKE rêvait de faire le portrait de John Garfield au cinéma. • PETER O'TOOLE joue du schwam, une flûte médiévale. • JACK ALBERTSON et sa collection des chapeaux qu'il a portés en 45 ans de show business. • La vente de deux millions de disques a permis aux CARPENTERS d'acheter cette maison de Downey. • Posant dans son appartement de Rome, SOPHIA LOREN présente les différentes récompenses qu'elle a obtenues, dont un Oscar sur l'étagère du haut. • LEVAR BURTON se détend en jouant des percussions.

ROBERT BLAKE, *Gene Trindl* 1976

PETER O'TOOLE, *Pictorial Press* 1961

JACK ALBERTSON, *Renie Mendez* 1975

RICHARD AND KAREN CARPENTER, *Robert Trendler* 1971

SOPHIA LOREN, *Omnia* 1962

LEVAR BURTON AND WINTER CHATMAN, *John R. Hamilton* 1977

SUSAN SARANDON, *Barbara Zitwer* 1980

MARSHA MASON, *Robert Touchstone* 1981

DEBRA WINGER, *Orlando* 1973

MARGOT KIDDER, *Orlando* 1968

ANNE BANCROFT, *Don Ornitz* 1965

LASSIE, *Bill Kobrin* 1965

LASSIE, arguably the most famous animal in films and TV, poses in front of his portrait in the home of owner and trainer Rudd Weatherwax. This Lassie is the grandson of the star of the movie LASSIE COME HOME. The original Lassie was contracted to be a stand-in for the pedigreed female already signed as the star but it became apparent that Weatherwax's collie was far superior and the roles were switched. Since then, through numerous LASSIE sequels and the long-running TV series, the role of the female collie has been played by a male. • GOLDIE HAWN, still a bachelor girl, has early morning coffee before reporting for work on the Rowan and Martin TV show LAUGH-IN. • Dancer JULIET PROWSE combines relaxation with exercise. • ANN MILLER, at home with Jasmine and Cinderella at the Mayflower Hotel in New York during the Broadway run of SUGAR BABIES.

LASSIE, das wohl berühmteste Tier aus Film und Fernsehen, posiert vor seinem Porträt im Haus seines Besitzers und Trainers Rudd Weatherwax. Dieser Lassie ist der Enkel des Hundes, der in HEIMWEH (LASSIE COME HOME) der Filmstar war. Ursprünglich war er für das reinrassige Weibchen, das bereits als Star unter Vertrag stand, als Double verpflichtet worden. Allerdings wurde bald klar, dass der Collie von Weatherwax der Hündin weitaus überlegen war und so wurden die Rollen vertauscht. Seitdem wurde die Rolle der weiblichen Lassie sowohl in zahlreichen LASSIE-Folgen als auch in der lang laufenden Fernsehserie von einem Rüden gespielt. • GOLDIE HAWN, immer noch Junggesellin, trinkt am frühen Morgen Kaffee, bevor sie sich für die Fernsehshow LAUGH-IN von Rowan und Martin zur Arbeit meldet. • Tänzerin JULIET PROWSE kombiniert Entspannung mit Gymnastik. • ANN MILLER, mit Jasmine und Cinderella im Mayflower Hotel in New York, während der Broadway-Aufführung von SUGAR BABIES.

LASSIE, sans aucun doute l'animal le plus célèbre du cinéma et de la télévision, pose devant son portrait dans la maison de son propriétaire et entraîneur Rudd Weatherwax. Cette Lassie est le petit-fils de la vedette du film LA FIDÈLE LASSIE (LASSIE COME HOME), qui devait être la doublure de la chienne de race déjà engagée comme vedette. Il devint toutefois rapidement évident que le colley de Weatherwax était de bien loin supérieur à la vedette, et leurs rôles furent inversés. Depuis lors, dans toutes les nombreuses suites de LASSIE et la longue série télé, le rôle du colley femelle a toujours été tenu par un chien mâle. • GOLDIE HAWN, alors célibataire, prend son petit-déjeuner avant de partir travailler dans le show télé de Rowan et Martin, LAUGH-IN. • La danseuse JULIET PROWSE se détend en faisant ses exercices. • ANN MILLER prend ses aises avec Jasmine et Cinderella au Mayflower Hotel de New York lors du lancement de SUGAR BABIES à Broadway.

JULIET PROWSE, *Don Ornitz* 1960

GOLDIE HAWN, *Bill Bridges* 1968

ANN MILLER, *Judie Burstein* 1989

FRANK SINATRA AND KIRK DOUGLAS, *Peter Douglas* 1974

When KIRK DOUGLAS invited his Palm Springs neighbor FRANK SINATRA to help celebrate his and wife Anne's anniversary, Sinatra insisted upon making the meal. Spaghetti, of course – his mother's recipe. • JOAN CRAWFORD carves the ham she didn't bake for CLARK GABLE. • CARROLL BAKER and husband JACK GARFEIN study a script during dinner. • MARIO LANZA and wife Betty sample a roast. • RON HOWARD and bride Cheryl share kitchen chores.

Als KIRK DOUGLAS seinen Nachbarn in Palm Springs, FRANK SINATRA, zu sich nach Hause einlud, um den Hochzeitstag von sich und seiner Frau Anne zu feiern, bestand Sinatra darauf, das Abendessen zuzubereiten. Spaghetti natürlich – nach dem Rezept seiner Mutter. • JOAN CRAWFORD schneidet den Schinken auf, den sie nicht für CLARK GABLE gebacken hatte. • CARROLL BAKER und Ehemann JACK GARFEIN besprechen beim Abendessen ein Skript. • MARIO LANZA und Frau Betty probieren ein Stück Braten. • RON HOWARD und Braut Cheryl teilen sich die Küchenpflichten.

Lorsque KIRK DOUGLAS invita FRANK SINATRA, son voisin de Palm Springs, pour célébrer son anniversaire et celui de sa femme Anne, Frank insista pour préparer le déjeuner. Des spaghetti, évidemment, suivant la recette de sa mère. • JOAN CRAWFORD découpe un jambon qu'elle n'avait pas préparé pour CLARK GABLE. • CARROLL BAKER et son mari JACK GARFEIN étudient un script tout en dînant. • MARIO LANZA et sa femme Betty goûtent à leur rôti. • RON HOWARD et son épouse Cheryl partagent les joies ménagères.

JOAN CRAWFORD AND CLARK GABLE, *Nate Cutler* 1944

CARROLL BAKER AND JACK GARFEIN, *Doris Nieh* 1961

MARIO AND BETTY LANZA, *Globe Archive* 1952

RON AND CHERYL HOWARD, *Bob Noble* 1976

ELIZABETH TAYLOR AND NICK GRIPPO, *Robert Landau* 1982

PAT AND ELOISE O'BRIEN, *Lou Friedman* 1976

SAMMY DAVIS JR., *Robert Stein* 1981

FRED MACMURRAY AND JUNE HAVER, *Larry Barbier Jr.* 1961

ANTHONY PERKINS, *Don Ornitz* 1960

GENE AND INA MAE AUTRY, *Globe Archive* 1960

GERTRUDE BERG, *Bill Kobrin* 1962

MICHAEL LANDON, *Larry Barbier Jr.* 1960

DICK AND TOMMY SMOTHERS, *Jay Thompson* 1974

HERVE VILLECHAIZE, *Steve Schatzberg* 1980

GEORGE CLOONEY, *Lynn McAfee* 1986

All the furnishings in 3'10" HERVE VILLECHAIZE'S San Fernando Valley ranch are normal size so he uses a stool to check his pot of chili. • A young GEORGE CLOONEY gives a peek into a typical bachelor's refrigerator.

Alle Möbel im Hause des ca. 1,20 Meter großen HERVE VILLE-CHAIZE, der im San Fernando Valley lebt, sind normal groß. Des-halb benötigt er einen Stuhl, um nach dem Chili auf dem Herd zu schauen. • Ein junger GEORGE CLOONEY schaut in den für einen Junggesellen typisch aussehenden Kühlschrank.

HERVE VILLECHAIZE (env. 1,20 m) doit utiliser un escabeau pour surveiller la cuisson de son chili car tout le mobilier de son ranch, situé dans la vallée de San Fernando, est de dimension normale. • GEORGE CLOONEY jeune présente un réfrigérateur typique de célibataire.

ROBERT REDFORD built his dream house near Provo, Utah, on 40 acres of land he discovered while skiing in the national forest area. • CLARK GABLE digs an irrigation ditch on his 22-acre ranch in the San Fernando Valley. • RONALD REAGAN installs a TV antenna at Yearling Row, his 305-acre ranch in the Santa Monica mountains. • Horticulturist RAYMOND BURR took pride in orchid breeding, had five greenhouses full of them on his estate. • E.G. MARSHALL chops firewood on his upstate New York estate.

ROBERT REDFORD baute sein Traumhaus in der Nähe von Provo, Utah, auf einem 40 Morgen großen Land, das er während des Skifahrens in der Gegend eines Naturschutzgebietes entdeckt hatte. • CLARK GABLE gräbt einen Bewässerungskanal auf seiner 22 Morgen großen Ranch im San Fernando Valley. • RONALD REAGAN installiert eine Fernsehantenne in der Nähe von Yearling Row, seiner 305 Morgen großen Ranch in den Bergen von Santa Monica. • Hobbygärtner RAYMOND BURR war stolz auf seine Orchideenzüchtung und besaß auf seinem Landgut fünf Gewächshäuser voller Orchideen. • E.G. MARSHALL hackt auf seinem Grundstück im Norden des Staates New York Feuerholz.

ROBERT REDFORD a fait construire la maison de ses rêves près de Provo (Utah) sur un terrain de 20 hectares qu'il a découvert en skiant dans la forêt nationale. • CLARK GABLE creuse un canal d'irrigation sur son ranch de 11 hectares, situé dans la vallée de San Fernando. • RONALD REAGAN installe une antenne de télévision à Yearling Row, son ranch de 150 hectares, édifié dans les montagnes de Santa Monica. • RAYMOND BURR, passionné d'horticulture, est fier des orchidées qu'il cultive dans les cinq serres de son domaine. • E.G. MARSHALL joue au bûcheron dans sa propriété du nord de l'État de New York.

ROBERT REDFORD, *William Claxton* 1965

CLARK GABLE, *Nate Cutler* 1947

RONALD REAGAN, *Dick Miller* 1958

RAYMOND BURR, *Gene Trindl* 1965

E.G. MARSHALL, *Stuart Smith* 1962

JAMES COBURN, *William Claxton* 1965

SHIRLEY MACLAINE, *Larry Barbier Jr.* 1954

DAVID SOUL AND FAMILY, *Bill Greenslade* 1975

MARTHA RAYE, *Jack Stager* 1954

CAROL BURNETT IN CENTRAL PARK, *Jay Thompson* 1959 >>

DICK VAN DYKE, *Richard Hewett* 1967

LOUIS AND LUCILLE ARMSTRONG, *Paul Slade* 1960

DELLA REESE, *Bob Noble* 1976

RICHARD GERE, *John R. Hamilton* 1978

DICK VAN DYKE and sons Barry and Chris, daughters Stacey and Carrie Beth in a family jam session. • LOUIS ARMSTRONG plays for wife Lucille at their home in Queens. • DELLA REESE at her piano. • RICHARD GERE in his first Hollywood apartment. • TUESDAY WELD washes her brand new car. • LEE MAJORS in his bedroom. • ANTHONY PERKINS in his New York apartment. • JANE SEYMOUR on her patio.

DICK VAN DYKE, Söhne Barry und Chris, Töchter Stacey und Carrie Beth bei einem Familienkonzert. • LOUIS ARMSTRONG spielt für seine Frau Lucille zu Hause in Queens. • DELLA REESE an ihrem Klavier. • RICHARD GERE in seinem ersten Apartment in Hollywood. • TUESDAY WELD wäscht ihr nagelneues Auto. • LEE MAJORS in seinem Schlafzimmer. • ANTHONY PERKINS in seinem Apartment in New York. • JANE SEYMOUR auf der Veranda.

DICK VAN DYKE et ses fils Barry et Chris, ses filles Stacey et Carrie Beth lors d'un concert familial. • LOUIS ARMSTRONG joue pour sa femme Lucille dans leur maison de Queens. • DELLA REESE au piano. • RICHARD GERE dans son premier appartement de Hollywood. • TUESDAY WELD lave sa nouvelle voiture. • LEE MAJORS dans sa chambre. • ANTHONY PERKINS dans son appartement de New York. • JANE SEYMOUR dans son patio.

TUESDAY WELD, *Bill Kobrin* 1960

LEE MAJORS, *Gene Trindl* 1966

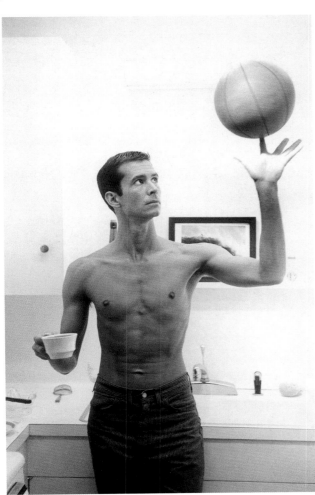

ANTHONY PERKINS, *Jack Stager* 1958

JANE SEYMOUR, *Bob Noble* 1977

GALE STORM AND LEE BONNELL, *Larry Barbier Jr.* 1956

PETER FONDA, *Omnia* 1969

DIANA ROSS, *Harry Langdon* 1974

ELVIS PRESLEY, *Globe Archive* 1958

CHEVY CHASE, *Susan Murphy* 1976

DOLORES DEL RIO, *Herm Lewis* 1966

CESAR ROMERO, *Nate Cutler* 1984

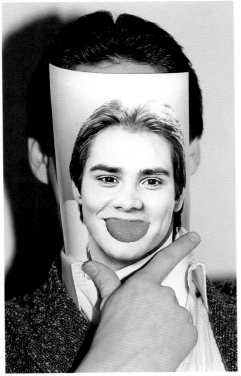

JIM CARREY, *Robert Landau* 1984

YUL AND JACQUELINE BRYNNER, *Cameraphoto Venezia* 1979

REDD FOXX, *Walter Zurlinden* 1972

MICHAEL JACKSON, *Echave* 1972

Long famous for his bald pate, YUL BRYNNER wondered aloud during the shoot what he would look like with long hair. Wife Jacqueline obliged. • Nightclub comedian turned TV star, REDD FOXX isn't shy about showing his tattoo. • Photography was MICHAEL JACKSON'S hobby. One of the Jackson Five when this was shot, Michael sits below his portrait of Diana Ross. • In home sittings, one of the formula shots was the subject showing his wardrobe. BURT REYNOLDS is happy to do so, totally oblivious to the fact that one of his toupees is in full view.

Der durch seinen Kahlkopf bekannte YUL BRYNNER fragt sich während der Dreharbeiten, wie er wohl mit Haaren aussehen würde. Frau Jacqueline ist dieser Idee nicht abgeneigt. • Der vom Nachtclub-Komödianten zum Fernsehstar gewordene REDD FOXX scheut sich nicht, sein Tattoo zur Schau zu stellen. • Fotografieren war eins von MICHAEL JACKSONS Hobbys. Zum Zeitpunkt dieser Aufnahme war Michael noch einer der Jackson Five. Er sitzt hier unter dem Porträt von Diana Ross. • Zu den Standard-Shootings in Eigenheimen gehörte auch ein Foto, das den Kleiderschrank des Stars zeigte. BURT REYNOLDS tut dies gerne und ihm ist nicht einmal bewusst, dass eines seiner Toupets zu sehen ist.

Célèbre pour son crâne chauve, YUL BRYNNER se demande quelle allure il aurait avec des cheveux aussi longs que ceux de son épouse Jacqueline. • Comédien de cabaret devenu vedette de télévision, REDD FOXX n'est pas peu fier de montrer ses tatouages. • La photographie était le violon d'Ingres de MICHAEL JACKSON. Michael, qui appartenait encore au groupe des Jackson Five lorsque cette photo a été prise, est assis sous le portrait qu'il a fait de Diana Ross. • La présentation de sa garde-robe par la vedette était l'un des thèmes les plus fréquemment réalisés lors des séances de pose « à la maison ». BURT REYNOLDS se prête facilement au jeu sans se rendre compte que l'on aperçoit une de ses perruques sur l'étagère.

BURT REYNOLDS, *Gene Trindl* 1970

GREER GARSON, *Larry Barbier Jr.* 1950

LIBERACE, *Nelson Tiffany* 1959

ENGELBERT HUMPERDINCK, *Richard Corkery* 1984

PHYLLIS DILLER, *Jay Thompson* 1966

DENNIS AND DAVID HOPPER, *Dick Miller* 1959

MIKE CONNORS, *Gene Trindl* 1970

FABIAN AND HIS BROTHER, *Jack Stager* 1959

TONY CURTIS, *Orlando* 1967

DENNIS HOPPER and Michelle Phillips in their Taos, New Mexico home, formerly the home of writer D.H. Lawrence. • KIRK DOUGLAS brushes his teeth while studying the script for SPARTACUS. • PETER USTINOV in his favorite place to write.

DENNIS HOPPER und Michelle Phillips in ihrem Haus in Taos, New Mexico, das früher einmal dem Schriftsteller D.H. Lawrence gehörte. • KIRK DOUGLAS putzt sich die Zähne, während er das Drehbuch zu SPARTACUS liest. • PETER USTINOV an dem Ort, an dem er am liebsten schreibt.

DENNIS HOPPER et Michelle Phillips dans leur demeure de Taos (Nouveau-Mexique), qui appartint à l'écrivain D.H. Lawrence. • KIRK DOUGLAS se brosse les dents tout en lisant le script de SPARTACUS. • Le lieu de travail préféré de PETER USTINOV.

DENNIS HOPPER AND MICHELLE PHILLIPS, *Orlando* 1971

KIRK DOUGLAS, *Don Ornitz* 1959

PETER USTINOV, *William Read Woodfield* 1959

JAMES AND PORTLAND MASON, *Don Ornitz* 1950

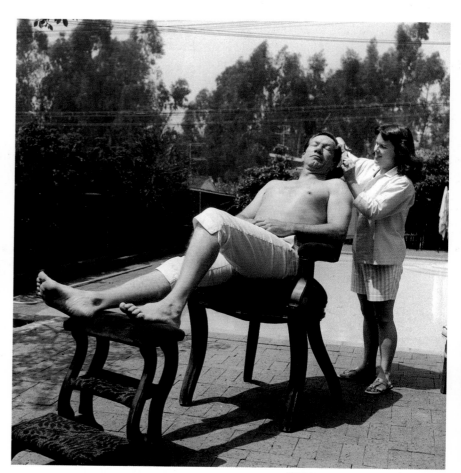

RICHARD AND CLAIRE BOONE, *Dick Miller* 1957

MAUREEN O'SULLIVAN AND MIA FARROW, *Don Ornitz* 1964

CLINT AND MAGGIE EASTWOOD, *Larry Barbier Jr.* 1959

GUY MADISON AND GAIL RUSSELL, *Nate Cutler* 1949

MARLO THOMAS, *Jay Thompson* 1966

JIMMY AND KRISTY McNICHOL, *Nate Cutler* 1977

JANE WYMAN, *Bruce McBroom* 1975

ROBBIE BENSON, *John Partipilo* 1976

DOUG McCLURE AND BARBARA LUNA, *John R. Hamilton* 1962

CHARLES FARRELL, *Don Ornitz* 1963

ERNEST BORGNINE, *Bill Greenslade* 1966

TREVOR HOWARD, RICHARD WIDMARK, *Larry Barbier Jr.* 1956

BETTY WHITE, *Herb Ball* 1953

CHAD EVERETT AND SHELBY GRANT, *Nate Cutler* 1970

SISSY SPACEK AND JACK FISK, *Steve Schatzberg* 1979

BILL BIXBY, *Gene Trindl* 1975

ANNE BAXTER AND DAUGHTER KATRINA, *Dick Miller* 1959

GEORGE MONTGOMERY, *Don Ornitz* 1953

PEGGY LEE, *Larry Barbier Jr.* 1956

BILL BIXBY AND BRENDA BENET, *Gene Trindl* 1971

AVA GARDNER, *Globe Archive* 1958

EVA GABOR, *John R. Hamilton* 1968

GEORGE C. SCOTT AND TRISH VAN DEVERE, *Globe Archive* 1979

ANDY GRIFFITH, *Globe Archive* 1968

DEBORAH KERR AND PETER VIERTEL, *PIP* 1965

HENRY WINKLER, *John R. Hamilton* 1974

MACDONALD CAREY, *Lynn McAfee* 1989

JOHN AND NANCY RITTER, *Gene Trindl* 1978

ROBERT URICH AND HEATHER MENZIES, *Bruce Herman* 1974

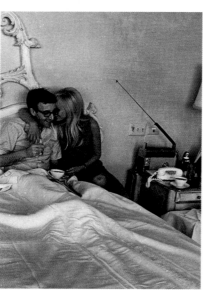

PETER SELLERS AND BRITT EKLAND, *Doris Nieh* 1964

LESLEY ANN WARREN, *Bill Greenslade* 1968

PAULA PRENTISS gets a suprise. In the middle of the layout, RICHARD BENJAMIN suddenly poured a pitcher of water over his wife. When asked about it 30 years later, Benjamin had no recollection whatsoever but, he smiled: "Guess it was OK. She didn't divorce me."

PAULA PRENTISS wird überrascht. Ohne Vorwarnung leert RICHARD BENJAMIN eine Kanne mit Wasser über den Kopf seiner Frau. 30 Jahre später darauf angesprochen, konnte sich Benjamin nicht mehr an diesen Zwischenfall erinnern, räumte aber lächelnd ein, dass „es in Ordnung gewesen sein muss – sie hat sich nicht von mir scheiden lassen".

RICHARD BENJAMIN surprend PAULA PRENTISS en pleine scéance de photos. Soudain, Richard Benjamin asperge d'eau son épouse. Lorsqu'on lui demanda pourquoi, 30 ans plus tard, Benjamin ne se souvenait plus du tout cet incident mais expliqua : « Il n'y a pas dû y avoir de problème puisqu'elle n'a pas divorcé ! ».

<< PAULA PRENTISS AND RICHARD BENJAMIN, *Don Ornitz* 1961

Although GIG YOUNG, ARLENE DAHL and GOLDIE HAWN were gifted Sunday painters, several celebrities took their painting very seriously and enjoy professional status. • ELKE SOMMER has had exhibitions in Los Angeles, Chicago, Rome, Berlin and Munich. • TOM TRYON was an accomplished illustration artist and writer of six successful novels. • Painting was just a hobby for ANTHONY QUINN in his early years but later he became a painter and sculptor of reputation. • Musician and composer DUKE ELLINGTON displays Satin Doll, inspired by his famous composition. • KIM NOVAK with her portrait of director Richard Quine and his son. • JAMES MASON'S paintings were used in the film BIGGER THAN LIFE. • PEGGY LEE works on a portrait of General Moshe Dayan. • RED SKELTON was well known for his paintings of clowns.

Obgleich GIG YOUNG, ARLENE DAHL und GOLDIE HAWN begabte Sonntagsmaler waren, so nahmen andere Berühmtheiten ihre Malerei sehr ernst und genossen sogar ein gewisses fachliches Ansehen. • ELKE SOMMER hat bereits in Los Angeles, Chicago, Rom, Berlin und München ausgestellt. • TOM TRYON war ein fähiger Illustrationskünstler und Schriftsteller sechs erfolgreicher Romane. • Malen war für ANTHONY QUINN in seinen jungen Jahren lediglich ein Hobby. Später wurde er allerdings ein renommierter Maler und Bildhauer. • Musiker und Komponist DUKE ELLINGTON führt Satin Doll vor, inspiriert durch seine berühmte Komposition. • KIM NOVAK mit ihrem Porträt von Regisseur Richard Quine und seinem Sohn. • JAMES MASONS Bilder wurden in dem Film EINE HANDVOLL HOFFNUNG (BIGGER THAN LIFE) verwendet. • PEGGY LEE arbeitet an einem Porträt von General Moshe Dayan. • RED SKELTON war bekannt für seine Clown-Bilder.

Si GIG YOUNG, ARLENE DAHL et GOLDIE HAWN sont des peintres du dimanche talentueux, d'autres acteurs-vedette ont pris la peinture très au sérieux et sont passés professionnels. • ELKE SOMMER a exposé à Los Angeles, Chicago, Rome, Berlin et Munich. • TOM TRYON, illustrateur accompli, écrivit six romans à succès. • Alors que la peinture n'était au début qu'un passe-temps pour ANTHONY QUINN, il finit par devenir un peintre et un sculpteur réputé. • Le musicien DUKE ELLINGTON présente Satin Doll, inspiré par sa célèbre composition. • KIM NOVAK avec le portrait qu'elle a réalisé du metteur en scène Richard Quine et de son fils. • Les tableaux de JAMES MASON servirent au décor du film DERRIÈRE LE MIROIR (BIGGER THAN LIFE). • PEGGY LEE travaille sur un portrait du général Moshe Dayan. • RED SKELTON se rendit célèbre pour ses portraits de clowns.

ELKE SOMMER, *Herm Lewis* 1970

GIG YOUNG, *Bill Kobrin* 1965

TOM TRYON, *Bill Kobrin* 1969

ANTHONY QUINN, WIFE KATHARINE AND DAUGHTER VALENTINA, *Larry Barbier Jr.* 1949

ARLENE DAHL, *Larry Barbier Jr.* 1953

DUKE ELLINGTON, *Tom Caffrey* 1975

KIM NOVAK, *PIP* 1962

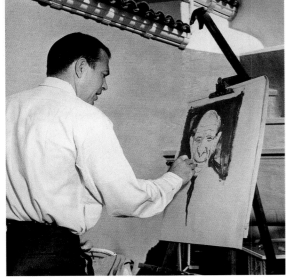

JAMES MASON, *Don Ornitz* 1955

PEGGY LEE, *Bill Greenslade* 1969

RED SKELTON, *John R. Hamilton* 1964

TONY CURTIS, *Don Ornitz* 1969

TONY BENNETT, *Globe Archive* 1980

HENRY FONDA, *Herm Lewis* 1969

PETER FALK, *Vera Anderson* 1984

TONY CURTIS exhibits his work in galleries in Beverly Hills and Las Vegas. • TONY BENNETT studied art before embarking on a show business career. • HENRY FONDA was famed for giving his paintings to costars of his films. • In the mid-60s PETER FALK discovered a talent for drawing which will be on display in a book of his work.

TONY CURTIS stellt seine Arbeiten in Galerien in Beverly Hills und Las Vegas aus. • TONY BENNETT studierte Kunst, bevor er seine Karriere im Showbusiness begann. • HENRY FONDA war berühmt für das Verschenken seiner Bilder an seine Filmpartner. • Mitte der 60er Jahre entdeckte PETER FALK ein Talent für das Zeichnen. Seine Zeichnungen werden in einem Buch über seine Bilder zu sehen sein.

TONY CURTIS a exposé son œuvre dans des galeries de Beverly Hills et de Las Vegas. • TONY BENNETT fit des études d'art avant de débuter une carrière dans le show business. • HENRY FONDA avait l'habitude d'offrir ses tableaux à ses partenaires. • PETER FALK se découvrit un talent de dessinateur au milieu des années 1960 ; ses œuvres seront publiées en livre.

KATHARINE HEPBURN AND KATHARINE HOUGHTON, *Don Ornitz* 1967

JAMES CAGNEY, *Globe Archive* 1963

GOLDIE HAWN, *Bill Kobrin* 1965

KIM NOVAK, *Joel Thomas* 1969

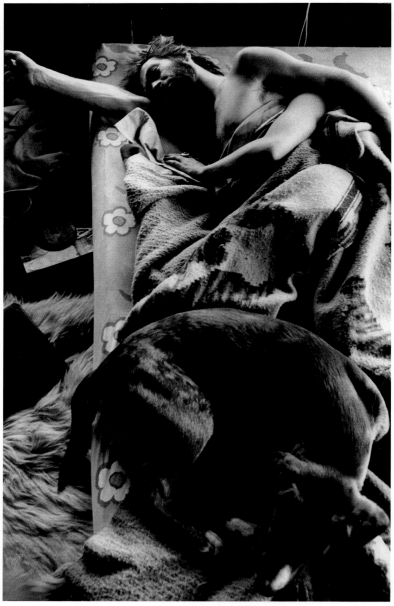

DAVID CARRADINE AND BARBARA HERSHEY, *Ron Thal* 1972

JOSEPH AND LENORE COTTEN, *Dick Miller* 1955

JOSEPH COTTEN AND PATRICIA MEDINA, *Bill Kobrin* 1961

When she moved away from Hollywood in 1961, KIM NOVAK made her home at Gull House on the northern California coast at Carmel. The solar-heated outdoor tub was made from a redwood wine barrel. • Sometimes a photographer establishes a close rapport with the stars he's covering enabling him to shoot more intimate coverage. Such was Ron Thal's relationship with DAVID CARRADINE and BARBARA HERSHEY, whom he was covering during their movie BOXCAR BERTHA. Thal frequently arrived at the couple's home to find them and their dog still asleep. • JOSEPH COTTEN did two home sittings in his Italian villa in Pacific Palisades. Everything is much the same – the painted vaulted ceiling, French windows, carved mantle and art work by Utrillo – in both sittings. Except the wives.

Als KIM NOVAK 1961 aus Hollywood wegzog, richtete sie sich ihr Zuhause in Gull House an der nördlichen Küste Kaliforniens bei Carmel ein. Die Außenwanne mit Solarheizung wurde aus einem Redwood-Weinfass gebaut. • Manchmal gelingt es einem Fotografen, eine engere Beziehung mit den Stars aufzubauen, die ihm die Möglichkeit eröffnet, intimere Bilder zu machen. Ron Thal hatte eine solche Beziehung zu DAVID CARRADINE und BARBARA HERSHEY, die er beide während den Dreharbeiten zum Film DIE FAUST DER REBELLEN (BOXCAR BERTHA) coverte. Thal fuhr einige Male zum Haus des Pärchens und fand dieses und ihren Hund noch schlafend vor. • JOSEPH COTTEN nahm an zwei Foto-Shootings in seiner italienischen Villa in Pacific Palisades teil. Fast nichts hat sich zwischen den Aufnahmen geändert – die bemalte gewölbte Zimmerdecke, französische Fenster, die gemeißelte Kamineinfassung und Kunstwerke von Utrillo – in beiden Shootings. Nur die Ehefrauen sind nicht dieselben.

Ayant quitté Hollywood en 1961, KIM NOVAK partit s'installer à Gull House, à Carmel, sur la côte nord de la Californie. Le baquet de la douche, dont l'eau est uniquement chauffée par le soleil, est réalisé dans un tonneau en séquoia. • Il arrive parfois que se créent des liens étroits entre un photographe et les vedettes avec lesquelles il travaille, ce qui lui permet évidemment d'assurer un reportage plus intime qu'à l'ordinaire. Ce fut le cas de Ron Thal lorsqu'il suivit DAVID CARRADINE et BARBARA HERSHEY lors du tournage du film BERTHA BOXCAR (BOXCAR BERTHA); il arriva fréquemment à Thal de se rendre dans la maison du couple pour les trouver ainsi tous deux endormis avec leur chien. • JOSEPH COTTEN accepta deux fois qu'on réalise un reportage chez lui, dans sa villa de style italien de Pacific Palisades. Rien n'avait changé entre les deux séances – les mêmes plafond voûté et peint, fenêtres à la française, manteau de cheminée sculpté et tableau d'Utrillo – sauf son épouse !

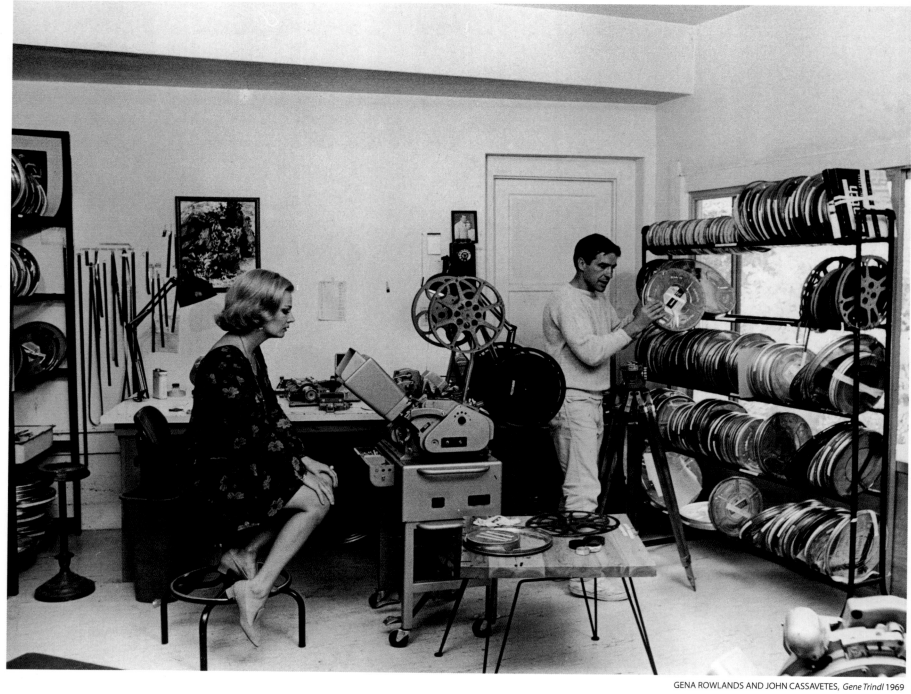

GENA ROWLANDS AND JOHN CASSAVETES, *Gene Trindl* 1969

JOHN CASSAVETES and wife GENA ROWLANDS turned their garage into a full-fledged editing room where they cut his first feature, FACES, on the moviola that she gave him for Christmas.

JOHN CASSAVETES und Frau GENA ROWLANDS bauten ihre Garage in ein voll ausgestattetes Schnittstudio um, in dem sie seinen ersten Spielfilm GESICHTER (FACES) auf der Moviola schnitten, die sie ihm zu Weihnachten geschenkt hatte.

C'est dans leur garage, transformé en salle de montage et où règne le Moviola qu'elle lui a offert pour Noël, que JOHN CASSAVETES et son épouse GENA ROWLANDS ont terminé FACES, leur premier film.

DAVID AND CHERYL LADD, *Bruce Herman* 1975

LORENZO LAMAS, *Steve Schatzberg* 1980

TAMMY GRIMES, *Richard Hewett* 1967

JANE FONDA AND ROGER VADIM, *Bruce McBroom* 1969

LINDA LAVIN, *John Partipilo* 1976

GLENN FORD, *Don Ornitz* 1971

RICHARD BEYMER, *Larry Barbier Jr.* 1959

ROCK HUDSON, *Guy Webster* 1970

SANDRA DEE AND MOTHER MARY DOUVAN, *Lawrence Schiller* 1962

MARLON BRANDO, *Ray Falk* 1956

MARY MARTIN, *Frank Diernhammer* 1972

TONY CURTIS AND CHRISTINE KAUFMANN, *Jean Marchand* 1962

JENNIFER JONES, *Hans Albers* 1975

As the wife of Norton Simon, JENNIFER JONES owns one of the most outstanding private art collections in the world. She sits beneath Matisse's "Petite Odalisque à la robe violette." • RICHARD BEYMER gives a bachelor's twist to bed-making. • ROCK HUDSON in the master bedroom of his Mediterranean style house. • SANDRA DEE and mom MARY DOUVAN share an intimate moment. • MARLON BRANDO in his apartment in Kyoto, Japan, during the filming of SAYONARA. • MARY MARTIN at Nosa Fazenda, her 15,000-acre ranch in Brazil. • Newlyweds TONY CURTIS and CHRISTINE KAUFMANN cut up.

Als Frau von Norton Simon besitzt JENNIFER JONES eine der herausragendsten Kunst-Privatkollektionen der Welt. Hier sitzt sie unter Matisse's „Petite Odalisque à la robe violette." • RICHARD BEYMER macht sein Bett nach Junggesellenart. • ROCK HUDSON im Hauptschlafzimmer seines Hauses im mediterranen Stil. • SANDRA DEE und Mutter MARY DOUVAN in einem liebevollen Augenblick. • MARLON BRANDO in seinem Apartment in Kyoto, Japan, während der Dreharbeiten zu SAYONARA. • MARY MARTIN bei Nosa Fazenda, ihrer 15.000 Morgen großen Ranch in Brasilien. • Das frisch verheiratete Pärchen TONY CURTIS und CHRISTINE KAUFMANN.

JENNIFER JONES, l'épouse de Norton Simon, posséde une des plus belles collections d'art au monde. On la voit ici assise sous le tableau de Matisse « Petite Odalisque à la robe violette ». • RICHARD BEYMER a trouvé une nouvelle manière de faire son lit. • ROCK HUDSON dans la grande chambre de sa maison de style méditerranéen. • SANDRA DEE et sa mère MARY DOUVAN partagent un instant d'intimité. • MARLON BRANDO dans son appartement de Kyoto (Japon), lors du tournage de SAYONARA. • MARY MARTIN à Nosa Fazenda, son ranch brésilien de 7 500 hectares. • Jeunes mariés, TONY CURTIS et CHRISTINE KAUFMANN font les pitres.

ANITA BRYANT AND FAMILY, *Bob Sherman* 1977

LOUISE FLETCHER AND PARENTS, *H.L. Paravicini* 1976

DIANE LADD AND LAURA DERN, *Bob Noble* 1984

PAT AND SHIRLEY BOONE, *Gene Trindl* 1965

MICHAEL CAINE, *Orlando* 1966

MICHAEL CAINE takes a sentimental journey as he stands on the site of the cold-water flat in London's Elephant and Castle area where he grew up. The building was bombed out during World War II and never rebuilt. • ANITA BRYANT and family at daily prayers. • LOUISE FLETCHER brought her best actress Oscar for ONE FLEW OVER THE CUCKOO'S NEST home to Birmingham, Alabama, to share with her deaf parents, Reverend and Mrs. Robert Fletcher, for whom she gave her acceptance speech in sign language. • LAURA DERN gets grooming tips from mom DIANE LADD. • PAT BOONE and wife SHIRLEY, praying together in their bedroom, devote an hour each day to prayer and meditation.

MICHAEL CAINE wird nostalgisch als er an den Ort, an dem er groß geworden ist, zurückkehrt – eine Wohnung im Londoner Viertel Elephant und Castle, in der es damals nur kaltes Wasser gab. Das Gebäude wurde während des Zweiten Weltkrieges ausgebombt und nie wieder aufgebaut. • ANITA BRYANT und Familie beim täglichen Gebet. • LOUISE FLETCHER brachte ihren Oskar, mit dem sie als beste Schauspielerin in EINER FLOG ÜBER DAS KUCKUCKSNEST (ONE FLEW OVER THE CUCKOO'S NEST) ausgezeichnet worden war, nach Hause in Birmingham, Alabama. Sie wollte ihre Freude mit ihren taubstummen Eltern teilen, Reverend und Mrs. Robert Fletcher, für die sie ihre Dankesrede in Zeichensprache gegeben hatte. • LAURA DERN bekommt von Mutter DIANE LADD Schönheitstipps. • PAT BOONE und Frau SHIRLEY beim gemeinsamen Gebet in ihrem Schlafzimmer. Sie nehmen sich jeden Tag eine Stunde Zeit zum Beten und Meditieren.

MICHAEL CAINE fait une promenade sentimentale dans le quartier Elephant et Castle de Londres à l'endroit où se trouvait le misérable appartement dans lequel il grandit. L'immeuble fut bombardé pendant la Seconde Guerre mondiale et jamais reconstruit. • ANITA BRYANT et famillie lors de la prière quotidienne. • LOUISE FLETCHER a ramené chez elle, à Birmingham (Alabama), l'Oscar de la meilleure actrice, remporté pour VOL AU-DESSUS D'UN NID DE COUCOU (ONE FLEW OVER THE CUCKOO'S NEST). Elle traduit son discours en langage des signes pour ses parents sourds, le révérend Robert Fletcher et son épouse. • LAURA DERN reçoit des conseils de beauté de sa mère DIANE LADD. • PAT BOONE et son épouse SHIRLEY consacrent chaque jour une heure à la prière et à la méditation.

CHARLOTTE RAE AND KATHLEEN VILLELLA, *Robert Landau* 1980

WALTER BRENNAN, *Larry Barbier Jr.* 1959

STEVE AND NEILE McQUEEN, *Larry Barbier Jr.* 1958

ANGIE DICKINSON, *Don Ornitz* 1971

TED DANSON, *Frank Carroll* 1982

DAVID ROSE, *Lee Sporkin* 1956

CHARLOTTE RAE exercises with trainer KATHLEEN VILLELLA. • Three-time Oscar winner WALTER BRENNAN rides the swing he built for his three children 37 years earlier. • STEVE McQUEEN has a morning workout while wife NEILE waits with the orange juice. • ANGIE DICKINSON keeps a daily exercise routine. • TED DANSON tries out his daughter's new slide. • Composer DAVID ROSE built a miniature track encircling his Sherman Oaks estate, complete with a steam engine capable of pulling a load of 100 persons.

CHARLOTTE RAE trainiert mit ihrem Trainer KATHLEEN VILLELLA. • Dreifacher Oskar-Gewinner WALTER BRENNAN auf der Schaukel, die er vor 37 Jahren für seine drei Kinder gebaut hatte. • STEVE McQUEEN beim morgentlichen Fitness-Training, während Frau NEILE bereits mit dem Orangensaft wartet. • ANGIE DICKINSON trainiert konsequent jeden Tag. • TED DANSON probiert die neue Rutsche seiner Tochter aus. • Komponist DAVID ROSE baute eine Miniatur-Eisenbahnstrecke, die um seinen gesamten Grundbesitz in Sherman Oaks herum verlief. Komplett mit Dampfmaschine ausgestattet war der Zug in der Lage, 100 Personen zu ziehen.

CHARLOTTE RAE en pleine séance de gymnastique avec son entraîneur KATHLEEN VILLELLA. • WALTER BRENNAN, trois fois récompensé par un Oscar, s'amuse sur la balançoire qu'il a construite pour ses trois enfants, 37 ans plus tôt. • STEVE MCQUEEN fait ses exercices matinaux tandis que sa femme NEILE attend avec son jus d'orange. • ANGIE DICKINSON entretient quotidiennement sa forme. • TED DANSON essaie le nouveau toboggan de sa fille. • Le compositeur DAVID ROSE a construit une voie de chemin de fer miniature qui fait le tour de sa propriété de Sherman Oaks, sur laquelle il fait circuler un train à vapeur capable de transporter 100 voyageurs.

MERV AND JULANN GRIFFIN, *Jack Stager* 1962

JAMES AND LOIS GARNER, *Don Ornitz* 1966

MERV GRIFFIN with wife JULANN in their New Jersey house, the home of the last man to be hanged in that state. • JAMES GARNER and wife LOIS survey the progress on their new house under construction.

MERV GRIFFIN mit Frau JULANN in ihrem Haus in New Jersey. In diesem Haus lebte zuvor der Mann, der als Letzter im Staate New Jersey erhängt wurde. • JAMES GARNER und Frau LOIS besichtigen die Fortschritte beim Bau ihres neuen Hauses.

MERV GRIFFIN et sa femme JULANN dans leur maison du New Jersey, où vécut le dernier homme à avoir été pendu dans cet État. • JAMES GARNER et son épouse LOIS surveillent l'avancement des travaux de leur nouvelle maison.

BETTE DAVIS AND GARY MERRILL, *Photo Trends* 1951

BRIAN AND VICTORIA KEITH, *Bill Kobrin* 1970

BETTE DAVIS and GARY MERRILL share lunch with workmen restoring the 19th-century house which is to be their new home in Maine. • Just returned from their honeymoon, BRIAN and VICTORIA KEITH pose for their first sitting as husband and wife.

BETTE DAVIS und GARY MERRILL beim Mittagessen mit den Bauarbeitern, die ihr zukünftiges Zuhause in Maine, ein Haus aus dem 19. Jahrhundert, restaurieren. • Gerade erst frisch aus den Flitterwochen zurück, posieren BRIAN und VICTORIA KEITH schon für ihr erstes Porträt als Mann und Frau.

BETTE DAVIS et GARY MERRILL partagent leur déjeuner avec les ouvriers qui restaurent la maison du XIXᵉ siècle qu'ils viennent d'acheter dans le Maine. • À peine de retour de leur lune de miel, BRIAN et VICTORIA KEITH posent pour la première fois comme mari et femme.

JERRY MATHERS, *Larry Barbier Jr.* 1958

SALLY KELLERMAN, *Guy Webster* 1970

ALLEN LUDDEN AND BETTY WHITE, *Richard DeNeut* 1972

JACK LEMMON, *Larry Barbier Jr.* 1959

HAROLD LLOYD, *Larry Barbier Jr.* 1962

BORIS AND EVELYN KARLOFF, *Frank Cannon* 1961

RICHARD AND SYBIL BURTON, *Globe Archive* 1959

SONNY AND CHER, *Jay Thompson* 1964

JOHN FORD, *Lee Sporkin* 1968

AARON SPELLING AND CAROLYN JONES, *Don Ornitz* 1960

JOHN FORD lived in the same house over 25 years, with no pool or fancy grounds, furnished modestly with personal memorabilia including this miniature stagecoach from one of his most successful movies. • TV producer AARON SPELLING was still an actor when this sitting showing him practicing yoga with wife CAROLYN JONES was shot. • One of the few superstar directors, ALFRED HITCHCOCK, who gained his greatest fame by his droll hosting of his TV series, here mimics the famous profile opening of that show.

Preceding pages: JERRY MATHERS had a collection of self-made planes and rocket ships. • SALLY KELLERMAN organizes her tape collection. • ALLEN LUDDEN and BETTY WHITE shared one of Hollywood's happiest marriages while enjoying successful TV careers. They also shared an appreciation for the OZ books and own several collections of the series. • JACK LEMMON checks out his new Japanese telescope. • One of the kings of silent comedy, HAROLD LLOYD shows his pride and joy, the family Christmas tree laden with ornaments from all over the world. The fully decorated tree remained up all year round. • BORIS and EVELYN KARLOFF share tea at the Château Mârmont. • RICHARD and SYBIL BURTON at their home in Switzerland. • The first home sitting with SONNY and – before the "renovations" started – CHER .

JOHN FORD lebte über 25 Jahre lang in demselben Haus, ohne Pool oder großem Grundstück, lediglich mit persönlichen Souvenirs ausgestattet, inklusive dieser Miniatur-Postkutsche aus einem seiner erfolgreichsten Filme. • Fernsehproduzent AARON SPELLING war zur der Zeit, als dieses Foto gemacht wurde, noch Schauspieler. Hier sieht man ihn beim Yoga mit seiner Frau CAROLYN JONES. • Einer der wenigen Superstars unter den Regisseuren war ALFRED HITCHCOCK, der seinen größten Ruhm als Gastgeber seiner Fernsehserien erlangt. Er imitiert auf diesem Foto den berühmten Beginn der Show, der ihn im Seitenprofil zeigt.

Vorherige Seiten: JERRY MATHERS hatte eine Sammlung von selbst gemachten Flugzeugen und Weltraumfahrzeugen. • SALLY KELLERMAN bringt Ordnung in ihre Kassettenkollektion. • ALLEN LUDDEN und BETTY WHITE führten nicht nur in Hollywood eine der glücklichsten Ehen, sondern waren auch beide erfolgreiche Fernsehstars. Sie waren beide Fans der OZ-Bücher, von denen sie mehrere Sammlungen hatten. •. JACK LEMMON probiert gerade sein neues japanisches Teleskop aus. • Einer der Könige der Stummfilmkomödie, HAROLD LLOYD, zeigt seinen ganzen Stolz und seine ganze Freude, den Weihnachtsbaum der Familie, beladen mit Ornamenten aus der ganzen Welt. Der dekorierte Baum blieb das ganze Jahr über stehen. • BORIS und EVELYN KARLOFF beim Teetrinken im Château Marmont. • RICHARD und SYBIL BURTON zu Hause in der Schweiz. • Das erste Porträtfoto zu Hause bei SONNY und CHER – vor ihrer „Restaurierung".

JOHN FORD a vécu plus de 25 ans dans la même maison, sans piscine ni parc, modestement meublée de souvenirs personnels, dont cette maquette de diligence provenant d'un de ses plus célèbres films. • Le producteur de télévision AARON SPELLING était encore acteur lors de cette photo, où on le voit faire du yoga avec son épouse CAROLYN JONES. • ALFRED HITCHCOCK, l'un des rares metteurs en scène à être devenu une superstar et dont la célébrité doit beaucoup à ses étranges apparitions dans les séries télévisées, offre à la caméra le même profil par lequel ouvrait le générique de ses émissions.

Pages précédentes: JERRY MATHERS présente sa collection de maquettes d'avions et de fusées. • SALLY KELLERMAN range sa collection de cassettes. • ALLEN LUDDEN et BETTY WHITE ont réussi l'un des plus heureux mariages de Hollywood tout en menant une magnifique carrière à la télévision. Ils partagent également le même goût pour les livres dont ils possèdent plusieurs collections. • JACK LEMMON vérifie ici son nouveau télescope japonais. • HAROLD LLOYD, l'un des rois du burlesque muet, montre sa fierté et sa joie devant l'arbre de Noël familial, couvert de décorations du monde entier et qu'il conservera ainsi toute l'année. • BORIS et EVELYN KARLOFF prennent le thé au Château Marmont. • RICHARD et SYBIL BURTON dans leur propriété en Suisse. • La première séance de pose avec SONNY et CHER – avant ses travaux de « restauration».

ALFRED HITCHCOCK, *Frank Carroll* 1960 >>

EDWARD G. ROBINSON, *Nelson Tiffany* 1965

EDWARD G. ROBINSON was perhaps Hollywood's premier art collector. Here he shows the bronze sculpture "Grande Figura Seduta" created by Emilio Grecco in 1951.

EDWARD G. ROBINSON war wahrscheinlich Hollywoods erster Kunstsammler. Auf diesem Foto zeigt er die von Emilio Grecco im Jahre 1951 entworfene Bronzeskulptur „Grande Figura Seduta".

EDWARD G. ROBINSON fut peut-être le plus grand collectionneur d'art de Hollywood. Il présente ici une sculpture en bronze - « Grande Figura Seduta » – créée par Emilio Grecco en 1951.

DIAHANN CARROLL, *Jay Thompson* 1968

ROSALIND RUSSELL, HUSBAND FREDERICK BRISSON AND SON LANCE, *Frank Bez* 1962

AGNES MOOREHEAD, *Larry Barbier Jr.* 1960

DANNY THOMAS, *Nate Cutler* 1987

MARY MARTIN AND NOEL COWARD IN JAMAICA, *Tom Caffrey* 1956

CYD CHARISSE, *Don Ornitz* 1960

TONY RANDALL WITH WIFE FLORENCE AND GUESTS DODIE HEATH AND BARBARA BEL GEDDES, *Dick Miller* 1958

ANDRÉ AND DORY PREVIN, *Irv Steinberg* 1969

STEVE McQUEEN AND ALI MACGRAW, *Nate Cutler* 1972

EDITH HEAD, *John R. Hamilton* 1973

VINCENTE MINNELLI, *John R. Hamilton* 1975

ANNE BAXTER, *John R. Hamilton* 1973

BURL IVES, *John R. Hamilton* 1973

MAE WEST, *Jay Thompson* 1965

MAE WEST insisted upon posing on four inches of unseen wood block to give her height during this sitting in her Santa Monica home. Later, while approving the photos, she stopped at a shot of her face framed in billowy white and commented that it looked like she had been photographed through a cloud. The photographer explained that he'd used a long lens which threw a bowl of white flowers in the foreground out of focus giving it that effect. He mentioned that a similar effect could be had by smearing vasoline on the lens. "Oh, yeah?" she nodded, "so it's good for that too!"

MAE WEST bestand darauf, auf einem gut versteckten, 10 cm hohen Holzblock zu posieren, um für die Aufnahme in ihrem Haus in Santa Monica größer zu wirken. Später, bei Begutachtung der Fotos zur Veröffentlichung, stockte sie bei einem Bild, auf dem ihr Gesicht in einem wogenden Weiß eingerahmt zu sein schien. Sie sagte, dass es so aussehen würde, als ob sie durch eine Wolke hindurch fotografiert worden wäre. Der Fotograf erklärte, dass er für diese Aufnahme ein langes Objektiv benutzt hatte. Dadurch wäre ein Strauß weißer Blumen, der sich im Vordergrund des Motivs befunden hätte, unscharf abgebildet worden. Er sagte, dass ein ähnlicher Effekt durch das Auftragen von Vaseline auf die Kameralinse erzielt werden könnte. „Ach, ja?" nickte sie, „es ist also auch für so etwas gut!"

Lors de cette séance de photos dans sa demeure de Santa Monica, MAE WEST insista pour poser juchée sur un bloc de bois de dix centimètres afin de paraître plus grande. Par la suite, en regardant les épreuves soumises à son accord, elle tomba en arrêt devant son visage encadré de volutes blanches et s'exclama qu'elle avait l'impression d'avoir été photographiée à travers un nuage. Le photographe lui expliqua qu'il avait utilisé à dessein une longue focale laissant dans le flou un vase de fleurs blanches au premier plan. Lorsqu'il eut indiqué qu'on pouvait obtenir le même effet en mettant de la vaseline sur l'objectif, elle s'exclama « Oh, oui ? C'est bon pour ça aussi ! »

SHIRLEY JONES, *Richard Hewett* 1970

SHIRLEY JONES tries to settle down with her script of THE CHEYENNE SOCIAL CLUB but Bronze, a Great Dane who thinks he's a lap dog, has other ideas. ● RED SKELTON and his menagerie of pets. ● KIM NOVAK lives in modern Noah's Ark fashion with a Siamese, a Great Dane, a Highland Terrier, mynah bird – and an African pygmy goat ● ROSSANO BRAZZI shares milk with a stray kitten in his home in Hawaii during the filming of SOUTH PACIFIC. ● ERIK ESTRADA and his best friend Don't Cry. HERB SHRINER offers Daffodil, his pet duck, a drink in his dressing room. ● PAUL LYNDE grooms his Dandie Dinmont, Harry. ● EFREM ZIMBALIST JR. and his wife STEPHANIE tend to one of the animals in what amounts to a miniature zoo in their French farmhouse in rural San Fernando Valley. ● IMOGENE COCA and her pet duck, Grover Cleveland. ● ELVIS PRESLEY and his menagerie of stuffed animals.

SHIRLEY JONES versucht, sich mit ihrem Skript für GESCHOSSEN WIRD AB MITTERNACHT (THE CHEYENNE SOCIAL CLUB) zu befassen, aber Bronze, eine deutsche Dogge, die sich als Schoßhündchen fühlt, hat andere Pläne. ● RED SKELTON und seine Haustier-Menagerie. ● KIM NOVAK lebt im modernen Arche-Noah-Stil mit einer siamesischen Katze, einer deutschen Dogge, einem Hochlandterrier, einem Hirtenstar – und einer afrikanischen Pygmäenziege. ● ROSSANO BRAZZI teilt seine Milch während der Dreharbeiten zu SOUTH PACIFIC mit einem herumstreunenden Kätzchen in seinem Hause in Hawaii. ● ERIK ESTRADA und sein bester Freund Don't Cry. ● HERB SHRINER bietet seiner Hausente Daffodil einen Drink im Umkleideraum an. ● PAUL LYNDE macht seinen Dandie Dinmont, Harry, zurecht. ● EFREM ZIMBALIST JR. und seine Frau STEPHANIE kümmern sich um eines der vielen Tiere auf ihrem Wohnsitz im französischen Landhausstil im ländlichen San Fernando Valley. Die Anzahl der Tiere, die die beiden besaßen, uferte fast in einen Miniaturzoo aus. ● IMOGENE COCA und ihre Hausente, Grover Cleveland. ● ELVIS PRESLEY und seine Stofftier-Menagerie.

SHIRLEY JONES voudrait bien travailler sur le script de ATTAQUE AU CHEYENNE-CLUB (THE CHEYENNE SOCIAL CLUB) mais son Danois Bronze, qui se prend pour un chien d'agrément, ne l'entend pas de cette oreille. ● RED SKELTON et sa ménagerie d'animaux familiers. ● KIM NOVAK vit dans une sorte de moderne arche de Noé avec un Siamois, un Danois, un Highland Terrier, un mainate et une chèvre pygmée d'Afrique. ● Lors du tournage de SOUTH PACIFIC à Hawaii, ROSSANO BRAZZI partage son lait avec un chaton qu'il a recueilli. ● ERIK ESTRADA et son meilleur ami Don't Cry. ● HERB SHRINER offre un verre à Daffodil, son canard apprivoisé, venu dans sa loge. ● PAUL LYNDE fait la toilette de Harry, un Dandie-Dinmont Terrier. ● EFREM ZIMBALIST JR. et sa femme STEPHANIE s'occupent d'un des animaux du zoo miniature de la ferme française située dans la vallée de San Fernando. ● IMOGENE COCA et son canard apprivoisé, Grover Cleveland. ● ELVIS PRESLEY et sa ménagerie d'animaux en peluche.

RED SKELTON, *Larry Barbier Jr.* 1953

KIM NOVAK, *Joel Thomas* 1969

ROSSANO BRAZZI, *Werner Stoy* 1957

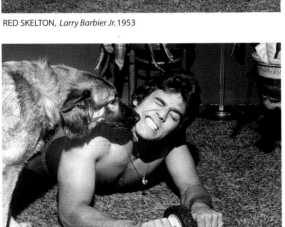

ERIK ESTRADA, *Ralph Dominguez* 1977

HERB SHRINER, *Nate Cutler* 1952

PAUL LYNDE, *Gene Trindl* 1972

EFREM AND STEPHANIE ZIMBALIST JR., *Gene Trindl* 1960

IMOGENE COCA, *Bill Kobrin* 1963

ELVIS PRESLEY, *Globe Archive* 1955

ROY ROGERS AND TRIGGER, *Bill Kobrin* 1962

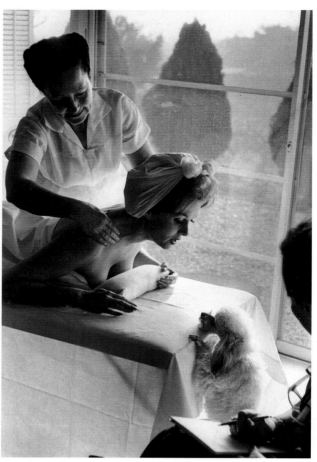

RHONDA FLEMING, *Bill Kobrin* 1964

BETTY GRABLE AND HARRY JAMES WITH JAMES SESSION, *Jerry Jackson* 1952

PERRY KING AND VALENTINO, *John R. Hamilton* 1978

SANDRA DEE, *Don Ornitz* 1959

MIKE MYERS, *Lisa Rose* 1995

DENNIS FRANZ, *John R. Hamilton* 1995

LORNE AND NANCY GREENE, *Bill Kobrin* 1964

DEIDRE HALL WITH PHAEDRA, *Bob Noble* 1979

PIPER LAURIE AND SOKOSHIA, *Dick Miller* 1958

A wildlife conservationist, GARDNER McKAY shares his 5-acre estate with two cheetahs and two lions. Here he is with 6-year-old Kenya. • URSULA ANDRESS, a lover of exotic animals, with her pet ocelot, Tiger. • AMANDA BLAKE had a regular menagerie of exotic animals in her home including this cheetah.

Als Tierschützer teilt GARDNER McKAY seinen fünf Morgen großen Besitz mit zwei Geparden und zwei Löwen. Hier sieht man ihn mit der sechs Jahre alten Kenya. • URSULA ANDRESS, Liebhaberin exotischer Tiere, hier mit ihrem zahmen Ozelot namens Tiger. • AMANDA BLAKE hatte eine regelrechte Menagerie exotischer Tiere in ihrem Haus, dazu gehört auch ein Gepard.

Grand défenseur de la faune et de la flore, GARDNER McKAY partageait sa propriété de 2,5 hectares avec deux lions et deux guépards, dont Kenya, âgée de 6 ans. • URSULA ANDRESS, passionnée d'animaux sauvages, avec Tiger, son ocelot apprivoisé. • AMANDA BLAKE entretenait dans sa maison une véritable ménagerie d'animaux exotiques dont ce guépard.

URSULA ANDRESS, *William Claxton* 1967

GARDNER McKAY, *Bill Greenslade* 1970

AMANDA BLAKE, *Don Jones* 1974

TIPPI HEDREN, *Gene Trindl* 1972

MELANIE GRIFFITH, *Gene Trindl* 1972

TIPPI HEDREN AND MELANIE GRIFFITH, *Gene Trindl* 1972

TIPPI HEDREN and her family literally lived with a house full of lions for months before the filming of husband Noel Marshall's ROAR started. Tippi wanted to become acquainted with her "costars", Neil, a large and superbly trained lion, and three cubs. The cubs would congregate in the master bedroom and, when efforts were made to evict them, could tear bedspreads, sheets and pillows apart in seconds. Tippi grew quite fond of Neil as Tippi's daughter, MELANIE GRIFFITH, did of the cubs.

TIPPI HEDREN und ihre Familie lebten vor dem Beginn der Dreharbeiten zu ROAR – EIN ABENTEUER (ROAR), den ihr Ehemann Noel Marshall drehte, monatelang regelrecht in einem Haus voller Löwen. Tippi wollte sich somit an ihre „Filmpartner" Neil, einen großen und hervorragend dressierten Löwen, und drei Löwenbabys gewöhnen. Die Löwenbabys versammelten sich im Schlafzimmer und konnten – wenn sie zum Verlassen des Zimmers gezwungen wurden – innerhalb weniger Sekunden Tagesdecken, Betttücher und Kissen zerreißen. Tippi schloss Neil in ihr Herz, genauso wie Tippis Tochter, MELANIE GRIFFITH, die Löwenbabys in ihr Herz schloss.

TIPPI HEDREN vécut avec sa famille dans une maison pleine de lions avant que ne commence le tournage de ROAR par son mari Noel Marshall. Elle voulait ainsi s'habituer à ses futurs « partenaires », Neil, un grand lion très bien dressé, et trois lionceaux qui aimaient s'installer sur le lit de la grande chambre mais pouvaient saccager couverture, draps et oreillers en quelques secondes si on tentait de les en chasser. Tippi aimait beaucoup Neil tandis que sa fille, MELANIE GRIFFITH, préférait les lionceaux.

STEVE McQUEEN, *William Claxton* 1963

DEAN MARTIN, *Larry Barbier Jr.* 1962

JOHN AND BONNIE RAITT, *Herb Ball* 1954

ROGER SMITH, *Larry Barbier Jr.* 1961

PETER AND PATRICIA LAWFORD, *Larry Barbier Jr.* 1955

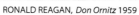

RONALD REAGAN, *Don Ornitz* 1959

RONALD AND NANCY REAGAN, *Don Ornitz* 1959

RONALD REGAN, during his G.E. THEATER days, with wife NANCY DAVIS poolside at their Bel Air home. • KIRK DOUGLAS is "helped" into the pool by sons MICHAEL, JOEL and ERIC. • JAMIE LEE CURTIS in the pool of mom Janet Leigh's home. •ESTHER WILLIAMS teaches her sons Eric and Ben Jr. to swim. • JAMES MACARTHUR and son take a giant leap.

RONALD REGAN, in seinen G.E.-THEATER-Tagen, mit Ehefrau NANCY DAVIS am Pool ihrer Wohnung in Bel Air. • KIRK DOUGLAS wird von seinen Söhnen MICHAEL, JOEL und ERIC ins Wasser befördert. • JAMIE LEE CURTIS im Hauspool ihrer Mutter Janet Leigh. • ESTHER WILLIAMS bringt ihren Söhnen Eric und Ben Jr. das Schwimmen bei. • JAMES MACARTHUR und Sohn wagen einen gewaltigen Sprung ins Wasser.

RONALD REGAN, à l'époque du G.E. THEATER, avec son épouse NANCY DAVIS, à la piscine de leur maison de Bel Air. • KIRK DOUGLAS est «plongé» dans la piscine par ses fils MICHAEL, JOEL et ERIC. • JAMIE LEE CURTIS dans la piscine de sa mère Janet Leigh. • ESTHER WILLIAMS apprend à nager à ses fils Eric et Ben Jr. • JAMES MACARTHUR plonge avec son fils.

KIRK, MICHAEL, JOEL AND ERIC DOUGLAS, *Don Ornitz* 1966

JAMIE LEE CURTIS, *John Partipilo* 1977

ESTHER WILLIAMS AND SONS, *Larry Barbier Jr.* 1954

JAMES AND CHARLES MACARTHUR, *Bill Greenslade* 1969

HELEN HAYES, *Ted Wick* 1988

ED ASNER, *J.D. Hall* 1985

MICHAEL JACKSON, *Michael Montfort* 1972

LAWRENCE WELK AND FAMILY, *Gene Trindl* 1965

In her 80s, HELEN HAYES retired to her second home, a hacienda in "the city of flowers" – Cuernavaca, Mexico. • ED ASNER considers a swim but stops short of getting wet. • MICHAEL JACKSON at the family pool in Encino. • LAWRENCE WELK with wife Fern and their grandchildren at the indoor pool in their Santa Monica home. • ROBERT and ROSEMARIE STACK strike a typical pose beside their pool. The Stacks share one of hollywood's longest marriages. In the year 2000 they celebrated their 44th anniversary.

Als 80-Jährige zog sich HELEN HAYES in ihr zweites Zuhause zurück – ein Landgut in „der Stadt der Blumen", Cuernavaca, Mexiko. • ED ASNER überlegt sich, ob er schwimmen gehen soll, lässt es dann aber kurz vor dem Nasswerden bleiben. • MICHAEL JACKSON am Familienpool in Encino. • LAWRENCE WELK mit seiner Frau Fern und ihren Enkelkindern am Pool in ihrem Haus in Santa Monica. • ROBERT und ROSEMARIE STACK nehmen eine typische Pose neben ihrem Pool ein. Die Stacks führen eine der längsten Ehen in Hollywood. Im Jahr 2000 feiern sie ihren 44. Hochzeitstag.

HELEN HAYES prit sa retraite à 80 ans dans sa maison secondaire, une hacienda de Cuernavaca, la « cité des fleurs », au Mexique. • ED ASNER se serait bien baigné mais a renoncé par peur de se mouiller. • MICHAEL JACKSON devant la piscine familiale à Encino. • LAWRENCE WELK, son épouse Fern et leurs petits-enfants au bord de la piscine intérieure de leur maison de Santa Monica. • ROBERT et ROSEMARIE STACK prennent une pose typique à côté de leur piscine. Le mariage des Stack est l'un de ceux qui durent depuis le plus longtemps à Hollywood. En l'an 2000, ils ont fêté leur 44e anniversaire de mariage.

ROBERT AND ROSEMARIE STACK, *Larry Barbier Jr.* 1956

WALTER AND CHARLES MATTHAU, *Jay Thompson* 1965

CHARLTON, LYDIA AND FRAZIER HESTON, *Don Ornitz* 1959

WALTER MATTHAU plays with son CHARLES in the pool of their Palm Springs home. In the 1990s director Charles Matthau directed his father in several films. • CHARLTON HESTON and son Frazier in the pool of the house BEN HUR built. • And DAN BLOCKER hits the pool BONANZA built. • RAY BOLGER in his first and only home sitting. Not that he had refused before, he told the photog, but simply because he had never been asked.

WALTER MATTHAU spielt mit seinem Sohn CHARLES im Pool ihres Hauses in Palm Springs. In den 90ern dirigierte Regisseur Charles Matthau seinen Vater durch einige Filme. • CHARLTON HESTON und sein Sohn Frazier im Pool des Hauses, das von den Einnahmen für den Spielfilm BEN HUR gebaut wurde. • DAN BLOCKER springt in den Pool, der von den Einnahmen des Spielfilms BONANZA gebaut wurde. • RAY BOLGER in seinem ersten und letzten Foto-Interview im Eigenheim. Es ist nicht etwa so, dass er es vorher abgelehnt hätte, aber er sei vorher nie gefragt worden, erzählte er den Fotografen.

WALTER MATTHAU joue avec son fils CHARLES dans la piscine de leur maison de Palm Springs. Dans les années 1990, Charles dirigera son père dans plusieurs films. • CHARLTON HESTON et son fils Frazier dans la piscine de la maison qui a été construite avec les revenus du film BEN HUR. • Et DAN BLOCKER sautant dans celle dont la construction a été financée grâce au cachet de BONANZA. • RAY BOLGER lors de sa seule et unique séance de pose dans l'intimité. Ce n'est pas qu'il ait déjà refusé, expliqua-t-il au photographe, mais simplement qu'on ne lui avait jamais demandé.

DAN BLOCKER, *Gerald Smith* 1960

ROBERT LANSING AND ROBERT JR., *Bill Kobrin* 1964

RAY BOLGER, *Don Ornitz* 1954

JOHN BERADINO AND JOHN ANTHONY, *Ron Grover* 1976

JACK WEBB, *Larry Barbier Jr.* 1953

JUNE LOCKHART, *Bill Kobrin* 1963

BURT REYNOLDS, *Gene Trindl* 1971

EARL HOLLIMAN, *Dick Miller* 1958

JOAN COLLINS, *Bill Kobrin* 1962

POLLY BERGEN, *Bill Kobrin* 1962

JACK WEBB pushes his dachshund Patsy around the family pool. • JUNE LOCKHART and her swimming cat, George, who June said preferred a cat-dip to catnip. • BURT REYNOLDS swims with Bertha, his beagle. • EARL HOLLIMAN enjoys a swim at his Laurel Canyon home with his diving dog Charley Brown. • JOAN COLLINS happily grooms Happy • POLLY BERGEN cools off with her children. • ROBERT CUMMINGS with his kids.

JACK WEBB schiebt seinen Dackel Patsy durch den Familienpool. • JUNE LOCKHART mit ihrer schwimmenden Katze George. • BURT REYNOLDS schwimmt mit seinem Beagle Bertha. • EARL HOLLIMAN genießt das Baden mit seinem tauchenden Hund Charley Brown in seinem Zuhause in Laurel Canyon. • JOAN COLLINS frisiert fröhlich ihren Hund Happy • POLLY BERGEN nimmt mit ihren Kindern ein kühles Bad. • ROBERT CUM-MINGS mit seinen Kindern.

JACK WEBB promène son teckel Patsy dans la piscine familiale. • JUNE LOCKHART et George, son chat nageur. • BURT REYNOLDS nage avec son beagle Bertha. • EARL HOLLIMAN se détend avec son chien Charley Brown dans la piscine de sa maison de Laurel Canyon. • JOAN COLLINS coiffe joyeusement son chien Happy. • POLLY BERGEN se détend avec ses enfants. • ROBERT CUMMINGS et ses enfants.

ROBERT CUMMINGS, *Don Ornitz* 1961

FRANK AND NANCY SINATRA WITH TINA, NANCY JR., AND FRANK JR., *Herb Ball* 1950

DEBORAH KERR AND DAUGHTERS MELANIE AND FRANCESCA, *Ossie Scott* 1954

One of TV longest-running family comedies, THE ADVENTURES OF OZZIE AND HARRIET, was the real life Nelson family on the air with the two young boys, David and Ricky, growing up before their parents' – and the televisions audience's – eyes.
• Bobby sox idol and, at the time still a family man, FRANK SINATRA poses with wife NANCY and children NANCY JR., FRANK JR. and TINA. • One of Britain's gifts to the colonies, DEBORAH KERR, here with daughters Melanie and Francesca, was a favorite of Globe's photographers.

Eine der am längsten im Fernsehen laufenden Familienserien war das alltägliche, reale Leben der Familie Nelson. In THE ADVENTURES OF OZZIE AND HARRIET wuchsen die beiden Söhne David und Ricky nicht nur vor den Augen ihrer Eltern, sondern auch vor den Augen der Fernsehzuschauer, auf. • Mädchenschwarm FRANK SINATRA, zu dieser Zeit schon verheiratet, lässt sich hier mit Ehefrau NANCY und den Kindern NANCY JR., FRANK JR. und TINA fotografieren. • DEBORAH KERR, Großbritanniens Beitrag zu Hollywood, war ein Liebling der Globe-Fotografen, hier mit den Töchtern Melanie und Francesca.

La série télévisée THE ADVENTURES OF OZZIE AND HARRIET, diffusée depuis très longtemps, faisait partager aux téléspectateurs la vie quotidienne de la famille Nelson. Les deux jeunes garçons, David et Ricky, grandissaient sous les yeux de leurs parents et des spectateurs. • L'idole de toutes les jeunes filles, FRANK SINATRA, déjà marié à cette époque, pose avec son épouse NANCY et ses enfants NANCY JR., FRANK JR. et TINA. • DEBORAH KERR, d'orgine anglaise, ici avec ses filles Melanie et Francesca, était la favorite des photographes de Globe.

<< THE NELSON FAMILY: OZZIE AND HARRIET, RICKY AND DAVID, *Globe Archive* 1952

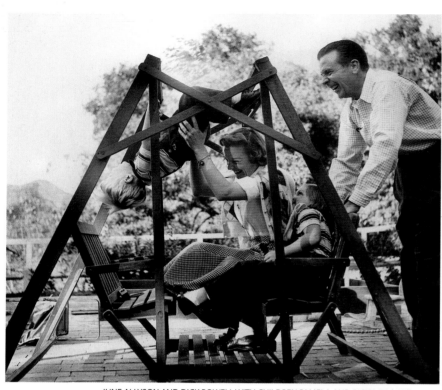

JUNE ALLYSON AND DICK POWELL WITH CHILDREN PAMELA AND RICKY, *Dick Miller* 1953

JOEL AND JODY McCREA, *Dick Miller* 1957

ART LINKLETTER AND GRANDCHILDREN, *Gene Trindl* 1965

ERROL FLYNN WITH WIFE PATRICE WYMORE AND DAUGHTER DEIDRE, *Larry Barbier Jr.* 1950

CHARLES BRONSON AND DAUGHTER SUZANNE, *Larry Barbier Jr.* 1961

GEORGE GOBEL WITH WIFE ALICE, CHILDREN LESLIE, GEORGIA AND GREGG, *Dick Miller* 1956

JOHN DAVIDSON AND DAUGHTER JENNIFER, *Gene Trindl* 1977

EDDIE AND EDWARD ALBERT, *Larry Barbier Jr.* 1959

PETER AND SUSAN FONDA WITH CHILDREN JUSTIN AND BRIDGET, *Peter Sorel* 1971

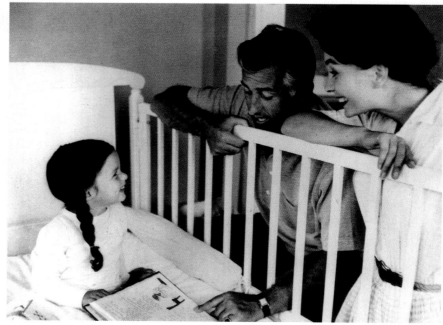

STEWART GRANGER AND JEAN SIMMONS WITH DAUGHTER TRACY, *Miller Services* 1956

CINDY WILLIAMS, *Michael Going* 1974

MIA FARROW WITH HER CHILDREN, *Vera Anderson* 1983

WILLIAM HOLDEN WITH WIFE BRENDA MARSHALL AND CHILDREN, *Chic Donchin* 1951

SID CAESAR AND FAMILY, *Gilloon* 1952

FREDRIC MARCH AND FLORENCE ELDRIDGE, *Interphoto* 1965

FREDRIC MARCH and wife FLORENCE ELDRIDGE pose for their grandsons at their Milford, Connecticut estate. • PETER FONDA on the grassy hillside of his home with wife SUSAN and children, JUSTIN and a future third generation acting Fonda, BRIDGET. • JEAN SIMMONS and STEWART GRANGER bid daughter Tracy goodnight. • CINDY WILLIAMS and sister Carol have a friendly fight over Cindy's hat collection. • MIA FARROW would have seemed an unlikely candidate for earth mother but she seems to fit the role well. Here she is with her twins, Matthew and Sascha (father is composer-conductor André Previn), adopted son Moses and adopted daughters Lark, Daisy and Soon Yi. • WILLIAM HOLDEN, wife BRENDA MARSHALL and kids Scott and Virginia are held by a story told by second son West, off camera. • SID CAESAR at home in New York with wife Florence, children Michelle and Rick.

FREDRIC MARCH und seine Frau FLORENCE ELDRIDGE posieren für ihre Enkelsöhne auf ihrem Anwesen in Milford, Connecticut. • PETER FONDA mit seiner Frau SUSAN, seinen Kindern JUSTIN und einer zukünftigen Fonda-Schauspielerin der dritten Generation, BRIDGET, auf dem grasbewachsenen Hang seines Hauses. • JEAN SIMMONS und STEWART GRANGER wünschen ihrer Tochter Tracy eine gute Nacht. • CINDY WILLIAMS und Schwester Carol streiten sich liebevoll um Cindys Hutkollektion. • Wer hätte in MIA FARROW eine Urmutter gesehen, aber sie scheint diese Rolle gut auszufüllen. Hier sieht man sie mit ihren Zwillingen Matthew und Sascha, deren Vater der Komponist und Dirigent André Previn ist, ihrem Adoptivsohn Moses und den Adoptivtöchtern Lark, Daisy und Soon Yi. • WILLIAM HOLDEN, seine Frau BRENDA MARSHALL und die Kinder Scott und Virginia hören gespannt einer Geschichte zu, die vom zweiten Sohn West (nicht im Bild) erzählt wird. • SID CAESAR mit seiner Frau Florence und den Kindern Michelle und Rick zu Hause in New York.

FREDRIC MARCH et son épouse FLORENCE ELDRIDGE posent pour leurs petits-enfants dans leur propriété de Milford (Connecticut). • PETER FONDA sur les pentes herbues de sa maison avec son épouse SUSAN et ses enfants JUSTIN et BRIDGET, la troisième génération d'acteurs de la famille Fonda. • JEAN SIMMONS et STEWART GRANGER souhaitent une bonne nuit à leur fille Tracy. • CINDY WILLIAMS et sa sœur Carol se disputent amicalement la collection de chapeaux de Cindy. • Qui aurait pu imaginer MIA FARROW dans le rôle d'une mère mais elle semble bien s'en acquitter. Elle se trouve, ici, entre ses deux jumeaux, Matthew et Sascha (leur père est le compositeur et chef d'orchestre André Previn) et ses enfants adoptifs Moses, Lark, Daisy et Soon Yi. • WILLIAM HOLDEN, son épouse BRENDA MARSHALL et leurs enfants Scott et Virginia semblent passionnés par l'histoire que raconte leur deuxième fils West (hors-champ). • SID CAESAR chez lui à New York avec son épouse Florence et ses enfants Michelle et Rick.

MIKE DOUGLAS and wife GENEVIEVE are entertained by the antics of daughter Kelly. • LEE GRANT and future actress DINAH MANOFF. • DOROTHY McGUIRE and daughter TRACY SWOPE at the beach at LaJolla, California, where Dorothy founded the famed LaJolla Playhouse. • ALAN LADD and son DAVID check egg production on their Palm Springs ranch. • MELISSA GILBERT was already appearing on LITTLE HOUSE ON THE PRAIRIE but her sister, SARA, had to wait a few years before starting her acting career. • Supper time for PATTI PAGE and CHARLES O'CURRAN means keeping watchful eyes on KATHLEEN and DANIEL. • Backyard football with JACK KLUGMAN and son DAVID. • PATTY DUKE, who lived with her managers JOHN and ETHEL ROSS, is seen here in a happy "family" moment, which was far from the truth.

LEE GRANT AND DAUGHTER DINAH MANOFF, *Gene Trindl* 1967

MIKE AND GENEVIEVE DOUGLAS WITH DAUGHTER KELLY, *Tom Caffrey* 1968

DOROTHY McGUIRE AND TRACY SWOPE, *NBC* 1955

ALAN AND DAVID LADD, *Don Ornitz* 1957

MIKE und GENEVIEVE DOUGLAS erfreuen sich an ihrer Tochter Kelly. • LEE GRANT und die zukünftige Schauspielerin DINAH MANOFF. • DOROTHY McGUIRE und Tochter TRACY SWOPE in LaJolla, Kalifornien, wo DOROTHY das berühmte LaJolla mitbegründete. • ALAN LADD und Sohn DAVID im Hühnerstall auf ihrer Ranch in Palm Springs. • MELISSA GILBERT war bereits aus UNSERE KLEINE FARM (LITTLE HOUSE ON THE PRAIRIE) bekannt, als sie für dieses Porträt posierte. Ihre Schwester SARA hingegen begann ihre Karriere als Schauspielerin erst später. • Beim Abendessen müssen PATTI PAGE und CHARLES O'CURRAN ein wachsames Auge auf ihre Kinder KATHLEEN und DANIEL werfen. • JACK KLUGMAN und sein Sohn DAVID spielen American Football. • PATTY DUKE lebte mit ihren Managern JOHN und ETHEL ROSS zusammen. Das Bild „glückliche Familie" täuscht.

MELISSA AND SARA GILBERT, *Bob Noble* 1976

MIKE et GENEVIEVE DOUGLAS admiratifs devant les exercices de gymnastique de leur fille Kelly. • LEE GRANT et la future actrice DINAH MANOFF. • DOROTHY McGUIRE et sa fille TRACY SWOPE sur la plage de LaJolla (Californie), dont le célèbre théâtre fut créé grâce à Dorothy. • ALAN LADD et son fils DAVID contrôlent la production d'œufs des poules de leur ranch de Palm Springs. • MELISSA GILBERT jouait dans LA PETITE MAISON DANS LA PRAIRIE lorsqu'elle participa à cette séance de pose, mais sa sœur SARA allait devoir attendre encore quelques années avant de se lancer dans la carrière d'actrice. • Pour PATTI PAGE et son mari le chorégraphe CHARLES O'CURRAN, le dîner oblige à une surveillance constante de KATHLEEN et DANIEL. • Une partie de football américain dans le jardin pour JACK KLUGMAN et son fils DAVID. • PATTY DUKE, qui vivait avec ses agents JOHN et ETHEL ROSS, semble connaître ici un moment de bonheur en famille – ce qui était loin d'être la réalité.

PATTI PAGE AND CHARLES O'CURRAN WITH CHILDREN KATHLEEN AND DANIEL, *Bill Kobrin* 1965

JACK AND DAVID KLUGMAN, *Bill Kobrin* 1965

ETHEL ROSS AND PATTY DUKE, *Jack Stager* 1963

DANNY THOMAS AND FAMILY, *Larry Barbier Jr.* 1958

DANNY THOMAS always tried out a new script for MAKE ROOM FOR DADDY on his family, wife Rosemarie and children Theresa, Tony and Margaret, later known as MARLO THOMAS.

DANNY THOMAS probierte ständig ein neues Skript zu MAKE ROOM FOR DADDY an seiner eigenen Familie, Frau Rosemarie und Kindern Theresa, Tony und Margaret, die später als MARLO THOMAS bekannt wurde, aus.

DANNY THOMAS lit le script de MAKE ROOM FOR DADDY pour connaître, comme d'habitude, la réaction de sa famille : son épouse Rosemarie et ses enfants Theresa, Tony et Margaret (plus tard célèbre sous le nom de MARLO THOMAS).

INGRID BERGMAN AND ISABELLA ROSSELLINI, *C. Kindahl* 1967

JACK BENNY WITH HIS GRANDCHILDREN, *Nate Cutler* 1955

ANN BLYTH WITH CHILDREN TIMOTHY, MAUREEN AND KATHLEEN, *Larry Barbier Jr.* 1958

ROBERT AND LISA RYAN, *Larry Barbier Jr.* 1955

MARY TYLER MOORE and her 6-year-old son RICHIE are pals for this single parent layout entitled "Life Without Father" for LADIES HOME JOURNAL. • Late-blooming family man JIMMY DURANTE makes sand castles with daughter CeCe near his summer home in Del Mar, California. Photog Kobrin remembers Durante rushed through the layout so he could make the first race at nearby Del Mar track. • SALLY FIELD and her two sons, PETER and ELIJAH CRAIG, near their beach house. Elijah is now the actor Eli Craig. • No matter where he worked, RICHARD HARRIS brought his family with him. During the location filming of HAWAII, their home was the oldest house on the island which once belonged to the sea captain-shipping magnate played by Harris in the film.

MARY TYLER MOORE und ihr 6 Jahre alter Sohn Richie posieren als Kumpel für die Zeitschrift LADIES HOME JOURNAL unter dem Titel „Leben ohne Vater", eine Ausgabe speziell für allein erziehende Eltern. • Der spät zu Vaterfreuden gekommene JIMMY DURANTE baut mit seiner Tochter CeCe Sandburgen in der Nähe seines Sommerferienhauses in Del Mar, Kalifornien. Fotograf Kobrin erinnert sich daran, dass Durante durch den Fototermin hetzte, um es zum ersten Wettrennen bei der nahe gelegenen Rennbahn Del Mar zu schaffen. • SALLY FIELD und ihre beiden Söhne, PETER und ELIJAH CRAIG, in der Nähe ihres Strandhauses. Elijah ist jetzt bekannt als Schauspieler Eli Craig. • Egal wo er arbeitete, RICHARD HARRIS nahm seine Familie immer mit sich mit. Während der Filmaufnahmen zu HAWAII, die vor Ort gemacht wurden, quartierten sie sich im ältesten Haus der Insel ein. Es gehörte einst dem Seefahrer und Magnat, den Harris im Spielfilm verkörperte.

MARY TYLER MOORE et son fils Richie, âgé de 6 ans, posent en grands copains sur cette photo intitulée « La vie sans père » pour le LADIES HOME JOURNAL. • JIMMY DURANTE, qui eut des enfants sur le tard, construit un château de sable avec sa fille CeCe près de sa maison d'été de Del Mar (Californie). Kobrin, le photographe, se souvient que Durante précipita la séance pour pouvoir assister à la première course à Del Mar. • SALLY FIELD et ses deux fils, PETER et ELIJAH CRAIG (aujourd'hui l'acteur Eli Craig), près de leur maison de plage. • Où qu'il travaille, RICHARD HARRIS amenait sa famille avec lui. La maison qu'ils occupèrent pendant le tournage de HAWAII était la plus ancienne de l'île et avait appartenu au marin et magnat du commerce maritime qu'il incarnait dans le film.

MARY TYLER MOORE AND SON RICHIE MEEKER, *Don Ornitz* 1962

JIMMY DURANTE AND DAUGHTER CECE, *Bill Kobrin* 1965

SALLY FIELD WITH PETER AND ELIJAH CRAIG, *Betty Graham* 1973

RICHARD HARRIS AND FAMILY, *Bill Kobrin* 1965

JAMES AND GLORIA STEWART, SONS MICHAEL AND RONALD, *Nate Cutler* 1957

JOHN AND JULIE FORSYTHE, DAUGHTERS DALL AND BROOKE, *Larry Barbier Jr.* 1959

Easter Sunday mornings with JIMMY STEWART and JOHN FORSYTHE and their families. • One of Hollywood's acting dynasties, the BRIDGES family boasts three first rate actors: father LLOYD and sons BEAU and JEFF, who was known as Lloyd Jr. when this layout was shot. With them mom Dorothy and sister Lucinda.

Ostersonntag mit JIMMY STEWART, JOHN FORSYTHE und ihren Familien. • Die Familie BRIDGES, eine der Schauspieler-dynastien Hollywoods, rühmt sich mit drei erstklassigen Schauspielern: Vater LLOYD und Söhne BEAU und JEFF, der als Lloyd Jr. bekannt war, als dieses Foto geschossen wurde. Bei ihnen stehen Mutter Dorothy und Schwester Lucinda.

Dimanche de Pâques avec JIMMY STEWART et JOHN FORSYTHE et leurs familles. • La famille BRIDGES, une des dynasties d'acteurs à Hollywood, a donné trois acteurs de premier plan: LLOYD, le père, et ses fils BEAU et JEFF (dit Lloyd Jr. lorsque cette photo a été prise), accompagnés de Dorothy, la mère, et Lucinda, la sœur.

THE BRIDGES FAMILY, *Russ Meyer* 1958

ELIZABETH MONTGOMERY WITH SONS WILLIAM AND ROBERT, *Orlando* 1966

JAMES AND JOSH BROLIN, *Gene Trindl* 1970

ELIZABETH MONTGOMERY prepares for Halloween with sons William and Robert. • JAMES BROLIN, who played a doctor on MARCUS WELBY, MD, watches son JOSH play one too. But Josh grew up to be an actor instead.

ELISABETH MONTGOMERY bereitet sich mit ihren Söhnen William and Robert auf Halloween vor. • JAMES BROLIN, der einen Arzt in der Fernsehserie MARCUS WELBY, MD darstellte, beobachtet wie sein Sohn JOSH Doktor spielt. Später wurde Josh stattdessen Schauspieler.

ELISABETH MONTGOMERY se prépare à fêter Halloween avec ses fils William et Robert. • JAMES BROLIN, qui interprète un médecin dans la série télévisée MARCUS WELBY, MD regarde son fils JOSH jouer au docteur – mais lorsque celui-ci grandit, il préféra devenir acteur.

VAN, EVIE AND SCHUYLER JOHNSON, *Larry Barbier Jr.* 1952

EVE ARDEN WITH SONS DUNCAN AND DOUGLAS, *Larry Barbier Jr.* 1960

JOHN AND PILAR WAYNE WITH CHILDREN MARISA AND ETHAN JOHN, *Beth Koch* 1969

THE OSMOND BROTHERS, *John R. Hamilton* 1969

BURT AND BILL LANCASTER, *Don Ornitz* 1954

ROBERT YOUNG AND FAMILY, *NBC* 1956

KURT RUSSELL AND FAMILY, *Globe Archive* 1963

TONY AND MARC DANZA, *Bob Noble* 1979

JANE, PETER AND HENRY FONDA, *Don Ornitz* 1962

HENRY FONDA and his acting offspsring JANE and PETER in the only sitting they ever did together. During the shoot, Peter revealed to photog Ornitz that Henry was loathe to give him and his sister compliments: "If he thought we'd done a good job, we'd hear it from his agent." • GARY COLEMAN shares an affectionate moment with his mother and father but all was not as peaceful as it looks here. Ten years later the pint-sized actor sued his estranged parents for mismanaging his earnings and won control over his career and income. • ROBERT REDFORD has an animated breakfast with son Jamie and daughter Shauna in their Utah retreat. • DONNA REED, everyone's favorite TV mom, cuddles with daughters Penny and Mary Ann.

HENRY FONDA und sein Schauspieler-Nachwuchs JANE und PETER beim einzigen Fototermin, den sie jemals zusammen abhielten. Während des Shootings verriet Peter Fotograf Ornitz, dass Henry es verabscheuen würde, ihm und seiner Schwester Komplimente zu machen: „Wenn er der Meinung wäre, dass wir unseren Job gut gemacht haben, dann würden wir es von seinem Agenten zu hören bekommen." • GARY COLEMAN in einem liebevollen Augenblick mit seiner Mutter und seinem Vater, aber nicht alles war so friedlich wie es hier aussieht. Zehn Jahre später verklagt der kleine Schauspieler seine Eltern wegen Missmanagements seines Einkommens und gewann somit die Kontrolle über seine Karriere und sein Einkommen. • ROBERT REDFORD bei einem lebhaften Frühstück mit Sohn Jamie und Tochter Shauna in ihrem Zufluchtsort in Utah. • DONNA REED, beliebteste Fernsehmutter aller, beim Kuscheln mit ihren zwei Töchtern Penny und Mary Ann.

GARY COLEMAN AND PARENTS, *Gene Trindl* 1981

HENRY FONDA et ses enfants, les acteurs JANE et PETER, au cours de la seule séance photos qui les ait jamais réunis. Peter révéla à Ornitz, le photographe, que Henry répugnait à leur faire des compliments : « S'il pense que nous avons bien travaillé, nous le saurons par son agent. » • GARY COLEMAN partage un tendre moment avec son père et sa mère, mais tout n'était pas aussi paisible qu'il y paraît. Dix ans plus tard, l'acteur nain gagnait le procès intenté à ses parents pour mauvaise gestion et reprenait le contrôle de sa carrière et de ses revenus. • ROBERT REDFORD prend un petit-déjeuner animé avec son fils Jamie et sa fille Shauna dans leur retraite de l'Utah. • DONNA REED, la maman de télévision favorite, câline ses filles Penny et Mary Ann.

ROBERT REDFORD AND CHILDREN, *William Claxton* 1965

DONNA REED AND CHILDREN, *Don Ornitz* 1962

JERRY LEWIS AND FAMILY, *Don Ornitz* 1959

NAT "KING" COLE WITH DAUGHTERS CAROL AND NATALIE, *Paul Bailey* 1955

GENE BARRY AND FAMILY, *Larry Barbier Jr.* 1958

EARTHA KITT AND DAUGHTER KIT, *Marti Cole* 1963

HAL MARCH WITH SONS PETER AND JEFFREY, *Jack Stager* 1957

STUART WHITMAN AND FAMILY, *Larry Barbier Jr.* 1958

MICHAEL CRAWFORD AND FAMILY, *Richard Fitzgerald* 1970

DENNIS DAY AND FAMILY, *Larry Barbier Jr.* 1953

GLEN CAMPBELL AND FAMILY, *Jay Thompson* 1968

SHIRLEY TEMPLE AND FAMILY, *Don Ornitz* 1965

When SHIRLEY TEMPLE, perhaps the most beloved of all Hollywood child stars, retired she became the wife of Charles Black and raised three children in the hills of Burlingame in northern California. At the time of this photo, she had come out of retirement to host SHIRLEY TEMPLE'S FAIRY TALES on NBC. Later she exchanged show business for politics, holding several posts during the Reagan and Bush administrations, including ambassadorships to Ghana and Czechoslovakia and Secretary of Protocol.

Als sich SHIRLEY TEMPLE, der vielleicht beliebteste aller Kinderstars Hollywoods, aus dem Filmgeschäft zurückzog, wurde sie die Frau von Charles Black und zog drei Kinder in den Hügeln von Burlingame in Nordkalifornien groß. Zum Zeitpunkt dieses Fotos war sie aus ihrem Ruhestand zurückgekehrt, um Gastgeberin der SHIRLEY TEMPLE'S FAIRY TALES auf NBC zu sein. Später wechselte sie vom Showgeschäft zur Politik und besetzte während der Amtszeiten von Reagan und Bush mehrere Positionen, inklusive zweier Botschafterposten für Ghana und die Tschechoslowakei. Zudem war sie Staatsprotokollantin.

SHIRLEY TEMPLE, sans doute l'enfant star préférée d'Hollywood, abandonna la scène pour épouser Charles Black et partit élever ses trois enfants dans la région vallonnée de Burlingame (dans le nord de la Californie). Au moment de cette photo, elle animait l'émission SHIRLEY TEMPLE'S FAIRY TALES sur NBC. Elle passa ensuite du show business à la politique, occupant plusieurs postes sous les administrations Reagan et Bush, dont ceux d'ambassadeur au Ghana et en Tchécoslovaquie et de chargée du Protocole.

ROBERT AND JIM MITCHUM, *Don Ornitz* 1958

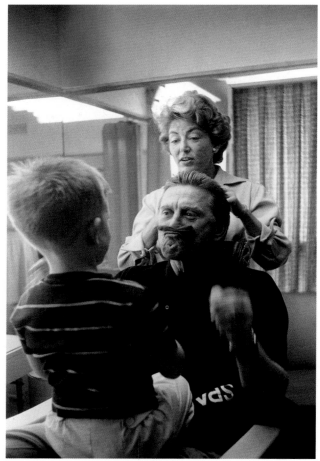

KIRK, ANNE AND PETER DOUGLAS, *William Read Woodfield* 1960

VANESSA REDGRAVE AND NATASHA RICHARDSON, *Lino Nanni* 1970

ROBERT MITCHUM and his look-alike son JIM, who followed briefly in the old man's footsteps. • KIRK DOUGLAS gets a trim from wife ANNE and uses the trimmings to create a mustache. • Young NATASHA RICHARDSON is piggy-backed by mother VANESSA REDGRAVE. • DEBBIE REYNOLDS was a single parent to daughter CARRIE FISHER and son TODD FISHER. • JANET LEIGH takes daughters JAMIE LEE and KELLY CURTIS for a spin. • RICHARD BURTON has his hands full trying to feed daughter JESSICA. • GEORG STANFORD BROWN and TYNE DALY listen to lessons. • Mother's Day with ROSEMARY CLOONEY. Gift-givers are husband JOSE FERRER, kids MIGUEL, GABRIEL and MARIA. • MARJORIE LORD has help in the kitchen from her teenaged daughter Anne, later known as ANNE ARCHER.

ROBERT MITCHUM mit seinem ihm ähnlich sehenden Sohn JIM, der nur kurz in die Fußstapfen seines Vaters trat. • KIRK DOUGLAS bekommt von seiner Frau ANNE einen Haarschnitt verpasst und verwendet die abgeschnittenen Haare als Schnurrbart. • Die junge NATASHA RICHARDSON wird von ihrer Mutter VANESSA REDGRAVE huckepack getragen. • DEBBIE REYNOLDS war allein erziehende Mutter für Tochter CARRIE FISHER und Sohn TODD FISHER. • JANET LEIGH macht mit ihren Töchtern JAMIE LEE und KELLY CURTIS eine Spritztour. • RICHARD BURTON hat beim Versuch, seine Tochter JESSICA zu füttern, alle Hände voll zu tun. • GEORG STANFORD BROWN und TYNE DALY üben mit ihren Kindern. • Muttertag mit ROSEMARY CLOONEY. Ehemann JOSE FERRER und die Kinder MIGUEL, GABRIEL und MARIA verteilen Geschenke. • MARJORIE LORD bekommt von ihrer Tochter Anne in der Küche Hilfe. Anne, die auf diesem Bild noch ein Teenager ist, wird später als ANNE ARCHER bekannt.

ROBERT MITCHUM et JIM, son fils et sosie, qui suivit brièvement les traces de son père. • KIRK DOUGLAS se fait couper les cheveux par son épouse ANNE et utilise une de ses mèches en guise de moustache. • VANESSA REDGRAVE porte sa fille NATASHA RICHARDSON. • DEBBIE REYNOLDS élevait seule sa fille CARRIE FISHER et son fils TODD FISHER. • JANET LEIGH emmène JAMIE LEE et KELLY CURTIS faire un tour de mobylette. • RICHARD BURTON s'efforce de faire manger sa fille JESSICA. • GEORG STANFORD BROWN et TYNE DALY font leurs devoirs. • Fête des Mères avec ROSEMARY CLOONEY, qui reçoit des cadeaux de son mari JOSE FERRER, et de ses enfants MIGUEL, GABRIEL et MARIA. • MARJORIE LORD se fait aider à la cuisine par sa fille Anne, alors adolescente et qui se fera connaître sous le nom de ANNE ARCHER.

DEBBIE REYNOLDS WITH CARRIE AND TODD FISHER, *Don Ornitz* 1959

JANET LEIGH WITH JAMIE LEE AND KELLY CURTIS, *Bill Kobrin* 1963

RICHARD AND JESSICA BURTON, *Marcello Geppetti* 1952

GEORG STANFORD BROWN AND TYNE DALY WITH DAUGHTERS ALISABETH AND KATHRYNE, *Eugene Coeal* 1974

JOSE FERRER AND ROSEMARY CLOONEY WITH MIGUEL, GABRIEL AND MARIA, *NBC* 1957

MARJORIE LORD AND ANNE ARCHER, *Ken Parker* 1962

Martial arts expert BRUCE LEE shot to stardom in the popular kung fu movies of the early 70s. He tragically died of a heart attack in 1973. Here he instructs his young son BRANDON in the art of karate. When he grew up, Brandon Lee also became an expert in martial arts and was just beginning a promising movie career when a freak accident caused his death on the set of THE CROW. • CLINT EASTWOOD, who once dug holes for swimming pools for a living, saw his career skyrocket when he left Hollywood to star in low-budget "spaghetti westerns" in Italy. Here Clint, his wife Maggie and son Kyle stroll their land in the Carmel area of northern California.

Der Kampfsportexperte BRUCE LEE wurde in den frühen 70er Jahren durch seine populären Kung-Fu-Filme berühmt. 1973 starb er tragischerweise an einem Herzanfall. Hier lehrt er seinen jungen Sohn BRANDON die Karatekunst. Brandon Lee wurde später auch ein Kampfsportexperte und war gerade im Begriff, eine viel versprechende Filmkarriere zu starten, als er bei einem außergewöhnlichen Unfall bei den Dreharbeiten zu DIE KRÄHE (THE CROW) ums Leben kam. • CLINT EASTWOOD, der früher einmal seinen Lebensunterhalt mit dem Schaufeln von Löchern für Swimmingpools verdiente, kehrte Hollywood den Rücken und gelang durch einen in Italien gedrehten „Italowestern" schnell zu Ruhm. Hier sieht man Clint, seine Frau Maggie und Sohn Kyle auf ihrem Grundstück in der Gegend von Carmel in Nordkalifornien spazieren gehen.

Empereur des arts martiaux, BRUCE LEE connut la célébrité dans les années 1970 grâce à ses films de kung fu puis mourut tragiquement d'une crise cardiaque en 1973. On le voit ici enseigner le karaté à son jeune fils BRANDON, qui deviendra également un expert en arts martiaux ; il entamait une carrière prometteuse au cinéma lorsqu'il décéda mystérieusement sur le tournage de THE CROW. • CLINT EASTWOOD, qui commença par gagner sa vie en creusant des piscines, a vu sa carrière monter en flèche lorsqu'il quitta Hollywood pour devenir la vedette de « westerns spaghetti » à petit budget tournés en Italie. On voit ici Clint, son épouse Maggie et son fils Kyle se promener aux environs de Carmel, dans le nord de la Californie.

CLINT, MAGGIE AND KYLE EASTWOOD, *Douglas Jones* 1971

GEORGE MONTGOMERY AND DINAH SHORE WITH CHILDREN JOHN DAVID AND MELISSA, *Larry Barbier Jr.* 1958

JOHN AND PATTI DEREK WITH CHILDREN RUSS AND SEAN, *Larry Barbier Jr.* 1950

STELLA AND ANDREW STEVENS, *Rick Strauss* 1959

WILLIAM SHATNER AND FAMILY, *Bill Greenslade* 1966

MADELEINE CARROLL AND DAUGHTER, *Globe Archive* 1948

EVA MARIE SAINT AND SON DARREL, *Frank Bez* 1958

LARRY HAGMAN AND FAMILY, *Gene Trindl* 1966

SHIRLEY MACLAINE AND SACHI PARKER, *Dick Miller* 1958

SHIRLEY MACLAINE AND SACHI PARKER, *Dick Miller* 1991

LARRY HAGMAN gets the royal treatment from wife Maj, daughter Heidi and son Preston. ● After their famous LIFE magazine cover, Dick Miller shot SHIRLEY MACLAINE and her daughter SACHI PARKER in the Santa Monica apartment Shirley had just bought. It was a mother-daughter dress-up layout with Sachi trying on Shirley's hats and shoes. Thirty-four years later, Shirley and Sachi repeated the layout. Same apartment, same photographer, same tension. Different hats.

LARRY HAGMAN wird von seiner Frau Maj, Tochter Heidi und Sohn Preston königlich verwöhnt. ● Nachdem das berühmte Titelblatt von LIFE MAGAZINE bereits erschienen war, fotografierte Dick Miller SHIRLEY MACLAINE und ihrer Tochter SACHI PARKER in ihrem Santa Monica Apartment, das Shirley gerade gekauft hatte. Auf diesem Foto machen sich Mutter und Tochter fein, wobei Sachi Shirleys Hüte und Schuhe anprobiert. 34 Jahre später wiederholten Shirley und Sachi das Foto. Dasselbe Apartment, derselbe Fotograf, dieselbe Aufregung, aber verschiedene Hüte.

LARRY HAGMAN est traité comme un prince par son épouse Maj, sa fille Heidi et son fils Preston. ● Après leur célèbre photo de couverture du magazine LIFE, Dick Miller photographia SHIRLEY MACLAINE et sa fille SACHI PARKER dans l'appartement de Santa Monica que la vedette venait d'acheter, Sachi essayant les chapeaux et les chaussures de Shirley. Trente-quatre ans plus tard, Shirley et Sachi reprirent la pose sur le même thème dans le même appartement, avec le même photographe et la même excitation ... mais d'autres chapeaux.

TOM HANKS AND RITA WILSON AT ST. SOPHIA GREEK ORTHODOX CATHEDRAL, LOS ANGELES, *Ralph Dominguez* 1988

DUSTIN AND LISA HOFFMAN, *Alan Grisbrook* 1979

WEDDINGS AND BABIES

Coverage of Hollywood weddings and babies was and is of special interest to both the national and fan magazines and both sets of publications have always been counted on to bid for exclusive first rights for such layouts. The name value of the star in question usually dictates how high the bidding can go.

Photographers have always found that celebrities behaved less like stars at these moments than at any other time. The most glamorous gods and goddesses of the screen were truly just like the fans at their weddings and when they were showing off their newborn, which was the usual order of events in the early days.

HOCHZEITEN UND BABYS

Die Berichterstattung über Hochzeiten und Babys in Hollywood waren und sind sowohl für die überregionalen Zeitschriften als auch für die Fanzeitschriften von besonderem Interesse. Von beiden erhoffte man sich immer, dass sie viel Geld für die Exklusivrechte an einem solchen Bericht bieten würden. Der Bekanntheitsgrad des betreffenden Stars bestimmte gewöhnlich die Höhe des zu zahlenden Entgelds.

Fotografen hatten schon immer das Gefühl, dass sich die Berühmtheiten in solchen Momenten am wenigsten wie Stars benahmen als zu irgendeinem anderen Zeitpunkt. Die schillerndsten Götter und Göttinnen der Leinwand verhielten sich in Wahrheit genauso wie ihre Fans bei deren Hochzeiten und beim Vorzeigen des Neugeborenen, was die früher übliche Reihenfolge war.

MARIAGES ET NAISSANCES

Les reportages sur les mariages et les naissances de Hollywood ont toujours intéressé autant les fanzines que les magazines nationaux. Et les agences photographiques étaient pratiquement sûres que ces publications feraient une offre pour en acquérir les droits d'exclusivité, le niveau minimum des enchères étant généralement dicté par la notoriété de la star en question.

Les photographes ont toujours constaté que même les personnalités les plus glamour de l'écran se comportent alors moins en stars que d'habitude au moment de la cérémonie de leur mariage ou à la présentation de leur nouveau-né, ce qui était de l'ordre naturel des choses à cette époque.

BOB NEWHART AND VIRGINIA QUINN, *Bill Kobrin* 1963

JUDY GARLAND AND MARK HERRON, *J. Cook* 1966

MICHAEL CALLAN AND PATRICIA HARTY, *Gene Trindl* 1973

BARBARA EDEN AND CHARLES FEGERT, *Larry Barbier Jr.* 1958

SUZANNE SOMERS AND ALAN HAMEL, *Bob Noble* 1977

DOROTHY MALONE AND JACQUES BERGERAC, *AFP* 1959

PEGGY LEE, *Nate Cutler* 1955

BOB NEWHART and VIRGINIA QUINN wed at St. Victor's Catholic Church in West Hollywood. • JUDY GARLAND married third husband MARK HERRON at the Little Church of the West in Las Vegas. • Home weddings for MICHAEL CALLAN and bride PATRICIA HARTY and for BARBARA EDEN and CHARLES FEGERT. • SUZANNE SOMERS and ALAN HAMEL were married in a Jewish ceremony by a Catholic priest from Scotland who gave the blessing in Hebrew with an Irish lilt. • DOROTHY MALONE and JACQUES BERGERAC wed at St. Therese Church in Hong Kong. • PEGGY LEE tosses the bride's bouquet following her marriage to BRAD DEXTER.

BOB NEWHART und VIRGINIA QUINN heiraten in der St. Victor's Catholic Church in West Hollywood. • JUDY GARLAND heiratet ihren dritten Ehemann MARK HERRON in der Little Church of the West in Las Vegas. • Hochzeiten zu Hause für MICHAEL CALLAN und Braut PATRICIA HARTY und für BARBARA EDEN und CHARLES FEGERT. • SUZANNE SOMERS und ALAN HAMEL wurden in einer jüdischen Zeremonie von einem katholischen Priester aus Schottland vermählt. Er gab seinen Segen auf Hebräisch, allerdings mit dem singenden Tonfall der Iren. • DOROTHY MALONE und JACQUES BERGERAC heiraten in der St. Therese Church in Hongkong. • PEGGY LEE wirft den Brautstrauß kurz nach der Vermählung mit BRAD DEXTER in die Luft.

BOB NEWHART et VIRGINIA QUINN se marièrent à l'église catholique St. Victor de West Hollywood. • JUDY GARLAND épouse son troisième mari, MARK HERRON, dans la Little Church of the West de Las Vegas. • Double mariage à domicile pour MICHAEL CALLAN et PATRICIA HARTY ainsi que BARBARA EDEN et CHARLES FEGERT. • SUZANNE SOMERS et ALAN HAMEL furent mariés suivant le rite judaïque par un prêtre de l'Église catholique d'Écosse qui les bénit en hébreu avec un accent irlandais. • DOROTHY MALONE et JACQUES BERGERAC se marièrent à l'église St. Therese de Hong Kong. • PEGGY LEE lance son bouquet après son mariage avec BRAD DEXTER.

MICHAEL AND DIANDRA DOUGLAS, *Michael Montfort* 1977

LEE MAJORS AND FARRAH FAWCETT, *Bruce McBroom* 1973

ANN BLYTH, PATRICK McNULTY, MICHAEL WILDING , ELIZABETH TAYLOR, *Nate Cutler* 1953

RUSS TAMBLYN AND VENETIA STEVENSON, *Ossie Scott* 1956

ROGER AND MARY MILLER WITH WILLIE NELSON, *Nate Cutler* 1978

JOAN CRAWFORD AND ALFRED STEELE, *Nate Cutler* 1955

JACK AND FELICIA LEMMON IN PARIS, *Globe Archive* 1962

JON PETERS AND LESLEY ANN WARREN, *Nate Cutler* 1967

MARISA PAVAN AND JEAN PIERRE AUMONT WITH PIER ANGELI, *Burr Jerger* 1956

STEFANIE POWERS, WILLIAM HOLDEN, CYNTHIA AND GLENN FORD, *Nate Cutler* 1977

SAMMY DAVIS JR. AND MAY BRITT, *Russ Meyer* 1960

CELINE DION AND RENE ANGELIL, *Andrea Renault* 1994

EDDIE AND NICOLE MURPHY, *John Barrett* 1993

KATE WINSLET AND JIM THREAPLETON, *Jeff Gilbert* 1998

PETER AND ELETHA FINCH, *Elio Sorci* 1973

DEBBY BOONE AND MIGUEL FERRER, *Gene Trindl* 1979

NATALIE WOOD AND RICHARD GREGSON, *Jay Thompson* 1975

The DEBBY BOONE-MIGUEL FERRER wedding at the Hollywood Presbyterian Church united two show business families. Her parents are Pat and Shirley Boone, his parents Jose Ferrer and Rosemary Clooney. • NATALIE WOOD and RICHARD GREGSON wed in a Russian Orthodox ceremony at the Holy Virgin Mary Church in Los Angeles. In the wedding party: Robert Redford and Mart Crowley. • The marriage of ARNOLD SCHWARZENEGGER and MARIA SHRIVER united the Republicans and Democrats.

Die Hochzeit von DEBBY BOONE und MIGUEL FERRER in der presbyterianischen Kirche von Hollywood vereinigte zwei Familien aus dem Showgeschäft. Ihre Eltern sind Pat und Shirley Boone, seine Eltern Jose Ferrer und Rosemary Clooney. • NATALIE WOOD und RICHARD GREGSON heiraten in einer russisch-orthodoxen Zeremonie in der Holy Virgin Mary Church in Los Angeles. Mit von der Partie bei der Hochzeit sind Robert Redford und Mart Crowley. • Die Hochzeit von ARNOLD SCHWARZENEGGER und MARIA SHRIVER vereinigte Republikaner und Demokraten.

Le mariage entre DEBBY BOONE et MIGUEL FERRER à l'église presbytérienne de Hollywood réunit deux familles du spectacle. Les parents de la mariée sont en effet Pat et Shirley Boone, et ceux du marié Jose Ferrer et Rosemary Clooney. • NATALIE WOOD et RICHARD GREGSON se marièrent suivant le rite orthodoxe russe à l'église Holy Virgin Mary de Los Angeles. On reconnaît Robert Redford et Mart Crowley dans l'assistance. • L'union de ARNOLD SCHWARZENEGGER et de MARIA SHRIVER consacre celle des Républicains et des Démocrates.

ARNOLD SCHWARZENEGGER AND MARIA SHRIVER, *John Barrett* 1986

RUE McCLANAHAN AND GUS FISHER, *Nate Cutler* 1976

SUZANNE PLESHETTE AND TROY DONAHUE, *Nate Cutler* 1964

FRANK SINATRA AND MIA FARROW, *Nate Cutler* 1966

DEAN MARTIN, PIER ANGELI
AND VIC DAMONE, *Larry
Barbier Jr.* 1954

ROMAN POLANSKI und SHARON TATE heirateten standesamtlich in Chelsea, London. • RUE McCLANAHAN und ihr fünfter Bräutigam GUS FISHER teilen sich den Hochzeitskuchen mit ihren Mitarbeitern der Serie MAUDE. • SUZANNE PLESHETTE und TROY DONAHUE heirateten im Januar und ließen sich im September scheiden. • FRANK SINATRA und MIA FARROW heirateten im Sands Hotel in Las Vegas. • DEAN MARTIN umarmt VIC DAMONE'S Braut PIER ANGELI.

ROMAN POLANSKI and SHARON TATE wed at the Chelsea Registry Office in London. • RUE McCLANAHAN and fifth bridegroom GUS FISHER share wedding cake with her coworkers on the MAUDE Show. • SUZANNE PLESHETTE and TROY DONAHUE wed in January, divorced in September. • FRANK SINATRA and MIA FARROW married at the Sands Hotel in Las Vegas. • DEAN MARTIN embraces VIC DAMONE'S bride PIER ANGELI.

ROMAN POLANSKI et SHARON TATE se marièrent au Chelsea Registry Office de Londres. • RUE McCLANAHAN et son cinquième mari GUS FISHER découpent leur gâteau de mariage, accompagnés par les partenaires de Rue dans la série télé MAUDE. • SUZANNE PLESHETTE et TROY DONAHUE se marièrent en janvier et divorcèrent en septembre. • FRANK SINATRA et MIA FARROW s'unirent au Sands Hotel de Las Vegas. • DEAN MARTIN embrasse PIER ANGELI, la nouvelle épouse de VIC DAMONE.

<< SHARON TATE AND ROMAN POLANSKI, *Sylvia Norris* 1968

DEBBIE REYNOLDS AND HARRY KARL, *Nate Cutler* 1960

FRED MACMURRAY AND JUNE HAVER, *Larry Barbier Jr.* 1954

DEAN AND CATHERINE MAE MARTIN, *Nate Cutler* 1973

ANOUK AIMEE AND ALBERT FINNEY, *Androe Csillag* 1970

HENRY AND ALFREDA FONDA, *Globe Archive* 1957

RUSS MEYER AND EDY WILLIAMS, *Nate Cutler* 1970

ETHEL MERMAN and ERNEST BORGNINE dance at their wedding reception at Chasen's restaurant in Beverly Hills. The dance lasted almost as long as the marriage. They separated 17 days later.

ETHEL MERMAN und ERNEST BORGNINE tanzen auf ihrem Hochzeitsempfang im Chasen's Restaurant in Beverly Hills. Der Tanz dauerte fast genauso lang wie ihre Ehe. 17 Tage später trennten sie sich voneinander.

ETHEL MERMAN et ERNEST BORGNINE dansent lors de leur réception de mariage au restaurant Chasen à Beverly Hills. Leur mariage fut presque aussi long que cette danse, puisqu'ils se séparèrent 17 jours plus tard.

ETHEL MERMAN AND ERNEST BORGNINE, *Bill Kobrin* 1964

SAMMY AND ALTOVISE DAVIS, *Nate Cutler* 1977

TINA LOUISE AND LES CRANE, *Nate Cutler* 1966

LINDA DARNELL AND MERLE ROBERTSON, *Nate Cutler* 1957

JANE RUSSELL AND ROGER BARRETT, *Bill Greenslade* 1968

SAMMY DAVIS JR. and wife ALTOVISE reaffirm their marriage vows seven years after their wedding. • TINA LOUISE and LES CRANE with Jim Backus, Bob Denver, Natalie Schafer, Dawn Wells, Alan Hale Jr. Nervous bride: LINDA DARNELL with MERLE ROBERTSON. • Nervous bridegroom: JANE RUSSELL with ROGER BARRETT.

SAMMY DAVIS JR. und Frau ALTOVISE beteuern sich ihre Liebe noch einmal sieben Jahre nach ihrer Hochzeit. TINA LOUISE und Bräutigam LES CRANE mit Jim Backus, Bob Denver, Natalie Schafer, Dawn Wells und Alan Hale Jr. • Nervöse Braut: LINDA DARNELL mit MERLE ROBERTSON. • Nervöser Bräutigam: JANE RUSSELL mit ROGER BARRETT.

Sept ans après leur union, SAMMY DAVIS JR. et son épouse ALTOVISE renouvelèrent leurs vœux de mariage. • TINA LOUISE et son mari LES CRANE entourés par Jim Backus, Bob Denver, Natalie Schafer, Dawn Wells et Alan Hale Jr. • Jeune mariée troublée: LINDA DARNELL avec MERLE ROBERTSON. • JANE RUSSELL et ROGER BARRETT, jeune marié troublé.

JAMES CAAN AND SHEILA RYAN, *Gary Thompson* 1976

PETER FALK AND SHERA DANESE, *Nate Cutler* 1977

ANTHONY FRANCIOSA AND JUDY BALABAN, *George E. Joseph* 1962

ANN-MARGRET AND ROGER SMITH, *Globe Archive* 1967

DEBBIE REYNOLDS AND EDDIE FISHER, *George Mattson* 1955

EDDIE FISHER AND ELIZABETH TAYLOR, *Larry Barbier Jr.* 1959

DEBBIE REYNOLDS and EDDIE FISHER wed at Grossiner's Country Club. • Just hours after Eddie won a Nevada divorce from Debbie he married ELIZABETH TAYLOR in a 15 minute Jewish ceremony in Las Vegas. • NATALIE WOOD and ROBERT WAGNER cut the cake at their first wedding. The couple divorced in 1963 and remarried in 1972.

DEBBIE REYNOLDS und EDDIE FISHER heirateten im Grossiner's Country Club. • Just nachdem Eddie in Nevada eine Scheidung von Debbie hinter sich gebracht hatte, heiratete er ELIZABETH TAYLOR in einer 15 Minuten langen jüdischen Zeremonie in Las Vegas. • NATALIE WOOD und ROBERT WAGNER schneiden auf ihrer ersten Hochzeit den Kuchen an. Das Paar ließ sich im Jahre 1963 scheiden und heiratete dann im Jahre 1972 erneut.

DEBBIE REYNOLDS et EDDIE FISHER se marièrent au Grossiner's Country Club. • Eddie épousa ELIZABETH TAYLOR lors d'une cérémonie juive de 15 minutes à Las Vegas quelques heures après avoir obtenu le divorce au Nevada contre Debbie. • NATALIE WOOD et ROBERT WAGNER découpent le gâteau de leur premier mariage. Ils divorcèrent en 1963 et se remarièrent en 1972.

NATALIE WOOD AND ROBERT WAGNER, *Larry Barbier Jr.* 1957

PRISCILLA AND ELVIS PRESLEY, *Nate Cutler* 1967

DAVID CASSIDY AND KAY LENZ, *Zinmaster* 1977

TOMMY SANDS AND NANCY SINATRA JR., *Nate Cutler* 1960

LUCILLE BALL AND GARY MORTON, *Jack Stager* 1961

JACK CASSIDY AND SHIRLEY JONES, *Don Ornitz* 1956

LYNDA CARTER AND RON SAMUEL, *Gene Trindl* 1977

GARY MORTON and JACK CASSIDY carried their brides, LUCILLE BALL and SHIRLEY JONES, over the threshold the conventional way. • LYNDA CARTER reverses the gesture, but then she played Wonder Woman.
JULIET MILLS and MAXWELL CAULFIELD wed at Point Dume, high on a cliff overlooking the Pacific ocean. • In a bizarre move even for Hollywood, TINY TIM and MISS VICKY were married on the Johnny Carson TONIGHT show. • DIAHANN CARROLL removes her garter following her wedding to Vic Damone.

GARY MORTON und JACK CASSIDY tragen ihre Bräute LUCILLE BALL und SHIRLEY JONES auf ganz konventionelle Art und Weise über die Türschwelle. • LYNDA CARTER vertauscht die Rollen als Wonder Woman.
JULIET MILLS und MAXWELL CAULFIELD heirateten im Point Dume, hoch oben auf einem Kliff mit Blick über den Pazifischen Ozean. • Selbst in einer für Hollywood bizarren Art und Weise, gaben sich TINY TIM und MISS VICKY in der Johnny-Carson-Show TONIGHT das Jawort. • DIAHANN CARROLL zieht sich nach ihrer Hochzeit mit Vic Damone das Strumpfband aus.

Suivant la tradition, GARY MORTON et JACK CASSIDY portent chacun leur jeune épouse, LUCILLE BALL et SHIRLEY JONES, pour franchir le pas de la porte de leur maison. • Mais LYNDA CARTER, qui incarnait alors Wonder Woman, se doit d'inverser les rôles.
JULIET MILLS et MAXWELL CAULFIELD se marièrent à Point Dume, au sommet d'une falaise dominant l'océan Pacifique. • Créant la surprise même pour Hollywood, TINY TIM et MISS VICKY se marièrent lors du show Johnny Carson TONIGHT. • DIAHANN CARROLL enlève sa jarretière après son mariage avec Vic Damone.

JULIET MILLS AND MAXWELL CAULFIELD, *Jonathan Mills*, 1980

TINY TIM AND MISS VICKY, *NBC* 1969

MARIAH CAREY AND TOMMY MOTTOLA, *Steve Trupp* 1993

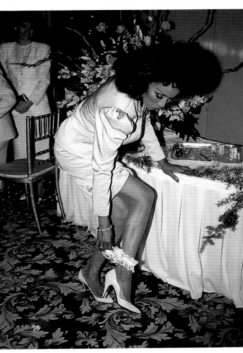

DIAHANN CARROLL, *Globe Archive* 1987

VANESSA WILLIAMS AND RICK FOX, *John Barrett* 1999

JANET LEIGH AND ROBERT BRANDT, *Larry Barbier Jr.* 1962

JAMES DARREN, *Jack Stager* 1960

JANET LEIGH and ROBERT BRANDT apply for their marriage license. • JAMES DARREN rehearses before his wedding to Evy Norlund. • STEFANIE POWERS shops for trousseau and wedding accessories prior to her marriage to Gary Lockwood. • SUE LYON and HAMPTON FANCHER III at the marriage license bureau.

JANET LEIGH und ROBERT BRANDT beantragen ihre Eheerlaubnis. • JAMES DARREN übt vor seiner Hochzeit mit Evy Norlund noch einmal den Ablauf der Zeremonie. • STEFANIE POWERS kauft vor ihrer Hochzeit mit Gary Lockwood ihre Aussteuer und Hochzeitszubehör. • SUE LYON und HAMPTON FANCHER III im Amt für Eheerlaubnis.

JANET LEIGH et ROBERT BRANDT signent leur licence de mariage. • JAMES DARREN répète la cérémonie avec Evy Norlund. • STEFANIE POWERS achète son trousseau et ses accessoires de mariage avant d'épouser Gary Lockwood. • SUE LYON et HAMPTON FANCHER III au bureau des licences de mariage.

STEFANIE POWERS, *Ron Thal* 1966

MARRIAGE LICENSES

HAMPTON FANCHER III AND SUE LYON, *Ron Joy* 1964

RICK NELSON AND KRISTIN HARMON, *Bill Kobrin* 1963

MICHAEL AND PAT YORK, *Richard Polak* 1968

MICHAEL LANDON, *Gary Null* 1983

PHIL AND EVELYN SILVERS, *David Workman* 1956

RICK NELSON and his bride KRISTIN leave St. Martin of Tours Church in Brentwood. • MICHAEL YORK wed photographer PATRICIA McCALLUM (she was a Globe photographer then) on his 26th birthday. • MICHAEL LANDON tosses his bride CINDY'S garter over his shoulder at his Malibu home. • PHIL SILVERS and bride EVELYN call her mother following their marriage.

RICK NELSON und seine Braut KRISTIN verlassen die Kirche St. Martin of Tours in Brentwood. • MICHAEL YORK heiratete an seinem 26. Geburtstag die Fotografin PATRICIA McCALLUM (sie war zu dieser Zeit Globe-Fotografin). • MICHAEL LANDON wirft in seinem Zuhause in Malibu das Strumpfband seiner Braut CINDY über seine Schulter. • PHIL SILVERS und Braut EVELYN rufen nach ihrer Hochzeit EVELYNS Mutter an.

RICK NELSON et son épouse KRISTIN quittent l'église St. Martin of Tours de Brentwood. • MICHAEL YORK a épousé la photographe PATRICIA McCALLUM (qui travaillait alors pour Globe) le jour de ses 26 ans. • MICHAEL LANDON lance la jarretière de son épouse CINDY dans sa maison de Malibu. • PHIL SILVERS et son épouse EVELYN appellent la mère de la nouvelle mariée.

RITA HAYWORTH AND DICK HAYMES, *Globe Archive* 1953

MICKEY AND MARGIE ROONEY, *Nate Cutler* 1966

TONY AND LESLIE CURTIS, *Nate Cutler* 1968

LANA TURNER AND ROBERT EASTON, *Nate Cutler* 1965

DENNIS AND HENRY HOPPER, *Andrea Renault* 1996

It was the fourth marriage for both RITA HAYWORTH and DICK HAYMES. Together they racked up twelve. • MARGIE LANG was the fifth of MICKEY ROONEY'S nine brides. • LESLIE ALLEN the third of five wives for TONY CURTIS. • LANA TURNER went to the altar seven times. Number six was ROBERT EASTON. • DENNIS HOPPER arrives at Boston's historic Old South Church with his son HENRY for his fifth wedding ceremony.

Es war sowohl die vierte Ehe für RITA HAYWORTH als auch für DICK HAYMES. Zusammen brachten sie es auf zwölf Ehen. • MARGIE LANG war die fünfte von MICKEY ROONEYS insgesamt neun Bräuten. • LESLIE ALLEN war die dritte von insgesamt fünf Ehefrauen von TONY CURTIS. • LANA TURNER ging sieben Mal zum Altar. Nummer sechs war ROBERT EASTON. • DENNIS HOPPER erscheint in Begleitung seines Sohnes HENRY in Bostons historischer Old South Church zu seiner fünften Hochzeit.

Quatrième mariage pour RITA HAYWORTH comme pour DICK HAYMES, qui en totalisèrent douze à eux deux. • MARGIE LANG devenait la cinquième des neuf femmes de MICKEY ROONEY. • LESLIE ALLEN fut la troisième des cinq femmes de TONY CURTIS. • LANA TURNER passa sept fois devant l'autel, étant accompagnée par ROBERT EASTON pour son sixième mariage. • Pour son cinquième mariage, DENNIS HOPPER est arrivé à l'église historique de Old South de Boston accompagné de son fils HENRY.

ROSEMARIE AND DANNY THOMAS, *Nate Cutler* 1996

RICHARD BURTON AND ELIZABETH TAYLOR, *Globe Archive* 1975

ELIZABETH TAYLOR and RICHARD BURTON at their second wedding, the sixth of her eight, the third of his four. • DANNY and ROSEMARIE THOMAS celebrate their 50th wedding anniversary. They hold the photograph taken on their wedding day.

ELIZABETH TAYLOR und RICHARD BURTON bei ihrer zweiten Hochzeit, die sechste ihrer insgesamt acht Hochzeiten, die dritte seiner vier. • DANNY und ROSEMARIE THOMAS feiern ihre goldene Hochzeit. In der Hand halten sie das Foto, das an ihrem Hochzeitstag aufgenommen wurde.

ELIZABETH TAYLOR et RICHARD BURTON lors de leur second mariage, le sixième sur huit pour elle et le troisième sur quatre pour lui. • DANNY et ROSEMARIE THOMAS célèbrent leur 50e anniversaire de mariage. Ils tiennent à la main la photo prise le jour de la cérémonie.

AMANDA BLAKE AND MR. BLACKWELL, *Orlando* 1964

AUDREY HEPBURN AND DR. ANDREA DOTTI, *Globe Archive* 1969

LIZA MINNELLI AND JACK HALEY JR., *Nate Cutler* 1974

JEFF AND SUSAN BRIDGES, *Nate Cutler* 1977

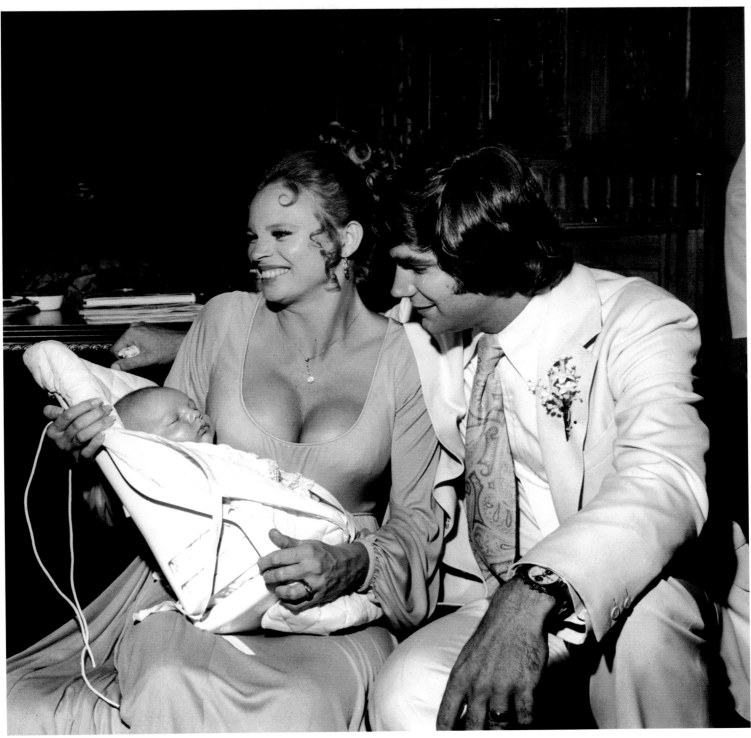

JULIET PROWSE AND JOHN McCOOK, *Nate Cutler* 1972

On the day JULIET PROWSE and JOHN McCOOK were to be married, the ceremony had to be cancelled because of the arrival of their son Seth. When the wedding was rescheduled, Seth was on hand to sleep through the ceremony and reception.

Am Tag, an dem JULIET PROWSE und JOHN McCOOK vermählt werden sollten, musste die Zeremonie wegen der Geburt ihres Sohnes Seth abgesagt werden. Als die Hochzeit zu einem neuen Termin stattfand, war Seth dabei und verschlief Zeremonie und Hochzeitsempfang.

JULIET PROWSE et JOHN McCOOK durent reporter leur mariage à cause de la naissance de leur fils Seth, qui dormit tout le temps de la cérémonie et de la réception qui unit plus tard ses parents.

PATRICIA NEAL AND LUCY DAHL, *Pictorial Press* 1965

PATRICIA NEAL holds her infant daughter LUCY, the "miracle baby" she was carrying when she was felled by the three massive strokes in 1964 which left her disabled for many months. Her recovery and reemergence into both family and professional life is one of the most moving of Hollywood's real life dramas.

PATRICIA NEAL hier mit ihrer Tochter LUCY, dem „Wunderbaby". Während ihrer Schwangerschaft im Jahre 1964 erlitt Patricia drei massive Schlaganfälle, die sie für viele Monate arbeitsunfähig machten. Ihre Genesung und Rückkehr in die Familie und ins Berufsleben ist eines der bewegendsten, tatsächlich geschehenen Hollywood-Dramen.

PATRICIA NEAL avec sa fille LUCY, ce « bébé du miracle » dont elle était enceinte en 1964 lorsqu'elle subit trois attaques qui la laissèrent paralysée pendant plusieurs mois. Sa guérison et son retour à une vie (professionnelle et privée) normale en font l'héroïne de l'un des drames les plus émouvants de Hollywood.

JANE FONDA AND VANESSA VADIM, *Bruce McBroom* 1969

ANDY AND NOELLE WILLIAMS, *Doris Nieh* 1965

CAROL LYNLEY WITH DAUGHTER JILL, *William Claxton* 1964

SHIRLEY MACLAINE WITH STEPHANIE SACHIKO PARKER, *Larry Barbier Jr.* 1956

BEAU AND CASEY BRIDGES, *Orlando* 1969

NATALIE WOOD WITH NATASHA GREGSON, *Orlando* 1970

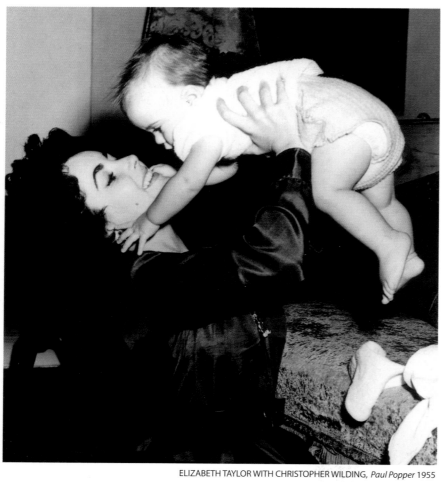

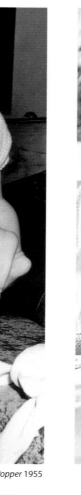

ELIZABETH TAYLOR WITH CHRISTOPHER WILDING, *Paul Popper* 1955

JULIE ANDREWS AND EMMA WALTON, *Bill Kobrin* 1964

CAROL BURNETT AND CARRIE HAMILTON, *Jay Thompson* 1965

ANGIE DICKINSON AND BURT BACHARACH WITH LEA NIKKI, *Orlando* 1967

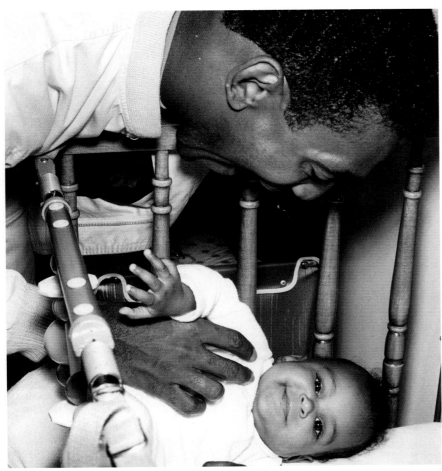

BILL AND ERICA COSBY, *Sylvia Norris* 1965

RICHARD THOMAS WITH SON RICHARD JR. AND TRIPLETS BARBARA, GWYNETH AND PILAR, *Nate Cutler* 1981

DEAN AND JEANNE MARTIN WITH DEAN PAUL, *Globe Archive* 1951

WILL "SUGARFOOT" HUTCHINS AND DAUGHTER JENNIFER, *Paul Bailey* 1965

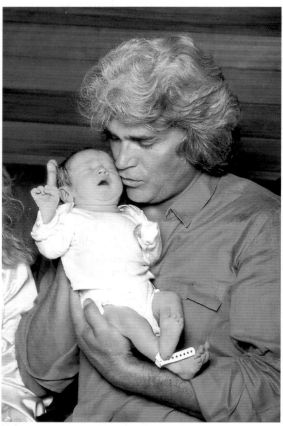

MICHAEL AND SEAN LANDON, *Frank Carroll* 1988

LYNN REDGRAVE WITH DAUGHTER ANNABEL, *Nate Cutler* 1981

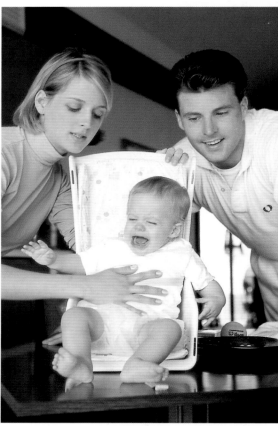

RICK AND KRISTIN NELSON WITH TRACY, *Bill Kobrin* 1963

KAREN BLACK, L. MINOR (KIT) CARSON WITH HUNTER MINOR NORMAN, *Bob Noble* 1976

MICHAEL AND PAULA COLE WITH JENNIFER HOLLY, *Peter Sorel* 1971

CARL WEATHERS WITH MATTHEW AND JASON, *Steve Schatzberg* 1979

TONY CURTIS is taught how to change a diaper in a class for expectant fathers before the birth of his and Janet Leigh's first child.

TONY CURTIS lernt, in einem Kurs für werdende Väter, wie man Windeln wechselt. Die Geburt seines und Janet Leighs ersten Kindes steht bald bevor.

TONY CURTIS apprend à langer dans une classe pour futurs pères peu avant la naissance de son premier enfant avec Janet Leigh.

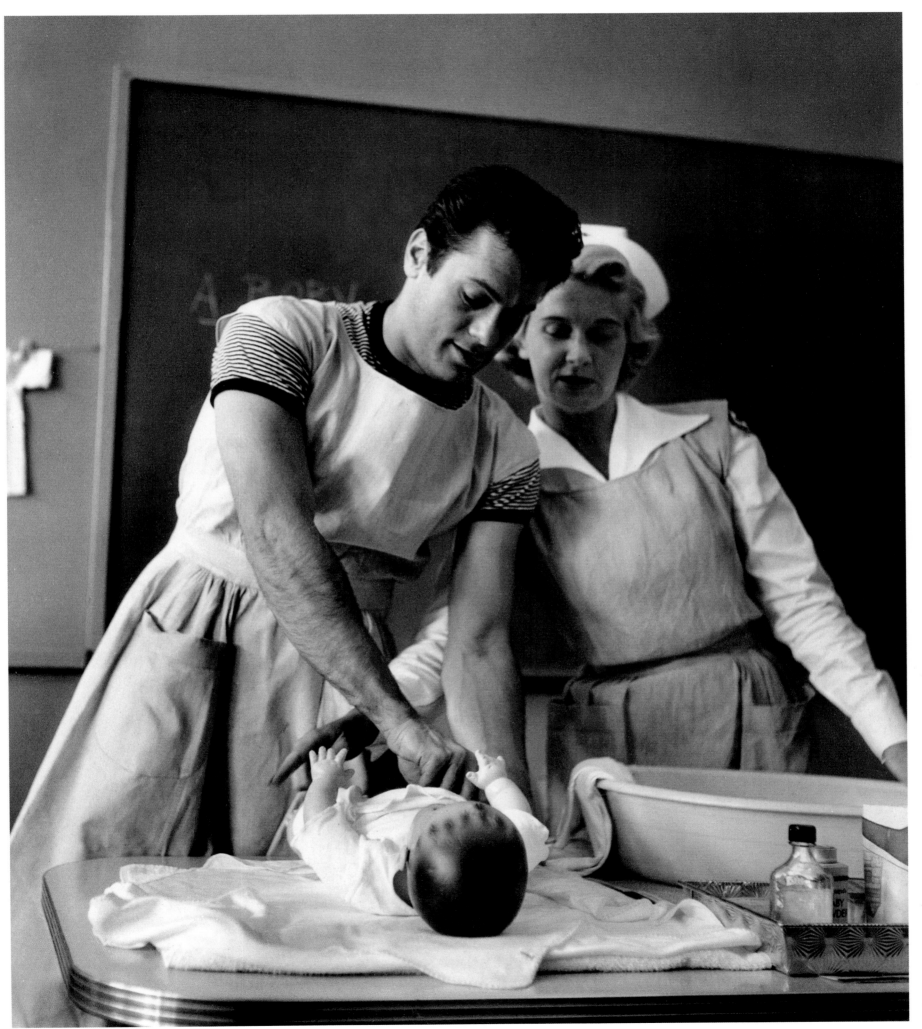

TONY CURTIS, *Larry Barbier Jr.* 1959

NICK AND CAROL ADAMS WITH JEB, *Larry Barbier Jr.* 1961

HOPE LANGE WITH SON CHRISTOPHER MURRAY, *Don Ornitz* 1957

AMY IRVING, STEVEN SPIELBERG AND SON MAX, *Alan Davidson* 1985

BARBARA HERSHEY SEAGULL (as she was known then) demonstrates just how much home sittings had changed by the 70s. Not only was she an unmarried mother, Barbara was not shy about nursing her son Free during the layout.

BARBARA HERSHEY SEAGULL (unter diesem Namen war sie damals bekannt) demonstriert, wie sehr sich Foto-Shootings in den 70er verändert hatten. Sie war nicht nur eine unverheiratete Mutter, sondern hatte auch keine Scheu, ihren Sohn Free während der Aufnahme zu stillen.

Cette photo de BARBARA HERSHEY SEAGULL (son nom à cette époque), mère célibataire en train d'allaiter son fils Free pendant la prise, témoigne de l'évolution du photoreportage dans les années 1970.

BARBARA HERSHEY AND SON FREE, *Jim McHugh* 1973

JACK AND CHRISTOPHER LEMMON, *Larry Barbier Jr.* 1954

SOPHIA LOREN AND CARLO PONTI JR., *Globe Archive* 1973

VIC AND JENNIFER MORROW, *Bill Kobrin* 1963

TERRY MOORE WITH STUART AND GRANT CRAMER, *Bill Kobrin* 1962

DESI ARNAZ AND LUCILLE BALL WITH DESI JR., *Nate Cutler* 1953

LIV ULLMANN AND LINN BERGMAN, *Joel Elkins* 1970

JACK LEMMON takes son CHRISTOPHER for a ride. • SOPHIA LOREN holds her firstborn. • VIC MORROW with his rambunctious daughter, the future JENNIFER JASON LEIGH. • TERRY MOORE with sons. The one getting his hair combed became an actor. • LUCILLE BALL and DESI ARNAZ with son DESI JR. at his christening. • LIV ULLMANN'S daughter LINN tries out mama's fur hat. Linn's father is Swedish director Ingmar Bergman.

JACK LEMMON dreht mit seinem Sohn CHRISTOPHER eine Runde. • SOPHIA LOREN hält ihr Erstgeborenes. • VIC MORROW mit seiner lebhaften Tochter, der zukünftigen JENNIFER JASON LEIGH. • TERRY MOORE mit seinen Söhnen. Der, der gekämmt wird, wurde später Schauspieler. • LUCILLE BALL und DESI ARNAZ mit Sohn DESI JR. bei seiner Taufe. • LIV ULLMANNS Tochter LINN probiert Mamis Pelzhut aus. Linns Vater ist der schwedische Filmregisseur Ingmar Bergman.

JACK LEMMON promène son fils CHRISTOPHER. • SOPHIA LOREN avec son premier-né. • VIC MORROW avec son exubérante fille, la future JENNIFER JASON LEIGH. • TERRY MOORE avec ses fils. Celui qui se fait peigner, devint plus tard acteur. • LUCILLE BALL et DESI ARNAZ lors du baptême de leur fils DESI JR. • LINN, la fille de LIV ULLMANN et d'Ingmar Bergman, le metteur en scène suédois, essaie la toque de fourrure de sa mère.

DAVID BIRNEY AND MEREDITH BAXTER WITH TWINS MOLLIE AND PETER, *Glenn Birney* 1984

JIM WITH HEIDI AND TIMOTHY HUTTON, *Don Ornitz* 1960

JAYNE MANSFIELD AND ZOLTAN HARGITAY, *Larry Barbier Jr.* 1969

TONY CURTIS AND JANET LEIGH WITH DAUGHTERS KELLY AND JAMIE LEE, *Dick Miller* 1958

ED BEGLEY WITH WIFE HELEN AND CHILDREN ED BEGLEY JR. AND MAUREEN, *Jay Thompson* 1964

BARBARA EDEN AND MATTHEW ANSARA, *Orlando* 1967

JOHN AND ETHAN JOHN WAYNE, *Bernie Abramson* 1962

JOHN WAYNE holds son ETHAN JOHN. He was to have been christened John Ethan Wayne but director John Ford changed that. Ford's present was a silver cup inscribed with the child's initials and he said he couldn't bring himself to have the cup etched J.E.W. so he insisted that Wayne reverse the names. • JIM HUTTON plays on Malibu beach with his two young children, daughter Heidi and the future Oscar winner TIMOTHY HUTTON. • JAMIE LEE CURTIS makes her debut with parents TONY CURTIS and JANET LEIGH and sister KELLY. • ED BEGLEY holds daughter Maureen as wife Helen looks on with son ED BEGLEY JR.

JOHN WAYNE hält Sohn ETHAN JOHN. Er sollte eigentlich John Ethan Wayne getauft werden, aber Filmregisseur John Ford änderte das. Ford schenkte einen silbernen Becher mit den Initialen des Kindes. Er sagte, er hätte sich nicht überwinden können, J.E.W. in den Becher eingravieren zu lassen. Deshalb drängte er darauf, den Namen umzustellen. • JIM HUTTON spielt mit Tochter Heidi und Sohn TIMOTHY, zukünftiger Oscar-Gewinner, am Strand von Malibu. • JAMIE LEE CURTIS macht ihr Debüt mit Eltern TONY CURTIS und JANET LEIGH und Schwester KELLY. • ED BEGLEY hält Tochter Maureen, während Frau Helen mit Sohn ED BEGLEY JR. zusieht.

JOHN WAYNE et son fils ETHAN JOHN. L'enfant devait s'appeler John Ethan Wayne mais le réalisateur John Ford ayant déjà acheté une timbale en argent gravée aux initiales E.J.W., il insista pour que John Wayne modifie l'ordre des prénoms. • JIM HUTTON joue sur la plage de Malibu avec ses deux jeunes enfants, sa fille Heidi et son fils TIMOTHY HUTTON, futur primé aux Oscars. • JAMIE LEE CURTIS fait ses débuts avec ses parents TONY CURTIS et JANET LEIGH, et sa sœur KELLY. • ED BEGLEY tient dans ses bras sa fille Maureen sous le regard de son épouse Helen et de son fils ED BEGLEY JR.

FRANKIE AVALON WITH FRANKIE JR., *Gene Trindl* 1965

CARY GRANT, *Sylvia Norris* 1966

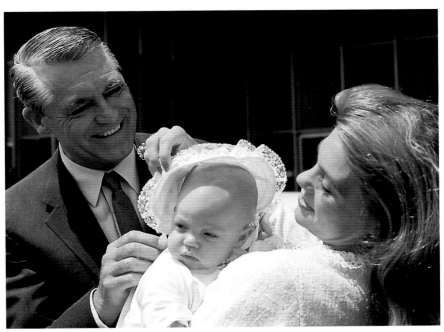

CARY GRANT AND DYAN CANNON WITH JENNIFER, *Sylvia Norris* 1966

ROY AND ROBIN ELIZABETH ROGERS, *Dick Miller* 1957

JAMES AND TARA CAAN, *John R. Hamilton* 1966

CARY GRANT, wife DYAN CANNON and baby JENNIFER aboard the British liner Oriana bound for England where Cary introduced his only child to her 89-year-old grandmother. • Cowboy star ROY ROGERS with 6-month-old daughter ROBIN ELIZABETH. • JAMES CAAN with daughter TARA on the set of El DORADO. • ROD STEIGER has a difference of opinion with son DAVID, who was born in the actor's 68th year.

CARY GRANT, Frau DYAN CANNON und Baby JENNIFER an Bord des britischen Linienschiffs Oriana auf dem Weg nach England. Dort stellt Cary sein einziges Kind der 89 Jahre alten Groß-mutter vor. • Cowboystar ROY ROGERS mit seiner sechs Monate alten Tochter ROBIN ELIZABETH. • JAMES CAAN mit seiner Tochter TARA bei den Dreharbeiten zu EL DORADO. • ROD STEIGER hat eine Meinungsverschiedenheit mit Sohn DAVID, der erst im 68. Lebensjahr des Schauspielers geboren wurde.

CARY GRANT, accompagné de son épouse DYAN CANNON et de sa fille JENNIFER, se rend en Angle-terre à bord du paquebot britannique Oriana pour présenter son seul fils à sa grand-mère, alors âgée de 89 ans. • ROY ROGERS, la vedette des westerns, avec sa fille de 6 mois, ROBIN ELIZABETH. • JAMES CAAN et sa fille TARA sur le tournage de El DORADO. • ROD STEIGER discute avec son fils DAVID, né alors que l'acteur avait 68 ans.

ROD AND DAVID STEIGER, *Lisa Rose* 1994

ANNETTE FUNICELLO AND JACK GILARDI WITH GINA, *Gene Trindl* 1966

EDD "KOOKIE" BYRNES AND SON LOGAN, *Gene Trindl* 1966

MARGARET O'BRIEN AND DAUGHTER MARA, *Nate Cutler* 1976

DEBBIE REYNOLDS AND EDDIE FISHER WITH CARRIE, *Larry Barbier Jr.* 1956

SHIRLEY JONES WITH SHAUN, PATRICK AND RYAN CASSIDY, *Larry Barbier Jr.* 1968

GEORGE, MARION AND ELIZABETH SEGAL, *Globe Archive* 1958

JIMMY DURANTE'S expression says it all. The Schnoz is the proudest of new papas at the christening of his adopted daughter CeCe. CeCe's famous godparents are comedian DANNY THOMAS and gossip columnist Louella Parsons.

JIMMY DURANTES Gesichtsausdruck sagt alles. Er ist der stolzeste aller neuen Väter bei der Taufe seiner adoptierten Tochter CeCe. Ihre berühmte Paten sind Komödiant DANNY THOMAS und Klatschgeschichten-Kolumnistin Louella Parsons.

L'expression de JIMMY DURANTE est explicite. Le « Schnoz » est le plus fier des pères lors du baptême de sa fille adoptive CeCe. Les célèbres parrain et marraine de CeCe sont le comédien DANNY THOMAS et l'échotière Louella Parsons.

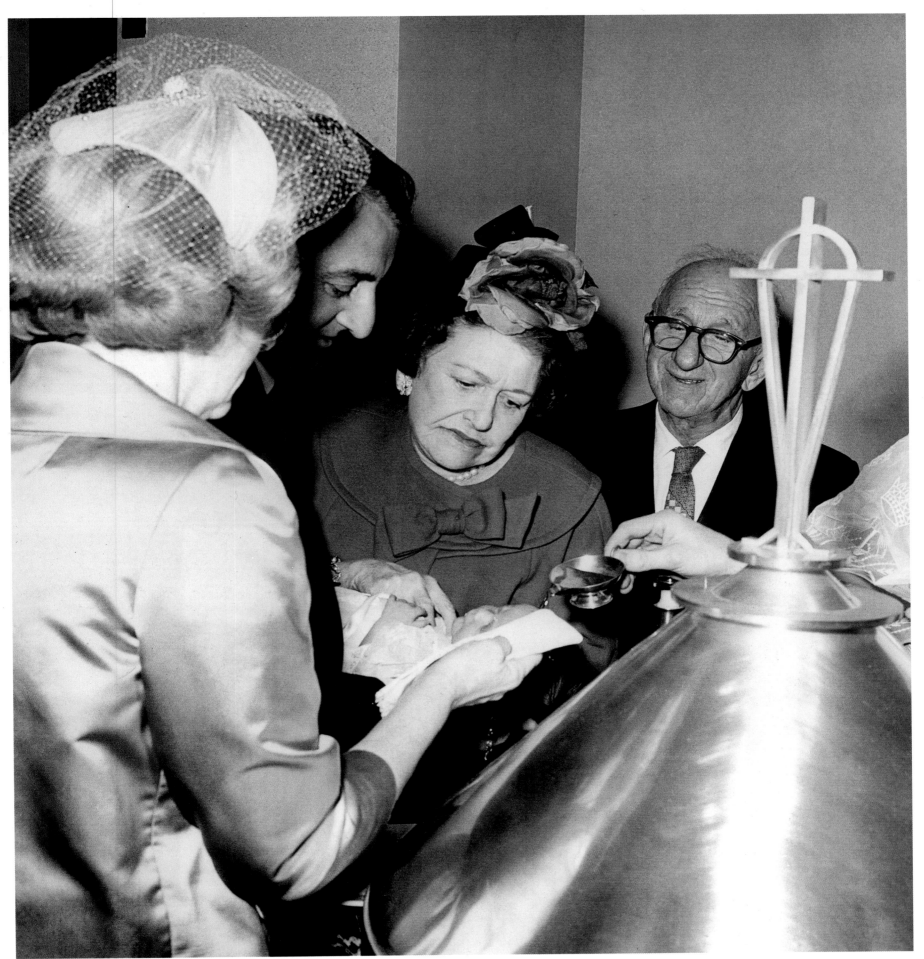

JIMMY DURANTE AND MARGE WITH DANNY THOMAS AND LOUELLA PARSONS, *Nate Cutler* 1961

DUSTIN HOFFMAN, *Robert Goldberg* 1971

FRED ALLEN, *Globe Archive* 1948

GINA LOLLOBRIGIDA, *Leo Fuchs* 1958

SITTING AWAY FROM HOME

Occasionally a star would not be available for a home sitting. The home itself might be off limits for photography or perhaps too many layouts had been done there. In the case of the younger players their homes might not be deemed "right" (read "nice enough") for a layout. But studio and personal publicists were loathe to lose magazine space in those days and alternate suggestions were offered.

"A Day in the Life of..." was a popular substitute. This could incorporate anything from a shopping spree to a visit to a local art gallery or a workout at a gym. Graduation day and a child's first haircut could be special. Parks and zoos made for interesting and fun pictures. Marineland and Pacific Ocean Park were homes away from home for us. And since Globe had stringers throughout the world, vacations could make the best layouts of all.

PRIVATES FERN DES EIGENHEIMS

Ab und zu war ein Star für Fotos in seinen eigenen vier Wänden nicht zu haben. Es konnte sein, dass das Haus zum Fotografieren nicht zur Verfügung stand oder dort schon zu viele Reportagen gemacht worden waren. Im Falle der jüngeren Schauspieler kam es vor, dass die Häuser dafür nicht „richtig" waren (das bedeutet nicht „schön genug"). Aber das Studio oder die Agenten wollten damals ungerne auf den Platz in den Zeitschriften verzichten und somit wurden Alternativen angeboten.

„Ein Tag im Leben von ..." war ein beliebter Ersatz. Dabei konnte es sich um alles Mögliche handeln, von einem Einkaufsbummel bis zu einem Besuch in einer örtlichen Kunstgalerie oder einem Training im Fitnesscenter. Der Tag der Abschlussfeier oder der erste Haarschnitt des Kindes konnten ebenfalls etwas Besonderes sein. Parks und Zoos waren für interessante und lustige Bilder geeignet. Marineland und Pacific Ocean Park waren Heime fern des Eigenheims. Und da Globe-Reporter rund um die Welt hatte, gaben Urlaubsreisen die besten Fotos ab.

L'INTIMITÉ À L'EXTÉRIEUR

Il arrivait qu'il ne soit ni possible ni souhaitable de procéder à des séances de photos au domicile d'une star, soit qu'elle ait interdit d'y photographier soit que le décor ait déjà servi de trop nombreuses fois. Dans le cas des plus jeunes acteurs, leur maison pouvait ne pas être jugée suffisamment «convenable» (c'est-à-dire «belle») pour y réaliser un reportage photo. Mais, comme les agents de publicité des Studios et les attachés de presse répugnaient à perdre l'espace alloué par le magazine, ils proposaient généralement des solutions de remplacement.

«Une journée particulière dans la vie de ...» était un des thèmes alternatifs les plus fréquemment employés. Cette rubrique permettait de traiter de n'importe quel sujet, depuis les courses dans les magasins à la visite d'une galerie d'art ou une séance d'entraînement au gymnase. Une cérémonie de remise de diplômes ou la première séance chez le coiffeur d'un enfant pouvaient faire l'objet d'un reportage spécial tandis que la visite d'un parc ou d'un zoo donnait souvent lieu à des photos intéressantes et drôles. Marineland et le Pacific Ocean Park nous devinrent bientôt des décors familiers. Les lieux de vacances des stars étaient le cadre idéal, Globe disposant de correspondants dans le monde entier.

ANN-MARGRET, *Don Ornitz* 1961

JOANNE WOODWARD, *Don Ornitz* 1959

EVA MARIE SAINT, *Don Ornitz* 1959

DENNIS AND JOEY COLE, *Gene Trindl* 1967

CLAUDIA CARDINALE, *Don Dornan* 1966

JANE POWELL AND SON GERRY STEFAN, *Larry Barbier Jr.* 1956

Before she had made one movie, Globe was hired to shoot a variety of layouts to introduce ANN-MARGRET to the public. Here she's on a tour of fashion shops. • JOANNE WOODWARD shops Venice Beach. • EVA MARIE SAINT shops Beverly Hills. • DENNIS COLE fits son Joey's military school uniform. • CLAUDIA CARDINALE, on her first trip to Las Vegas, shops for souvenirs. • JANE POWELL and her son GERRY STEFAN at Uncle Bernie's Toy Store.

Um ANN-MARGRET vor ihrem ersten Film der Öffentlichkeit vorzustellen, wurde Globe mit einer Fotoreportage über sie beauftragt. Hier ist sie beim Einkaufsbummel. • JOANNE WOODWARD kauft in Venice Beach ein. • EVA MARIE SAINT beim Einkauf in Beverly Hills. • DENNIS COLE kontrolliert die Militär-Schuluniform von Sohn Joey. • CLAUDIA CARDINALE geht auf ihrer ersten Reise nach Las Vegas auf Souvenirsuche. • JANE POWELL und ihr Sohn GERRY STEFAN in Onkel Bernies Spielzeugladen.

L'agence Globe fut choisie pour présenter ANN-MARGRET au public avant même qu'elle ait fait un film ; on la voit ici faire le tour des boutiques. • JOANNE WOODWARD fait les magasins de Venice Beach. • EVA MARIE SAINT fait du shopping à Beverly Hills. • DENNIS COLE fait essayer son uniforme d'école militaire à son fils Joey. • CLAUDIA CARDINALE cherche un souvenir à rapporter de son premier séjour à Las Vegas. • JANE POWELL et son fils GERRY STEFAN au magasin de jouets Uncle Bernie's.

ERNEST AND NANCY BORGNINE, *Larry Barbier Jr.* 1956

PAUL ANKA, *Larry Barbier Jr.* 1958

STEVE MARTIN, *Nate Cutler* 1972

SUSAN ST. JAMES, *Judie Burstein* 1981

Uncle Bernie's was *the* toy store in Beverly Hills and a popular site for a family layout at the time ERNEST BORGNINE took his daughter shopping there. A visit to Uncle Bernie's never failed to bring out the kid in the parent. • PAUL ANKA at Sy Devore's Men's Shop in Hollywood. • STEVE MARTIN in his local supermarket. • SUSAN ST. JAMES on East 42nd Street in New York City.

Uncle Bernie's war *der* Spielzeugladen in Beverly Hills und ein gefragter Ort für Familienfotos. ERNEST BORGNINE macht mit seiner Tochter einen Einkaufsbummel bei Uncle Bernie's. Ein Besuch in diesem Spielzeugladen brachte immer das Kind im Erwachsenen hervor. • PAUL ANKA im Sy Devore's Shop für Männermode in Hollywood. • STEVE MARTIN in seinem lokalen Supermarkt. • SUSAN ST. JAMES auf der 42. Straße von New York City.

Uncle Bernie's, *le* célèbre magasin de jouets de Beverly Hills, servait souvent de cadre aux séances de photos en famille, comme ce jour où ERNEST BORGNINE, qui y avait amené sa fille, retrouve son âme d'enfant. • PAUL ANKA chez Sy Devore's, une boutique pour hommes de Hollywood. • STEVE MARTIN dans son supermarché de quartier. • SUSAN ST. JAMES sur la 42e Rue Est à New York.

ROD TAYLOR, *Eric Skipsey* 1975

ROBERT CONRAD AND VAN WILLIAMS, *Bill Kobrin* 1961

ERIK ESTRADA, *Gene Trindl* 1979

"A Day at the Gym" layouts with ROD TAYLOR, ROBERT CONRAD and VAN WILLIAMS who work out at the Warner Brothers studio facility, and ERIK ESTRADA and ROGER MOORE at the Beverly Hills Health Club.

„Ein Tag im Fitness-Club" Fotoreportagen mit ROD TAYLOR, ROBERT CONRAD und VAN WILLIAMS, die im Sportklub der Warner Brothers Studios trainieren, ERIK ESTRADA und ROGER MOORE im Beverly Hills Health Club.

Quelques séances sur le thème « Un jour en salle de gymnastique » avec ROD TAYLOR, ROBERT CONRAD, VAN WILLIAMS au gymnase du studio de la Warner Brothers, ERIK ESTRADA et ROGER MOORE au Beverly Hills Health Club.

ROGER MOORE, *Larry Barbier Jr.* 1960

MAY BRITT, SAMMY DAVIS JR. AND JAY SEBRING, *Winson Muldrow* 1962

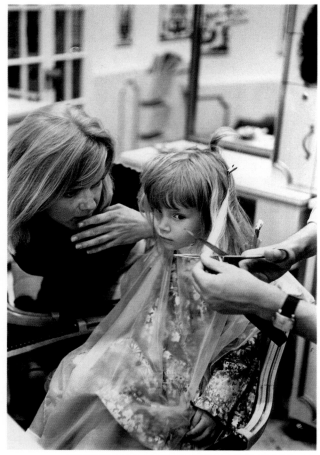

ANNE FRANCIS AND DAUGHTER JANE ELIZABETH, *Bill Kobrin* 1965

SAMMY DAVIS JR., with wife MAY BRITT at his side, has his hair styled by JAY SEBRING. • ANNE FRANCIS' daughter Jane is a bit apprehensive at her first haircut but MAMIE VAN DOREN'S son Perry is downright unhappy about it. • SHIRLEY MACLAINE cuts up with hair stylist George MASTERS. • ZSA ZSA GABOR – what can you say? • DINAH SHORE makes fun out of a wash and set. • DOROTHY MALONE and daughters MIMI and DIANE enjoy a sauna at the Lake Arrowhead Country Club.

SAMMY DAVIS JR., mit Frau MAY BRITT an seiner Seite, geht zum Haarstylisten JAY SEBRING. • ANNE FRANCIS' Tochter Jane ist ein wenig besorgt um ihre Haare, aber MAMIE VAN DORENS Sohn ist regelrecht unglücklich darüber. • SHIRLEY MACLAINE lacht mit Haarstylisten GEORGE MASTERS. • ZSA ZSA GABOR – was kann man sagen? • DINAH SHORE hat Spaß bei ihrem Friseurbesuch. • DOROTHY MALONE und Töchter MIMI und DIANE genießen am Lake Arrowhead Country Club ein Saunabad.

SAMMY DAVIS JR., son épouse MAY BRITT près de lui, se fait coiffer par JAY SEBRING. • Si Jane, la fille de ANNE FRANCIS, montre un peu d'appréhension lors de sa première coupe de cheveux, Perry, le fils de MAMIE VAN DOREN, n'est pas du tout content. • SHIRLEY MACLAINE chez le coiffeur GEORGE MASTERS. • ZSA ZSA GABOR – que peut-on dire? • DINAH SHORE s'amuse chez son coiffeur. • DOROTHY MALONE et ses filles MIMI et DIANE au sauna du Lake Arrowhead Country Club.

MAMIE VAN DOREN AND SON PERRY ANTHONY, *Nate Cutler* 1957

SHIRLEY MACLAINE WITH GEORGE MASTERS, *William Claxton* 1960

ZSA ZSA GABOR, *Larry Barbier Jr.* 1960

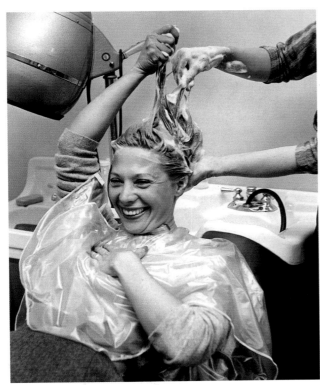

DINAH SHORE, *Globe Archive* 1956

DOROTHY MALONE WITH DAUGHTERS MIMI AND DIANE, *Bill Kobrin* 1965

JODIE FOSTER, *Bob Patterson* 1980

JODIE FOSTER was valedictorian of her high school graduation class at College Lycée Français in Los Angeles. • NATALIE WOOD drives her high school graduation gift from exercises at Van Nuys High School. • SANDRA DEE attended New York Professional School but left before graduation. She got her diploma at University High School in West Los Angeles. • FABIAN in gym class at Southern Philadelphia High School. • BROOKE SHIELDS at her graduation from Princeton University.

JODIE FOSTER war Abschiedsrednerin der High School-Abschlussklasse am College Lycée Français in Los Angeles. • NATALIE WOOD fährt ihr High-School Abschlussgeschenk nach ihrem Training an der Van Nuys High School nach Hause. • SANDRA DEE besuchte die New York Professional School, verließ diese aber vor einem Abschluß. Sie erhielt ihr Diplom von der University High School im Westen von Los Angeles. • FABIAN in einer Gymnastikstunde in der Southern Philadelphia High School. • BROOKE SHIELDS bei ihrer Abschlussfeier an der Princeton University.

JODIE FOSTER sortit major de sa promotion au Lycée Français de Los Angeles. • NATALIE WOOD conduit la voiture qu'elle a reçue pour son diplôme après la cérémonie de remise à la Van Nuys High School. • SANDRA DEE suivit les cours de la New York Professional School mais la quitta avant d'y passer son diplôme, qu'elle obtint à la University High School de West Los Angeles. • FABIAN en cours de gymnastique à la Southern Philadelphia High School. • BROOKE SHIELDS lors de la remise des diplômes à la Princeton University.

NATALIE WOOD, *Larry Barbier Jr.* 1955

SANDRA DEE, *Don Ornitz* 1959

FABIAN, *Jack Stager* 1958

BROOKE SHIELDS, *John Barrett* 1985

JEANNE MOREAU, *Orlando* 1969

SIMONE SIGNORET AND YVES MONTAND, *Len Sirman* 1960

WOODY ALLEN WITH DAUGHTER DYLAN, *Dave Parker* 1989

PHIL SILVERS, *Marvin Koner* 1957

JOHN TRAVOLTA, *Robert Fitzgerald* 1976

DOLORES HART, *Larry Barbier Jr.* 1958

JEANNE MOREAU acts the tourist and checks the hand and footprints at Grauman's Chinese Theater in Hollywood. • SIMONE SIGNORET and YVES MONTAND at the Seine near their home in Paris. • WOODY ALLEN with adopted daughter Dylan in London. • PHIL SILVERS in New York's 59th Street automat. • JOHN TRAVOLTA displays his first poster on the street in Manhattan. • DOLORES HART designed greeting cards bearing her cartoons, named them Sweetharts and put them on the market.

JEANNE MOREAU gibt sich als Touristin und sieht sich die Hand- und Fußabdrücke vor dem Grauman's Chinese Theater in Hollywood an. • SIMONE SIGNORET und YVES MONTAND an der Seine ganz in der Nähe ihres Pariser Hauses. • WOODY ALLEN mit Adoptivtochter Dylan in London. • PHIL SILVERS auf der 59. Straße in New York. • JOHN TRAVOLTA zeigt sein erstes Poster auf der Straße in Manhattan. • DOLORES HART entwarf Grußkarten mit ihren Karikaturen, nannte sie Sweetharts und brachte sie auf den Markt.

JEANNE MOREAU joue les touristes et compare ses empreintes de main et de pied à celles imprimées dans le béton du Grauman's Chinese Theater de Hollywood. • SIMONE SIGNORET et YVES MONTAND sur les quais de la Seine, près de leur appartement parisien. • WOODY ALLEN à Londres avec Dylan, sa fille adoptive. • PHIL SILVERS devant un distributeur de la 59ᵉ Rue à New York. • JOHN TRAVOLTA montre sa première affiche dans une rue de Manhattan. • DOLORES HART dessinait des cartes de vœux, qu'elle appelait Sweetharts, et vendait ensuite.

JEANNE CRAIN, here with husband PAUL BRINKMAN and sons MICHAEL and TIMOTHY, lamented that her studio bosses could never see her playing a mother. • CLINT EASTWOOD pays a visit to Marineland of the Pacific and gets a lesson in fast draw. • OLIVIA DeHAVILLAND, a Los Angeles visitor from Paris, takes her two children, Benjamin and Giselle, to Jungleland for a family layout. Photographer Kobrin was very solicitous and told Olivia it would be all right if she didn't get close to the animals. But the lady was nowhere as jumpy as he was and even got the giraffe to drink out of her cup.

JEANNE CRAIN, hier mit Ehemann PAUL BRINKMAN und Söhnen MICHAEL und TIMOTHY, bedauerte, dass ihre Studiobosse sie nie für die Rolle als Mutter vorsahen. • CLINT EASTWOOD besucht das Marineland of the Pacific und lernt, wie man eine Waffe zieht. • OLIVIA DeHAVILLAND aus Paris besucht Los Angeles und nimmt ihre beiden Kinder Benjamin und Giselle ins Jungleland mit, um dort eine Familien-Fotoreportage machen zu lassen. Fotograf Kobrin war sehr besorgt und sagte Olivia, dass er mit allem einverstanden wäre, so lange sie nicht zu nahe an die Tiere herangehen würde. Aber Olivia war nicht halb so nervös wie er und brachte die Giraffe sogar dazu, aus ihrem Becher zu trinken.

JEANNE CRAIN, ici avec son mari PAUL BRINKMAN et ses fils MICHAEL et TIMOTHY, se plaignait que les patrons des studios ne veuillent pas lui faire jouer une mère de famille. • CLINT EASTWOOD prend une leçon de tir rapide à Marineland Pacifique. • OLIVIA DeHAVILLAND, venue exprès à Los Angeles depuis Paris, emmène ses deux enfants, Benjamin et Gisele, au Jungleland pour une séance de photos en famille ; très inquiet, le photographe Kobrin avait dit à Olivia que tout irait bien si elle ne s'approchait pas trop des animaux, mais elle n'en fit qu'à sa tête et donna même à boire à la girafe dans son gobelet.

JEANNE CRAIN AND FAMILY, *Larry Barbier Jr.* 1953

CLINT EASTWOOD AND FRIEND, *Bill Kobrin* 1963

OLIVIA DeHAVILLAND AND CHILDREN, *Bill Kobrin* 1965

GEORGE PEPPARD, *Don Ornitz* 1962

FESS PARKER, *Larry Barbier Jr.* 1958

CLIFF ROBERTSON, *Larry Barbier Jr.* 1962

LEE J. COBB, *Bill Kobrin* 1964

CAROL BURNETT AND GARRY MOORE, *Jerry Yulsman* 1959

GENE AND MIRIAM NELSON, *Don English* 1952

PETULA CLARK AND CLAUDE WOLFE WITH DAUGHTERS BARBARA AND CATHRINE, *Orlando* 1970

SHEREE NORTH, *Russ Meyer* 1958

GEORGE PEPPARD on board The Gambit. • FESS PARKER sails northern California waters. • CLIFF ROBERTSON'S weekend passions were flying and sailing. • LEE J. COBB aboard his 35-foot sailboat Delia. • CAROL BURNETT is GARRY MOORE'S guest aboard his 35-foot yacht Red Wing. • GENE and MIRIAM NELSON catch large mouth black bass at Lake Mead, Nevada. • PETULA CLARK and family at Lake Tahoe. • SHEREE NORTH on the SS Leilani during a cruise to Acapulco.

GEORGE PEPPARD an Bord der Gambit. • FESS PARKER segelt auf norkalifornischen Gewässern. • CLIFF ROBERTSONS Wochenendleidenschaften waren das Fliegen und Segeln. • LEE J. COBB an Bord seiner 11m langen Delia. • CAROL BURNETT als Gast bei GARRY MOORE auf seiner 11m langen Yacht Red Wing. • GENE und MIRIAM NELSON angeln Barsche am Lake Mead, Nevada. • PETULA CLARK und Familie am Lake Tahoe. • SHEREE NORTH an Deck der SS Leilani bei einer Kreuzfahrt nach Acapulco.

GEORGE PEPPARD à bord du Gambit. • FESS PARKER sur son voilier en Californie du nord. • Les deux passions de CLIFF ROBERTSON étaient le bateau et l'avion. • LEE J. COBB sur Delia, son voilier de 35 pieds (11 m). • CAROL BURNETT est l'invitée de GARRY MOORE sur Red Wing, son yacht de 35 pieds. • GENE et MIRIAM NELSON ont pêché des perches dans le lac Mead (Nevada). • PETULA CLARK et sa famille sur le lac Tahoe. • SHEREE NORTH sur le pont supérieur du paquebot SS Leilani lors d'une croisière à Acapulco.

MARIA SCHELL, *Rick Strauss* 1958

DENNIS HOPPER, *William Claxton* 1963

CAROL LAWRENCE AND ROBERT GOULET, *Jack Stager* 1970

BARBARA STANWYCK AND RICHARD McKENZIE, *John R. Hamilton* 1970

On her first visit to Hollywood, MARIA SCHELL wanted to sample an American drive-in. • DENNIS HOPPER in front of a display of his "assemblage", so-named because it combines photographs and other objects to form a unique composition. • Home on the road: Husband and wife team ROBERT GOULET and CAROL LAWRENCE travel with sons Christopher and Michael in a trailer home which doubles as their dressing room during their summer stock engagements. • BARBARA STANWYCK sits for her portrait by RICHARD McKENZIE in his studio.

Während ihres ersten Besuches in Hollywood wollte MARIA SCHELL ein amerikanisches Drive-In ausprobieren. • DENNIS HOPPER vor seiner "Sammlung". Sein Kunstwerk wurde so genannt, weil es Fotografien und andere Objekte zu einer einzigartigen Komposition vereinte. • Zu Hause auf der Landstraße: Das Ehepaar ROBERT GOULET und CAROL LAWRENCE reisen mit ihren Söhnen Christopher und Michael in einem Wohnwagen, der während ihrer zahlreichen Auftritte im Sommer auch als ihre Umkleidekabine dient. • BARBARA STANWYCK wird von RICHARD McKENZIE in seinem Studio porträtiert.

MARIA SCHELL voulut absolument essayer un drive-in américain lors de sa première visite à Hollywood. • DENNIS HOPPER devant un de ses «assemblages», une composition mêlant photographies et autres objets. • ROBERT GOULET et CAROL LAWRENCE voyagent avec leurs fils Christopher et Michael dans une caravane qui leur sert également de loge pendant leurs tournées d'été. • BARBARA STANWYCK pose dans l'atelier du peintre RICHARD McKENZIE.

NANCY KWAN, *Nancy Kwan* 1971

RICHARD MULLIGAN, *Rolf Konow* 1981

LANA TURNER, *Herb Ball* 1957

FAYE DUNAWAY, *Cirrus McAnson* 1968

NANCY KWAN, an occasional Globe contributor, photographed herself on the Great Wall of China. • RICHARD MULLIGAN and the Little Mermaid in Copenhagen. • LANA TURNER gets her shots for a trip to South America. • FAYE DUNAWAY receives the traditional greeting upon her arrival in Bombay, India.

NANCY KWAN war eine gelegentliche Mitarbeiterin bei Globe. Sie fotografierte sich selber auf der Chinesischen Mauer. • RICHARD MULLIGAN und die Kleine Meerjungfrau in Kopenhagen. • LANA TURNER läßt sich anlässlich ihrer Reise nach Südamerika impfen. • FAYE DUNAWAY wird bei ihrer Ankunft in Bombay, Indien, auf traditionelle Art und Weise begrüßt.

NANCY KWAN, qui travaillait parfois pour Globe, se photographie sur la Grande Muraille de Chine. • RICHARD MULLIGAN et la petite Sirène de Copenhague. • LANA TURNER fait ses vaccinations avant de partir en Amérique du Sud. • FAYE DUNAWAY est accueillie à la manière traditionnelle lors de son arrivée à Bombay (Inde).

RICHARD BURTON, *Bruce Kerner* 1965

ELIZABETH TAYLOR, RICHARD BURTON AND FAMILY, *Herm Lewis* 1963

When RICHARD BURTON filmed THE NIGHT OF THE IGUANA in Mismaloya, Mexico, wife ELIZABETH TAYLOR and the kids joined him in nearby Puerto Vallarta. The Burtons liked the area so much they later vacationed and ultimately bought a home there. Several Globe photographers were sent down to shoot the family. Herm Lewis introduced himself to Burton outside Casa Kimberly, the Burton house and told him of his mission. Burton to Lewis: "Well, if you wait around, I'll see what I can do." Lewis waited in front of the house for three days when suddenly Burton appeared on the balcony and shouted for him to get his camera out. In a flash, the whole family, Liza Todd, Christopher and Michael Wilding, and Maria Burton, piled into the family jeep. Herm got his shot.

Rome adventures: ELEANOR PARKER, husband PAUL CLEMENTS and their children. • STEVE ALLEN, JAYNE MEADOWS and their kids try watermelon on the street. BOBBY DARIN throws three coins in the fountain. • BETTE DAVIS and daughter BD at the Fountain of Trevi in Rome.

ELIZABETH TAYLOR AND LIZA TODD, *Ron Joy* 1964

ELEANOR PARKER AND FAMILY, *Herbert Fried* 1959

STEVE ALLEN, JAYNE MEADOWS AND SONS, *Herbert Fried* 1958

BOBBY DARIN, *Leo Fuchs* 1961

BETTE DAVIS AND DAUGHTER BD, *Herbert Fried* 1958

Als RICHARD BURTON DIE NACHT DES LEGUAN (THE NIGHT OF THE IGUANA) in Mismaloya, Mexiko, filmte, trafen sich Frau ELIZABETH TAYLOR und die Kinder im nahe gelegenen Puerto Vallarta mit ihm. Die Burtons mochten die Gegend so sehr, dass sie später dort Urlaub machten und letztendlich dort ein Haus kauften. Mehrere Fotografen wurden nach Mexiko geschickt, um Fotos von der Familie zu schießen. Vor der Casa Kimberly, dem Haus der Burtons, stellt Herm Lewis sich Burton vor und erzählt ihm von seinem Auftrag. Burton sagte daraufhin: „Nun ja, wenn du ein bisschen wartest, werde ich mal sehen, was sich machen lässt." Lewis wartete drei Tage lang vor dem Haus, als Burton plötzlich auf dem Balkon auftauchte und ihm zurief, dass er seine Kamera herausnehmen sollte. In Windeseile stieg die gesamte Familie in den Familienjeep ein, Liza Todd, Christopher, Michael Wilding und Maria Burton. Herm bekam seinen Schnappschuss.

Abenteurer in Rom: ELEANOR PARKER mit ihrem Ehemann PAUL CLEMENTS und ihren Kindern. • STEVE ALLEN, JAYNE MEADOWS und ihre Kinder probieren auf der Straße Wassermelone. • BOBBY DARIN wirft drei Münzen in den Brunnen. • BETTE DAVIS und ihre Tochter BD am Trevibrunnen in Rom.

RICHARD BURTON, qui tournait LA NUIT DE L'IGUANE (THE NIGHT OF THE IGUANA) à Mismaloya (Mexique), fut rejoint par son épouse ELIZABETH TAYLOR et ses enfants près de Puerto Vallarta, un endroit qu'ils apprécièrent tant qu'ils revinrent y passer des vacances et s'y achetèrent une maison. De nombreux photographes de Globe y furent envoyés pour photographier la famille. Herm Lewis se présenta à la Casa Kimberly, leur résidence, et expliqua sa mission à Burton. Le dernier dit à Lewis : « Bon, attendez un peu, je vais voir ce que je peux faire. » Lewis attendit trois jours devant la demeure lorsque Richard Burton apparut soudain au balcon et lui cria de se tenir prêt. Quelques secondes plus tard, toute la famille, avec Liza Todd, Christopher et Michael Wilding et Maria Burton, s'entassa dans la jeep familiale et Herm fit sa photo.

Vacances romaines : ELEANOR PARKER avec son mari PAUL CLEMENTS et leurs enfants. • STEVE ALLEN, JAYNE MEADOWS et leurs enfants goûtent à des pastèques vendues dans la rue. • BOBBY DARIN jette trois pièces dans la fontaine de Trevi à Rome, tout comme BETTE DAVIS et sa fille.

FRED ASTAIRE AND HERMES PAN, *Don Ornitz* 1959

HOLLYWOOD
AT WORK

DORIS DAY AND ROCK HUDSON, *Dick Miller* 1959

DORIS DAY and ROCK HUDSON break each other up on the set of PILLOW TALK. Hudson told photog Miller: "Doris and I can't look at each other. You know that sweet agony of laughing when you're not supposed to? Well, that's what Doris and I have." • FRED ASTAIRE and HERMES PAN work out a routine on their feet as Hollywood gypies watch.

DORIS DAY und ROCK HUDSON lachen sich während der Dreharbeiten zu BETTGEFLÜSTER (PILLOW TALK) kaputt. Hudson sagte dem Fotografen Miller: „Doris und ich können uns nicht anschauen. Kennen Sie die süße Qual, gerade dann lachen zu wollen, wenn Sie es nicht dürfen? Tja, das ist das, was Doris und ich gerade durchmachen." • FRED ASTAIRE und HERMES PAN bei ihren Tanzübungen und werden dabei beobachtet.

DORIS DAY et ROCK HUDSON sont pris de fou rire sur le plateau de CONFIDENCES SUR L'OREILLER (PILLOW TALK). Hudson a d'ailleurs raconté à Miller, le photographe : « Doris et moi ne pouvons pas nous regarder sans éclater de rire. Vous savez ce que c'est que d'être pris de fou rire sans pouvoir s'en empêcher ? Et bien, ça nous arrive tout le temps. » • FRED ASTAIRE et HERMES PAN sont observés pendant leurs exercises de danse.

GARY COOPER, *Don Ornitz* 1955

OFF CAMERA

Studio publicity departments were kept busy in the 30s and 40s dispensing publicity shots of their stars "at work." These were posed, rather stilted shots (considered campy today) and the editors of the emerging picture magazines soon grew tired of them. They wanted features that were more candid and less controlled, unretouched, unaltered and unrestrained by studio flacks.

Globe began to cover interesting films being shot at the studios and offered the coverage to the major national magazines. This coverage was generally free from studio interference and had a candid feel that met with enormous approval from the publications' readership. It was also exclusive. There was no worry that the same shot would pop up in a competitive magazine.

During this period Hollywood's major studios were producing all the important pictures. In the mid-50s a new breed of production company loomed on the scene – the independent. Overnight a new notion of shooting on location rather than in the studio took shape.

One of these independent companies was Aspen Productions, formed by directors Mark Robson and Robert Wise. Aspen's first venture was RETURN TO PARADISE with Gary Cooper. The entire film was to be shot on location – in British Samoa, no less – before the age of jet travel. Aspen's publicity man, Ted Loeff, knew that the future of this company was dependent upon the success of RETURN TO PARADISE and he also knew that none of the leading national magazines would assign a staffer to cover the filming.

Loeff's solution to the problem opened the arena for a new kind of Hollywood photojournalist – the "special photographer." Loeff retained Globe Photos' Don Ornitz to cover the entire production of RETURN TO PARADISE with the provision that Globe would have the right to distribute Ornitz' coverage to publications throughout the world for a specified period of time. After that, the photos would be made available to the production company for publicity, promotion and advertising use.

Ornitz' coverage was so successful that United Artists, the distribution company, which had no overhead staff personnel and thus was more flexible than the major companies, adopted the "special photographer" concept for all their films.

In addition to Ornitz, the new photographic pioneers in the virgin land were Bob Willoughby, Orlando,

FERN DER FILMKAMERA

Die Werbeabteilungen der Filmstudios waren in den 30er und 40er Jahren damit beschäftigt, Pressefotos ihrer Stars „bei der Arbeit" anzufertigen. Diese waren übertriebene und gestellte Schnappschüsse, die man heutzutage als theatralisch bezeichnen würde, und die Herausgeber der neu aufkommenden Illustrierten waren diese Art Fotos bald überdrüssig. Sie wollten Artikel, die weniger kontrolliert und natürlich wirkten und von den Filmstudios unretuschiert, unverändert und unkontrolliert gelassen wurden.

Globe begann damit, interessante Filme, die in Filmstudios gedreht wurden, abzulichten, und bot diese Fotoberichte dann den großen nationalen Zeitschriften an. Die Filmstudios mischten sich normalerweise nicht in die Berichterstattung ein, wodurch die Reportagen eine viel natürlichere Atmosphäre widerspiegelten, die bei der Leserschaft sehr gut ankam. Die Reportage war auch exklusiv, denn man brauchte sich keine Sorgen machen, dass dieselbe Aufnahme in einer konkurrierenden Zeitschrift auftauchen würde.

In dieser Zeit wurden alle wichtigen Filme in Hollywood von den großen Studios produziert. Mitte der 50er Jahre entstand eine neue Gattung der Produktionsgesellschaft – die unabhängige Filmgesellschaft. Quasi über Nacht bevorzugte man den Dreh vor Ort, anstelle von Studioaufnahmen.

Eine dieser unabhängigen Filmgesellschaften war Aspen Productions, gegründet von den Filmregisseuren Mark Robson und Robert Wise. Aspens erstes Projekt war der Film RÜCKKEHR INS PARADIES (RETURN TO PARADISE) mit Gary Cooper, und der gesamte Film sollte vor Ort gedreht werden – auf den britischen Samoa-Inseln –, und dies vor dem Zeitalter des Flugverkehrs! Aspens Werbefachmann, Ted Loeff, wusste, dass die Zukunft seiner Filmgesellschaft vom Erfolg des Films RÜCKKEHR INS PARADIES abhing, und er wusste auch, dass keine der national führenden Zeitschriften einen Journalisten zur Berichterstattung über den Film schicken würde.

Loeffs Lösung des Problems erschuf in Hollywood eine neue Art Fotojournalist – den „Spezial-Fotografen". Loeff beauftragte den Fotografen Don Ornitz von Globe Photos, über die gesamte Produktion von RÜCKKEHR INS PARADIES zu berichten. Dies geschah unter der Bedingung, dass Globe Ornitz' Berichterstattung über einen bestimmten Zeitraum hinweg an Magazine in der

HORS CHAMP

Dans les années 1930–1940, les départements de publicité des studios s'occupèrent de fournir des portraits des stars « au travail ». Ces photos étant posées et assez théâtrales – à la limite plutôt kitsch – les rédactions des magazines photo s'en fatiguèrent rapidement. Ils voulaient des scènes « improvisées » et d'apparence plus naturelle, moins retouchées et moins contrôlées par les attachés de presse des Studios.

Globe entreprit de couvrir les films les plus intéressants tournés par les Studios et offrit les reportages aux grands magazines nationaux. Ces photographies, généralement réalisées en dehors de toute interférence des Studios, donnaient une image naturelle des stars et étaient particulièrement appréciées des lecteurs. Vendues sous couvert d'exclusivité, il n'y avait pas de risque que la même photo soit publiée dans un magazine concurrent.

À cette époque, tous les films importants étaient produits par les grandes compagnies de Hollywood. Vers le milieu des années 1950 apparaissent des producteurs de films d'un nouveau type, appelés indépendants, qui introduisent du jour au lendemain la notion moderne de tournage en extérieur plutôt qu'en studio.

Aspen Productions, créée par les réalisateurs Mark Robson et Robert Wise, est l'une de ces compagnies indépendantes. Leur premier projet fut RETOUR AU PARADIS (RETURN TO PARADISE) avec Gary Cooper; la totalité du film fut tourné en extérieur, dans les Samoa britanniques. L'agent de publicité d'Aspen, Ted Loeff, savait parfaitement que du succès de RETOUR AU PARADIS dépendait l'avenir de sa compagnie mais qu'aucun des principaux magazines nationaux n'enverrait un correspondant aussi loin, à une époque où les jets n'existaient pas encore, pour couvrir le tournage.

La solution trouvée par Loeff – le « photographe spécial » – institua un nouveau style de photojournalisme à Hollywood. Loeff engagea en effet Don Ornitz, qui travaillait pour Globe Photos, afin de couvrir la totalité du tournage de RETOUR AU PARADIS et en offrant l'assurance que Globe pourrait distribuer les photos du reportage aux publications de son choix mais pendant une durée limitée. À l'expiration de cette période, les photos appartiendraient à la société de production pour ses besoins en publicité et promotion.

Le reportage d'Ornitz eut tant de succès que le distributeur United Artists, qui ne disposait d'aucun photographe permanent et pouvait donc s'adapter plus

GARY COOPER, *Don Ornitz* 1955

William Claxton, Gene Trindl, Jack Hamilton, William Read Woodfield, Bill Kobrin, Larry Barbier Jr., Dick Miller, Ron Thal, Richard Hewett, Lawrence Schiller, Russ Meyer (who went on to a successful career as a director of sexy, exploitation movies) and Frank Bez, who specialized in portraiture and glamour photography. All of them regularly covered films in Hollywood and became media stars themselves.

When motion picture production in Europe burgeoned, Globe opened an office in London where it assigned such top photographers as Joel Elkins, Ruan O'Lochlainn, Alex Lowe, David Hurn, Leo Fuchs, Tazio Secchiaroli, Pat McCallum and Richard Polak.

The job of the "special" was to produce picture stories or features on a film during the production: major essays on the stars for cover stories (Cooper back to nature in South Seas waters, Fred Astaire creating a dance number, Marilyn Monroe's relationship with her backstage guru Paula Strasberg) or stories on the stars preparing for a particular challenge (Bette Davis or Marlon Brando learning to be hoofers, Natalie Wood becoming a fencer, Joan Crawford mastering jujitsu), or tiny vignettes for one page fillers (known as "floaters" in journalistic slang). In short, everything the studio's unit photographer, who was busy recording each scene in "stills", could not shoot. It was an all-encompassing view of motion picture making up close with all its attendant backstage excitement, its energy and tension, its sober dedication and silly camaraderie.

Special photography captured the *spirit* of movie making.

ganzen Welt vertreiben durfte. Danach standen die Fotos der Produktionsgesellschaft zu Reklame-, Promotions- und Werbezwecken zur Verfügung.

Ornitz' Berichterstattung war so erfolgreich, dass United Artists, die Vertriebsgesellschaft, die keine festen Mitarbeiter hatte und somit flexibler als die großen Filmgesellschaften war, das Konzept des „Spezial-Fotografen" auf alle Filme anwendete.

Außer Ornitz waren die fotografischen Pioniere Bob Willoughby, Orlando, William Claxton, Gene Trindl, Jack Hamilton, William Read Woodfield, Bill Kobrin, Larry Barbier Jr., Dick Miller, Ron Thal, Richard Hewett, Lawrence Schiller, Russ Meyer (der später eine erfolgreiche Karriere als Regisseur von Pornofilmen machte) und Frank Bez, der sich auf die Porträt- und Glamour-fotografie spezialisiert hatte. Jeder von ihnen berichtete regelmäßig über die Filme in Hollywood und wurde selbst zum Medienstar.

Als die Filmproduktion in Europa zu expandieren begann, eröffnete Globe ein Büro in London. Dieses Büro verpflichtete Top-Fotografen wie Joel Elkins, Ruan O'Lochlainn, Alex Lowe, David Hurn, Leo Fuchs, Tazio Secchiaroli, Pat McCallum und Richard Polak.

Die Arbeit eines „Spezialisten" bestand darin, die Produktion eines Filmes mit Fotoreportagen und Sonderbeiträgen zu begleiten: komplexe Essays über Stars für Titelblatt-Aufmacher (Cooper findet in der Südsee zurück zur Natur, Fred Astaire kreiert eine Tanznummer, Marilyn Monroes Beziehung zu ihrem Backstage-Guru Paula Strasberg) oder Geschichten über Stars bei der Vorbereitung auf eine besondere Herausforderung (Bette Davis oder Marlon Brando erlernen das Tanzen, Natalie Wood lernt Fechten, Joan Crawford lernt Jiu-Jitsu) oder winzig kleine Vignetten, die gerade mal eine Seite füllten (Journalisten nennen sie auch „floaters"). Kurz gesagt, all das, was der Studiofotograf, der jede Szene in Standfotos festzuhalten hat, mit der Kamera nicht einfangen konnte. Es war ein allumfassender Blick auf das Filmemachen, der die Aufregung hinter den Kulissen, der die Energie und Spannung des Moments, der die ernsthafte Hingabe und die herzhafte Kameradschaft einfing.

Diese Art der Fotografie hielt die *Aura* der Filmproduktion fest.

facilement que les grandes compagnies, adopta le concept de « photographe spécial » pour tous ses films.

Outre Ornitz, les pionniers de ce type nouveau de photojournalisme furent Bob Willoughby, Orlando, William Claxton, Gene Trindl, Jack Hamilton, William Read Woodfield, Bill Kobrin, Larry Barbier Jr., Dick Miller, Ron Thal, Richard Hewett, Lawrence Schiller, Russ Meyer (qui allait connaître un certain succès comme réalisateur de films à tendance pornographique) et Frank Bez, qui se spécialisa dans le portrait et la photographie glamour. Comme ils couvraient tous régulièrement les tournages de Hollywood, ils devinrent à leur tour des vedettes des médias.

Lorsque l'Europe se lança à son tour dans la production de films, Globe ouvrit un bureau à Londres et y installa de grands photographes comme Joel Elkins, Ruan O'Lochlainn, Alex Lowe, David Hurn, Leo Fuchs, Tazio Secchiaroli, Pat McCallum et Richard Polak.

Le travail du « photographe spécial » consistait à faire la chronique en images d'un film pendant sa réalisation. Il pouvait s'agir de grandes compositions pour les couvertures de magazine et mettant une star en vedette (Cooper dans les mers du Sud, Fred Astaire créant un numéro de danse, les relations de Marilyn Monroe avec son gourou Paula Strasberg), de photoreportages sur les stars se préparant à un rôle particulier (Bette Davis ou Marlon Brando apprenant à danser, Natalie Wood pratiquant l'escrime ou Joan Crawford faisant du jiu-jitsu) ou encore de petites vignettes pour des articles bouche-trous d'une page (appelées « floaters » dans l'argot journalistique américain). En bref, il s'agissait de réaliser tout ce que ne pouvait pas faire un photographe de studio, travaillant chaque scène comme pour une « photo-réclame », et d'offrir au public une vision globale de la fabrication d'un film en rendant au mieux l'atmosphère des coulisses et toute l'excitation, l'énergie et la tension des acteurs, ainsi que leur dévouement profond et leur camaraderie affectée.

Ce nouveau genre de photographie « de plateau » veut saisir *l'esprit* de la réalisation cinématographique.

JAMES STEWART, GENE KELLY AND HENRY FONDA, *Don Ornitz* 1968

WARREN BEATTY, *Fred Schnell* 1964

During the location filming of RETURN TO PARADISE, GARY COOPER spends his off camera time reef fishing in the waters of British Samoa. Catch of the day is parrot fish. • Three giants of the screen, JAMES STEWART, HENRY FONDA and GENE KELLY, collaborated on THE CHEYENNE SOCIAL CLUB, Fonda and Stewart as stars, Kelly as their director. • WARREN BEATTY floats above the skyline of Chicago with the help of a trampoline during a break in the filming of MICKEY ONE.

Während der Außenaufnahmen von RÜCKKEHR INS PARADIES (RETURN TO PARADISE) verbringt GARY COOPER seine freie Zeit damit, in den Gewässern von British Samoa zu fischen. Der Fang des Tages ist ein Papageifisch. • Drei Leinwandgiganten, JAMES STEWART, HENRY FONDA und GENE KELLY, arbeiteten zusammen an GESCHOSSEN WIRD AB MITTERNACHT (THE CHEYENNE SOCIAL CLUB). Fonda und Stewart als Stars, Kelly als ihr Regisseur. • WARREN BEATTY schwebt während einer Pause zwischen den Dreharbeiten zu MICKEY ONE mit der Hilfe eines Trampolins über der Skyline von Chicago.

GARY COOPER a passé son temps à pêcher (ici un poisson perroquet) dans les eaux des Samoa britanniques pendant le tournage en extérieur de RETOUR AU PARADIS (RETURN TO PARADISE). • Trois géants du cinéma – HENRY FONDA et JAMES STEWART comme vedettes, et GENE KELLY en tant que réalisateur – ont participé au film ATTAQUE AU CHEYENNE-CLUB (THE CHEYENNE SOCIAL CLUB). • Bondissant sur un trampoline, WARREN BEATTY s'envole au-dessus des gratte-ciel de Chicago lors d'une pause pendant le tournage de MICKEY ONE.

LIZA MINNELLI AND JUDY GARLAND, *Globe Archive* 1964

MARLENE DIETRICH, *Carroll Seghers II* 1952

MARY TYLER MOORE, JAMES FOX AND JULIE ANDREWS, *Orlando* 1966

SOPHIA LOREN, *Bill Kobrin* 1959

A famous chest gets X-rayed. As part of the standard physical examination prior to the start of all film productions, SOPHIA LOREN gets an X-ray in her dressing room. Sophia was about to begin her role in HELLER IN PINK TIGHTS. • JUDY GARLAND and 13-year-old LIZA MINNELLI during rehearsal for their first appearance together at the London Palladium. • MARLENE DIETRICH in rehearsal for her one-woman show at the Sands Hotel in Las Vegas. • On a Universal sound stage, MARY TYLER MOORE, JAMES FOX, JULIE ANDREWS and the dancers led by DON CREIGHTON rehearse the Charleston for THOROUGHLY MODERN MILLIE, set in the 20s.

Eine berühmte Büste wird geröngt. Als Bestandteil der Standarduntersuchung vor Beginn jeder Filmproduktion, wird SOPHIA LOREN in ihrer Garderobe geröngt. Sophia stand kurz vor den Dreharbeiten zu DIE DAME UND DER KILLER (HELLER IN PINK TIGHTS). • JUDY GARLAND und ihre 13 Jahre alte Tochter LIZA MINNELLI proben zusammen für ihren ersten gemeinsamen Auftritt im Londoner Palladium. • MARLENE DIETRICH bei der Probe zu ihrer Einmann-Show im Sands Hotel in Las Vegas. • Auf einer Universal Musikbühne üben MARY TYLER MOORE, JAMES FOX, JULIE ANDREWS und die von DON CREIGHTON geleiteten Tänzer den Charleston für THOROUGHLY MODERN MILLIE, der in den 20ern spielt.

Le célèbre buste de SOPHIA LOREN passe aux rayons X lors de l'examen médical obligatoire avant toute production cinématographique. Sophia était sur le point de débuter le tournage de LA DIABLESSE EN COLLANT ROSE (HELLER IN PINK TIGHTS). • JUDY GARLAND et LIZA MINNELLI, alors âgée de 13 ans, lors des répétitions de leur premier spectacle ensemble au London Palladium. • MARLENE DIETRICH en répétition pour son « one woman show » au Sands Hotel de Las Vegas. • C'est dans une salle de tournage de Universal que MARY TYLER MOORE, JAMES FOX, JULIE ANDREWS et les danseurs dirigés par DON CREIGHTON ont répété le Charleston de MILLIE (THOROUGHLY MODERN MILLIE), créé dans les années 1920.

KATHARINE HEPBURN AND SPENCER TRACY, *Don Ornitz* 1967

WILLIAM HOLDEN AND AUDREY HEPBURN, *Don Ornitz* 1953

PAUL NEWMAN AND JOANNE WOODWARD, *Don Ornitz* 1960

Arguably Hollywood's best-loved team, KATHARINE HEPBURN and SPENCER TRACY on the set of GUESS WHO'S COMING TO DINNER?, their ninth and final film together. When the insurance company refused to insure the ailing Tracy, Hepburn and producer-director Stanley Kramer put up their own salaries to ensure Tracy would complete the film. He died two weeks after the end of production. • Not general knowledge until recently, this look between SABRINA co-stars WILLIAM HOLDEN and AUDREY HEPBURN signified a personal love affair. • Also not acting are PAUL NEWMAN and JOANNE WOODWARD, between takes on the set of FROM THE TERRACE.

Das wohl heiß geliebteste Team Hollywoods, KATHARINE HEPBURN und SPENCER TRACY, bei den Dreharbeiten zu RAT MAL, WER ZUM ESSEN KOMMT (GUESS WHO'S COMING TO DINNER?), ihrem neunten und letzten gemeinsamen Film. Als sich die Versicherung weigerte, den kränkelnden Tracy zu versichern, legten Hepburn und Produzent und Regisseur Stanley Kramer ihre Gehälter zusammen, um zu gewährleisten, dass Tracy den Film vollenden würde. Er starb zwei Wochen nach Beendigung der Dreharbeiten. • Was bis vor kurzem noch nicht bekannt war, ist, dass dieser Blick zwischen WILLIAM HOLDEN und AUDREY HEPBURN, die in dem Film SABRINA Filmpartner waren, eine persönliche Liebesbeziehung enthüllt. • Auch PAUL NEWMAN und JOANNE WOODWARD, hier in einer Pause bei den Dreharbeiten zu VON DER TERRASSE (FROM THE TERRACE), sind nicht nur auf der Leinwand ein Paar.

KATHARINE HEPBURN et SPENCER TRACY, qui ont formé sans aucun doute le couple le plus aimé de Hollywood, sur le plateau de DEVINE QUI VIENT DÎNER ? (GUESS WHO'S COMING TO DINNER?), leur neuvième et dernier film ensemble. Lorsque la compagnie d'assurance refusa de couvrir Tracy, alors souffrant, Hepburn et le réalisateur-producteur Stanley Kramer mirent leur propre cachet en jeu pour garantir le contrat. Tracy mourut deux semaines après la fin du tournage. • Ce regard entre WILLIAM HOLDEN et AUDREY HEPBURN, partenaires dans SABRINA, aurait dû révéler une liaison qu'on n'a apprise que récemment. • PAUL NEWMAN et JOANNE WOODWARD pendant une pause entre deux prises sur le tournage de DU HAUT DE LA TERRASSE (FROM THE TERRACE), forment un couple à la scène comme à la ville.

MIA FARROW, *Ron Thal* 1967

Ron Thal was hired by Paramount to produce some provocatively moody portraits of MIA FARROW in advance of the film ROSEMARY'S BABY. • For a special layout in LIFE magazine, William Read Woodfield created this shot highlighting a special plot element from THE MANCHURIAN CANDIDATE.

Ron Thal wurde von Paramount eingestellt, um für den Film ROSEMARY'S BABY von MIA FARROW einige provokante stimmungsvolle Porträtaufnahmen zu machen. • Für eine Sonderbeilage in LIFE machte William Read Woodfield diese Aufnahme, die ein besonderes Handlungselement des Films BOTSCHAFTER DER ANGST (THE MANCHURIAN CANDIDATE) hervorheben sollte.

Ron Thal fut engagé par la Paramount pour faire quelques portraits de Mia Farrow, provocateurs par leur atmosphère romantique, à l'occasion de la sortie du film ROSEMARY'S BABY. • Cette photographie, symbolique de l'ambiance de UN CRIME DANS LA TÊTE (THE MANCHURIAN CANDIDATE), fut réalisée par William Read Woodfield pour illustrer un reportage du magazine LIFE.

LAURENCE HARVEY AND FRANK SINATRA, *William Read Woodfield* 1962

KIRK DOUGLAS AND MICHAEL DOUGLAS, *Ron Thal* 1969

On location for his first film, HAIL HERO, MICHAEL DOUGLAS listens while Douglas pere lays a few pearls of acting wisdom down. • JAMES STACY returned to the screen in the western POSSE following his devastating motorcycle accident in which he lost an arm and a leg. The film was produced and directed by KIRK DOUGLAS. • FAYE DUNAWAY catches 40 winks while her BONNIE AND CLYDE cohorts, WARREN BEATTY and ARTHUR PENN, have a set-side conference. • SIDNEY POITIER between scenes of DUEL AT DIABLO. • RINGO STARR on the set of THE MAGIC CHRISTIAN. JULIE LONDON, with GARY COOPER on location for MAN OF THE WEST, is ready for a nap.

Am Drehort zu seinem ersten Film HAIL HERO bekommt MICHAEL DOUGLAS von seinem Vater KIRK Ratschläge. • JAMES STACY kehrte nach seinem verheerenden Motorradunfall, in dem er einen Arm und ein Bein verlor, mit einer Rolle in dem Western MÄNNER DES GESETZES (POSSE) zum Film zurück. KIRK DOUGLAS war Produzent und Regisseur des Films. • FAYE DUNAWAY zieht alle Blicke auf sich, während ihre Filmpartner in BONNIE AND CLYDE, WARREN BEATTY und ARTHUR PENN, eine Konferenz am Drehort abhalten. • SIDNEY POITIER bei den Dreharbeiten zu DUELL IN DIABLO (DUEL AT DIABLO). • RINGO STARR bei den Dreharbeiten zu THE MAGIC CHRISTIAN. • JULIE LONDON, hier mit GARY COOPER am Drehort von DER MANN AUS DEM WESTEN (MAN OF THE WEST), ist reif für ein Nickerchen.

MICHAEL DOUGLAS, qui tourne alors son premier film, HAIL HERO, écoute son père lui donner quelques conseils d'acteur. • JAMES STACY est revenu à l'écran dans le western LA BRIGADE DU TEXAS (POSSE) après un tragique accident de motocyclette où il perdit un bras et une jambe. Le film était produit et réalisé par KIRK DOUGLAS. • FAYE DUNAWAY fait un petit somme près de ses compagnons de BONNIE AND CLYDE, WARREN BEATTY et ARTHUR PENN. • SIDNEY POITIER entre deux prises de LA BATAILLE DE LA VALLÉE DU DIABLE (DUEL AT DIABLO). • RINGO STARR sur le plateau de THE MAGIC CHRISTIAN. • L'attente paraît longue pour JULIE LONDON, ici avec GARY COOPER sur le tournage de L'HOMME DE L'OUEST (MAN OF THE WEST).

KIRK DOUGLAS AND JAMES STACY, *Orlando* 1974

FAYE DUNAWAY, *Ron Thal* 1966

SIDNEY POITIER, *Winson Muldrow* 1966

RINGO STARR, *Bruce McBroom* 1968

JULIE LONDON AND GARY COOPER, *Dick Miller* 1958

ACTORS STUDIO, *Globe Archive* 1972

LEE STRASBERG conducts a class at the Actors Studio in New York. The class includes HARVEY KEITEL and DAVID GROH.
• On the set of his first film and on his first scooter, JAMES MACARTHUR and his mother, good scout HELEN HAYES.
• Wearing her BARBARELLA costume, JANE FONDA whips up lunch in her dressing room. • NOEL COWARD strikes a royal pose on the set of THE ITALIAN JOB. • One of Globe's jobs was to get magazine space for up and coming starlets. Here ELLEN McRAE poses while her publicist, MICKEY FREEMAN, looks on, as they say, admiringly. Later, she was signed for a film called THE LAST PICTURE SHOW and changed her name to ELLEN BURSTYN.

LEE STRASBERG gibt eine Unterrichtsstunde im Actors Studio in New York. HARVEY KEITEL und DAVID GROH sind ebenfalls anwesend. • Bei den Dreharbeiten seines ersten Filmes fährt JAMES MACARTHUR seine Mutter, HELEN HAYES, auf seinem ersten Motorroller spazieren. • JANE FONDA in ihrem BARBARELLA-Kostüm bereitet sich in ihrem Umkleideraum gerade ihr Mittagessen zu. • NOEL COWARD nimmt bei den Dreharbeiten zu CHARLIE STAUBT MILLIONEN AB (THE ITALIAN JOB) eine königliche Pose ein. • Eine von Globes Aufgaben war es, neue und zukünftige Stars in die Zeitschriften zu bringen. Hier posiert ELLEN McRAE, während ihr PR-Agent MICKEY FREEMAN sie bewundert. Später wurde sie für einen Film namens DIE LETZTE VORSTELLUNG (THE LAST PICTURE SHOW) engagiert und änderte ihren Namen in ELLEN BURSTYN.

LEE STRASBERG dirige une classe de l'Actors Studio de New York, à laquelle participent HARVEY KEITEL et DAVID GROH.
• JAMES MACARTHUR promène sa mère HELEN HAYES en scooter dans les décors de son premier film. • JANE FONDA, vêtue de son costume de BARBARELLA, prépare le déjeuner dans sa loge. • NOEL COWARD adopte une pose royale au milieu des décors de L'OR SE BARRE (THE ITALIAN JOB).
• L'une des tâches de Globe était d'obtenir de la place dans les magazines pour y publier des photos de starlettes futures ou confirmées. ELLEN McRAE pose ici pour son portrait sous le regard admiratif de son agent de publicité, MICKEY FREEMAN ; elle fut ensuite engagée pour LA DERNIÈRE SÉANCE (THE LAST PICTURE SHOW) et changea alors son nom en ELLEN BURSTYN.

HELEN HAYES AND JAMES MACARTHUR, *William Read Woodfield* 1957

JANE FONDA, *Globe Archive 1967*

NOEL COWARD, *Ruan O'Lochlainn* 1969

MICKEY FREEMAN AND ELLEN McRAE, *Gene Trindl* 1970

DEBORAH KERR, *Ken Danvers* 1959

JOHN WAYNE, *Don Ornitz* 1970

DEBORAH KERR and new friend on the Australian location of THE SUNDOWNERS.
• JOHN WAYNE in a bunny suit was enough reason for NBC to invite a photographer onto the set of ROWAN AND MARTIN'S LAUGH-IN. • AUDREY HEPBURN is taken to the location set of THE NUNS STORY Congo-style.

DEBORAH KERR und ihr neuer Freund bei den Dreharbeiten von DER ENDLOSE HORIZONT (THE SUNDOWNERS) in Australien. • JOHN WAYNE in einem Häschenkostüm – das war für NBC Grund genug, einen Fotografen zu den Dreharbeiten zu ROWAN AND MARTIN'S LAUGH-IN einzuladen. • AUDREY HEPBURN wird an den Drehort im Kongo-Stil zu GESCHICHTE EINER NONNE (THE NUNS STORY) gebracht.

DEBORAH KERR et son nouveau petit ami sur le tournage en extérieur des HORIZONS SANS FRONTIÈRES (THE SUNDOWNERS), en Australie. • Avec JOHN WAYNE dans un costume de lapin, la NBC n'a pas manqué de convoquer un photographe sur le tournage de ROWAN AND MARTIN'S LAUGH-IN. • AUDREY HEPBURN dans les décors de style congolais du film AU RISQUE DE SE PERDRE (THE NUNS STORY).

AUDREY HEPBURN, *Leo Fuchs* 1958

TONY CURTIS AND JACK LEMMON, *Dick Miller* 1959

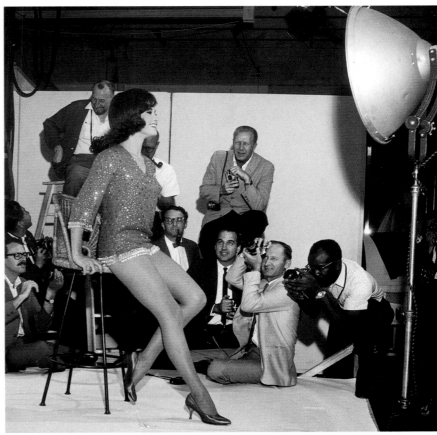

"MISS PINUP" MARY TYLER MOORE, *Nate Cutler* 1966

RED SKELTON AND WALTER BRENNAN, *Nate Cutler* 1954

JANE RUSSELL, BOB HOPE AND SHIRLEY MACLAINE, *Nate Cutler* 1959

WALT DISNEY, *Don Ornitz* 1959

Just days before Disneyland opened, WALT DISNEY walked through the entire park giving it a personal inspection.

Einige Tage vor der Eröffnung von Disneyland ging WALT DISNEY persönlich durch den Park, um alles zu inspizieren.

WALT DISNEY fait une tournée d'inspection de Disneyland quelques jours avant l'ouverture du parc.

FRANK BEZ AND LEE REMICK, *Dick Miller* 1965

DICK VAN DYKE AND MARY TYLER MOORE, *Frank Bez* 1962

For ESQUIRE magazine, Frank Bez shot LEE REMICK in a series of bathtub scenes as they might have been staged by several famous directors, including Japan's Akiro Kurosawa. • Also for ESQUIRE: ANDY WARHOL and sidekick NICO as Batman and Robin. • FOR THIS WEEK, DICK VAN DYKE and MARY TYLER MOORE spoof women drivers.

Für die Zeitschrift ESQUIRE schoss Frank Bez eine Serie von Badewannenszenen von LEE REMICK, wie sie auch von anderen berühmten Filmregisseuren, inklusive Japans Akiro Kurosawa, inszeniert worden wären. • Auch für ESQUIRE: ANDY WARHOL und NICO als Batman und Robin. • Für THIS WEEK parodieren DICK VAN DYKE und MARY TYLER MOORE weibliche Autofahrer.

Frank Bez a photographié LEE REMICK pour le magazine ESQUIRE dans une série de scènes de bain telles qu'elles auraient pu être mises en scène par des réalisateurs célèbres de l'époque, notamment le Japonais Akiro Kurosawa. • Également pour ESQUIRE : ANDY WARHOL et NICO en Batman et Robin ; et pour THIS WEEK, DICK VAN DYKE et MARY TYLER MOORE se moquant des femmes au volant.

ANDY WARHOL AND NICO, *Frank Bez* 1962

CANTINFLAS, *Gerard Decaux* 1959

Seminary schoolboys in Toledo, Spain, get an eyeful of movie presence as PEPE star CANTINFLAS takes a stroll. • 10-year-old RICKY MARTIN backstage at a Menudo concert. • ELIZABETH TAYLOR gives RICHARD BURTON'S cheek a pat on the set of CLEOPATRA. • VANESSA REDGRAVE and the 2nd assistant cameraman both tread water as a wet ISADORA scene gets slated. • BRAD PITT takes aim at the photographer on the New York set of THE DEVIL'S OWN.

Schuljungen eines Priesterseminars in Toledo, Spanien, bekommen PEPE-Star CANTINFLAS bei einem Spaziergang zu sehen. • Der 10-jährige RICKY MARTIN bei einem Menudo-Konzert hinter der Bühne. • ELIZABETH TAYLOR verpasst RICHARD BURTON während der Dreharbeiten zu CLEOPATRA einen leichten Klaps auf den Po. • VANESSA REDGRAVE und der 2. Kameraassistent gehen beide für eine Wasserszene für ISADORA baden. • BRAD PITT zielt bei den Dreharbeiten zu VERTRAUTER FEIND (THE DEVIL'S OWN) in New York auf den Fotografen.

De jeunes séminaristes reconnaissent CANTINFLAS, la vedette de PEPE, dans les rues de Tolède (Espagne). • RICKY MARTIN à l'âge de 10 ans dans les coulisses d'un concert de Menudo. • ELIZABETH TAYLOR «rajuste le costume» de RICHARD BURTON sur le tournage de CLÉOPÂTRE (CLEOPATRA). • VANESSA REDGRAVE et le 2ᵉ assistant caméra attendent dans l'eau le lancement d'une scène humide de ISADORA. • BRAD PITT vise le photographe sur le tournage à New York de ENNEMIS RAPPROCHÉS (DEVIL'S OWN).

RICKY MARTIN, *Globe Archive* 1984

RICHARD BURTON AND ELIZABETH TAYLOR, *Herschtrit* 1962

VANESSA REDGRAVE, *Norman Gryspeerdt* 1968

BRAD PITT, *Alex Olviera* 1997

DON FELD AND ANN-MARGRET, *Bill Kobrin* 1965

CARROLL BAKER AND EDITH HEAD, *William Claxton* 1963

CHARLTON HESTON, *Dick Miller* 1958

ANN-MARGRET and DON FELD begin the process of designing her wardrobe for THE CINCINNATI KID. • EDITH HEAD makes last minute changes in CARROLL BAKER's feathered costume for THE CARPETBAGGERS. • CHARLTON HESTON has a fitting even for the loin cloth he wears in BEN HUR. • During the Mexico location for her first English-language movie, VIVA MARIA, BRIGITTE BARDOT announced that Charlie Chaplin was the actor she most admired and Orlando, the special photographer on the movie, got an idea. He asked Bardot if she would recreate Chaplin's Little Tramp character for a layout and she readily agreed. She put together anything she could beg, borrow or steal for costume and props, even arose at 3am to get ready. The resulting photograph was published around the world.

ANN-MARGRET und DON FELD fangen an, ihre Kostüme für THE CINCINNATI KID zu entwerfen. • EDITH HEAD nimmt in letzter Minute Änderungen an CARROLL BAKERS gefedertem Kostüm für DIE UNERSÄTTLICHEN (THE CARPETBAGGERS) vor. • CHARLTON HESTON hat sogar ein spezielles Kostüm für seinen Film BEN HUR. • Während der Dreharbeiten zu ihrem ersten englischsprachigen Film VIVA MARIA, der in Mexiko gedreht wurde, sagte BRIGITTE BARDOT, dass Charlie Chaplin der Schauspieler sei, den sie am meisten bewundere. Orlando, der Spezial-Fotograf für VIVA MARIA, hatte daraufhin eine Idee. Er fragte Bardot, ob sie Chaplins Charakter aus Little Tramp für ein Fotoshooting nachstellen könne. Sie stimmte zu und brachte alle Kostüme und Requisiten zusammen, die sie erbetteln, leihen oder stehlen konnte. Sie stand sogar um 3 Uhr morgens auf, um sich fertig zu machen. Das daraus hervorgegangene Foto wurde in der ganzen Welt veröffentlicht.

ANN-MARGRET et DON FELD font les premiers essayages de costumes pour LE KID DE CINCINNATTI (THE CINCINNATI KID). • EDITH HEAD procède à quelques ajustements de dernière minute sur les plumes de CARROLL BAKER pour LES AMBITIEUX (THE CARPETBAGGERS). • CHARLTON HESTON doit aussi faire des essayages pour le pagne qu'il porte dans BEN HUR. Alors qu'elle tournait au Mexique son premier film en anglais, VIVA MARIA, BRIGITTE BARDOT dit un jour que Charlie Chaplin était l'acteur qu'elle admirait le plus. Orlando, le photographe du film, eut alors l'idée de demander à Bardot si elle voulait bien incarner le personnage de Charlot pour une série de photos. Elle accepta aussitôt et, ayant emprunté costume et accessoires, se leva même à 3 heures du matin pour être fin prête. La photo fit ensuite le tour du monde.

BRIGITTE BARDOT, *Orlando* 1964

CLINT EASTWOOD, *Douglas Jones* 1970

SIDNEY POITIER, *Ron Thal* 1966

CLINT EASTWOOD and photog Douglas Jones took a few minutes away from the filming of DIRTY HARRY to experiment. The result became the basis for the ad campaign for the movie. • A young citizen of Sparta, Illinois, looks up to his idol SIDNEY POITIER during the filming of IN THE HEAT OF THE NIGHT. • CHARLES BRONSON, his wife JILL IRELAND and their brood on the location of THE DUBIOUS PATRIOTS, in the wilds of Nevishir, Turkey.

CLINT EASTWOOD und Fotograf Douglas Jones nahmen sich während der Dreharbeiten zu DIRTY HARRY ein paar Minuten frei, um zu experimentieren. Das Resultat wurde die Basis für die Werbekampagne zum Film. • Ein junger Einwohner von Sparta, Illinois, bewundert bei den Dreharbeiten zu IN DER HITZE DER NACHT (IN THE HEAT OF THE NIGHT) sein Idol SIDNEY POITIER. • CHARLES BRONSON, seine Frau JILL IRELAND und ihre Kinder am Drehort zu ZWEI KERLE AUS GRANIT (THE DUBIOUS PATRIOTS) in der Wildnis von Nevishir in der Türkei.

Pendant le tournage de L'INSPECTEUR HARRY (DIRTY HARRY), CLINT EASTWOOD et le photographe Douglas Jones prirent quelques clichés qui servirent ensuite de base à la campagne de publicité du film. • Un jeune habitant de Sparta (Illinois) contemple son idole SIDNEY POITIER lors du tournage de DANS LA CHALEUR DE LA NUIT (IN THE HEAT OF THE NIGHT). • CHARLES BRONSON, son épouse JILL IRELAND et leurs enfants, sur le lieu de tournage des BAROUDEURS (THE DUBIOUS PATRIOTS), dans la région sauvage du Nevishir, en Turquie.

CHARLES BRONSON AND FAMILY, *Nancy Holmes* 1969

MARILYN MONROE AND PAULA STRASBERG, *Don Ornitz* 1959

JAMES DEAN, *Russ Meyer* 1955

Every minute between scenes of SOME LIKE IT HOT, MARILYN MONROE could be found in serious conversation with her confidante and coach PAULA STRASBERG, wife of Actors Studio founder Lee Strasberg. Here they huddle at the famous old Hotel Coronado in San Diego where much of the comedy was filmed. • JAMES DEAN on the Marfa, Texas, location of GIANT. It was no secret that director George Stevens fought with Dean from the first day of shooting. Stevens had little patience with the long behavioral exercises Dean insisted upon before filming a scene and having to take time to answer his constant questions about the technical side of moviemaking. The distraught Stevens told the young actor to get himself an 8mm camera and learn to make his own movies because he would probably never work in Hollywood again. Dean did just that, going out on Sundays to shoot, borrowing photographer Russ Meyer's tripod, and the relationship between actor and director calmed. Stevens was tragically correct in his prediction. GIANT was indeed Dean's last film. He was killed in an auto accident just days after completing it.

In jeder freien Minute der Dreharbeiten zu MANCHE MÖGEN'S HEISS (SOME LIKE IT HOT) konnte man MARILYN MONROE mit ihrer Vertrauten und Trainerin PAULA STRASBERG, Frau des Actors-Studio-Gründers Lee Strasberg, in ein tiefgründiges Gespräch vertieft sehen. Hier tuscheln sie am berühmten alten Hotel Coronado in San Diego, wo ein Großteil der Komödie gefilmt wurde. • JAMES DEAN in Marfa, Texas, den Drehort von GIGANTEN (GIANT). Es war kein Geheimnis, dass Filmregisseur George Stevens mit Dean vom ersten Tag des Shootings an stritt. Stevens hatte wenig Geduld für die langen Verhaltens- übungen, auf die Dean vor dem Filmen einer jeden Szene bestand und für Deans ständige Fragen zur Technik des Filme- machens. Der verzweifelte Stevens sagte dem jungen Schau- spieler, dass er sich eine 8mm-Kamera kaufen und lernen solle, seine eigenen Filme zu machen, weil er sehr wahrscheinlich sonst nie wieder in Hollywood arbeiten würde. Dean folgte sei- nem Rat. Er ging fortan sonntags nach draußen, um zu filmen. Dazu lieh er sich das Stativ des Fotografen Russ Meyer aus. Die Beziehung zwischen Filmregisseur und Schauspieler beruhigte sich daraufhin. Stevens hatte tragischerweise mit seiner Vorher- sage Recht: GIGANTEN war tatsächlich Deans letzter Film. Er kam bei einem Autounfall einige Tage nach Beendigung der Drehar- beiten ums Leben.

MARILYN MONROE discutait systématiquement entre chaque scène de CERTAINS L'AIMENT CHAUD (SOME LIKE IT HOT) avec sa confidente et entraîneuse PAULA STRASBERG, l'épouse du fondateur de l'Actors Studio Lee Strasberg, comme ici devant le célèbre vieil Hotel Coronado de San Diego, où presque toute la comédie fut filmée. • JAMES DEAN lors du tournage en exté- rieur de GÉANT (GIANT) à Marfa (Texas). Il fut évident dès le début du tournage que George Stevens, le réalisateur, ne s'en- tendait pas du tout avec Dean. Peu patient, Stevens n'appréciait pas les exercices que Dean voulait absolument faire avant chaque prise et refusait de perdre son temps à répondre à ses questions continuelles sur la technique de la réalisation. Agacé, Stevens dit finalement au jeune acteur qu'il ferait mieux de s'acheter une caméra 8mm et d'apprendre à faire ses propres films, car il ne travaillerait probablement plus jamais à Hollywood. L'idée plut aussitôt à Dean qui, ayant emprunté le trépied du photographe Russ Meyer, passa ensuite tous ses dimanches à filmer ; du coup, les relations entre l'acteur et le réalisateur s'améliorèrent. La prédiction de Stevens se révéla malheureusement exacte car GÉANT fut effectivement le dernier film de James Dean, qui se tua dans un accident de voiture à peine quelques jours après la fin du tournage.

CAROL CHANNING AND PAUL SOLEN, *Jack Stager* 1965

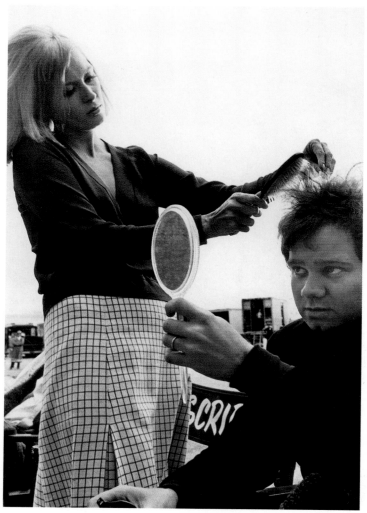

FAYE DUNAWAY AND MICHAEL J. POLLARD, *Ron Thal* 1966

PETER USTINOV, *William Read Woodfield* 1959

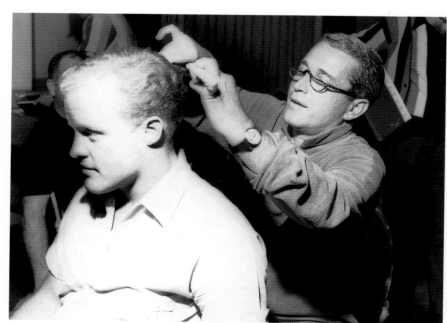

PHILLIP CROSBY AND PERRY COMO, *Bill Hill* 1962

CAROL CHANNING was the official barber for the cast of HELLO DOLLY. • MICHAEL J. POLLARD gets teased by FAYE DUNAWAY on the set of BONNIE AND CLYDE. • PETER USTINOV in curlers for SPARTACUS. • A barber by trade before turning singer, PERRY COMO trims PHILLIP CROSBY. • ROGER MOORE teaches LANA TURNER fine points of fencing for DIANE. • JANET LEIGH gets pointers for THE VIKINGS from KIRK DOUGLAS in Norway. • NATALIE'S instructor for THE GREAT RACE is Olympic fencing coach JOSEF VINCE. • Retired boxer MUSHY CALLAHAN takes it on the chin from student ELVIS PRESLEY, learning to box for KID GALAHAD.

ROGER MOORE AND LANA TURNER, *Globe Archive* 1955

JANET LEIGH, KIRK DOUGLAS AND TONY CURTIS, *William Read Woodfield* 1957

JOSEF VINCE AND NATALIE WOOD, *Orlando* 1965

MUSHY CALLAHAN AND ELVIS PRESLEY, *Globe Archive* 1962

CAROL CHANNING war die Friseurin für die Filmtruppe von HELLO DOLLY. • MICHAEL J. POLLARD wird von FAYE DUNAWAY frisiert. • PETER USTINOV bekommt für SPARTACUS Locken. • Bevor PERRY COMO Sänger wurde, arbeitete er als Friseur. Hier frisiert er PHILLIP CROSBY. • ROGER MOORE bringt LANA TURNER für DIANE – KURTISANE VON FRANKREICH das Fechten bei. • JANET LEIGH bekommt bei DIE WIKINGER in Norwegen von KIRK DOUGLAS Regieanweisungen. • NATALIES Fechtlehrer für DAS GROSSE RENNEN RUND UM DIE WELT ist der Olympiatrainer JOSEF VINCE. • Der pensionierte Boxer MUSHY CALLAHAN bekommt von ELVIS PRESLEY einige Schläge aufs Kinn ab.

CAROL CHANNING fut la coiffeuse des acteurs de HELLO DOLLY. • FAYE DUNAWAY sur le plateau de BONNIE AND CLYDE coiffe MICHAEL J POLLARD. • PETER USTINOV en bigoudis pour SPARTACUS. • PERRY COMO coupe les cheveux de PHILLIP CROSBY. • ROGER MOORE enseigne quelques parades d'escrime à LANA TURNER pour le film DIANE DE POITIERS. • JANET LEIGH reçoit des conseils de KIRK DOUGLAS pour le tournage des VIKINGS en Norvège. • Le professeur de NATALIE dans LA GRANDE COURSE AUTOUR DU MONDE était le directeur de l'équipe olympique d'escrime JOSEF VINCE. • ELVIS PRESLEY expédie une droite au menton de son professeur, le boxeur MUSHY CALLAHAN.

MARLON BRANDO AND MICHAEL KIDD, *Bob Willoughby* 1954

The idea of MARLON BRANDO singing and dancing in the film version of the musical GUYS AND DOLLS was big news. Bob Willoughby got permission to shoot the dance rehearsals with Broadway choreographer MICHAEL KIDD. At the first rehearsal Brando borrowed Willoughby's camera and followed Kidd around watching his every move through the viewfinder but never snapping the shutter, completely intimidating him. Then, satisfied that he could terrorize the dancer, Brando handed the camera back and got to work.

For THE CARETAKERS, in which she played a matron in a mental institution, JOAN CRAWFORD had to learn jujitsu. It took her only one lesson before she could throw the 200-pound instructor, Bruce Tegner.

Die Vorstellung, MARLON BRANDO in der Filmversion des Musicals SCHWERE JUNGS – LEICHTE MÄDCHEN (GUYS AND DOLLS) singen und tanzen zu sehen, war eine große Neuigkeit. Bob Willoughby bekam die Erlaubnis, die Tanzszenen mit dem Broadway-Choreografen MICHAEL KIDD zu fotografieren. Bei der ersten Probe lieh sich Brando Willoughbys Kamera aus und folgte Kidd auf Schritt und Tritt, schoss aber niemals ein Bild, was diesen sehr einschüchterte. Brando, zufrieden mit der Tatsache, den Tänzer auch terrorisieren zu können, gab die Kamera zurück und machte sich an die Arbeit.

Für FRAUEN, DIE NICHT LIEBEN DÜRFEN (THE CARETAKERS), in dem sie eine Aufseherin in einer Irrenanstalt spielte, musste JOAN CRAWFORD Jiu-Jitsu lernen. Sie benötigte nur eine Trainingsstunde, um den 90 Kilo schweren Lehrer Bruce Tegner aufs Kreuz zu legen.

Le fait que MARLON BRANDO chante et danse dans la version cinématographique de la comédie musicale BLANCHES COLOMBES ET VILAINS MESSIEURS (GUYS ET DOLLS) était un événement. Bob Willoughby eut l'autorisation d'assister aux répétitions conduites par MICHAEL KIDD, le chorégraphe de Broadway. Lors de la première séance, Brando emprunta l'appareil de Willoughby et suivit Kidd en observant chacun de ses mouvements à travers l'oculaire mais sans appuyer sur le déclencheur. Puis, assez satisfait d'avoir réussi à terroriser ainsi le danseur, Brando rendit l'appareil et se mit au travail.

JOAN CRAWFORD dut apprendre le jiu-jitsu pour THE CARETAKERS, dans lequel elle jouait la surveillante d'un hôpital psychiatrique. Il ne lui fallut toutefois qu'une leçon pour projeter en l'air les 90 kilos de son instructeur Bruce Tegner.

JOAN CRAWFORD AND BRUCE TEGNER, *Don Ornitz* 1962

ARNOLD SCHWARZENEGGER, *Michael Norcia* 1977

ANTHONY QUINN AND VALENTINA CORTESE, *Warsacki* 1964

DEAN MARTIN AND JERRY LEWIS, *Larry Barbier Jr.* 1953

ANTHONY QUINN entertains VALENTINA CORTESE on the set of THE VISIT. ● DEAN MARTIN and JERRY LEWIS entertain each other during SCARED STIFF. ● KIRK DOUGLAS shows off for PIER ANGELI between scenes of THE STORY OF THREE LOVES.

ANTHONY QUINN unterhält VALENTINA CORTESE bei den Dreharbeiten zu THE VISIT. ● DEAN MARTIN und JERRY LEWIS unterhalten sich gegenseitig während der Dreharbeiten zu STARR VOR ANGST (SCARED STIFF). ● KIRK DOUGLAS gibt in den Drehpausen von WAR ES DIE GROSSE LIEBE? (THE STORY OF THREE LOVERS) vor PIER ANGELI an.

ANTHONY QUINN distrait VALENTINA CORTESE sur le tournage de LA RANCUNE (THE VISIT). ● DEAN MARTIN et JERRY LEWIS se divertissent pendant les pauses de TU TREMBLES, CARCASSE (SCARED STIFF). ● KIRK DOUGLAS fait l'intéressant devant PIER ANGELI entre les prises de HISTOIRE DE TROIS AMOURS (THE STORY OF THREE LOVES).

KIRK DOUGLAS AND PIER ANGELI, *Larry Barbier Jr.* 1953

Journalists are an integral part of Hollywood. Here are a few of them doing their jobs: SIDNEY SKOLSKY interviews DEAN MARTIN on the set of WHO WAS THAT LADY? • ARMY ARCHERD and JOE HYAMS get MONROE and LOREN on tape. • Commenting on the interview process is ROBERT REDFORD on the set of JEREMIAH JOHNSON.

Journalisten sind ein wesentlicher Bestandteil Hollywoods. Hier sieht man einige von ihnen bei der Arbeit: SIDNEY SKOLSKY interviewt DEAN MARTIN am Drehort zu WER WAR DIE DAME? (WHO WAS THAT LADY?). • ARMY ARCHERD und JOE HYAMS interviewen MONROE und LOREN. • Am Drehort zu JEREMIAH JOHNSON: ROBERT REDFORD zu den Interviews.

Les journalistes font partie intégrante de la vie de Hollywood. On en voit ici quelques-uns en plein exercice de leur métier : SIDNEY SKOLSKY face à DEAN MARTIN sur le tournage de QUI ÉTAIT DONC CETTE DAME ? (WHO WAS THAT LADY?). • ARMY ARCHERD et JOE HYAMS enregistrant MARILYN MONROE et SOPHIA LOREN. • Quant à ROBERT REDFORD, il fait un autre genre de commentaire sur le tournage de JEREMIAH JOHNSON.

DEAN MARTIN AND SIDNEY SKOLSKY, *Bill Kobrin* 1960

ROBERT REDFORD, *Orlando* 1972

MARILYN MONROE AND ARMY ARCHERD, *Nate Cutler* 1960

SOPHIA LOREN AND JOE HYAMS, *Bill Kobrin* 1959

BILLY WILDER AND SHIRLEY MACLAINE, *Dick Miller* 1959

JOHN HUSTON, *Globe Archive* 1958

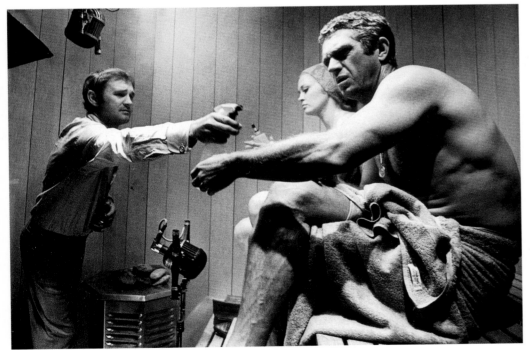

NORMAN JEWISON, FAYE DUNAWAY AND STEVE McQUEEN, *Ron Thal* 1967

BILLY WILDER and SHIRLEY MACLAINE cut up on the set of THE APARTMENT. • JOHN HUSTON has his picture taken with the African tribe he cast in THE ROOTS OF HEAVEN. • NORMAN JEWISON adds a few beads of sweat to his THOMAS CROWN AFFAIR stars FAYE DUNAWAY and STEVE McQUEEN.

BILLY WILDER und SHIRLEY MACLAINE scherzen bei den Dreharbeiten zu DAS APPARTEMENT (THE APARTMENT). • JOHN HUSTON lässt sich mit dem afrikanischen Stamm aus DIE WURZELN DES HIMMELS (THE ROOTS OF HEAVEN) ablichten. • NORMAN JEWISON fügt den Stars FAYE DUNAWAY und STEVE McQUEEN ein paar Schweißperlen für THOMAS CROWN IST NICHT ZU FASSEN (THE THOMAS CROWN AFFAIR) hinzu.

BILLY WILDER et SHIRLEY MACLAINE font les pitres pendant le tournage de LA GARÇONNIÈRE (THE APARTMENT). • JOHN HUSTON se fait prendre en photo avec la tribu d'Africains qu'il a engagée pour LES RACINES DU CIEL (THE ROOTS OF HEAVEN). • NORMAN JEWISON asperge de fausse sueur FAYE DUNAWAY et STEVE McQUEEN, les vedettes de son film L'AFFAIRE THOMAS CROWN (THE THOMAS CROWN AFFAIR).

KATHARINE HEPBURN, PETER O'TOOLE AND ANTHONY HARVEY, *Joel Elkins* 1966

CHARLES CHAPLIN AND SOPHIA LOREN, *Tazio Secchiaroli* 1966

KATHARINE HEPBURN AND ANTHONY HOPKINS, *Joel Elkins* 1966

CHARLES CHAPLIN AND MARLON BRANDO, *Tazio Secchiaroli* 1966

ANNE BANCROFT, SUE LYON, MILDRED DUNNOCK, IRENE TSU, FLORA ROBSON, MARGARET LEIGHTON, ANNA LEE AND JOHN FORD, *Don Ornitz* 1964

JOHN FORD was known throughout his career as a man's director yet he helmed the action drama SEVEN WOMEN with a strong all-woman cast including these ladies who are giving him their rapt attention. • ANTHONY HARVEY rehearsed PETER O'TOOLE, KATHARINE HEPBURN and ANTHONY HOPKINS on an unused sound stage in London for weeks prior to filming THE LION IN WINTER. Hepburn was especially helpful to Hopkins, who was making his film debut, by giving him tips on how to guard against having his scenes stolen by another actor which, she warned him, she'd probably do anyway. • The CHARLES CHAPLIN directorial touch in THE COUNTESS FROM HONG KONG got different reactions from his stars SOPHIA LOREN and MARLON BRANDO. Chaplin always showed his actors exactly what he wanted by acting out all parts in detail. Loren was delighted with his hands-on technique. Brando was not amused.

JOHN FORD war seine ganze Karriere hindurch dafür bekannt, in seinen Filmen hauptsächlich Männer mit von der Partie zu haben. In seinem Action-Drama SIEBEN FRAUEN (SEVEN WOMEN) hat er zum ersten Mal eine starke weibliche Besetzung, die ihm hier aufmerksam zuhört. • ANTHONY HARVEY probt Wochen vor den Dreharbeiten zu DER LÖWE IM WINTER (THE LION IN WINTER) ein Stück mit PETER O'TOOLE, KATHARINE HEPBURN und ANTHONY HOPKINS auf einer unbenutzten Bühne in London ein. Insbesondere für Hopkins war Hepburn eine große Hilfe. Er machte sein Filmdebüt und Hepburn gab ihm Tipps, wie man sich davor schützen könnte, dass der Filmpartner einem die Show stahl. Sie warnte ihn, dass sie es trotzdem versuchen würde. • CHARLES CHAPLIN Besonderheit, die in DIE GRÄFIN VON HONGKONG (THE COUNTESS FROM HONG KONG) erkennbar wird, provozierte unterschiedliche Reaktionen bei seinen Stars SOPHIA LOREN und MARLON BRANDO. Chaplin zeigte seinen Schauspielern immer genau, was er er wollte, indem er alles im Detail vorspielte. Loren war erfreut über seine Technik. Brando gefiel sie gar nicht.

Bien que JOHN FORD ait fait toute sa carrière en mettant en scène des hommes, il assura aussi la direction du film FRONTIÈRE CHINOISE (SEVEN WOMEN), à la distribution presque uniquement féminine qui ici l'écoute attentivement. • ANTHONY HARVEY fit répéter PETER O'TOOLE, KATHARINE HEPBURN et ANTHONY HOPKINS pendant des semaines dans une salle de tournage désaffectée de Londres avant de filmer UN LION EN HIVER (THE LION IN WINTER). Hepburn aida particulièrement Hopkins, qui faisait ses débuts au cinéma, en lui indiquant comment éviter qu'un autre acteur ne lui « vole » ses scènes – ce qu'elle essaierait d'ailleurs très probablement de faire, avoua-t-elle aussitôt. • La direction d'acteur de CHARLES CHAPLIN dans LA COMTESSE DE HONG KONG (THE COUNTESS FROM HONG KONG), provoqua des réactions différentes de ses vedettes SOPHIA LOREN et MARLON BRANDO. Si Loren était ravie que Chaplin indique très précisément ce qu'il voulait en jouant leurs rôles en détail, cela n'amusait pas beaucoup Brando.

JAKE LaMOTTA was a constant and very much felt presence on the set of RAGING BULL, his life story; here he is listening in on MARTIN SCORSESE directing ROBERT DeNIRO. • On the other hand, GEORGE RAFT made one appearance on the set of THE GEORGE RAFT STORY to teach his movie counterpart RAY DANTON to dance and wasn't seen again until the film was in the can. • An intimate moment on the set of JUDGEMENT AT NUREMBERG with MAXIMILIAN SCHELL, director STANLEY KRAMER and MONTGOMERY CLIFT.

JAKE LaMOTTA, MARTIN SCORSESE AND ROBERT DeNIRO, *Christine Loss* 1979

GEORGE RAFT AND RAY DANTON, *Bill Kobrin* 1962

JAKE LaMOTTA hört sich die Regieanweisungen von MARTIN SCORSESE an ROBERT DeNIRO an. LaMotta war sehr präsent bei den Dreharbeiten zu WIE EIN WILDER STIER (RAGING BULL), seiner Lebensgeschichte. • Auf der anderen Seite ließ sich GEORGE RAFT nur einmal bei den Dreharbeiten zu DER TANZENDE GANGSTER (THE GEORGE RAFT STORY) sehen, um RAY DANTON, der ihn im Film darstellt, das Tanzen beizubringen und wurde erst wieder gesehen, als der Film fertig war. • Ein liebevoller Moment bei den Dreharbeiten zu URTEIL VON NÜRNBERG (JUDGEMENT AT NUREMBERG) mit MAXIMILIAN SCHELL, Filmregisseur STANLEY KRAMER und MONTGOMERY CLIFT.

JAKE LaMOTTA, qui écoute MARTIN SCORSESE diriger ROBERT DeNIRO, marqua de sa présence constante et chaleureuse le tournage de RAGING BULL, qui raconte l'histoire de sa vie. • En revanche, pour DOMPTEUR DE FEMMES (THE GEORGE RAFT STORY), GEORGE RAFT n'apparût qu'une seule fois pour indiquer comment danser à RAY DANTON, son incarnation à l'écran; on ne le vit plus avant la fin du tournage. • Un moment d'intimité sur le tournage de JUGEMENT À NUREMBERG (JUDGEMENT AT NUREMBERG) avec MAXIMILIAN SCHELL, le réalisateur STANLEY KRAMER et MONTGOMERY CLIFT.

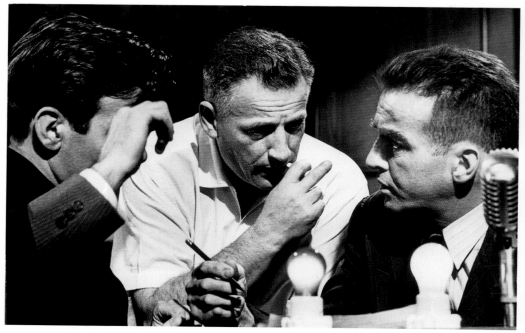

MAXIMILIAN SCHELL, STANLEY KRAMER AND MONTGOMERY CLIFT, *Don Ornitz* 1960

JEROME ROBBINS (WEST SIDE STORY), *Jack Harris* 1960

SYDNEY POLLACK AND BURT LANCASTER (THE SCALPHUNTERS), *Orlando* 1968

GEORGE CUKOR AND AUDREY HEPBURN (MY FAIR LADY), *Globe Archive* 1963

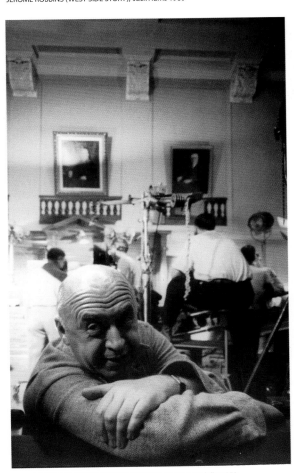

OTTO PREMINGER (ANATOMY OF A MURDER), *Lawrence Schiller* 1959

STANLEY KUBRICK, KIRK DOUGLAS AND JOHN IRELAND (SPARTACUS), *Don Ornitz* 1959

FRANCIS FORD COPPOLA (FINIAN'S RAINBOW), *Orlando* 1967

Ad art for the action comedy SERGEANTS THREE found rat-packers SINATRA, MARTIN and LAWFORD leaping into the air with the aid of a trampoline and enjoying it like kids. • JACK LEMMON and BILLY WILDER made seven movies together and were frequently the last to leave the set at the end of the day. Wilder felt Lemmon had the greatest rapport with an audience since Chaplin. "Just by looking at him, people can tell what goes on in his mind."

Bei PR-Aufnahmen für die Actionkomödie DIE SIEGREICHEN DREI (SERGEANTS THREE) sieht man SINATRA, MARTIN und LAWFORD auf einem Trampolin in die Luft springen, wobei sie sich wie kleine Kinder freuen. • JACK LEMMON und BILLY WILDER machten zusammen sieben Filme und waren häufig die Letzten, die den Drehort am Ende des Tages verließen. Wilder war der Meinung, dass Lemmon das beste Verhältnis seit Chaplin zu seinem Publikum hatte: „Man muss ihn nur ansehen, um zu wissen, was in seinem Kopf vorgeht."

SINATRA, MARTIN et LAWFORD s'amusent comme des enfants à bondir sur un trampoline pour les besoins de la publicité de la comédie LES TROIS SERGENTS (SERGEANTS THREE). • JACK LEMMON et BILLY WILDER, qui tournèrent sept films ensemble, étaient souvent les derniers à quitter le plateau à la fin de la journée. Wilder disait que Lemmon était l'acteur qui avait le meilleur contact avec le public depuis Chaplin : « Rien qu'en le voyant, les gens savent ce qu'ils pensent. »

FRANK SINATRA, DEAN MARTIN AND PETER LAWFORD, *William Read Woodfield* 1962

JACK LEMMON AND BILLY WILDER, *Orlando* 1965

JANE FONDA AND ANTHONY PERKINS IN CENTRAL PARK, *Jack Stager* 1959

RICHARD BEYMER AND SHARON TATE, *Winson Muldrow* 1963

THE DATE LAYOUT

The date layout was born in the late 1940s in the fan magazines, sired by major studios that in those days told – didn't ask – their contract players what they would do for publicity. They were cotton candy layouts that paired attractive young people in quasi-romantic situations, usually focusing on one couple but sometimes on a group, always evenly matched boy/girl. The reason for the date layout was promotion – publicity for a new film or a new contract player – and that the romantically portrayed couple might barely know one another was of no consequence. The fan mags devoted many pages each month to these little charades but they didn't have exclusive custody of them. Several of the national publications (most notably LOOK, PAGEANT, CORONET) ran them too. And they served their purpose well. More than a few young players, as yet unworthy of personal features and interviews in the magazines, solidified their status as up-and-coming stars by being on view in these layouts month after month until the fan magazines began to die off in the 70s.

"A Day at the Beach" was a favorite layout for two reasons. The location was free and it offered the chance for some cheese-and-beefcake. But it could just as easily be "A Day at Disneyland" or "A Day at the Farmer's Market" or a picnic in a park, a ride in the country or even a dip in the Marineland fish tank. Local restaurants, amusement parks and nearby resorts were available as location sites to cash in on free magazine publicity, known as "plugs". But a studio backlot or someone's pool would suffice as a location as long as the actors looked like they were having a good time together and the layout could end with a kiss.

The date layout was one stop, a rite of passage if you will, for most young actors on their way to stardom. Many became known to movie fans primarily through this exposure. And some achieved major stardom.

Granted, not every star did date layouts. But almost every star did.

DAS DATE-LAYOUT

Das so genannte Date-Layout wurde in den späten 40ern von den Fanzeitschriften entwickelt – ausgeklügelt von den großen Studios, die ihren vertraglich gebundenen Schauspielern zu dieser Zeit vorschrieben, was sie für Publicity zu tun hatten. Es handelte sich dabei um „Zuckerwatte-Layouts", die attraktive junge Leute in quasi romantischen Situationen zeigten. Der Blick war dabei normalerweise auf ein Paar gerichtet, manchmal auch auf eine Gruppe, wobei es immer gleich viel Männer und Frauen gab. Das Date-Layout war Werbung – für einen neuen Film oder einen neu unter Vertrag genommenen Schauspieler. Die Tatsache, dass sich das romantisch dargestellte Paar kaum kannte, spielte keine Rolle. Die Fanzeitschriften widmeten diesen kleinen Possen jeden Monat viele Seiten, aber sie verfügten über keine Exklusivrechte. Einige der nationalen Publikationen (vor allem LOOK, PAGEANT, CORONET) veröffentlichten sie ebenfalls. Und sie erfüllten ihren Zweck sehr gut. Viele der jungen Schauspieler, die noch nicht so bekannt waren, dass man ihnen in den Zeitschriften eigene Beiträge gewidmet oder Interviews mit ihnen veröffentlicht hätte, festigten ihren Status als zukünftige Stars dadurch, dass sie Monat für Monat auf diese Weise abgebildet wurden. Diese Praxis war üblich, bis die Fanzeitschriften in den 70ern aus der Mode kamen.

„Ein Tag am Strand" war aus zwei Gründen ein beliebtes Thema. Der Ort, an dem gedreht wurde, war kostenlos und man hatte die Gelegenheit, nackte Haut und Muskelprotze bewundern zu können. Es konnte aber genauso gut „Ein Tag in Disneyland" oder „Ein Tag auf dem Bauernmarkt", ein Picknick in einem Park, eine Landpartie oder sogar eine Tauchpartie im Marineland-Aquarium sein. Restaurants, Vergnügungsparks und nahe gelegene Urlaubsorte standen als Drehorte zur Verfügung, um aus der Zeitschriften-Publicity kostenlos Kapital zu schlagen (in der Branche „plugs" genannt). Aber auch das Filmgelände oder irgendein Swimmingpool waren ausreichend, so lange die Schauspieler aussahen, als hätten sie zusammen Spaß und so lange die Möglichkeit bestand, dass das Layout mit einem Kuss enden konnte.

Das Date-Layout war für die meisten jungen Schauspieler eine Etappe oder ein Ritual auf ihrem Weg zum Ruhm. Viele wurden hauptsächlich durch dieses Layout bei ihren Fans bekannt. Einige kamen ganz groß raus.

Zugegeben, nicht jeder Star war auf einem Date-Layout zu sehen. Aber fast jeder Star.

RENCONTRES

Les premières photos mettant en scène des couples de vedettes sont apparues dans les fanzines à la fin des années 1940, à une époque où les grandes compagnies dictaient à leurs acteurs sous contrat – et sans leur demander leur avis – ce qu'ils devaient faire et quelle image publique ils devaient présenter. On vit ainsi des photographies angéliques de beaux et romantiques jeunes gens, généralement en couple mais parfois en groupe comprenant toujours un même nombre de garçons que de filles. Qu'aucun d'eux ne se connaisse jamais vraiment avait assez peu d'importance, le seul objectif de ces photos étant de faire la promotion d'un nouveau film ou d'un nouvel acteur sous contrat. Si les fanzines consacraient de nombreuses pages chaque mois à ces petites charades, ils n'en avaient pas l'exclusivité et plusieurs revues nationales (notamment LOOK, PAGEANT et CORONET) publiaient également ce genre de photos. Elles remplissaient d'ailleurs parfaitement leur rôle et un certain nombre de jeunes acteurs, encore trop peu connus pour mériter de poser seul ou d'avoir une interview dans un magazine mais dont le public pouvait suivre l'évolution mois après mois (jusqu'à la disparition des fanzines dans les années 1970), purent asseoir grâce à elles leur réputation de future star.

« Une journée à la plage » était un des thèmes de prédilection des photographes pour deux raisons principales : il n'y avait rien à payer et cela permettait de faire quelques photos de garçons musclés et de belles jeunes filles montrant leurs appâts en maillot de bain. Le thème choisi pouvait tout aussi bien être « Une journée à Disneyland » ou « Une journée au marché », avoir pour prétexte un pique-nique dans un parc, une promenade à la campagne ou encore la visite des aquariums de Marineland, mais aussi les coulisses d'un studio ou les bords d'une simple piscine. La plupart des restaurants, parcs d'attraction et stations balnéaires proches acceptaient d'autant plus facilement de servir de décor que cela leur permettait de bénéficier d'une « réclame » gratuite dans les magazines. L'essentiel était que les figurants aient l'air de prendre du bon temps et que la scène se termine par un baiser.

Ces scènes constituaient une sorte de rituel, une étape obligée sur le chemin de la gloire pour la plupart des jeunes acteurs. C'est par ce biais « plastique » que nombre d'entre eux se firent connaître des cinéphiles. Certains sont même devenus des stars.

Il faut avouer que toutes les stars ne posèrent pas pour ce genre de scène, mais presque toutes.

TED HARTLEY AND VICKI FEE, *Gene Trindl* 1966

DIANE McBAIN AND RICHARD BEYMER, *Larry Barbier Jr.* 1959

FABIAN AND MARTA KRISTEN, *Larry Barbier Jr.* 1961

EDD BYRNES AND DOROTHY PROVINE, *Larry Barbier Jr.* 1960

TERRY MOORE AND ROBERT WAGNER, *Jack Stager* 1953

LINDA CRISTAL AND ALEJANDRO REY, *Bill Greenslade* 1968

RALPH TAEGER, PAT HOBBS, CHICKIE LIND AND JAMES COBURN, *Bill Kobrin* 1961

AVA GARDNER AND BURT LANCASTER, *Globe Archive* 1946

MICKEY ROONEY AND ELAINE MENCKEN, *Don Ornitz* 1952

MICHAEL DANTE, NINA SHIPMAN, JAMES FRANCISCUS, LORI NELSON, BURT REYNOLDS AND CATHY CASE, *Larry Barbier Jr.* 1959

NATALIE WOOD AND TAB HUNTER, *Larry Barbier Jr.* 1956

Shortly after this layout was shot, ELAINE became the fourth of MICKEY'S nine wives. • Boy-girl group dates were popular with personal press agents who could get several of their clients covered in one layout. TAB HUNTER probably holds the date layout record, with Rock Hudson, Terry Moore, Fabian and NATALIE WOOD close runners-up. • BARBARA STANWYCK is a name one wouldn't quickly associate with date layouts and this one with BOB STACK wasn't strictly a date – more like an afternoon with Beverly Hills neighbors.

Kurz nach Erscheinen dieser Fotoreportage wurde ELAINE die vierte von MICKEYS neun Frauen. • Gruppen-Verabredung mit Jungen und Mädchen waren sehr beliebt, da die Presseagenten bei diesen Veranstaltungen mehrere ihrer Stars in einem Artikel präsentieren konnten. Die Anzahl von TAB HUNTERS Auftritten in Fotoreportagen über Verabredungen ist rekordverdächtig, dicht gefolgt von Rock Hudson, Terry Moore, Fabian und NATALIE WOOD. • BARBARA STANWYCK ist ein Name, den man nicht so schnell mit Date-Layouts in Verbindung bringen würde und diese Verabredung mit BOB STACK war streng genommen auch keine Verabredung – es war mehr ein Nachmittag mit Nachbarn aus Beverly Hills.

ELAINE devint la quatrième des neufs épouses de MICKEY peu de temps après que cette photo a été prise. • Les photos de groupe entre garçons et filles étaient appréciées par les agents de presse, qui pouvaient ainsi obtenir une couverture médiatique pour plusieurs de leurs clients à la fois. TAB HUNTER détient probablement le record des photos de couple, suivi de près par Rock Hudson, Terry Moore, Fabian et NATALIE WOOD. • BARBARA STANWYCK est un nom que l'on n'associe pas immédiatement aux photos de couple et sa rencontre avec BOB STACK n'était pas vraiment un rendez-vous d'amoureux mais plutôt un après-midi entre voisins de Beverly Hills.

BARBARA STANWYCK AND ROBERT STACK, *Larry Barbier Jr.* 1954

JEAN PAUL BELMONDO AND URSULA ANDRESS, *Maynard Frank Wolfe* 1965

VICTORIA SHAW, ROGER SMITH, TY HARDIN AND ANDRA MARTIN, *Rick Strauss* 1959

GOLDIE HAWN AND DENNIS COLE, *Gene Trindl* 1968

TAB HUNTER AND TERRY MOORE, *Globe Archive* 1954

MICHAEL CALLAN AND JUNE BLAIR, *Larry Barbier Jr.* 1958

SAL MINEO AND NATALIE WOOD, *Globe Archive* 1955

FABIAN AND TUESDAY WELD, *Dick Miller* 1959

CAROL LYNLEY AND BRANDON DeWILDE, *Rick Strauss* 1959

KATHY NOLAN AND ANDY WILLIAMS, *Larry Barbier Jr.* 1958

FRANCE NUYEN AND ROBERT CULP, *Don Ornitz* 1967

MARY ANN MOBLEY AND TRINI LOPEZ, *Ron Thal* 1965

DOLORES HART AND MAXIMILIAN SCHELL, *Dick Miller* 1960

CONNIE FRANCIS AND ERIC FLEMING, *Larry Barbier Jr.* 1959

LINDA CRISTAL AND ROCK HUDSON, *Don Ornitz* 1960

SANDRA DEE AND BOBBY DARIN, *Leo Fuchs* 1960

MILLIE PERKINS AND DEAN STOCKWELL, *Lawrence Schiller* 1958

TERRY MOORE AND DOUGLAS DICK, *Theda and Emerson Hall* 1949

DOLORES HART and MAXIMILIAN SCHELL at the Farmer's Market. • CONNIE FRANCIS and ERIC FLEMING at Grauman's Chinese Theater. • ROCK HUDSON and LINDA CRISTAL on a sailing date. • SANDRA DEE and BOBBY DARIN in Rome. • MILLIE PERKINS and DEAN STOCKWELL at Pacific Ocean Park. • TERRY MOORE and DOUGLAS DICK at a petting zoo.

DOLORES HART und MAXIMILIAN SCHELL auf dem Bauernmarkt. • CONNIE FRANCIS und ERIC FLEMING vor Graumans Chinese Theater. • ROCK HUDSON und LINDA CRISTAL auf einer Segeltour. • SANDRA DEE und BOBBY DARIN in Rom. • MILLIE PERKINS und DEAN STOCKWELL im Pacific Ocean Park. • TERRY MOORE und DOUGLAS DICK in einem Tierpark.

DOLORES HART et MAXIMILIAN SCHELL au marché. • CONNIE FRANCIS et ERIC FLEMING au Grauman's Chinese Theater. • ROCK HUDSON et LINDA CRISTAL voguent ensemble. • SANDRA DEE et BOBBY DARIN à Rome. • MILLIE PERKINS et DEAN STOCKWELL au Pacific Ocean Park. • TERRY MOORE et DOUGLAS DICK au zoo.

VENETIA STEVENSON AND RUSS TAMBLYN, *Larry Barbier Jr.* 1955

GEORGE HAMILTON AND SUSAN KOHNER, *Don Ornitz* 1960

JOHNNY CARSON AND JILL COREY, *Nate Cutler* 1960

TAB HUNTER AND DEBBIE REYNOLDS, *Nate Cutler* 1951

TROY DONAHUE AND JOAN STALEY, *Larry Barbier Jr.* 1960

SCOTT BRADY AND DOROTHY MALONE, *Larry Barbier Jr.* 1950

ROBERT FULLER, CONNIE STEVENS, BURT REYNOLDS, LORI NELSON, *Nate Cutler* 1959

ROCK HUDSON AND BARBARA RUICK, *Don Ornitz* 1952

DIANE BAKER AND MARK DAMON, *Nate Cutler* 1957

GRACE KELLY AND JEAN PIERRE AUMONT, *Jack Stager* 1953

SHIRLEY KNIGHT, DICK SARGENT, DOROTHY PROVINE, RAY STRICKLYN WITH MICHAEL AND DODIE LANDON, *Larry Barbier Jr.* 1958

JOHN SAXON AND DOLORES HART, *Larry Barbier Jr.* 1960

KIRK DOUGLAS AND ELSA MARTINELLI, *Don Ornitz* 1952

DYAN CANNON AND JEAN-JACQUES WARD, *Rick Strauss* 1959

BOBBY DARIN AND GINGER BARNES, *Bernard Wagner* 1959

JOHN SAXON and KIRK DOUGLAS "teach" DOLORES HART and ELSA MARTINELLI to fish. • DYAN CANNON underwater at Marineland of the Pacific. • BOBBY DARIN and showgirl GINGER BARNES in Las Vegas.

JOHN SAXON und KIRK DOUGLAS „lehren" DOLORES HART und ELSA MARTINELLI das Fischen. • DYAN CANNON unter Wasser im Marineland of the Pacific. • BOBBY DARIN und Showgirl GINGER BARNES in Las Vegas.

JOHN SAXON et KIRK DOUGLAS « apprennent » à pêcher à DOLORES HART et ELSA MARTINELLI. • DYAN CANNON en plongée au Marineland Pacifique. • BOBBY DARIN et la danseuse GINGER BARNES à Las Vegas.

RICHARD BEYMER AND LINDA EVANS, *Bill Kobrin* 1962

FARLEY GRANGER AND BETH BRICKELL, *Gene Trindl* 1964

HUGH O'BRIAN AND STELLA STEVENS, *Rick Strauss* 1958

TAB HUNTER AND VENETIA STEVENSON, *Walt Davis* 1958

CONNIE STEVENS AND GLENN FORD, *Herman Leonard* 1962

JOHN PHILLIP LAW AND LUDMILA MIKAEL, *John Prosser* 1967

TINA LOUISE AND EARL HOLLIMAN, *Larry Barbier Jr.* 1958

MARY ANN MOBLEY AND RICHARD CHAMBERLAIN, *Jay Thompson* 1965

What could be more romantic than Paris? Ask GLENN and CONNIE or JOHN and LUDMILA. • TINA LOUISE and EARL HOLLIMAN in a western ghost town. • RICHARD CHAMBERLAIN and MARY ANN MOBLEY in Griffith Park.

Was könnte romantischer sein als Paris? Fragen Sie GLENN und CONNIE oder JOHN und LUDMILA. • TINA LOUISE und EARL HOLLIMAN in einer Western-Geisterstadt. • RICHARD CHAMBERLAIN und MARY ANN MOBLEY im Griffith Park.

Quoi de plus romantique que Paris? Demandez à GLENN et CONNIE ou à JOHN et LUDMILA. • TINA LOUISE et EARL HOLLIMAN dans une ville fantôme. • RICHARD CHAMBERLAIN et MARY ANN MOBLEY au Griffith Park.

STELLA STEVENS AND STEPHEN BOYD, *Don Ornitz* 1960

ROCK HUDSON AND LORI NELSON, *Don Ornitz* 1952

GEORGE MAHARIS AND CAROL BYRON, *Bill Kobrin* 1961

RICHARD CHAMBERLAIN AND MYRNA FAHEY, *Bill Kobrin* 1962

DAVID HASSELHOFF AND ROBERTA LEIGHTON, *Steve Schatzberg* 1979

RUSS TAMBLYN AND JAN CAWLEY, *Larry Barbier Jr.* 1956

DIANE McBAIN AND VAN WILLIAMS, *Bill Kobrin* 1962

BARRY BOSTWICK AND SUSAN SARANDON, *Kelly Sebring* 1975

MARA CORDAY, GEORGE NADER, PHYLLIS GATES AND ROCK HUDSON, *Larry Barbier Jr.* 1955

JAN CHANEY, TAB HUNTER, ANTHONY PERKINS AND NORMA MOORE, *Nate Cutler* 1957

Double date in Palm Springs: ROCK HUDSON and GEORGE NADER with MARA CORDAY and PHYLLIS GATES. • Double date at the Ice Capades: TAB HUNTER and TONY PERKINS with JAN CHANEY and NORMA MOORE.

Doppelte Verabredung in Palm Springs: ROCK HUDSON und GEORGE NADER mit MARA CORDAY und PHYLLIS GATES. • Doppelte Verabredung bei den Ice Capades: TAB HUNTER und TONY PERKINS mit JAN CHANEY und NORMA MOORE.

Double rencontre à Palm Springs: ROCK HUDSON et GEORGE NADER avec MARA CORDAY et PHYLLIS GATES. • Double rencontre encore à Ice Capades: TAB HUNTER et TONY PERKINS avec JAN CHANEY et NORMA MOORE.

ELIZABETH TAYLOR, *Globe Archive* 1952

GLAMOUR

Of all the photographic coverage of Hollywood stars of the 1930s and 40s, perhaps the most representative as well as the best remembered comes under the heading of "glamour" photography. Hollywood glamour photography was exclusively about creating illusion in those days. Shot in still galleries, it paid strict attention to posed formality. The meticulously made up actresses were carefully lighted, the frames perfectly composed, and should there be even the most minute imperfection, the resulting photographs were turned over to the retoucher before being released to publications.

When photojournalistic techniques gained popularity with magazine editors, there began a market for a more realistic approach to glamour photography as well. They wanted pictures that avoided the artificiality of the gallery shot. Candid glamour photography was born and given a new name: cheesecake. Major magazines like ESQUIRE, ARGOSY and PLAYBOY published not single cheesecake photos but cheesecake layouts, features that spotlighted an actress in a series of sexy shots. When photojournalists turned their cameras to the glamour field, something quite personal was created. There was an informality of pose. Available light replaced studio lamps. Location became important. Smaller cameras and faster film allowed both the photographer and the subjects a freedom to move, to take chances, and to capture the immediacy of a moment. The actresses, as alluring and beautiful as always, now seemed more accessible.

Globe photographers utilized both techniques with a decided preference for location shoots. Don Ornitz created a portable studio with frames holding a variety of colorful background material so he could have the best of both worlds. Frank Bez built a studio with one entire wall of glass to allow him to take advantage of available light. William Claxton, Orlando, Ron Thal and William Read Woodfield had little use for the studio. They did their most provocative glamour photography on location. The only drawback was being slave to the weather.

When Richard Polak, one of Globe's English photographers working out of its London office, mourned the lack of a studio for a glamour shoot, he was told that his California counterparts didn't need an indoor studio. Their studio was the great outdoors. Polak looked out at the drizzling London sky and wondered if anyone had noticed that his studio had a leaky roof.

GLAMOUR

Von allen Fotoreportagen über die Hollywood-Stars der 30er und 40er Jahre sind die am repräsentativsten und in bester Erinnerung geblieben, die man als „Glamour" bezeichnet. Die Glamourfotografie Hollywoods beschäftigte sich damit, Illusionen zu schaffen. In Studios aufgenommen, legte man viel Wert auf posierte Förmlichkeit. Die zurechtgemachten Schauspielerinnen wurden sorgfältig beleuchtet, die Hintergründe perfekt hergerichtet und bei der kleinsten Unvollkommenheit wurden die gemachten Fotos zum Retuschieren geschickt, bevor sie zur Veröffentlichung freigegeben wurden.

Als fotojournalistische Techniken unter den Zeitschriftenherausgebern an Popularität gewannen, entstand ein Markt für eine realistischere Glamourfotografie. Die Herausgeber waren an Fotos interessiert, die die Künstlichkeit der Studiofotos vermieden. Eine freizügigere Glamourfotografie mit dem Namen „cheesecake" entstand. Die großen Zeitschriften, wie ESQUIRE, ARGOSY und PLAYBOY, veröffentlichten keine einzelnen „cheesecake"-Fotos, sondern ganze „cheesecake layouts" – Sonderbeiträge, die eine Schauspielerin in einer Reihe von aufreizenden Fotos zeigten. Als sich die Fotojournalisten der Glamourfotografie zuwandten, entstand etwas Persönliches. Es gab auf einmal eine gewisse Ungezwungenheit, was die Posen anbelangte. Natürliches Licht ersetzte die Studiobeleuchtung. Der Ort, an dem die Fotos gemacht wurden, gewann an Wichtigkeit. Kleinere Kameras und schnellerer Film gaben Fotografen und Modellen mehr Bewegungsfreiheit, mehr Möglichkeiten, auch einmal etwas zu riskieren und die Unmittelbarkeit eines Moments einzufangen. Die Schauspielerinnen, verführerisch und schön wie immer, schienen nun zugänglicher zu sein.

Globe-Fotografen verwendeten beide Techniken, bevorzugten allerdings das Fotografieren vor Ort. Don Ornitz erfand ein tragbares Studio mit vielfältigen, farbenfrohen Hintergründen. So hatte er beides auf einmal. Frank Bez baute ein Studio mit einer voll verglasten Wand und nutzte so natürliches Licht. William Claxton, Orlando, Ron Thal und William Read Woodfield konnten mit einem Studio wenig anfangen. Sie schossen ihre provokativsten Glamourfotos vor Ort. Allerdings war man so der Willkür des Wetters ausgeliefert.

Als Richard Polak, einer von Globes englischen Fotografen, der von seinem Büro aus in London arbeitete, das Fehlen eines Studios für Glamourfotos beklagte, erklärte man ihm, dass seine Kollegen in Kalifornien ein solches Studio nicht bräuchten. Ihr Studio sei die freie Natur. Polak schaute auf den Londoner Nieselregen und fragte sich, ob jemand bemerkt hatte, dass das Dach seines Studios eine undichte Stelle hatte.

GLAMOUR

De tous les reportages photographiques réalisés sur les stars de Hollywood des années 1930 et 1940, ceux dont on se souvient le mieux et qui sont sans doute les plus représentatifs de cette époque appartiennent au genre dit de la « photographie glamour ». Ces clichés, qui n'avaient d'autre but que de créer une illusion tout hollywoodienne, étaient toujours réalisés en studio. La composition s'efforçait de mettre en valeur des actrices soigneusement maquillées et aux poses d'un formalisme strict. S'il y avait la moindre imperfection, la photographie passait d'abord à la retouche avant d'être publiée.

Appréciant de plus en plus la nouvelle vogue du photojournalisme, les rédactions des magazines voulurent alors une approche plus réaliste de la photographie glamour et demandèrent à leurs auteurs des images libérées de l'artificialité de la séance en studio : le genre «glamour» (dit « cheesecake ») était né. Les grands magazines comme ESQUIRE, ARGOSY ou PLAYBOY ne se contentèrent pas de ne publier qu'une seule photo glamour mais proposèrent à leurs lecteurs des reportages de plusieurs pages consacrés à une actrice, mise en valeur par une série de poses « sexy ». Adaptant leur technique à ce nouveau genre, les photojournalistes créèrent un style illustratif où la pose était simplifiée, voire improvisée, où l'éclairage ambiant devait pallier l'absence de projecteurs et où le décor de la scène prenait plus d'importance. L'emploi d'appareils photo plus petits et de films plus sensibles autorisa une plus grande liberté de mouvements au photographe et à ses sujets et permit de mieux saisir l'immédiateté d'un moment. Tout aussi séduisantes et sensuelles que d'habitude mais plus « naturelles », les actrices semblèrent désormais plus accessibles au public.

Les photographes de Globe utilisèrent ces deux techniques. Don Ornitz inventa un « studio » portable équipé de panneaux sur lesquels il pouvait adapter différents décors d'arrière-plan, tandis que Frank Bez imagina un atelier dont une paroi était vitrée pour tirer parti de toute la lumière possible. William Claxton, Orlando, Ron Thal et William Read Woodfield avaient en revanche assez peu l'habitude de travailler en studio et réalisèrent en extérieur leurs photos glamour. Les conditions météorologiques étaient le principal obstacle à ce mode opératoire.

Richard Polak, l'un des photographes anglais extérieurs à Globe, se plaignait de ne pas disposer d'un studio adapté à la réalisation de photos glamour alors que le climat dont jouissaient ses collègues de Californie leur permettait de travailler au grand air. Polak regarda alors le ciel menaçant au-dessus de Londres et il se demanda si quelqu'un avait remarqué que le toit de son studio avait des fuites.

ANGIE DICKINSON, *Frank Bez* 1960

ELKE SOMMER, *Joe Hyams* 1970

JANE FONDA, *Frank Bez* 1962

CARROLL BAKER, *John R. Hamilton* 1963

TINA LOUISE, *Russ Meyer* 1958

VICTORIA PRINCIPAL, *Globe Archive* 1969

ESTHER WILLIAMS, *Globe Archive* 1952

CANDICE BERGEN, *Don Ornitz* 1968

MARIANNA HILL, *Frank Bez* 1967

SONDRA LOCKE, *Frank Bez* 1968

NATALIE WOOD, *Helen Miljakovich* 1970

KIM NOVAK, *Frank Bez* 1964

JOAN COLLINS, *Bill Kobrin* 1962

JILL ST. JOHN, *Russ Meyer* 1958

CLAUDIA CARDINALE, *Orlando* 1964

GAYLE HUNNICUTT, *Ron Thal* 1969

RAQUEL WELCH, *Don Ornitz* 1966

JOCELYN LANE, *Orlando* 1969

VENETIA STEVENSON, *Don Ornitz* 1960

JULIE NEWMAR, *Don Ornitz* 1959

JANE RUSSELL, *Globe Archive* 1956

CYD CHARISSE, *Orlando* 1965

ELIZABETH TAYLOR, *Globe Archive* 1954

RITA HAYWORTH, *Globe Archive* 1952

MARTHA HYER, *Larry Barbier Jr.* 1954

JAYNE MANSFIELD, *William Read Woodfield* 1956

DARYL HANNAH, *Dustin Pittman* 1984

BRIGITTE BARDOT, *Orlando* 1964

MAMIE VAN DOREN, *Bill Crespinel* 1967

STELLA STEVENS, *Orlando* 1967

MARILYN MONROE, *Globe Archive* 1960

SHARON TATE, *Jim Silke* 1969

GINA LOLLOBRIGIDA, *Orlando* 1967

JACQUELINE BISSET, *John R. Hamilton* 1968

FRANCE NUYEN, *Werner Stoy* 1957

NOBU McCARTHY, *William Claxton* 1958

NANCY KWAN, *Orlando* 1959

LESLEY ANN WARREN, *Ron Thal* 1970

VIKKI DOUGAN, *Don Ornitz* 1957

EDY WILLIAMS, *Jay Arnold* 1969

RHONDA SHEAR, *Bob Noble* 1980

RAQUEL WELCH, *Frank Bez* 1964

THE ROMANCE COVER

Nestled in the myriad magazine display at local news-stands and markets was a unique group of publications known as Romance Magazines. Now extinct, but once numbering at least two dozen titles monthly, the romance magazines were aimed exclusively at the female audience. With titles like TRUE LOVE and REAL ROMANCE, they were, cover to cover, romantic fiction pieces of the most extravagant and syrupy nature. And almost all text. They did run, however, a pretty girl on each cover and Globe photographers shot the lion's share of these. With strong contacts at studios and model agencies, Globe had a seemingly never-ending supply of cover candidates.

Some of the lovely gals went on to enjoy major film careers on both sides of the camera after being seen on these covers. One, Sherry Lansing, is the chairman of Paramount Pictures. Globe photographers Don Ornitz and Frank Bez put the youthful Raquel Welch on the covers of 22 magazines in a single year. The producer of the film version of Polly Adler's A HOUSE IS NOT A HOME called Globe one day and asked how he could contact her. The rest, as they say, is history.

DAS ROMANTISCHE TITELBLATT

Eingebettet in die lange Reihe der Zeitschriftenauslagen an Kiosken und in Supermärkten, konnte man eine Gruppe von Publikationen finden, die als Liebesromane bekannt waren. Diese Art Liebesromane gibt es heute nicht mehr, damals wurden monatlich mindestens zwei Dutzend Titel veröffentlicht, die sich ausschließlich an die weibliche Leserschaft richteten. Mit Titeln wie TRUE LOVE und REAL ROMANCE waren sie romantische Fiktionen der extravagantesten und schmalizigsten Art. Sie bestanden fast ausschließlich aus Text. Auf jedem Titelblatt befand sich ein hübsches Mädchen und Globe-Fotografen schossen den Löwenanteil dieser Bilder. Durch Kontakte zu Studios und Modelagenturen hatte Globe einen scheinbar endlosen Vorrat an Titelblattkandidatinnen.

Manche dieser hübschen Mädels kamen nach ihrem Erscheinen auf diesen Titelblättern im Filmgeschäft sowohl vor wie hinter der Kamera ganz groß raus. Eine von ihnen, Sherry Lansing, ist heute Präsidentin von Paramount Pictures. Die Globe-Fotografen Don Ornitz und Frank Bez setzten die jugendliche Raquel Welch in einem einzigen Jahr auf die Titelblätter von 22 Zeitschriften. Der Produzent der Filmversion von Polly Adler's MADAME P. UND IHRE MÄDCHEN (A HOUSE IS NOT A HOME) rief eines Tages Globe an, um zu fragen, wie er sie kontaktieren könne. Der Rest ist, wie man so schön sagt, in die Geschichte eingegangen.

LA PRESSE DU CŒUR

Parmi les innombrables magazines exposés dans les kiosques à journaux se trouvait autrefois un ensemble de publications désignées sous le terme générique de «presse du cœur». Ces magazines mensuels, aujourd'hui disparus, mais dont on comptait autrefois près de deux douzaines de titres, s'adressaient exclusivement à un lectorat féminin. Portant les noms de TRUE LOVE ou REAL ROMANCE, ils offraient à chaque numéro des fictions romantiques à l'eau de rose des plus extravagantes mais très peu illustrées, à l'exception de la photo d'une jolie fille en couverture, dont la fourniture était assurée pour l'essentiel par des photographes de Globe. Grâce aux contacts étroits qu'elle entretenait avec les studios et les agences de mannequins, Globe disposait d'une réserve de candidates apparemment infinie.

Certaines de ces charmantes jeunes filles firent d'ailleurs une grande carrière dans le cinéma aussi bien devant que derrière la caméra après avoir été ainsi remarquées. L'une d'entre elles, Sherry Lansing, est la présidente de Paramount Pictures. Don Ornitz et Frank Bez, deux photographes de Globe, placèrent ainsi la même année la jeune Raquel Welch en couverture de 22 magazines. L'ayant remarquée, le producteur de LA MAISON DE MADAME ADLER (A HOUSE IS NOT A HOME), film tiré du livre de Polly Adler, appela Globe pour savoir comment contacter cette jeune beauté. Le reste appartient à l'histoire…

DIANE McBAIN, *Frank Bez* 1958

CHRISTINA FERRARE, *Frank Bez* 1966

TUESDAY WELD, *Frank Bez* 1957

CYBILL SHEPHERD, *Ron Joy* 1971

JOEY HETHERTON, *Don Ornitz* 1961

GAYLE HUNNICUTT, *Frank Bez* 1964

CAROL LYNLEY, *William Claxton* 1959

CHERYL MILLER, *Frank Bez* 1964

SHARON FARRELL, *Don Ornitz* 1962

ANGEL TOMKINS, *Jay Arnold* 1970

VENETIA STEVENSON, *Don Ornitz* 1965

SHERRY LANSING, *Frank Bez* 1965

BURT LANCASTER, *Nate Cutler* 1961

BURT LANCASTER (best actor for ELMER GANTRY) races back-stage to retrieve the Oscar he left behind in the press room.

BURT LANCASTER (bester Schauspieler in ELMER GANTRY) rennt hinter die Bühne, um seinen Oscar zu holen. Er hatte ihn im Presseraum liegen gelassen.

BURT LANCASTER (consacré meilleur acteur pour ELMER GAN-TRY) traverse les coulisses pour aller récupérer l'Oscar qu'il a oublié dans la salle de presse.

DESI ARNAZ AND LUCILLE BALL, *Nate Cutler* 1958

REWARDS

In "There's No Business Like Show Business" Irving Berlin trumpeted the difference between show folk and the butchers, bakers and clerks of this world: While the rest of us get paid for our work, the denizens of show business are doubly rewarded. They not only get paid, they get applause.

Applause is something Hollywood never gets enough of and can be counted on to turn out for. Back in the "Golden Age" there were just a few ceremonies to attend, but times have changed. Today, 3182 industry awards are handed out each year at 332 ceremonies worldwide in 144 countries and in 25 of the 52 United States.

Awards are made to all members of the Hollywood community from actors to stuntmen, from animals to stand-ins (yes, there is an award from the Association of Stand-Ins, acknowledging contributions of those sturdy folk who "stand in" for the stars while the lights are set up). Awards are given by guilds and academies, newspapers and magazines, critics, universities, foundations as well as some unexpected donors (the company that manufactures Snickers candy bars and Alamo-Rent-A-Car present awards).

There are even awards made to the worst films and performances of the year by the Golden Raspberry Group (the Razzies) and, from the Boring Institute, for the most boring films of the year. These, not surprisingly, don't get a turnout.

But most of the presentations bring celebrities out in droves. Hollywood likes awards and, to paraphrase the famous line in FIELD OF DREAMS – if you build one, they will come.

AUSZEICHNUNGEN

In „There's No Business Like Show Business" trompetete Irving Berlin den Unterschied zwischen den Leuten vom Showgeschäft und den Metzgern, Bäckern und Angestellten dieser Welt hinaus: Während die Normalsterblichen für ihre Arbeit bezahlt werden, werden die Filmstars doppelt entlohnt: Sie bekommen nicht nur Geld, sondern auch noch Applaus.

Vom Applaus bekommt Hollywood nie genug und man kann darauf zählen, dass es sich um weiteren bemüht. Im Goldenen Zeitalter musste man nur wenigen Zeremonien beiwohnen, aber die Zeiten haben sich geändert. Nicht weniger als 3382 Auszeichnungen werden jährlich weltweit in 332 Zeremonien, in 144 verschiedenen Ländern und 25 der 52 amerikanischen Bundesstaaten, vergeben.

Diese Auszeichnungen werden an alle Mitglieder der Hollywood-Gemeinde vergeben, von Schauspielern bis zu Stuntmännern und -frauen, von Tieren bis zu Doublen (ja, es gibt eine Auszeichnung von der Association of Stand-Ins, die die Beiträge dieser standhaften Menschen, die für die Stars einspringen, während noch an der Beleuchtung gearbeitet wird, anerkennen). An diesen Auszeichnungen arbeiten Gilden und Akademien, Zeitungen und Zeitschriften, Kritiker, Universitäten, Stiftungen und unerwartete Spender (z.B. die Hersteller von Snickers-Schokoriegeln und die Mietwagenfirma Alamo präsentieren Auszeichnungen).

Von der Golden Raspberry Group (the Razzies) werden jedes Jahr Auszeichnungen an die schlechtesten Filme und darstellerischen Leistungen vergeben und von dem Boring Institute werden die langweiligsten Filme des Jahres prämiert – aber die werden nicht bejubelt.

Alle anderen Auszeichnungen schaffen das. Hollywood mag Auszeichnungen und, um die berühmte Zeile aus dem Film FELD DER TRÄUME (FIELD OF DREAMS) zu umschreiben – wenn man einen hat, werden andere folgen.

RÉCOMPENSES

Dans sa chanson «There's No Business Like Show Business», Irving Berlin souligne la différence entre les gens du spectacle et les autres (bouchers, boulangers ou fonctionnaires): si tous sont payés pour ce qu'ils font, les acteurs sont doublement récompensés. Ils reçoivent en plus des applaudissements.

Hollywood ne s'est jamais rassasié d'applaudissements et les recherche toujours avidement. Alors qu'il n'existait que quelques cérémonies à l'époque de l'âge d'or, on dénombre aujourd'hui 3182 prix distribués chaque année au cours de 332 festivals organisés dans 144 pays et 25 des 52 états des États-Unis.

Ces récompenses sont attribuées à tous les métiers du cinéma, des acteurs aux cascadeurs et des animaux aux doublures (il existe en effet un prix attribué par l'Association of Stand-Ins reconnaissant la contribution de ces obscurs figurants qui servent de «doublure lumière» aux stars lors de la mise au point de l'éclairage). Ces prix sont décernés chaque année non seulement par des guildes et des académies, des journaux et des magazines, des critiques, des universités, des fondations, etc., mais aussi par des promoteurs plus surprenants comme le fabricant de barres chocolatées Snickers ou le loueur de voitures Alamo-Rent-A-Car.

Des prix sont même décernés aux plus mauvais films et aux pires acteurs de l'année par le Golden Raspberry Group (les «Razzies») ou au film le plus ennuyeux de l'année par le Boring Institute. Les lauréats ne tirent évidemment aucune gloire de ces récompenses et l'assistance reste assez clairsemée!

Toutes les autres cérémonies attirent en revanche une foule de célébrités d'Hollywood. Ils adorent tant les prix que, pour paraphraser une célèbre réplique de JUSQU'AU BOUT DU RÊVE (FIELD OF DREAMS), si vous en créez un, ils viendront tous.

TOM HANKS, *Fitzroy Barrett* 1996

GWYNETH PALTROW AND BEN AFFLECK, *Lisa Rose* 1999

KEVIN COSTNER, *Craig Skinner* 1991

DOLLY PARTON, *Nate Cutler* 1983

MORGAN FREEMAN, *Bob Noble* 1989

HILARY SWANK AND CHAD LOWE, *Nina Prommer* 2000

The People's Choice award, based on popularity by public vote, was twice given to TOM HANKS. • Named best actress (for SHAKESPEARE IN LOVE) by the Screen Actors Guild, GWYNETH PALTROW gets a peck from boyfriend BEN AFFLECK. • KEVIN COSTNER is the fourth actor-director to win the coveted Directors Guild Award (for DANCES WITH WOLVES). • DOLLY PARTON at the American Music Awards. • The Image Award is presented by the NAACP in recognition of accurate portrayals of African Americans in films. MORGAN FREEMAN is a two-time winner. • The Independent Spirit Awards, established in 1984 by the Independent Filmmaking Advocacy, recognizes achievement by non-studio filmmakers. HILARY SWANK holds her plexiglass bird as 1999's best actress (BOYS DON'T CRY).

TOM HANKS erhielt zweimal die Auszeichnung People's Choice. Diese Auszeichnung basiert auf der Beliebheit des Stars beim Publikum. • GWYNETH PALTROW wurde als beste Schauspielerin (SHAKESPEARE IN LOVE) durch den Screen Actors Guild ausgezeichnet. Hier bekommt sie ein Küsschen von ihrem Freund BEN AFFLECK. • KEVIN COSTNER ist der vierte Schauspieler und Regisseur, der den begehrten Directors Guild Award für den Film DER MIT DEM WOLF TANZT (DANCES WITH WOLVES) erhielt. • DOLLY PARTON bei den American Music Awards. • Der Image Award wird durch die NAACP vergeben. Er zeichnet die akkurate Darstellung von Afroamerikanern in Filmen aus. MORGAN FREEMAN ist zweimaliger Gewinner. • Die Independent Spirit Awards, 1984 durch die Independent Filmmaking Advocacy gegründet, zeichnet Leistungen von unabhängigen Filmemachern aus. HILARY SWANK hält ihren Plexiglasvogel, mit dem sie zur besten Schauspielerin des Jahres 1999 ausgezeichnet wurde (BOYS DON'T CRY).

Le People's Choice, décerné par le public à l'acteur le plus populaire, fut décerné deux fois à TOM HANKS. • Nommée meilleure actrice (SHAKESPEARE IN LOVE) par la Screen Actors Guild, GWYNETH PALTROW est également récompensée par son ami BEN AFFLECK. • KEVIN COSTNER est le quatrième acteur-réalisateur à remporter le Directors Guild Award pour DANSE AVEC LES LOUPS (DANCES WITH WOLVES). • DOLLY PARTON aux American Music Awards. • MORGAN FREEMAN a obtenu deux fois l'Image Award, décerné par la NAACP pour distinguer un rôle d'Afro-américain au cinéma. • L'Independent Spirit Awards, créé en 1984 par l'Independent Filmmaking Advocacy, récompense les films réalisés par des metteurs en scène indépendants des studios. HILARY SWANK tient l'Oiseau de plexiglas qu'elle a reçu en 1999 au titre de meilleure actrice (BOYS DON'T CRY).

MADONNA, *Fitzroy Barrett* 1998

KEVIN SPACEY, *Fitzroy Barrett* 1999

ANTHONY HOPKINS AND JODIE FOSTER, *Fitzroy Barrett* 1999

ALAIN DELON AND GREGORY PECK, *Imapress* 1995

SANDRA BULLOCK, *Fitzroy Barrett* 1995

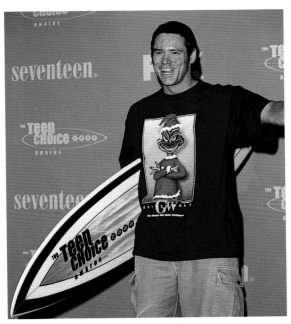
JIM CARREY, *Fitzroy Barrett* 2000

A 4-Grammy win for MADONNA. • The Hollywood Walk of Fame, lining Hollywood Boulevard with sidewalk stars bearing the names of famous players, was the brainchild of the Hollywood Chamber of Commerce to restore glamour to the fading street. When KEVIN SPACEY received his star, he brought his mother, acknowledging that she was the one who drove him to acting classes when he was a youngster. • JODIE FOSTER is recipient of the American Cinematheque Award at the 14th annual Moving Picture Ball. • ALAIN DELON congratulates GREGORY PECK French style at the 20th anniversary of the Cesar Awards. • SANDRA BULLOCK and her MTV award, which represents the choice of MTV viewers for their favorite performers. • JIM CARREY looks like a poster boy for acne, with fake braces and phony pimples provided by a Hollywood makeup pro, at the 2000 Teen Choice awards, one of several annual events voted on by teenagers.

Eine vierfache Grammy-Auszeichnung für MADONNA. • Der Hollywood Walk of Fame, der die Bürgersteige des Hollywood Boulevards mit Namen berühmter Schauspieler schmückt, war das Geistesprodukt der Handelskammer Hollywoods. Er sollte wieder Glanz in die verblasste Straße bringen. Als KEVIN SPACEY seinen Stern erhielt, brachte er seine Mutter mit, denn sie war es, so sagte er, die ihn zur Schauspielschule getrieben hat als er noch ein Junge war. • JODIE FOSTER erhält den American Cinematheque Award auf dem 14. Moving Picture Ball, der jährlich stattfindet. • ALAIN DELON gratuliert GREGORY PECK in französischer Manier am 20. Jahrestag der Cesar Awards. • SANDRA BULLOCK und ihre MTV-Auszeichnung, die die Wahl der MTV-Zuschauer ihres Lieblingskünstlers darstellt. • JIM CARREY sieht bei den Teen Choice Award – eine von mehreren jährlichen Veranstaltungen, bei der Teenager abstimmen – im Jahre 2000, professionell zurecht gemacht, wie ein Junge aus, der Reklame für Akne macht, mit seiner falschen Zahnspange und den Pickeln.

Quatre victoires aux Grammy pour MADONNA. • Le Hollywood Walk of Fame, ce trottoir de Hollywood Boulevard dont les dalles étoilées portent les noms d'acteurs célèbres, est né d'une idée de la Chambre de commerce d'Hollywood pour redonner un certain éclat à cette avenue. • KEVIN SPACEY offrit son étoile à sa mère pour la remercier de lui avoir fait suivre des cours de comédie lorsqu'il était jeune. • JODIE FOSTER reçoit le American Cinematheque Award lors du 14ᵉ bal annuel du cinéma. • ALAIN DELON félicite GREGORY PECK dans un style purement français, lors du 20ᵉ anniversaire des césars. • SANDRA BULLOCK et son MTV award, qui représente le choix des téléspectateurs de MTV pour leur performance favorite. • JIM CARREY ressemble à une publicité d'adolescent avec appareil dentaire et boutons d'acné dus à une séance de maquillage, lors du Teen Choice de l'an 2000, l'un des événements annuels qui requièrent le vote de jeunes adolescents.

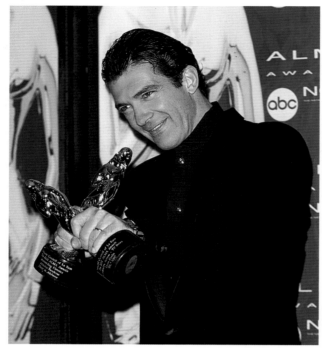

ANTONIO BANDERAS, *Fitzroy Barrett* 2000

RICARDO MONTALBAN, *Tom Rodriguez* 1998

CLINT WALKER, *Fitzroy Barrett* 1997

MELVIN AND MARIO VAN PEEBLES, *Fitzroy Barrett* 1995

The Golden Eagle, presented by NOSOTROS, and the ALMA (American Latino Media Arts) awards, recognize achievement by Latin performers who have improved the image of Hispanics in movies and television. ANTONIO BANDERAS takes home two ALMA, but only one has his name on it. • RICARDO MONTAL-BAN, who founded NOSOTROS in 1980, is given a Golden Eagle for lifetime achievement. With him are BARBARA SINATRA and MARIA CONCHITA ALONSO. • CLINT WALKER holds his Golden Boot, awarded by the Motion Picture and Television Fund for achievement in the field of westerns. • MELVIN and MARIO VAN PEEBLES take a father and son win at the 17th annual Cable Ace awards, which recognizes excellence on cable TV.

Der Golden Eagle, der von NOSOTROS vergeben wird, und die ALMA (American Latino Media Arts) Awards zeichnen die Leistungen lateinamerikanischer Darsteller aus, die das Image der hispanischen Bevölkerung in Film und Fernsehen verbessern. ANTONIO BANDERAS nimmt zwei ALMA mit, aber nur einer trägt seinen Namen. • RICARDO MONTALBAN, der NOSOTROS 1980 gründete, wird für sein Lebenswerk mit dem Golden Eagle ausgezeichnet. Dabei sind BARBARA SINATRA und MARIA CONCHITA ALONSO. • CLINT WALKER hält den Golden Boot, der vom Motion Picture and Television Fund für Leistungen in der Kategorie Western vergeben wird. • MELVIN und MARIO VAN PEEBLES gewinnen bei den jährlichen 17. Cable Ace Awards, die schauspielerische Leistungen im Kabelfernsehen auszeichnet.

Les Golden Eagle, décernés par NOSOTROS, et les prix de l'ALMA (American Latino Media Arts), distinguent des acteurs latins dont la composition valorise l'image des Hispaniques au cinéma et à la télévision. Si ANTONIO BANDERAS a remporté deux ALMA, un seul porte son nom. • Accompagné par BARBARA SINATRA et MARIA CONCHITA ALONSO, RICARDO MONTALBAN, fondateur de NOSOTROS en 1980, obtient un Golden Eagle pour sa carrière exceptionnelle. • CLINT WALKER admire la Golden Boot, un prix décerné par le Motion Picture et Television Fund pour les acteurs de Western. • MELVIN et MARIO VAN PEEBLES, père et fils, obtiennent un prix lors des 17e Cable Ace, décernés chaque année pour récompenser des acteurs de la télévision par câble.

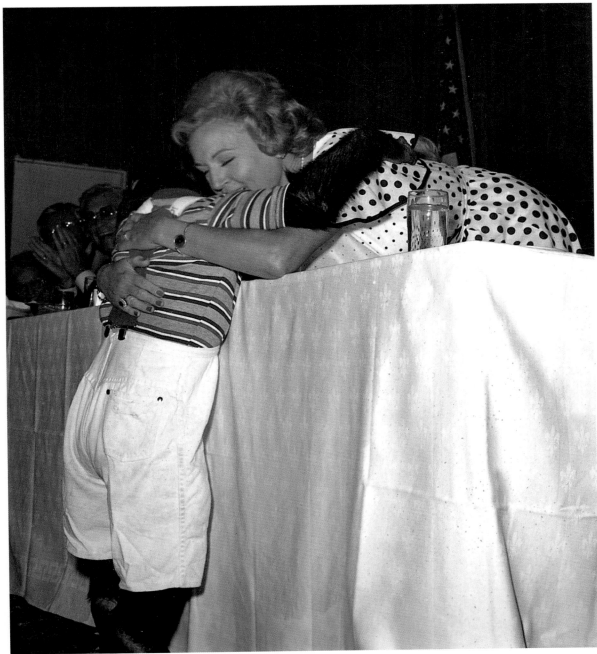

BING CROSBY AND JUDY GARLAND, RED SKELTON, *Nate Cutler* 1955

ALEC BALDWIN AND GLENN CLOSE, *Adam Scull* 1992

BETTY WHITE AND PEGGY, *Nate Cutler* 1954

The Patsy awards are given to animal performers by the American Humane Association. BETTY WHITE congratulates Patsy winner PEGGY, whose screen name was BONZO. • Awards were once handed out by many national magazines, the most important being the LOOK award. In 1955, BING CROSBY, JUDY GARLAND and RED SKELTON were the recipients. Crosby and Garland were also up for Oscars that year but when they lost to Marlon Brando and Grace Kelly, Judy asked Bing, "What do we do now?" "I don't know about you," answered Crosby, "but I'm going to renew my subscription to LOOK." • ALEC BALDWIN lifts GLENN CLOSE and her Tony nomination plaque.

Die Patsy Awards werden von der American Humane Association an die besten Tierdarsteller vergeben. BETTY WHITE gratuliert der Gewinnerin des Patsy, PEGGY, deren Leinwandname BONZO war. • Auszeichnungen wurden früher von vielen nationalen Zeitschriften verteilt. Einer der wichtigsten war der LOOK Award. 1955 erhielten BING CROSBY, JUDY GARLAND und RED SKELTON diesen Award. Crosby und Garland waren in demselben Jahr auch auf der Oscar-Liste, verloren ihn aber an Marlon Brando und Grace Kelly. Judy fragte Bing:„Was machen wir jetzt?" „Ich weiß nicht, was du machen wirst, aber ich werde LOOK neu abonnieren", antwortete Crosby. • ALEC BALDWIN hebt GLENN CLOSE und ihre Tony-Auszeichnung empor.

BETTY WHITE félicite PEGGY – dont le nom à l'écran était BONZO – lauréat d'un des Patsy Awards décernés par l'American Humane Association aux animaux de films. • Parmi les nombreux prix décernés autrefois par des magazines, le plus recherché était celui attribué par LOOK, que reçurent notamment BING CROSBY, JUDY GARLAND et RED SKELTON en 1955. Nominés aux Oscars la même année mais finalement battus par Marlon Brando et Grace Kelly, Judy demanda alors à Bing: « Qu'est-ce qu'on fait maintenant ? » « Toi, je ne sais pas, répondit Crosby, « mais moi je vais renouveler mon abonnement à LOOK. » • ALEC BALDWIN porte GLENN CLOSE tenant sa plaque de nomination au Tony Award.

SUSAN SARANDON, *Lisa Rose* 1999

SIDNEY POITIER, *Nate Cutler* 1967

MEL GIBSON, *Lisa Rose* 1993

KIRK DOUGLAS, *Nate Cutler* 1962

MERYL STREEP, *Lisa Rose* 1994

CHARLTON HESTON, *Nate Cutler* 1962

ROSALIND RUSSELL, *Nate Cutler* 1959

FRANK SINATRA, *Nate Cutler* 1965

JOHN TRAVOLTA, *Nate Cutler* 1980

JACK NICHOLSON, *Nate Cutler* 1974

DENZEL WASHINGTON, *Fitzroy Barrett* 1998

PAUL NEWMAN AND JOANNE WOODWARD, *Nate Cutler* 1957

In 1927, as she was exiting Sid Grauman's Chinese Theater on Hollywood Boulevard, silent screen star Norma Talmadge accidentally stepped into a square of freshly laid cement and left her dainty footprint. A tradition was born, for instead of having the cement smoothed out, Grauman decided to create a forecourt in his movie palace where stars could plant their hand- and footprints for posterity.

Im Jahre 1927, als sie die Aufmerksamkeit vor Sid Graumans Chinese Theater auf dem Hollywood Boulevard erregte, trat der Stummfilmstar Norma Talmadge versehentlich in frisch gegossenen Zement und hinterließ so ihren zierlichen Fußabdruck. Eine Tradition enstand. Anstatt den Zement glätten zu lassen, entschied sich Grauman dafür, einen Vorhof in seinem Filmpalast zu kreieren, in dem die Stars ihre Hand- und Fußabdrücke für die Nachwelt hinterlassen konnten.

C'est en 1927, alors qu'elle sortait du Chinese Theater de Sid Grauman, sur Hollywood Boulevard, que la vedette du muet Norma Talmadge marcha accidentellement dans un carré de ciment frais et y laissa l'empreinte de ses pieds. Une tradition était née car, au lieu d'effacer ces traces, Grauman décida d'inviter les stars à marquer de leurs empreintes de pieds et de mains les dalles de la place devant son cinéma.

SID CAESAR AND PHIL SILVERS, *Nate Cutler* 1958

MARY TYLER MOORE AND DICK VAN DYKE, *Nate Cutler* 1967

Emmy wins for their pairing on THE DICK VAN DYKE SHOW have DICK VAN DYKE and MARY TYLER MOORE literally jumping for joy. • Two kings in the realm of TV comedy, SID CAESAR and PHIL SILVERS each won two Emmys the same year.

Die Auszeichnung mit einem Emmy für die Darstellung eines Paares in THE DICK VAN DYKE SHOW lassen DICK VAN DYKE und MARY TYLER MOORE regelrecht vor Freude in die Höhe springen. • Zwei Könige im Reich der Fernsehkomödie, SID CAESAR und PHIL SILVERS, gewannen beide zwei Emmys im selben Jahr.

DICK VAN DYKE et MARY TYLER MOORE sautent littéralement de joie après avoir reçu un Emmy pour le couple qu'ils forment à la télévision dans le DICK VAN DYKE SHOW. • Princes de la comédie télévisée, SID CAESAR et PHIL SILVERS remportent chacun deux Emmy la même année.

KIRSTIE ALLEY, *Lisa Rose* 1994

MICHAEL J. FOX, *Ralph Dominguez* 1986

CARL REINER, *Nate Cutler* 1962

Acceptance speeches are usually long-winded, rambling and unremembered. A few of the shortest, most precise and notable Emmy acceptances were: KIRSTIE ALLEY: „I'd like to thank my husband Parker for giving me the big one for the last eight years." • MICHAEL J. FOX: „I feel four feet tall!" • CARL REINER: „I wish someone had told me. I would have worn my hair!"

Dankesreden sind gewöhnlich lang, umständlich und werden schnell vergessen. Einige der kürzesten, präzisesten und beachtenswertesten Emmy-Ansprachen waren: KIRSTIE ALLEY: „Ich danke meinem Ehemann Parker, der mir in den letzten acht Jahren sein Bestes gegeben hat." • MICHAEL J. FOX: „Ich fühle mich ganz klein!" • CARL REINER: „Ich wünschte, das hätte mir jemand erzählt – dann hätte ich meine Haare getragen!"

Les discours de remerciement des artistes sont souvent trop longs, décousus et rapidement oubliés. On se rappelle toutefois, parmi les mots les plus courts et les plus notables prononcés aux Emmy, ceux de KIRSTIE ALLEY : « Je voudrais remercier mon mari, Parker, de m'avoir donné « le plus gros » de lui-même ces huit dernières années. » ; de MICHAEL J. FOX : « J'ai l'impression de faire 1,20 mètres ! », ou de CARL REINER : « J'aurais préféré que quelqu'un me prévienne ! J'aurais mis mes cheveux ! »

SYLVESTER STALLONE, *Steve Finn* 1986

DONNA REED AND LORNE GREENE, *Nate Cutler* 1964

ELIZABETH TAYLOR, *Richard Chambury* 2000

"SYLVESTER STALLONE" is carried into Madame Tussaud's Wax Museum in London. • DONNA REED and LORNE GREENE hold their Golden Apples, presented by the Hollywood Women's Press Club to the stars voted most cooperative to the press. The group also presented a "Sour Apple" to the least cooperative but the recipient didn't show up to claim it. Cooperation with the media as the criterion for the awards faded as club membership tipped in favor of publicists over journalists. What PR is going to allow her client tagged "uncooperative?" • Dame ELIZABETH TAYLOR, with sons CHRISTOPHER and MICHAEL WILDING JR., following the London-born star's investiture as Dame Commander of the British Empire at Buckingham Palace.

„SYLVESTER STALLONE" wird in das Wachsmuseum der Madame Tussaud in London getragen. • DONNA REED und LORNE GREENE halten ihre Golden Apples, die durch den Frauenpresseclub Hollywoods an die Stars, die sich der Presse gegenüber kooperativ verhalten, vergeben werden. Die Gruppe vergibt auch einen „sauren Apfel" an diejenigen, die unkooperativ sind, allerdings ließen sich diese Gewinner nicht blicken. Die Kooperation mit den Medien schwand als Kriterium für die Auszeichnungen, als sich die Mehrzahl der Clubmitglieder von den Journalisten zu Gunsten der PR-Agenten verschob. Welcher PR-Agent möchte seinen Star schon als „unkooperativ" abgestempelt sehen? • Dame ELIZABETH TAYLOR mit Söhnen CHRISTOPHER und MICHAEL WILDING JR., die der Ernennung des in London geborenen Stars zur Dame Commander of the British Empire im Buckingham Palace beiwohnen.

« SYLVESTER STALLONE » est emmené à Londres au musée de cire de Madame Tussaud. • DONNA REED et LORNE GREENE présentent le Golden Apple qu'ils viennent de remporter. Le Hollywood Women's Press Club, qui décerne ce prix aux vedettes qui se montrent les plus coopératives avec la Presse, attribue également une « Sour Apple » aux moins aimables – mais l'artiste choisi vient alors rarement réclamer sa récompense. Aujourd'hui, les médias jouant un rôle de plus en plus important, c'est plutôt les bons rapports avec les publicitaires qu'avec les journalistes qui justifient l'attribution du prix par les membres du club. Quel attaché de presse va permettre en effet que son client soit mal vu par les médias ? • Dame ELIZABETH TAYLOR, avec ses fils CHRISTOPHER et MICHAEL WILDING JR., après l'élévation de la vedette d'origine londonienne au titre de Commandeur de l'Empire britannique à Buckingham Palace.

SHARON STONE AND RIP TORN, *Lisa Rose* 1995

SEAN CONNERY, *Lisa Rose* 1988

DUSTIN HOFFMAN, SIR LAURENCE OLIVIER, *Nate Cutler* 1977

HALLE BERRY, *Fitzroy Barrett* 2000

For years the Hollywood Foreign Press Association handed out its annual Golden Globes at a private dinner and earned a well-deserved reputation as the best party in town.

Jahrelang verteilte der Ausländische Presseverband Hollywoods seine jährlichen Golden Globes bei einem privaten Abendessen – eine Veranstaltung, die sich zu Recht den Ruf erwarb, die beste Party der Stadt zu sein.

La Hollywood Foreign Press Association décerne depuis des années ses Golden Globes lors d'une soirée privée, qui a gagné une réputation d'excellence méritée.

GREGORY PECK, JOAN CRAWFORD, PATTY DUKE AND ED BEGLEY, *Nate Cutler* 1963

LANA TURNER AND RED BUTTONS, *Nate Cutler* 1958

EDMUND GWENN AND GLORIA GRAHAME, *Nate Cutler* 1953

PATRICIA NEAL, *Globe Archive* 1964

JULIE CHRISTIE AND DON BESSANT, *Nate Cutler* 1966

JULIE ANDREWS AND AUDREY HEPBURN, *Nate Cutler* 1965

WILLIAM HOLDEN AND BARBARA STANWYCK, *Nate Cutler* 1979

In earlier days special backstage moments at the Academy of Motion Picture Arts & Sciences Oscar presentations were captured by a mere handful of photographers. The winners – and losers – were the news then. In recent years, although hundreds of photographers cover, there is only an occasional chance for that special photo and even less chance that it will be published. Today the gluttonous interest in what the stars are wearing has turned the Oscar event into a giant fashion show. Magazines that once devoted entire sections to the winners now run page upon page of what was worn instead.

JOAN CRAWFORD, not nominated although her WHATEVER HAP-PENED TO BABY JANE? costar Bette Davis was, got her revenge by accepting the Oscar for absent winner Anne Bancroft. • Cute shots like LANA TURNER coveting RED BUTTONS' Oscar and EDMUND GWENN paying tribute to winner GLORIA GRAHAME are rare in today's atmosphere. • The Oscar PATRICIA NEAL was unable to accept in person was delivered to her home in England, where she introduces the golden boy to her children Theo, Lucy and Tessa. • JULIE CHRISTIE and boyfriend DON BESSANT at the Governor's Ball. • Class act: AUDREY HEPBURN, not nominated for the film version of MY FAIR LADY, congratulates the lady who originated the role on Broadway, JULIE ANDREWS, winner for MARY POPPINS. • WILLIAM HOLDEN and BARBARA STANWYCK were close friends since GOLDEN BOY, his first film, in 1939. He came close to being fired until she stepped in. He always bemoaned the fact that Stanwyck had never won. After his death, she was awarded a special Oscar and in her acceptance speech, she acknowledged Holden: "Tonight, my golden boy, you got your wish."

Früher wurden bei der Oscarvergabe der Academy of Motion Picture Arts & Sciences die Reaktionen hinter der Bühne nur von wenigen Fotografen eingefangen. Die Gewinner – und Verlierer – waren die Neuigkeiten. Obwohl heutzutage Hunderte von Foto-grafen dabei sind, gibt es selten die Chance, ein besonderes Foto zu machen und die Möglichkeit, dass dieses Foto veröffentlicht wird, ist noch geringer. Das unersättliche Interesse an der Garderobe der Stars hat die Oscarverleihung in eine riesige Modenschau verwan-delt. Zeitschriften, die einst ganze Kolumnen den Gewinnern gewidmet haben, berichten Seite über Seite, was die Stars trugen.

JOAN CRAWFORD, die nicht für WAS GESCHAH WIRKLICH MIT BABY JANE? nominiert war, im Gegensatz zu ihrer Filmpartnerin Betty Davis, bekam ihre Revanche als sie den Oscar der abwesenden Anne Bancroft entgegennahm. • Süße Schnappschüsse wie diese – LANA TURNER begehrt den Oscar von RED BUTTONS und EDMUND GWENN verneigt sich vor der Gewinnerin GLORIA GRAHAME – sind rar geworden. • Der Oscar, der abwesenden PATRICIA NEAL, wurde zu ihr nach Hause nach England geschickt. Der Goldjunge wird den Kindern Theo, Lucy und Tessa vorgestellt. • JULIE CHRISTIE und Freund DON BESSANT auf dem Governor's Ball. • AUDREY HEPBURN, die nicht für MY FAIR LADY nominiert wurde, gratuliert JULIE ANDREWS für ihre Rolle am Broadway. Diese wurde im selben Jahr als beste Schauspielerin in MARY POPPINS ausgezeichnet. • WILLIAM HOLDEN und BARBARA STANWYCK waren seit seinem ersten Film GOLDEN BOY, 1939, eng befreundet. Er wurde beinahe gefeuert – bis sie dazu kam. Er bemängelte immer, dass Stanwyck nie einen gewann. Nach seinem Tod bekam sie einen besonderen Oscar. In ihrer Dankesrede sagte sie: „Heute Nacht, mein Goldjunge, geht dein Traum in Erfüllung."

Au début, seuls quelques photographes étaient en coulisses pour immortaliser les moments d'émotion au cours de la cérémonie des Oscars décernés par l'Academy of Motion Picture Arts & Sciences. Les gagnants – et les perdants – étaient alors souvent une surprise. Depuis quelques années, il devient difficile de faire une photo exceptionnelle, et encore plus qu'elle soit publiée. Aujourd'hui, l'in-térêt gourmand pour ce que portent les stars a transformé la soirée des Oscars en un gigantesque défilé de mode et des magazines qui consacraient autrefois des pages entières aux lauréats ne s'intéressent plus guère qu'à leurs vêtements.

JOAN CRAWFORD, qui n'était pas nominée pour QU'EST-IL ARRIVÉ À BABY JANE ? au contraire de sa partenaire Bette Davis, se console en acceptant l'Oscar au nom de la gagnante, Anne Bancroft, alors absente. • Des photos aussi charmantes que celles-ci – LANA TURNER protégeant l'Oscar de RED BUTTONS et EDMUND GWENN rendant hommage à GLORIA GRAHMAME – sont désormais plus rares dans l'atmosphère actuelle d'intense compétition. • L'Oscar que PATRICIA NEAL n'avait pu venir chercher en 1964 lui fut livré à domicile. Elle le présente à ses enfants. • JULIE CHRISTIE et son ami DON BESSANT examinent l'Oscar qu'elle a reçu. • AUDREY HEPBURN, qui n'avait pas été nominée pour MY FAIR LADY, félicite JULIE ANDREWS, de l'Oscar de la meilleure actrice qu'elle a obtenu pour MARY POPPINS. • WILLIAM HOLDEN et BARBARA STANWYCK étaient des amis intimes depuis 1939 et son premier film, L'ESCLAVE AUX MAINS D'OR, dont il avait failli être renvoyé. Il déplora toujours que Stanwyck n'ait jamais obtenu d'Oscar. En 1982, dans son dis-cours de remerciement pour l'Oscar d'honneur qui lui était décerné, elle s'adressa à Holden, mort un an plus tôt, en disant : « Ce soir, mon enfant chéri, ton vœu se réalise. »

ALFRED HITCHCOCK, *Nate Cutler* 1979

FRANK CAPRA, *Nate Cutler* 1982

STEVEN SPIELBERG, *Paul Drinkwater* 1998

JANE FONDA, BETTE DAVIS AND GEORGE STEVENS JR., *Bob Noble* 1977

The American Film Institute has honored the lifetime work of one member of the film community each year since its inception in 1986. ALFRED HITCHCOCK acknowledges the tribute with the help of cue cards. • AFI recognizes "the CAPRA touch." • STEVEN SPIELBERG gives an enthusastic thanks. • BETTE DAVIS, flanked by JANE FONDA and AFI president GEORGE STEVENS JR., was the third recipient – and first woman – to be honored.

Das American Film Institute (AFI) honoriert seit seiner Gründung im Jahre 1986 jedes Jahr das Lebenswerk eines Mitglieds der Filmgemeinde. ALFRED HITCHCOCK liest seine Dankesrede ab. • AFI erkennt den „CAPRA-Touch" an. • STEVEN SPIELBERG bedankt sich enthusiastisch. • BETTE DAVIS, umgeben von JANE FONDA und AFI-Präsident, GEORGE STEVENS JR., war die dritte Empfängerin – und erste Frau – die ausgezeichnet wurde.

L'American Film Institute honore depuis 1986 un membre de la communauté cinématographique pour l'ensemble de son œuvre. C'est par des panneaux qu'ALFRED HITCHCOCK a fait son discours. • Le talent de CAPRA est reconnu par l'AFI • STEVEN SPIELBERG remercie avec enthousiasme. • BETTE DAVIS, encadrée par JANE FONDA et GEORGE STEVENS JR., le président de l'AFI, fut la 3ᵉ récipiendaire – et la première femme – à être célébrée par l'institut.

NIGHT OF 100 STARS, *Globe Archive* 1990

KENNEDY HONORS, *Globe Archive* 1983

A tribute to eight of the most admired and successful people in the history of movies is part of the Night of 100 Stars. Honored were SIDNEY LUMET, SYLVESTER STALLONE, JANE FONDA, HELEN HAYES, KATHARINE HEPBURN, MICHAEL CAINE, JOSEPH L. MANKIEWICZ and LIV ULLMANN. • The prestigious Kennedy Honors, established in 1978, each year honors five outstanding performers for lifetime achievement in the arts. Honored at the 6th presentation at the Kennedy Center were VIRGIL THOMPSON, ELIA KAZAN, FRANK SINATRA, KATHERINE DUNHAM and JAMES STEWART, here with PRESIDENT and MRS. RONALD REAGAN.

Eine Hommage an acht der meist angesehensten und erfolgreichsten Menschen in der Filmgeschichte war Teil der jährlichen Nacht der 100 Stars. Ausgezeichnet wurden SIDNEY LUMET, SYLVESTER STALLONE, JANE FONDA, HELEN HAYES, KATHARINE HEPBURN, MICHAEL CAINE, JOSEPH L. MANKIEWICZ und LIV ULLMANN. • Die angesehenen Kennedy Honors, die im Jahre 1978 gegründet wurden, zeichnen jährlich fünf herausragende Darsteller für ihr Lebenswerk im Bereich der Kunst aus. Bei der 6. Verleihung am Kennedy Center wurden VIRGIL THOMPSON, ELIA KAZAN, FRANK SINATRA, KATHERINE DUNHAM und JAMES STEWART, hier mit Präsident RONALD REAGAN und dessen Frau, ausgezeichnet.

La cérémonie annuelle de la Night of 100 Stars est marquée par un hommage rendu aux huit hommes et femmes les plus admirés et à la carrière la plus réussie de l'histoire du cinéma. On reconnaît ici SIDNEY LUMET, SYLVESTER STALLONE, JANE FONDA, HELEN HAYES, KATHARINE HEPBURN, MICHAEL CAINE, JOSEPH L. MANKIEWICZ et LIV ULLMANN. • Les prestigieux Kennedy Honors, créés en 1978, consacrent chaque année cinq grands artistes pour l'œuvre accomplie. La 6ᵉ cérémonie, organisée au Kennedy Center, consacra ainsi VIRGIL THOMPSON, ELIA KAZAN, FRANK SINATRA, KATHERINE DUNHAM et JAMES STEWART, ici en compagnie de RONALD REAGAN, le président des États-Unis, et de son épouse.

WAR BOND TOUR, *J. Wallace Fassmann* 1943

JAMES CAGNEY on a war bond selling tour with other stars including LUCILLE BALL, FRED ASTAIRE, MICKEY ROONEY, DICK POWELL, BETTY HUTTON, PAUL HENREID and HARPO MARX.

JAMES CAGNEY, beim Verkauf von Kriegsanleihen, mit anderen Stars, inklusive LUCILLE BALL, FRED ASTAIRE, MICKEY ROONEY, DICK POWELL, BETTY HUTTON, PAUL HENREID und HARPO MARX.

JAMES CAGNEY fait une tournée de promotion des bons de guerre, accompagné par quelques autres vedettes : LUCILLE BALL, FRED ASTAIRE, MICKEY ROONEY, DICK POWELL, BETTY HUTTON, PAUL HENREID et HARPO MARX.

JACK NICHOLSON, *Milan Ryba* 1999

CONCERNS AND COMMITMENTS

Hollywood has always had an easy entre into the world of social conscience and politics via money and glamour. Aided by the media, celebrities become a bridge to Middle America, making people aware of issues. Their concerns may be varied but they share the passion that drives their commitment whether it be for a cause, a candidate, a duty or a personal dream.

Over many years the major impact of Hollywood stars was through giving money and raising money. Little by little, the arena expanded and celebrities began to endorse political candidates and ideologies. Stars became more and more visible on the commitment battlefield. There have always been some who have not been afraid to roll up their sleeves and get their hands dirty or let their shoe leather hit the asphalt for a cause they believe in. And where a celebrity treads, a photographer is sure to follow.

The value of film personalities in morale-building and fund-raising was first exploited by the Roosevelt White House which used Hollywood to rally the rest of the nation around a war. In all the years following, Hollywood has continued to stomp for funds and sympathy for victims of hunger, abuse and illness. All the big charities – cancer, heart, lung, multiple sclerosis and retinitis pigmentosa – boast their own passionate celebrity crusaders eager to help rid the world of disease. Comedian George Gobel once quipped that by the time he became a star all the good diseases were taken.

Jerry Lewis is almost better known as a fund raiser for muscular dystrophy than as a comic actor. Mention the pesticide Alar and people think of Meryl Streep. As the highly visible spokeswoman for Mothers and Others for Pesticide Limits, she created such a public stir that the manufacturers took Alar off the market. Ted Danson heads up the American Oceans Campaign and lobbies Congress to save our waterways. Elizabeth Taylor is widely recognized for her tireless campaign to fight AIDS and her high voltage stardom guarantees maximum coverage in the press. There's hardly a Hollywood star one can mention who has not lent his or her name to a worthy cause.

Why has charity always been in vogue? It must be admitted that positive publicity is one motivating factor but for most famous folk, activism comes from the heart. The earliest activists looked at their political engagements largely as an extension of their on-screen duties. When invited to appear at a rally or a public forum, they did little more than sparkle and sign autographs. Rarely did they offer their own views on matters of state. As late as the mid-1950s, with a few notable exceptions, Hollywood stars were used merely as decoration.

FÜRSORGE UND ENGAGEMENT

Hollywood übt seit jeher durch sein Geld und seinen Glanz Einfluss auf das soziale Bewusstsein und die Politik aus. Unterstützt von den Medien, beeinflussten Stars die amerikanische Mittelklasse und machten auf Probleme aufmerksam. Ihre Anliegen waren verschieden, gemeinsam war ihnen die Leidenschaft, mit der sie sich engagierten, sei es für eine politische Überzeugung, einen Kandidaten, eine soziale Aufgabe oder einen persönlichen Traum.

Viele Jahre lang erzielten die Hollywoodstars die größten Effekte, wenn sie spendeten oder Geld einsammelten. Langsam aber sicher weitete sich der Schauplatz aus und die Prominenten begannen, Politiker und Ideologien zu unterstützen. Das Engagement der Stars wurde immer sichtbarer. Es gab immer einige, die sich nicht zu schade waren, für eine Sache, an die sie glaubten, die Ärmel hochzukrempeln, sich die Hände schmutzig zu machen oder sich die Schuhsohlen abzulaufen. Und wo ein Star auch hingeht, ein Fotograf wird folgen.

Der Nutzen von Schauspielern, zur Stärkung der Moral und beim Sammeln von Spenden, wurde zuerst von der Roosevelt-Regierung erkannt. Sie nutzte Hollywood, um den Rest der Nation von einem Krieg zu überzeugen. Hollywood führte dieses Engagement fort und trat für Hilfsfonds ein und rief Sympathie für Hungeropfer, Missstände und Krankheiten hervor. Alle großen Wohlfahrtsverbände – gegen Krebs-, Herz- und Lungenleiden, multiple Sklerose und Retinitis Pigmentosa – brüsten sich mit den Prominenten, die sich dafür einsetzen, die Welt von Krankheiten zu befreien. Der Komiker George Gobel witzelte einmal, dass alle guten Krankheiten, als er ein Star wurde, schon von anderen Stars besetzt waren.

Jerry Lewis ist als Spendenbeschaffer für Muskelschwund fast bekannter als für seine komischen Rollen. Das Pestizid Alar wird unweigerlich mit Meryl Streep in Verbindung gebracht. Als Sprecherin von Mothers and Others for Pesticide Limits hat sie so einen Aufstand verursacht, dass die Hersteller Alar vom Markt nahmen. Ted Danson leitet die American Oceans Campaign und nimmt als Lobbyist Einfluss auf den Kongress für die Rettung der Wasserstraßen. Elizabeth Taylor ist überall für ihre Kampagne gegen AIDS bekannt und als Star garantiert sie eine maximale Berichterstattung in der Presse. Es gibt kaum eine Hollywood-Größe, die seinen oder ihren Namen nicht für eine gute Sache hergegeben hat.

Warum war Wohltätigkeit schon immer in Mode? Man weiß, dass positive Publicity motivierend ist, aber für die meisten Stars kommt ihr Engagement von Herzen. Die frühesten Aktivisten betrachteten ihr politisches Engagement als eine Erweiterung ihrer Pflichten aus der Bildschirmpräsenz. Wann immer sie bei einem Treffen oder

CAUSES ET ENGAGEMENTS

L'argent des Studios et le prestige du star system leur ont depuis toujours ouvert les portes des mondes de la politique et de l'action sociale. C'est bien souvent grâce aux stars du cinéma, aidées par les médias, que l'Amérique moyenne a pris conscience de ses problèmes de société. Si leurs sujets d'intérêt étaient très divers, toutes ces personnalités ont montré la même passion dans leurs engagements, qu'il s'agisse de soutenir une cause sociale ou un candidat politique, de réaliser une œuvre ou un rêve personnel.

La principale activité des grandes vedettes de Hollywood s'est longtemps cantonnée à la collecte de fonds et à leur distribution. Puis, elles en vinrent à soutenir des candidats et des idéologies politiques et à s'engager de plus en plus visiblement. Certaines de ces stars n'hésitèrent pas alors à s'investir personnellement ou à manifester dans la rue pour une cause en laquelle elles croyaient. Et là où va une célébrité, on peut être sûr qu'elle est suivie par un photographe.

C'est la Maison Blanche et le gouvernement Roosevelt qui, les premiers, utilisèrent les vedettes de cinéma pour renforcer le moral de la nation et collecter des fonds, qu'il s'agisse de défendre une cause ou à l'occasion d'un conflit. Ce furent les victimes de la faim, la lutte contre les injustices ou des maladies les années suivantes. Toutes les grandes opérations caritatives se glorifient de bénéficier de l'appui de croisés célèbres et passionnés, fiers d'aider à débarrasser le monde de la maladie. Le comédien George Gobel a dit en plaisantant qu'à l'époque où il est devenu une star toutes les bonnes maladies étaient déjà prises.

Jerry Lewis est presque mieux connu aux États-Unis pour aider à collecter des fonds destinés aux actions contre la dystrophie musculaire qu'en tant qu'acteur comique. Mentionnez le pesticide Alar et les Américains pensent aussitôt à Meryl Streep ; porte-parole de l'association « Mothers et Others for Pesticide Limits », elle a créé une telle agitation publique que le fabricant a retiré ce produit de la vente. Ted Danson, qui est à la tête de la campagne « American Oceans », organise le lobbying du Congrès pour préserver les eaux américaines. La notoriété d'Elizabeth Taylor, qui mène une campagne infatigable contre le SIDA, assure à son action une couverture médiatique maximum. En fait, il n'y a pas une vedette de Hollywood, ou presque, qui n'ait prêté son nom à une grande cause.

Si les actions caritatives ou la défense de grandes causes ont toujours été à la mode, c'est évidemment parce que toute publicité positive est motivante à l'égard du public bien qu'il ne fasse aucun doute que, pour les personnalités les plus célèbres, leur engagement vient d'abord du cœur. Autrefois, c'est-à-dire vers le milieu des années 1950, les vedettes considéraient leur activisme et leur engagement

BOB HOPE, *Globe Archive* 1968

The idea that fame carried intrinsic power was nurtured in the 1960s as a result of changes in both the film community and the political world, particularly the demise of the studio system and the emergence of actors as independent agents, as well as the rise to dominance of television in the exposure of causes and the spotlighting of political campaigns. No longer subject to the restrictions imposed by studio publicity departments on contractees, the stars learned to apply their celebrity more aggressively and the devil take the consequences. They became available to speak out for a cause they believed in, no matter if it was unpopular, or tubthump for a favored candidate, or demonstrate even if it meant getting arrested.

Historically, the shared attraction of politician and celebrity can be reduced to a simple equation: celebrities looked to politicians to validate them as part of the company of serious men and women and politicians looked to celebrities to validate them as part of the company of the famous. Much like the successful pairing of Ginger Rogers and Fred Astaire: he gave her class and she gave him sex appeal.

Throughout the 1970s, 1980s and 1990s, the belief that celebrity is a weapon that can be marshaled to attract attention permeated Hollywood and, as a result, stars became more visible and aggressive participants in American politics and movements critical of American policies here and abroad than ever before. And they have moved their forum to the street. Witness such names as Jane Fonda, Martin Sheen, Ed Asner, Valerie Harper, Burt Lancaster, Harry Belafonte, Jon Voight, Marlo Thomas and Susan Sarandon. They have not only brought issues to public attention but mobilized constituencies and challenged authority.

Charlton Heston once said, long before his 1998 election as president of the National Rifle Association: "I see nothing wrong with actors speaking out on causes – that's a fundamental right in our society and actors can exercise it as well as anyone else. The only obligation we have is not to make horses' asses of ourselves."

einem öffentlichen Forum erschienen, taten sie nicht mehr als zu lächeln und Autogramme zu geben. Selten offenbarten sie ihre persönlichen Ansichten zu Staatsangelegenheiten. Bis zur Mitte der 50er Jahre dienten die Stars – mit wenigen Ausnahmen – lediglich zur Dekoration.

Die Vorstellung, dass Ruhm auch Macht bedeutet, wurde von den Veränderungen der 60er Jahre genährt, insbesondere durch den Niedergang des Studiosystems und das damit einhergehende Auftauchen unabhängiger Schauspieler, aber auch durch die wachsende Bedeutung des Fernsehens und der Fokussierung auf politische Großveranstaltungen. Den Einschränkungen von Studiopresseabteilungen nicht länger ausgeliefert, lernten die Stars, ihren Ruhm zu nutzen und sich nicht um die Konsequenzen zu scheren. Sie setzten sich nun für eine Sache oder für ihren favorisierten Kandidaten ein – egal, ob es unpopulär war oder bedeutete, von der Polizei verhaftet zu werden.

Historisch gesehen kann die gegenseitige Anziehungskraft zwischen Politiker und Filmstar auf eine einfache Gleichung reduziert werden: Filmstars wollten von den Politikern als Teil der Gesellschaft seriöser Männer und Frauen anerkannt werden und Politiker hätten gerne zu der berühmten Gesellschaft dazugehört. Ganz wie das berühmte Paar Ginger Rogers und Fred Astaire: Er verlieh ihr Klasse und sie schenkte ihm Sexappeal.

In den 70er, 80er und 90er Jahren war Hollywood davon überzeugt, Ruhm sei ein Mittel zur Erregung von Aufmerksamkeit. Als Resultat sind Stars sichtbare und aggressive Akteure in der amerikanischen Politik und in Bewegungen, die sich mit der amerikanischen Politik, wie sie im In- und Ausland betrieben wird, auseinandersetzen. Und sie haben die Straße zu ihrem Forum gemacht. Man denke an Persönlichkeiten wie Jane Fonda, Martin Sheen, Ed Asner, Valerie Harper, Burt Lancaster, Harry Belafonte, Jon Voight, Marlo Thomas und Susan Sarandon, die die Öffentlichkeit nicht nur auf Probleme hinwiesen, sondern auch Wahlkreise mobilisierten und die Autoritäten herausforderten.

Charlton Heston sagte lange vor seiner Wahl zum Präsidenten der National Rifle Association 1998: „Ich sehe kein Problem mit den Schauspielern, die sich zu Problemen äußern – das ist ein fundamentales Recht unserer Gesellschaft und Schauspieler können wie jeder andere davon Gebrauch machen. Die einzige Verpflichtung, die wir haben, ist es, aus uns selbst keinen Idioten zu machen."

politique comme un prolongement obligé de leur travail à l'écran. Invitées à l'occasion de réunions publiques, elles ne faisaient alors pas grand chose de plus que d'apparaître et signer des autographes, rares étant celles qui osaient donner leur avis personnel sur les affaires. En réalité, à quelques exceptions notables, les stars de Hollywood étaient alors essentiellement engagées à titre décoratif.

L'idée que la participation d'une célébrité était un atout supplémentaire intrinsèque naquit dans les années 1960 à la suite des changements apparus à la fois dans la communauté du cinéma et du monde politique, notamment avec la fin du système des Studios et l'émergence d'acteurs indépendants, ainsi que de la domination de la télévision dans la publicité faite aux grandes causes et aux campagnes politiques. N'étant plus soumises aux contraintes imposées par les départements de publicité des studios, les stars apprirent à utiliser leur notoriété de manièr plus indépendante et plus personnelle. Les acteurs acceptèrent de s'exprimer en faveur d'une cause en laquelle ils croyaient, de manifester dans la rue ou encore de soutenir très démagogiquement leur candidat favori lors des élections.

D'un point de vue historique, l'attirance réciproque entre politiciens et vedettes peut se réduire à une simple équation : les célébrités ont besoin de la caution des politiciens pour s'affirmer comme des individus sérieux et les politiciens recherchent la compagnie des vedettes pour bénéficier de leur notoriété publique. Un peu à l'exemple du célèbre couple formé par Ginger Rogers et Fred Astaire : il lui donnait de la classe et elle lui apportait du sex appeal.

Dans les années 1970, 1980 et 1990, Hollywood étant persuadé que la célébrité est une arme dont on peut se servir pour canaliser l'attention du public, les stars adhèrent de manière plus active aux mouvements politiques qui élèvent une voix critique contre la politique américaine. Et, comme en témoignent Jane Fonda, Martin Sheen, Ed Asner, Valerie Harper, Burt Lancaster, Harry Belafonte, Jon Voight, Marlo Thomas ou Susan Sarandon, les acteurs n'hésitent pas à défier l'autorité et à déplacer le débat dans la rue pour mobiliser les électeurs.

Bien avant d'être élu président de la National Rifle Association en 1998, Charlton Heston déclarait : « Je ne vois rien de mal à ce que des acteurs se prononcent sur une cause ou une autre – c'est un droit fondamental offert par notre société, et les acteurs peuvent l'exercer au même titre que n'importe qui d'autre. La seule obligation que nous avons est de ne pas nous rendre ridicules. »

JAMES STEWART, *Harris/Ewing* 1943

CLARK GABLE, *Harris/Ewing* 1943

Air Force Captain JAMES STEWART was one of the first stars to enlist during World War II. He was discharged with the rank of full Colonel. • Captain CLARK GABLE at a press conference at the War Department.

Luftwaffenkapitän JAMES STEWART war einer der ersten Stars, die sich im Zweiten Weltkrieg meldeten. Er wurde als Oberst aus dem Dienst entlassen. • Hauptmann CLARK GABLE bei einer Pressekonferenz im Kriegsministerium.

JAMES STEWART fut l'une des premières vedettes à s'engager au début de la Seconde Guerre mondiale. Capitaine dans l'Air Force, il termina le conflit avec le grade de colonel. • Le capitaine CLARK GABLE lors d'une conférence de presse au ministère de la Guerre.

TYRONE POWER, *PFC Robert Estes* 1944

VICTOR MATURE, *Harris/Ewing* 1943

GENE KELLY, *Harris/Ewing* 1946

Marine First Lieutenant TYRONE POWER, a transport pilot in the Pacific, washes off the grime of dusty airfields on Saipan, Marianas. • Chief Petty Officer VICTOR MATURE, shows where pocketless gobs keep their cigarettes. • Lt. j.g. GENE KELLY happily leaves the Washington Naval Separation Center following his discharge from the navy.

Oberstleutnant der Marine, TYRONE POWER, der im Pazifik als Transportpilot eingesetzt wurde, wäscht sich den aufgewirbelten Staub von den Landebahnen in Saipan, Marianas ab. • Offizier VICTOR MATURE zeigt, wo Blaue Jungs ohne Taschen ihre Zigaretten aufbewahren. • Unteroffizier GENE KELLY verlässt nach seiner Entlassung aus der Navy hocherfreut das Washington Naval Separation Center.

TYRONE POWER, pilote d'avion de transport dans le Pacifique avec le grade de 1er lieutenant des US Marines, sous la douche de l'aérodrome de Saipan, dans les Mariannes. • Maître VICTOR MATURE montre où les marins, dont l'uniforme n'a pas de poches, rangent leurs cigarettes. • Démobilisé de la Marine et heureux, l'enseigne de vaisseau GENE KELLY quitte le Washington Naval Separation Center.

HELEN HAYES, *Harris/Ewing* 1944

BETTY GRABLE, *Globe Archive* 1944

LORETTA YOUNG, *Globe Archive* 1943

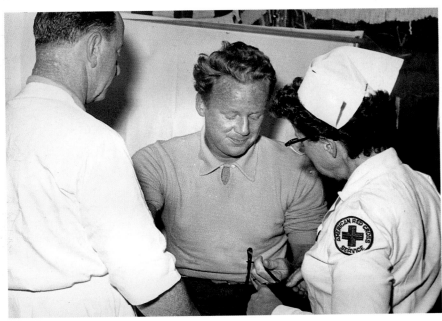

VAN JOHNSON, *Globe Archive* 1943

HELEN HAYES visited troops on military posts throughout the country. • Top WWII pinup BETTY GRABLE sings along with servicemen at the Hollywood Canteen, which provided food and entertainment to military personnel only by a lineup of famous names a raja's fortune couldn't have commanded – all for free. The "ticket" was a uniform. • LORETTA YOUNG allowed that "even though some of us couldn't sing or dance to entertain our service-men, we were welcomed at all the army posts where the boys just wanted to talk to someone from home." • VAN JOHNSON helps publicize blood drives by donating blood and being photo-graphed while he pumps away.

HELEN HAYES besuchte Truppen auf Militärbasen im ganzen Land. • Top-Pin-up-Girl während des Zweiten Weltkrieges, BETTY GRABLE, singt mit Soldaten in der Hollywood-Kantine. Hier wurde nicht nur für das leibliche Wohl des Militärpersonals gesorgt, sondern auch für deren Unterhaltung sorgte eine Reihe von bekannten Stars – alles kostenlos. Die „Eintrittskarte" war eine Uniform. • LORETTA YOUNG sagte, dass „auch wenn manche von uns nicht singen oder tanzen konnten, so waren wir doch immer willkommen, denn die Jungs waren froh, sich mit jemandem aus ihrer Heimat unterhalten zu können." • VAN JOHNSON unterstützt die Werbekampagne für das Blut-spenden. Hier wurde er während der Blutabnahme geknippst.

HELEN HAYES fait la tournée des postes militaires. • BETTY GRABLE, la pin-up de la Seconde Guerre mondiale, chante avec les soldats à la Hollywood Canteen, une cantine militaire où les célébrités (dans un générique qu'aucun studio n'aurait pu obtenir) servaient à manger et distrayaient gratuitement les soldats. Le seul « ticket » d'entrée était l'uniforme. • LORETTA YOUNG racontait que « alors que certains d'entre nous ne savaient ni chanter ni danser pour distraire les soldats des postes militaires où nous passions, nous étions quand même bien accueillis tant les gars avaient envie et besoin de parler à quelqu'un du pays. » • VAN JOHNSON participe à la campagne de promotion du don du sang en offrant le sien et en se laissant photographier pendant la transfusion.

ORSON WELLES, *Globe Archive* 1943

CECIL B. DeMILLE, *Harris/Ewing* 1947

ORSON WELLES, assisted by ELEANOR COUNTS and MERRY HAMILTON, during a levitation act in his Mercury Wonder Show which toured military bases. • CECIL B. DeMILLE, whose refusal to pay a one dollar union assessment cost him his job as host of the Lux Radio Theater, testifies before the Senate Labor Committee in opposition to union closed shop. • LAUREN BACALL decorates the piano at the National Press Club Canteen with Vice President HARRY S. TRUMAN at the keyboard.

ELEANOR COUNTS und MERRY HAMILTON assistieren ORSON WELLES bei einem Schwebe-Akt in seiner Mercury Wonder Show. Seine Show war auf allen Militärbasen zu sehen. • CECIL B. DeMILLE, weigerte sich, seiner Gewerkschaft einen 1-Dollar-Beitrag zu zahlen, was ihn seinen Job als Moderator des Lux Radio Theaters kostete. Hier sagt er vor dem Senatsausschuss für Arbeitsfragen gegen Unternehmen mit Gewerkschaftszwang aus. • LAUREN BACALL dekoriert das Klavier in der Kantine des Nationalen Presseclubs und Vize-Präsident HARRY S. TRUMAN spielt ihr etwas vor.

En tournée dans les bases militaires américaines, ORSON WELLES, assisté par ELEANOR COUNTS et MERRY HAMILTON, présente le numéro de lévitation de son spectacle Mercury Wonder. • CECIL B. DeMILLE, dont le refus de payer le dollar de sa cotisation syndicale lui coûta sa place d'animateur au Lux Radio Theater, témoigne contre la syndicalisation devant la commission sénatoriale du Travail. • LAUREN BACALL sur le piano de la National Press Club Canteen dont joue le vice-président HARRY S. TRUMAN.

LAUREN BACALL AND VICE PRESIDENT HARRY S. TRUMAN, *Harris/Ewing* 1945

HOUSE UN-AMERICAN ACTIVITIES COMMITTEE, *Harris/Ewing* 1948

STERLING HAYDEN, *Harris/Ewing* 1948

UTA HAGEN WITH JOHN AND ROBERTA GARFIELD, *Harris/Ewing* 1948

LARRY PARKS, *Harris/Ewing* 1948

ADOLPH MENJOU, *Harris/Ewing* 1947

Friendly witness ROBERT TAYLOR takes the oath from Representative J. PARNELL THOMAS, standing next to committee member Senator RICHARD NIXON, at the House Un-American Activities Committee hearings in Washington D.C. • STERLING HAYDEN, LARRY PARKS and ADOLPH MENJOU during their testimonies before the committee. • JOHN and ROBERTA GARFIELD and UTA HAGEN are concerned spectators. Garfield was at that time under subpoena to testify.

ROBERT TAYLOR leistet seinen Eid – als wohlwollender Zeuge – vor dem Abgeordneten J. PARNELL THOMAS. Neben ihm steht Ausschussmitglied Senator RICHARD NIXON. Die Anhörungen finden vor dem Ausschuss für Unamerikanische Aktivitäten in Washington D.C. statt. • STERLING HAYDEN, LARRY PARKS und ADOLPH MENJOU während ihrer Zeugenaussage vor der Kommission. • JOHN und ROBERTA GARFIELD und UTA HAGEN sind besorgte Zuschauer. Garfield war zu dieser Zeit zur Zeugenaussage vorgeladen.

ROBERT TAYLOR prête serment en tant que témoin « amical » devant le député J. PARNELL THOMAS, la commission des activités anti-américaines (House Un-American Activities Committee, HUAC), et le sénateur RICHARD NIXON, lors d'une séance d'audition à Washington D.C. • STERLING HAYDEN, LARRY PARKS et ADOLPH MENJOU pendant leur témoignage devant la HUAC. • JOHN GARFIELD, assigné à comparaître comme témoin ; son épouse, ROBERTA, et UTA HAGEN sont des spectatrices intéressées.

PATRICIA NEAL, *Globe Archive* 1955

MARTHA RAYE AND GENERAL WILLIAM WESTMORELAND, *Globe Archive* 1955

BARBARA STANWYCK, MAUREEN O'HARA AND LIONEL BARRYMORE, *Nate Cutler* 1954

SOPHIE TUCKER, *Nate Cutler* 1959

VIRGINIA MAYO, *Nate Cutler* 1955

DEBBIE REYNOLDS, *US Army* 1955

PATRICIA NEAL chows down with American soldiers on duty in Korea. • MARTHA RAYE receives thanks for her many tours of military bases overseas from General William Westmoreland. • War Bonds and Victory Bonds became US Defense Bonds in the 50s. New salesmen include BARBARA STANWYCK, MAUREEN O'HARA and LIONEL BARRYMORE. • The Last of the Red Hot Mamas, SOPHIE TUCKER never missed a week visiting war wounded at veteran's hospitals. Here she talks with vets at the Veterans Hospital in Los Angeles. • The Hollywood Canteen was mustered out in 1946 only to be born again in 1951 to host military men serving in the Korean Conflict. VIRGINIA MAYO greets marines just back from Korea. • DEBBIE REYNOLDS is greeted by soldiers as she arrives in Korea with the Johnny Grant USO-Camp Show. • Private ELVIS PRESLEY in boot camp at Ft. Hood, Texas. • The singing EVERLY BROTHERS, DON and PHIL, get shorn for duty as marine reservists at Camp Pendleton, California.

PATRICIA NEAL isst zusammen mit amerikanischen Soldaten, die in Korea im Einsatz waren. • General William Westmoreland bedankt sich bei MARTHA RAYE für ihre vielen Besuche auf Militärbasen in Übersee. • Kriegsanleihen und Siegesanleihen wurden Mitte der 50er Jahre amerikanische Verteidigungsanleihen. Zu den neuen Vertretern gehören BARBARA STANWYCK, MAUREEN O'HARA und LIONEL BARRYMORE. • Die letzte der Red Hot Mamas, SOPHIE TUCKER, versäumte es nie, verwundete Kriegsveteranen im Krankenhaus zu besuchen. Hier unterhält sie sich mit Veteranen im Krankenhaus von Los Angeles. • Die Hollywood-Kantine wurde 1946 geschlossen, allerdings 1951 wieder eröffnet, um Soldaten, die im Koreakrieg dienten, zu bewirten. VIRGINIA MAYO begrüßt Marinesoldaten, die gerade aus Korea zurückkommen. • DEBBIE REYNOLDS wird von Soldaten bei ihrer Ankunft mit der Johnny Grant USO-Camp Show in Korea begrüßt. • Gefreiter ELVIS PRESLEY im Boot Camp in Ft. Hood, Texas. • Den singenden EVERLY BROTHERS DON und PHIL werden für ihren Einsatz als Marinereservisten im Camp Pendleton, Kalifornien, die Haare geschoren.

PATRICIA NEAL fait la queue à la cantine avec les soldats américains engagés en Corée. • Le général William Westmoreland remercie MARTHA RAYE pour ces nombreux spectacles en tournée sur les bases militaires à l'étranger. • Les anciens War Bonds et Victory Bonds furent rebaptisés US Defense Bonds dans les années 1950. BARBARA STANWYCK, MAUREEN O'HARA et LIONEL BARRYMORE en deviennent les nouveaux « vendeurs ». • SOPHIE TUCKER, surnommée « The Last of the Red Hot Mamas » (La Dernière des Femmes Sexy), rendait visite chaque semaine aux blessés de guerre dans les hôpitaux militaires. Elle discute ici avec des vétérans du Veterans Hospital de Los Angeles. • La Hollywood Canteen fut démantelée en 1946 mais remise en service en 1951 pour accueillir les militaires engagés dans la guerre de Corée. VIRGINIA MAYO salue les Marines de retour d'Extrême-Orient. • DEBBIE REYNOLDS est saluée par des soldats américains lors de son arrivée en Coreé avec le Johnny Grant USO-Camp Show. • Le soldat ELVIS PRESLEY au camp d'entraînement de Fort Hood (Texas). • Les frères EVERLY, DON et PHIL, passent chez le coiffeur avant de reprendre du service comme réservistes de la Marine à Camp Pendleton (Californie).

ELVIS PRESLEY, *Globe Archive* 1958

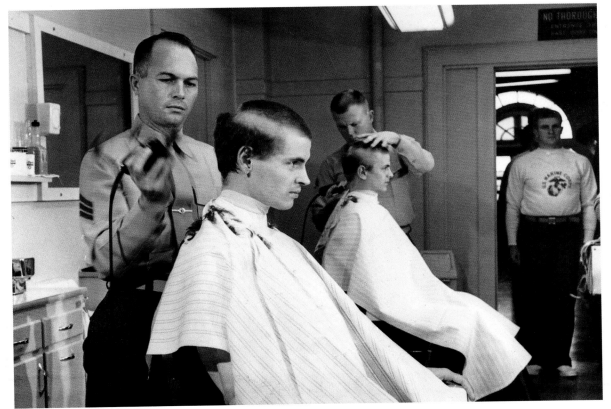

THE EVERLY BROTHERS, *Globe Archive* 1962

JANE RUSSELL, *Nate Cutler* 1955

THE THALIANS, *Nate Cutler* 1959

JANE RUSSELL was the founder of WAIF (Women's Adoption International Fund), the inter-country adoption service which found homes for homeless children throughout the world. • Breaking ground for the Thalians Mental Health Center at Cedars-Sinai Medical Center are Thalian president DEBBIE REYNOLDS, PATRICIA CROWLEY, BARBARA and MARGARET WHITING, and LORI NELSON. • DANNY KAYE, UNICEF'S international ambassador, amuses 6-year-old Boon-Ting and his friends during the filming of ASSIGNMENT CHILDREN, Kaye's documentary about Tungkaponghow Village in Thailand. Kaye served with UNICEF for 34 years. • CHARLES LAUGHTON toured the country, visiting the convalescent wards of military hospitals, with his readings from the Bible.

DANNY KAYE, *Harris/Ewing* 1954

CHARLES LAUGHTON, *Don Ornitz* 1956

JANE RUSSELL war die Gründerin des WAIF (Women's Adoption International Fund). Diese Organisation kümmerte sich um die Adoption von heimatlosen Kindern aus der ganzen Welt und vermittelte sie an Familien. ● Die Thalian-Vorsitzende DEBBIE REYNOLDS, PATRICIA CROWLEY, BARBARA und MARGARET WHITING und LORI NELSON beim ersten Spatenstich zum Fundament der Psychiatrischen Klinik, die die Organisation am Cedars-Sinai Medical Center ins Leben rief. ● DANNY KAYE, UNICEFS internationaler Botschafter, spielt mit dem 6 Jahre alten Boon-Ting und seinen Freunden während der Dreharbeiten zu ASSIGNMENT CHILDREN, Kayes Dokumentarfilm über das Dorf Tungkaponghow in Thailand. Kaye arbeitete 34 Jahre lang für UNICEF. ● CHARLES LAUGHTON reist durch das Land und besucht Patienten in Militärhospitälern und liest ihnen aus der Bibel vor.

JANE RUSSELL fut la fondatrice de la WAIF (Women's Adoption International Fund), une association s'occupant de trouver des familles aux enfants abandonnés. ● DEBBIE REYNOLDS, présidente de l'association Thalian, accompagnée par PATRICIA CROWLEY, BARBARA et MARGARET WHITING, et LORI NELSON creusent les fondations du service psychiatrique créé par l'association au Cedars-Sinai Medical Center. ● DANNY KAYE, ambassadeur international de l'UNICEF, joue avec Boon-Ting, âgé de 6 ans, et ses amis pendant le tournage de ASSIGNMENT CHILDREN, un documentaire qu'il a réalisé sur le village thaïlandais de Tungkaponghow. Kaye travailla 34 ans pour l'UNICEF. ● CHARLES LAUGHTON fait des lectures de la Bible dans les différents centres de convalescence des hôpitaux militaires américains.

MARTIN LUTHER KING MARCH ON WASHINGTON, *Tom Caffrey* 1963

MARLON BRANDO, ANTHONY FRANCIOSA, BURT LANCASTER, JAMES GARNER and HARRY BELAFONTE were among the Hollywood personalities who converged on the nation's capital for the Martin Luther King March on Washington. • MARLON BRANDO, Hollywood's chief advocate of civil rights causes, attends the funeral of Black Panther Bobby Hutton with Bill Brendt, Ken Denmon and Bobby Seale at Merritt Park in Oakland, California. • BRANDO joins the picket line for CORE, demonstrating for equal rights for housing.

MARLON BRANDO, ANTHONY FRANCIOSA, BURT LANCASTER, JAMES GARNER und HARRY BELAFONTE gehören zu den Hollywoodstars, die sich im März in der Landeshauptstadt zum Martin-Luther-King-Marsch versammeln. • MARLON BRANDO, Hollywoods Verfechter für Bürgerrechte, nimmt an der Beerdigung des Black-Panther-Mitglieds Bobby Hutton teil. Weitere Anwesende sind Bill Brendt, Ken Denmon und Bobby Seale im Merritt Park in Oakland, Kalifornien. • BRANDO schließt sich den Sympatisanten für CORE an und demonstriert für das gleiche Recht auf Unterkunft.

MARLON BRANDO, ANTHONY FRANCIOSA, BURT LANCASTER, JAMES GARNER et HARRY BELAFONTE firent partie des personnalités de Hollywood qui se rendirent dans la capitale des États-Unis pour participer à la marche de Martin Luther King. • Accompagné par Bill Brendt, Ken Denmon et Bobby Seale, MARLON BRANDO, grand défenseur des droits civils à Hollywood, assiste aux funérailles de Bobby Hutton, membre des Black Panther, au Merritt Park de Oakland (Californie). • BRANDO rejoint les sympathisants du CORE qui manifestent pour l'égalité des droits au logement.

MARLON BRANDO, *Jeffrey Blankfort* 1968

MARLON BRANDO, *John R. Hamilton* 1963

Do Democrats, like blondes, have more fun? Democrats FONDA, LOY and BACALL frolic at a rally for Adlai Stevenson's presidential bid at the Hollywood Bowl while Republicans DeFORE, COREY and the REAGANS give imitations of Mt. Rushmore at the Anti-Red Rally.

Haben Demokraten, genau wie Blondinen, mehr Spaß? Demokraten FONDA, LOY und BACALL unterhalten sich auf einer Präsidentschaftskampagne für Adlai Stevenson im Hollywood Bowl sehr ausgelassen. • Republikaner DeFORE, COREY und die REAGANS imitieren Mt. Rushmore bei der Anti-Kommunismus-Versammlung.

À voir la mine réjouie de FONDA, LOY et BACALL lors d'un meeting pour la course à la présidence de Adlai Stevenson au Hollywood Bowl, les Démocrates semblent plus gais que les Républicains DeFORE, COREY et les REAGAN, ici à une réunion anti-communiste.

HENRY FONDA, MYRNA LOY AND LAUREN BACALL, *Nate Cutler* 1956

DON DeFORE, NANCY REAGAN, RONALD REAGAN AND WENDELL COREY, *Bill Kobrin* 1962

LUCILLE BALL, *Dick Miller* 1959

AGNES MOOREHEAD, *Bill Kobrin* 1963

JEAN STAPLETON, *Globe Archive* 1970

When LUCILLE BALL'S Desilu Productions took over RKO Studios, she realized a longtime dream to open a workshop for talented young performers, much along the lines of the RKO Studio Club Theater where she had once been a Hollywood hopeful. Lucy taught many of the sessions with up and coming players like DICK KALMAN, JANICE CARROLL, STEVE MARLO and MAJEL BARRETT. The yawning young man is Turner Classic Movies host Robert Osborne. • AGNES MOOREHEAD and JEAN STAPLETON are two other major actresses who devoted time to teaching. Agnes had her own studio in Hollywood and Jean both acted and coached at the Totem Pole Theater in Lafayetteville, Pennsylvania. Her students are Linda Selman and John Ritter.

Als LUCILLE BALLS Desilu Productions die RKO Studios übernahmen, erfüllte sie sich einen Lebenstraum. In Anlehnung an das RKO Studio Club Theater, an dem Lucille einst hoffnungsvoll ihre Karriere begann, sollte ein Workshop für talentierte junge Darsteller eröffnet werden. Lucy gab viele der Unterrichtsstunden in Anwesenheit von schon etablierten und zukünftigen Stars wie DICK KALMAN, JANICE CARROLL, STEVE MARLO und MAJEL BARRETT. Der gähnende junge Mann ist Robert Osborne, der Gastgeber der Turner Classic Movies. • AGNES MOOREHEAD und JEAN STAPLETON sind zwei weitere berühmte Schauspielerinnen, die ihre Zeit dem Schauspielunterricht widmeten. Agnes hatte ihr eigenes Studio in Hollywood und Jean spielte und unterrichtete am Totem Pole Theater in Lafayetteville, Pennsylvania. Zu ihren Studenten gehören Linda Selman und John Ritter.

Lorsque sa société, Desilu Productions, reprend les Studios RKO, LUCILLE BALL peut réaliser le vieux rêve d'ouvrir une école pour les jeunes acteurs, à l'exemple du RKO Studio Club Theater où elle était devenue une des jeunes espoirs de Hollywood. Lucy assurait plusieurs des cours avec des acteurs confirmés ou en devenir comme DICK KALMAN, JANICE CARROLL, STEVE MARLO et MAJEL BARRETT. Le jeune homme en train de bâiller est Robert Osborne, des Turner Classic Movies. • AGNES MOOREHEAD et JEAN STAPLETON sont deux des principaux acteurs qui ont consacré leur temps à enseigner. Agnes possède son propre studio à Hollywood tandis que Jean joue et enseigne au Totem Pole Theater à Lafayetteville en Pensylvanie. Ses étudiants sont Linda Selman et John Ritter.

TUESDAY WELD AND BOB HOPE, *Globe Archive* 1963

MARY MARTIN, *Jerry Jackson* 1965

TUESDAY WELD gets a big welcome from soldiers during the BOB HOPE tour of Turkey, Libya and Greece. • MARY MARTIN brought HELLO DOLLY to Vietnam, touring military bases throughout the war torn country. She is here at the air base in Bien Hoa, where armed helicopters circled overhead for protection. • PHYLLIS DILLER visits with wounded and disabled servicemen in a South Vietnam military hospital during the Bob Hope Christmas tour to Southeast Asia.

TUESDAY WELD wird von Soldaten während der BOB-HOPE-Tournee in der Türkei, Lybien und Griechenland herzlich begrüßt. • MARY MARTIN brachte HELLO DOLLY nach Vietnam, zu einer Tournee durch die Militärbasen im vom Krieg verwüsteten Land. Hier befindet sie sich auf der Militärbasis in Bien Hoa, wo bewaffnete Helikopter aus Sicherheitsgründen in der Luft kreisten. • PHYLLIS DILLER besucht während der Bob-Hope-Weihnachtstournee durch den Südosten Asiens verwundete und arbeitsunfähige Soldaten in einem Krankenhaus in Südvietnam.

TUESDAY WELD, qui suit la tournée de BOB HOPE en Turquie, en Libye et en Grèce, est chaleureusement accueillie par les soldats. • MARY MARTIN a joué HELLO DOLLY en tournée dans les bases américaines du Viêtnam, comme ici la base aérienne de Bien Hoa ; des hélicoptères armés surveillèrent le camp depuis les airs pendant tout le spectacle. • PHYLLIS DILLER profite de la tournée de Noël de Bob Hope en Asie du Sud-Est pour rendre visite aux soldats blessés d'un hôpital militaire du Viêtnam-du-Sud.

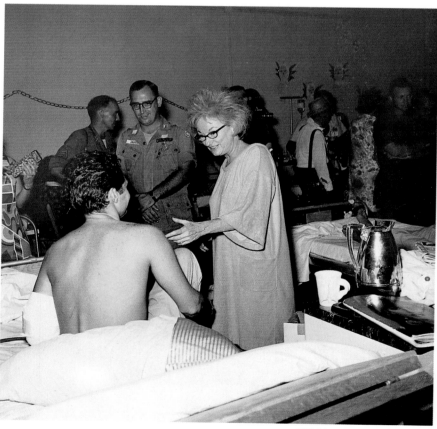

PHYLLIS DILLER, *Globe Archive* 1967

BARBARA STANWYCK, *Gene Trindl* 1966

DANNY THOMAS, *Globe Archive* 1960

BARBARA STANWYCK, a supporter of the Braille Institute in Los Angeles, is helped to feel-sight the world globe by adventitiously blind student Laura Haneline. • When DANNY THOMAS was a struggling entertainer, he prayed to St. Jude, patron saint of hopeless causes, for help in his career. When he became successful, Thomas vowed to build a shrine to the saint and in 1962 the St. Jude Children's Research Hospital, seeking cures for children with cancer and other catastrophic diseases, was opened. Here he proudly shows his barber the plans for the hospital. • JULIE ANDREWS, talking with children in Cambodia, was one of the prime movers behind Operation California, a huge airlift of foodstuffs and medical supplies to people in that country.

BARBARA STANWYCK, Mitglied des Braille Institute in Los Angeles, lässt sich von der blinden Studentin Laura Haneline beim Ertasten der Weltkugel helfen. • Als DANNY THOMAS ein am Hungertuch nagender Künstler war, betete er zu St. Jude, dem Schutzpatron hoffnungsloser Fälle, um Hilfe bei seiner Karriere. Als er erfolgreich wurde, schwur Thomas, dem Heiligen einen Schrein zu bauen. Im Jahre 1962 wurde das St. Jude Children's Research Hospital eröffnet, das speziell nach Heilungsmethoden für krebskranke und anderweitig schwer kranke Kinder forschte. Hier zeigt er seinem Friseur stolz die Baupläne für das Krankenhaus. • JULIE ANDREWS unterhält sich mit Kindern aus Kambodscha. Sie war eine der ersten Befürworterinnen für die Operation California, eine Luftbrücke, die die Menschen in Kambodscha mit Nahrungsmitteln und Medikamenten versorgte.

JULIE ANDREWS, *Tony Adams* 1980

BARBARA STANWYCK, qui soutient le Braille Institute de Los Angeles, apprend à reconnaître le globe au toucher, guidée par Laura Haneline, une étudiante devenue aveugle par accident. • À l'époque où DANNY THOMAS n'étant qu'un artiste tirant le diable par la queue, il avait pris l'habitude d'invoquer saint Jude, patron des causes désespérées, pour qu'il l'aide dans sa carrière. Lorsqu'il connut enfin le succès, Thomas fit le vœu de consacrer un monument au saint ; c'est ainsi qu'il ouvrit en 1962 le St. Jude Children's Research Hospital, où l'on soigne les enfants atteints du cancer et autres maladies graves. On voit ici Danny présenter fièrement les plans de l'hôpital à son coiffeur. • JULIE ANDREWS, qui parle ici avec des petits Cambodgiens, fut l'une des principales animatrices de l'Opération California, un vaste pont aérien d'aide alimentaire et sanitaire au Cambodge.

JANE FONDA, *Russell Reif* 1970

ANN-MARGRET, *US Army* 1966

BURT LANCASTER, *Nate Cutler* 1971

ERA BENEFIT, *Bob Noble* 1978

VANESSA REDGRAVE, *Globe Archive* 1970

JANE FONDA rides with wounded Vietnam veterans in a Memorial Day protest march in New York. • ANN-MARGRET entertains troops in Vietnam as part of Bob Hope's annual Christmas tour. • BURT LANCASTER speaks on behalf of Entertainment Industry for Peace and Justice at the home of director Richard Quine. • Supporters of the Equal Rights Amendment gathered at the home of MARLO THOMAS to raise funds for its passage. The fervent included ESTHER ROLLE, DAVID FROST, HARVEY KORMAN, DORY PREVIN, RENEE TAYLOR, JOE BOLOGNA, SHIRLEY MACLAINE, BELLA ABZUG, POLLY BERGEN, JANE FONDA, LILY TOMLIN, SUSAN BLAKELEY, ELLIOTT GOULD, JOHN RITTER, HENRY WINKLER. • VANESSA REDGRAVE leads protesters in the 1970 Peace Demonstration in London.

JANE FONDA auf einem Protestmarsch am Memorial Day in New York mit verwundeten Vietnamveteranen. • ANN-MARGRET unterhält Truppen in Vietnam anlässlich von Bob Hopes jährlicher Weihnachtstournee. • BURT LANCASTER spricht im Haus des Filmregisseurs Richard Quine im Namen der Unterhaltungsindustrie für Gerechtigkeit und Frieden. • Befürworter des Zusatzartikels für die Gleichberechtigung versammeln sich im Haus von MARLO THOMAS, um Gelder für die Verabschiedung des Gesetzes aufzubringen. Unter den Befürwortern befinden sich ESTHER ROLLE, DAVID FROST, HARVEY KORMAN, DORY PREVIN, RENEE TAYLOR, JOE BOLOGNA, SHIRLEY MACLAINE, BELLA ABZUG, POLLY BERGEN, JANE FONDA, LILY TOMLIN, SUSAN BLAKELEY, ELLIOTT GOULD, JOHN RITTER und HENRY WINKLER. • VANESSA REDGRAVE führt 1970 eine Friedensdemonstration in London an.

JANE FONDA manifeste avec les vétérans du Viêtnam lors d'une marche de protestation à New York le jour du Memorial Day. • ANN-MARGRET divertit les troupes au Viêtnam à l'occasion de la tournée de Noël de Bob Hope. • BURT LANCASTER parle en faveur de l'Entertainment Industry for Peace and Justice chez le metteur en scène Richard Quine. • Parmi ces partisans de l'Amendement pour l'égalité des Droits (Equal Rights Amendment), rassemblés chez Marlo Thomas pour recueillir des fonds, on reconnaît ESTHER ROLLE, DAVID FROST, HARVEY KORMAN, DORY PREVIN, RENEE TAYLOR, JOE BOLOGNA, SHIRLEY MACLAINE, BELLA ABZUG, POLLY BERGEN, JANE FONDA, LILY TOMLIN, SUSAN BLAKELEY, ELLIOTT GOULD, JOHN RITTER et HENRY WINKLER. • VANESSA REDGRAVE marche en tête d'une manifestation pour la Paix en 1970 à Londres.

MIKE FARRELL, *Robert Landau* 1979

BILL AND CAMILLE COSBY WITH JESSE JACKSON, *Nate Cutler* 1970

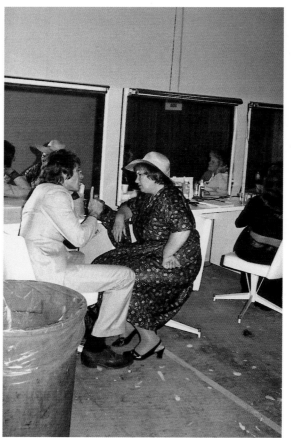

JANE FONDA, ANGELA DAVIS AND JEAN GENET, *Travis Lehman* 1970

WARREN BEATTY AND BELLA ABZUG, *Globe Archive* 1976

ELIZABETH TAYLOR, *Brad Markel* 1984

MIKE FARRELL takes to the streets in several Californian cities to urge a boycott on lettuce in support of Cesar Chavez and the United Farm Workers. • Civil rights leader Reverend JESSE JACKSON enlists the help of BILL and CAMILLE COSBY for Operation Breadbasket. • Writer Dalton Trumbo hosted a fundraiser for the legal defense of Black Panthers ANGELA DAVIS and Bobby Seale. Guests included JANE FONDA and French writer JEAN GENET. • WARREN BEATTY huddles with BELLA ABZUG backstage at the 1976 Democratic Telethon. • Generally credited with helping to bring AIDS awareness into the mainstream, ELIZABETH TAYLOR testifies before Congress on behalf of a bill that appropriated 875 million dollars for emergency AIDS care in areas hardest hit by the epidemic. That same year Taylor founded AmFAR (American Foundation for AIDS Research).

MIKE FARRELL geht in mehreren kalifornischen Städten auf die Straße, um zu einem Kopfsalat-Boykott zur Unterstützung von Cesar Chavez und den United Farm Workers aufzurufen. • Bürgerrechtler Reverend JESSE JACKSON erhält für den Einsatz Breadbasket die Hilfe von BILL und CAMILLE COSBY. • Schriftsteller Dalton Trumbo ist Gastgeber einer Spenden-aktion für den Rechtsbeistand der Black Panthers ANGELA DAVIS und Bobby Seale. Unter den Gästen waren auch JANE FONDA und der französische Schriftsteller JEAN GENET. • WARREN BEATTY diskutiert während einer Fernseh-Spenden-aktion 1976 mit BELLA ABZUG hinter der Bühne. • Es ist allge-mein bekannt, dass ELIZABETH TAYLOR die Aufmerksamkeit der Öffentlichkeit auf das Thema AIDS gelenkt hat. Hier sagt sie zu Gunsten eines Gesetzes, das 875 Millionen Dollar zur Soforthilfe in den am meisten betroffenen Gegenden dieser Epidemie zur Verfügung stellt, vor dem Kongress aus. Im selben Jahr gründete sie die AmFAR (American Foundation for AIDS Research).

MIKE FARRELL a manifesté dans les rues de plusieurs villes de Californie en faveur du boycott de la salade pour soutenir Cesar Chavez et les United Farm Workers. • Le révérend JESSE JACKSON explique l'Opération Breadbasket à BILL et CAMILLE COSBY. • L'écrivain Dalton Trumbo organise une collecte de fonds pour assurer la défense de ANGELA DAVIS et Bobby Seale, membres des Black Panthers. On note parmi ses invités JANE FONDA et l'écrivain français JEAN GENET. • WARREN BEATTY discute en coulisses avec BELLA ABZUG lors du Democratic Telethon de 1976. • ELIZABETH TAYLOR, qui a beaucoup œuvré pour sensibiliser l'opinion au Sida, plaide devant le Congrès pour l'attribution d'un crédit de 875 millions de dollars en faveur des soins d'urgence contre le Sida dans les régions les plus touchées par l'épidémie. Taylor fondera l'AmFAR (American Foundation for AIDS Research) la même année.

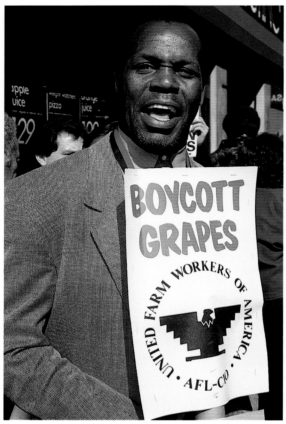

DANNY GLOVER, *Stephen Allen* 1988

PAUL NEWMAN, *John Barrett* 1986

ROBERT AND ALAN ALDA, *Nate Cutler* 1980

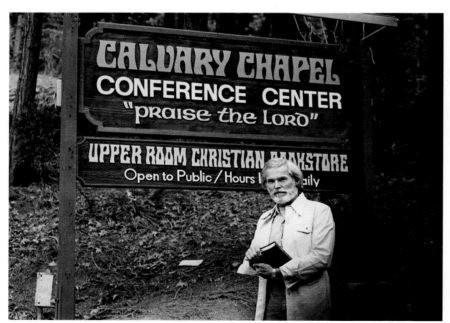

TY HARDIN, *Walter Zurlinden* 1985

EARL HOLLLIMAN, BENJI AND LASSIE, *Nate Cutler* 1982

BILLY CRYSTAL, WHOOPI GOLDBERG AND ROBIN WILLIAMS, *Robert Landau* 1986

DANNY GLOVER waves his Boycott Grapes sign in New York City. • PAUL NEWMAN samples his Oldstyle Picture Show Popcorn, one of several products he markets under the Newman's Own trademark, distributing 100% of the profits to charitable organizations outside the charity mainstream, like The Hole in the Wall Gang Camp in Ashford, Connecticut, for children with cancer. • ALAN ALDA joins dad ROBERT ALDA and fellow actors on the picket line of the 1980 Screen Actors Guild strike. • TV western star TY HARDIN became a reborn Christian and a minister in Lake Arrowhead, California. • EARL HOLLIMAN, with canine stars BENJI and LASSIE presides over Actors and Others For Animals, dedicated to the promotion of humane treatment for animals. • BILLY CRYSTAL, WHOOPI GOLDBERG and ROBIN WILLIAMS spearhead the annual telethon, Comic Relief, using humor to raise funds to aid the homeless in the United States.

DANNY GLOVER trägt sein Plakat Boycott Grapes in New York City. • PAUL NEWMAN stellt sich sein Oldstyle Picture Show Popcorn zusammen, ein Produkt, das er unter seinem Newman-Warenzeichen vermarktet. Der Gewinn geht an karitative Organisationen, die nicht dem Mainstream angehören. Dazu gehört u. a. The Hole in the Wall Gang Camp in Ashford, Connecticut, für krebskranke Kinder. • ALAN ALDA schließt sich 1980 seinem Vater ROBERT ALDA und befreundeten Schauspielern beim Streik der Screen Actors Guild an. • Der frühere Westernstar TY HARDIN fand zur Kirche zurück und wurde Pfarrer in Lake Arrowhead, Kalifornien. • EARL HOLLIMAN, hier mit BENJI und LASSIE, ist Vorsitzender des Verbandes „Schauspieler und Andere für Tiere", der die menschenwürdige Behandlung von Tieren fordert. • BILLY CRYSTAL, WHOOPI GOLDBERG und ROBIN WILLIAMS leiten die Spendenaktion Comic Relief, um Spenden für Obdachlose in den USA aufzubringen.

DANNY GLOVER manifeste pour le boycott du raisin à New York. • PAUL NEWMAN goûte à son popcorn Oldstyle Picture Show, qu'il commercialise sous la marque Newman's Own et dont la totalité des bénéfices de la vente est attribuée à des organisations caritatives moins classiques, comme l'association The Hole in the Wall Gang Camp de Ashford (Connecticut), qui s'occupe des enfants cancéreux. • ALAN ALDA rejoint son père ROBERT et ses amis acteurs lors de la grève de la Screen Actors Guild, en 1980. • TY HARDIN, vedette de westerns, a retrouvé le chemin de l'église en se faisant pasteur à Lake Arrowhead (Californie). • EARL HOLLIMAN, avec BENJI et LASSIE, préside l'association Actors and Others For Animals. • BILLY CRYSTAL, WHOOPI GOLDBERG et ROBIN WILLIAMS animent le téléthon annuel de Comic Relief, une association caritative qui utilise l'humour pour recueillir des fonds et aider les sans-abri des États-Unis.

JENNIFER LOVE HEWITT, *Milan Ryba* 1999

HARRISON FORD, *Nina Prommer* 1995

MARLEE MATLIN, *Milan Ryba* 1998

MINNIE DRIVER, *Milan Ryba* 1998

BETTE MIDLER, *Alex Oliveira* 1996

AUDREY HEPBURN, *John Barrett* 1991

JENNIFER LOVE HEWITT and MARLEE MATLIN serve up meals at the Los Angeles Mission's annual Thanksgiving Dinner for the homeless of Skid Row. • HARRISON FORD busses tables at the L.A. Mission. • MINNIE DRIVER is one of several celebrities who give weekly storybook readings for the children of Dolphin House, which provides for children of special needs. • BETTE MIDLER helps clean up Manhattan's Central Park as part of her commitment to her New York Restoration Project. • AUDREY HEPBURN, here at a volunteer rally at United Nations Plaza, became special ambassador to UNICEF in 1988. • MARTIN SHEEN is a primary advocate of causes and frequently marches for the environment, the homeless, nuclear disarmament and against US involvement in Nicaragua, the Gulf War and sanctions against Iraq. • EDWARD JAMES OLMOS works with kids from Para Los Ninos, entering its third decade of service to the needy in the inner city of Los Angeles. • ROBERT DUVALL marches with demonstrators demanding liberty for the oppressed in Puerto Rico. • JANE ALEXANDER appears before Congress as nominee for chairman of the National Endowment for the Arts. She was named to the post and served from 1993 to 1997. • MICHAEL J. FOX makes an appearance before the U.S. Senate to lobby for a hike in federal spending on Parkinsons Disease research. The plea from Fox, who suffers from Parkinsons, led to an initial increase of 10 million dollars.

JENNIFER LOVE HEWITT und MARLEE MATLIN geben anlässlich des jährlichen Dinner zum Erntedankfest in der Los Angeles Mission Essen an Obdachlose von Skid Row aus. • HARRISON FORD ist dort als Bedienung im Einsatz. • MINNIE DRIVER ist eine von mehreren Stars, die den Kindern vom Dolphin House jede Woche Geschichten vorlesen. Das Dolphin House nimmt sich Kindern mit speziellen Bedürfnissen an. • BETTE MIDLER hilft beim Sauberhalten des Central Park in Manhattan und leistet so ihren Anteil an ihrem New Yorker Restaurationsprojekt. • AUDREY HEPBURN, hier bei einer Versammlung am United Nations Plaza, wurde 1988 Botschafterin von UNICEF. • MARTIN SHEEN ist Verfechter aller Arten von Anliegen und marschiert regelmäßig für den Umweltschutz, Heimatlose, nukleare Abrüstung und Nichteinmischung der USA in Nicaragua, im Golfkrieg und für die Aufhebung der Sanktionen gegen den Irak. • EDWARD JAMES OLMOS arbeitet mit Kindern aus Para Los Ninos. Dies ist sein drittes Jahrzehnt im Dienste von Menschen in Not in der Innenstadt von Los Angeles. • ROBERT DUVALL demonstriert für die Freiheit der Unterdrückten in Puerto Rico. • JANE ALEXANDER tritt vor dem Kongress als Kandidatin für die Vorsitzende des Nationalen Schutzes der Kunst an. Sie wurde für den Posten gewählt und übte ihr Amt von 1993 bis 1997 aus. • MICHAEL J. FOX tritt vor dem US-Senat auf, um Spendengelder für die Forschung der Parkinson Krankheit aufzubringen. Der Appell von Fox, der selbst an der Krankheit leidet, führte zu einer anfänglichen Spendensumme von 10 Millionen Dollar.

Tandis que HARRISON FORD nettoie les tables, JENNIFER LOVE HEWITT et MARLEE MATLIN servent les repas lors du dîner annuel de Thanksgiving offert par la Mission de Los Angeles aux sans-abri de Skid Row. • MINNIE DRIVER est l'une des nombreuses personnalités à venir chaque semaine lire des contes à la Dolphin House, qui accueille des enfants ayant besoin de soins spécialisés. • À Manhattan, BETTE MIDLER participe au nettoyage de Central Park dans le cadre du New York Restoration Project qu'elle a mis sur pied. • AUDREY HEPBURN, ici lors d'un meeting de volontaires au United Nations Plaza, est devenue ambassadrice spéciale de l'UNICEF en 1988. • MARTIN SHEEN, l'un des champions des causes en tous genres, s'investit dans des actions en faveur de l'environnement, des sans-abri, du désarmement nucléaire ou contre l'implication américaine au Nicaragua, la guerre du Golfe ou les sanctions infligées à l'Irak. • EDWARD JAMES OLMOS, qui œuvre depuis 30 ans en faveur des nécessiteux de la ville de Los Angeles, est ici avec des enfants de l'association Para Los Ninos. • ROBERT DUVALL participe à la manifestation réclamant la liberté pour les oppressés à Puerto Rico • JANE ALEXANDER se présente devant le Congrès en tant que présidente du National Endowment for the Arts, un poste qu'elle occupa de 1993 à 1997. • MICHAEL J. FOX fait une apparition devant le Sénat américain pour soutenir la demande d'augmentation des dépenses fédérales pour la recherche contre la maladie de Parkinson. La plaidoirie de Fox, qui souffrait de ce mal, contribua à débloquer 10 millions de dollars.

MARTIN SHEEN, *John Barrett* 1984

EDWARD JAMES OLMOS, *Craig Skinner* 1991

ROBERT DUVALL, *Bill Crespinel* 1979

JANE ALEXANDER, *James M. Kelly* 1993

MICHAEL J. FOX, *James M. Kelly* 1999

PRESIDENT BILL CLINTON AND BARBRA STREISAND, *James M. Kelly* 1993

PIERCE BROSNAN, *Milan Ryba* 2000

KATHLEEN TURNER, *James M. Kelly* 1995

RICHARD GERE, *Adam Scull* 1989

AL PACINO, *Rita Katz* 1983

TIM ROBBINS, SUSAN SARANDON AND KURT VONNEGUT, *Adam Scull* 1991

PAUL NEWMAN AND CHRISTOPHER REEVE, *Janet C. Koltick* 1995

BARBRA STREISAND greets newly elected U.S. President BILL CLINTON at the inaugural gala in Washington D.C. • PIERCE BROSNAN spearheads the campaign to save the whales. • KATHLEEN TURNER speaks out for Healthy Women 2000, educational programs highlighting the most prominent and previously neglected health issues of women. • RICHARD GERE, president of the International Campaign for Tibet, at a demonstration of the rare Tibetian art form of butter sculpture with Tibetan monks from Gyute Tantric Monastery. • AL PACINO speaks at a tribute to Lee Strasberg benefiting the Actors Studio in New York. • With writer KURT VONNEGUT are SUSAN SARANDON and TIM ROBBINS who bring their son Jack to the Peace Rally at Columbia University. • PAUL NEWMAN looks on as CHRISTOPHER REEVE speaks before the American Paralysis Association.

BARBRA STREISAND begrüßt den frisch gewählten US-Präsidenten BILL CLINTON auf der Eröffnungsfeier in Washington D.C. • PIERCE BROSNAN leitet die Kampagne zur Rettung der Wale. • KATHLEEN TURNER setzt sich für Gesunde Frauen 2000 ein. Dabei handelt es sich um Bildungsprogramme, die die wichtigsten und zuvor vernachlässigten Gesundheitsprobleme von Frauen zur Sprache bringen. • RICHARD GERE, Präsident der Internationalen Kampagne für Tibet, sieht sich zusammen mit tibetischen Mönchen aus dem Kloster Gyute Tantricdie seltene Kunstform der Butterskulpturen an. • AL PACINO spricht bei einer Feier zu Ehren von Lee Strasberg zu Gunsten des Actors Studio in New York. • SUSAN SARANDON und TIM ROBBINS bringen ihren Sohn Jack in Begleitung des Schriftstellers KURT VONNEGUT zur Friedensdemonstration an der Columbia University. • PAUL NEWMAN ist bei der Rede von CHRISTOPHER REEVE vor der American Paralysis Association anwesend.

BARBRA STREISAND salue BILL CLINTON, qui vient d'être élu président des États-Unis, lors du gala inaugural à Washington D.C. • PIERCE BROSNAN en campagne pour le sauvetage des baleines. • KATHLEEN TURNER prononçant un discours lors du Healthy Women 2000, un ensemble de programmes éducatifs orientés vers les problèmes de santé des femmes. • RICHARD GERE, président de la Campagne internationale pour le Tibet, lors d'une manifestation sur l'art tibétain et ses sculptures à base de beurre, en présence des moines tibétains du monastère tantrique de Gyute. • AL PACINO prend la parole lors d'une soirée d'hommage à Lee Strasberg donnée en faveur de l'Actors Studio de New York. • SUSAN SARANDON et TIM ROBBINS, accompagnés par l'écrivain KURT VONNEGUT, sont venus avec leur fils Jack à la manifestation pour la Paix de la Columbia University. • PAUL NEWMAN regarde CHRISTOPHER REEVE pendant son discours devant l'American Paralysis Association.

HARRY HAMLIN, *Fitzroy Barrett* 2000

ALEC BALDWIN, *Andrea Renault* 1999

SALMA HAYEK, *Milan Ryba* 2000

HARRY HAMLIN speaks out at a rally in support of this year's SAG/AFTRA strike against advertisers. • ALEC BALDWIN is thrown in the Hudson River but it's all for a good cause. Baldwin, a conservationist, took the leap to support Riverkeepers, dedicated to cleaning up our waterways. • SALMA HAYEK, with JOHNNY GRANT, DANICA McKELLER and Garrett Morris, headlines the USO Operation Starlift, en route to visit peacekeeping troops in Bosnia, Macedonia and Kosovo.

HARRY HAMLIN spricht bei einer Versammlung zur Unterstützung des diesjährigen SAG/AFTRA-Streiks gegen Werbemacher. • ALEC BALDWIN wird für einen guten Zweck in den Hudson River gestoßen. Baldwin ist Umweltschützer und wagte den Sprung, um Riverkeepers, eine Organisation, die gegen die Verschmutzung von Gewässern kämpft, zu unterstützen. • SALMA HAYEK, mit JOHNNY GRANT, DANICA McKELLER und Garrett Morris, begleiten die USO Operation Starlift, die gerade auf dem Weg ist, Friedenstruppen in Bosnien, Mazedonien und im Kosovo zu besuchen.

HARRY HAMLIN prenant la parole lors d'une manifestation de soutien de la grève du SAG/AFTRA contre les publicitaires. • ALEC BALDWIN est jeté dans l'Hudson mais pour la bonne cause puisque c'est pour soutenir l'action des Riverkeepers, une unité spécialisée dans le nettoyage des cours d'eau. • SALMA HAYEK, avec JOHNNY GRANT, DANICA McKELLER et Garrett Morris, mettent en vedette l'opération Starlift de l'USO (United Service Organizations) avant d'aller voir les troupes américaines en Bosnie, en Macédoine et au Kosovo.

RM DOLORES HART, *Richard DeNeut* 2000

A rising young actress in the late 50s, DOLORES HART was considered heiress-apparent to the Grace Kelly mantle when she abruptly quit Hollywood in 1963 for a new life as a nun in the cloistered Benedictine Abbey of Regina Laudis in Bethlehem, Connecticut. Hollywood wags predicted she would last as long as June Haver, another film actress who had joined a religious order but left within a few months. In 1991, Reverend Mother Dolores Hart celebrated the silver jubilee of her first vows. Here Mother Dolores (center) joins Reverend Mother Benedict Duss, abbess of Regina Laudis (right), and other members of the community in rehearsal for their second recording of Gregorian chants entitled WOMEN IN CHANT: RECORDARE. The first, released in 1998, became a major hit in the commercial world of recorded music so she seems to be still in touch with show business.

In den späten 50er Jahren war DOLORES HART eine junge, aufstrebende Schauspielerin, die als würdige Nachfolgerin von Grace Kelly angesehen wurde, als sie plötzlich Hollywood verließ und 1963 ein neues Leben als Nonne im Benediktinerkloster Regina Laudis in Bethlehem, Connecticut, anfing. So mancher Witzbold aus Hollywood sagte voraus, dass sie dort genauso lange bleiben würde wie June Haver, eine weitere Filmschauspielerin, die einem religiösen Orden beigetreten war, diesen aber wieder innerhalb weniger Monate verließ. 1991 feierte die Mutter Oberin Dolores Hart ihr silbernes Jubiläum ihrer ersten Gelübde. Hier versammeln sich Mutter Dolores (Mitte) und Mutter Oberin Benedict Duss, Äbtissin von Regina Laudis (rechts), mit anderen Mitgliedern der Gemeinde, um für die zweite Aufnahme von gregorianischen Gesängen mit dem Titel WOMEN IN CHANT: RECORDARE zu proben. Die erste Aufnahme aus dem Jahre 1998 wurde in der ein großer kommerzieller Erfolg. Somit scheint sich Dolores Hart nicht ganz aus dem Showgeschäft zurückgezogen zu haben.

Jeune actrice montante de la fin des années 1950, DOLORES HART était considérée comme la digne héritière de Grace Kelly lorsqu'elle abandonna soudain Hollywood en 1963 pour devenir religieuse au monastère bénédictin Regina Laudis de Bethlehem (Connecticut). Les mauvaises langues de Hollywood prédirent qu'elle n'allait pas tenir plus longtemps que June Haver, une autre actrice qui était entrée dans les ordres mais en sortit au bout de quelques mois. En 1991, la révérende mère Dolores Hart célébrait son jubilée d'argent! On voit ici mère Dolores (au centre) avec la révérende mère Benedict Duss (à droite), abbesse de Regina Laudis, et d'autres religieuses de la communauté pendant les répétitions de leur second enregistrement de chants grégoriens intitulé WOMEN IN CHANT: RECORDARE. Le premier disque, publié en 1998, ayant été un succès, on pourrait dire que mère Dolores est restée d'une certaine manière en contact avec le monde du show business.

SOPHIA LOREN AND CARLO PONTI, *Bill Kobrin* 1961

HOLLYWOOD AT PLAY

THE BEVERLY HILTON

GEORGIE JESSEL, ROSALIND RUSSELL, GROUCHO MARX, FRANK SINATRA, DINAH SHORE, DEAN MARTIN, DANNY KAYE AND IRVING BERLIN, *Nate Cutler* 1964

The great IRVING BERLIN offers an impromptu concert at FRANK SINATRA'S party in his honor. Some high-priced talent joins him in song.

Der große IRVING BERLIN gibt ein spontanes Konzert bei der Party, die FRANK SINATRA zu seinen Ehren gab. Einige Stars singen mit.

Le grand IRVING BERLIN, accompagné par quelques artistes de talent, offre un concert impromptu lors de la soirée organisée en son honneur par FRANK SINATRA.

PAMELA ANDERSON AND BRETT MICHAELS, *John Barrett* 1996

REST AND REHABILITATION

By far the most in-demand area of Globe Photos' sixty years of documenting Hollywood life has been its candid coverage of the stars at play. Globe has long syndicated, to magazines and newspapers at home and abroad, a weekly service of celebrities at parties and premieres, in nightclubs and on baseball diamonds, in formal dress or kiddie costume, capturing spontaneous moments to be preserved in print for posterity.

For many of those years shot by one photographer, Nate Cutler, this service has continued decade after decade utilizing many top photographers on both U.S. coasts and overseas. These include Bob Noble, Fitzroy Barrett, Ralph Dominguez, Michael Ferguson, Lisa Rose, Tom Rodriguez, Milan Ryba, Travis Lehman and Nina Prommer on the west coast. In the east: John Barrett, Irv Steinberg, Andrea Renault, Adam Scull, Walter Weissman, Sonia Moskowitz, Henry McGee, James M. Kelly, Rose Hartman, Michael Norcia, Trish Meadows and Steve Trupp.

In Hollywood, parties aren't just social occasions. They can be important business opportunities, used to strengthen relationships, flatter the powerful and meet people who don't return phone calls. Mostly they are used as a spotlight to get attention for a new film or a new star or a new deal that may have been made at a previous party. This social arena, widened to include sporting activities, is a relatively painless way to get the job done and provides celebrities with a little rest and rehabilitation along the way.

RUHE UND ERHOLUNG

In den 60 Jahren, in denen Globe Photos das Leben in Hollywood dokumentiert hat, waren enthüllende Fotoreportagen aus dem Privatleben der Stars am meisten gefragt. Seit langem beliefert Globe Zeitschriften und Zeitungen aus dem In- und Ausland wöchentlich mit Artikeln über die Stars bei Partys und Premieren, in Nachtclubs und auf Baseballfeldern, in Gesellschaftsanzügen oder Freizeitkleidung, und hält so Augenblicke für die Nachwelt fest.

Viele Jahre hindurch schoss ein einziger Fotograf, Nate Cutler, diese Fotos. Dieser Service hatte über die Jahrzehnte Bestand und wird von vielen Top-Fotografen, die sowohl an der Ost- als auch an der Westküste der USA und in Übersee leben, bedient. Unter anderem von Spitzen-Fotografen wie Bob Noble, Fitzroy Barrett, Ralph Dominguez, Michael Ferguson, Lisa Rose, Tom Rodriguez, Milan Ryba, Travis Lehman und Nina Prommer an der Westküste und John Barrett, Irv Steinberg, Andrea Renault, Adam Scull, Walter Weissman, Sonia Moskowitz, Henry McGee, James M. Kelly, Rose Hartman, Michael Norcia, Trish Meadows und Steve Trupp an der Ostküste.

In Hollywood sind Partys nicht nur gesellschaftliche Anlässe. Sie bieten die Gelegenheiten, ins Geschäft zu kommen: Man kann Bekanntschaften festigen, den Mächtigen schmeicheln und Leute treffen, die einen doch nicht zurückrufen. Üblicherweise dienen Partys dazu, die Aufmerksamkeit auf einen neuen Film oder Schauspieler zu lenken oder auf ein Geschäft, das auf einer vorhergehenden Party geschlossen wurde. Diese gesellschaftliche Bühne beinhaltet sportliche Aktivitäten, bietet die Gelegenheit, auf eine relativ schmerzlose Art und Weise die Arbeit zu bewältigen und verschafft den Stars ein wenig Erholung und Ruhe.

REPOS ET RÉHABILITATION

Les photographies de stars en extérieur représentent sans doute le type d'illustration le plus demandé à Globe Photos au cours de ces soixante années d'activité. Globe a notamment fourni à la presse américaine et étrangère un service hebdomadaire de reportages sur les célébrités, en tenue classique ou en costume de fantaisie, réalisés lors de soirées mondaines ou de premières, dans des nightclubs ou sur un terrain de base-ball, qui permettaient de conserver à jamais pour la postérité ces moments de spontanéité qu'offraient les vedettes, prises sur le vif par le photographe.

Cette couverture événementielle, dont Nate Cutler s'est occupé pendant de nombreuses années, est alors assurée aux États-Unis et à l'étranger par nombre de photographes de premier plan. Sur la côte Ouest, on peut citer Bob Noble, Fitzroy Barrett, Ralph Dominguez, Michael Ferguson, Lisa Rose, Tom Rodriguez, Milan Ryba, Travis Lehman et Nina Prommer ; tandis que John Barrett, Irv Steinberg, Andrea Renault, Adam Scull, Walter Weissman, Sonia Moskowitz, Henry McGee, James M. Kelly, Rose Hartman, Michael Norcia, Trish Meadows et Steve Trupp s'occupent de la côte Est des États-Unis.

Les réceptions qui se donnent à Hollywood ne sont pas uniquement des réunions mondaines. Elles sont également l'occasion de traiter des affaires importantes, de nouer des relations ou de les renforcer, de courtiser les puissants et de rencontrer tous ceux qui ne répondent jamais au téléphone. Plus souvent encore, elles permettent de braquer les projecteurs de la presse événementielle sur un nouveau film, une nouvelle star ou la signature d'un nouveau contrat (éventuellement élaboré lors d'une soirée précédente). Cette arène sociale, qui s'élargit parfois aux activités sportives, est finalement, pour les vedettes, un moyen assez agréable et peu fatigant d'exercer son métier.

FRED ASTAIRE, *Nate Cutler* 1979

ADELE ASTAIRE, *Nate Cutler* 1979

FRED AND AVA ASTAIRE, *Nate Cutler* 1979

FRED ASTAIRE celebrates his 80th birthday with family, who join him in a test of skill in the game Pop. He had just learned that the newly revived LIBERTY magazine, a major publication of the 30s and 40s, had named him the performer of the half century. The editors invited him to attend a luncheon in his honor and during the whole birthday party he was grumbling about having to attend. Finally his exasperated daughter AVA said, "Daddy, if you don't want to go, don't go." Fred thought for a moment and answered, "If I don't go, it would be rude. And then they'll give it to someone else – which would be wrong."

FRED ASTAIRE feiert seinen 80. Geburtstag im Kreise der Familie. Fred hatte soeben herausgefunden, dass die wieder aufgelegte Zeitschrift LIBERTY, eine der großen Publikationen der 30er und 40er, ihn zum Darsteller des halben Jahrhunderts gewählt hatte. Um ihn zu ehren, luden ihn die Herausgeber zum Mittagessen ein und die ganze Geburtstagsparty hindurch beschwerte er sich darüber, daran teilnehmen zu müssen. Schließlich sagte ihm seine verärgerte Tochter AVA: „Papi, wenn du nicht dahin gehen willst, dann geh nicht." Fred dachte einen Moment lang nach und antwortete:„Es wäre unhöflich, wenn ich nicht gehen würde. Außerdem würden sie die Auszeichnung dann jemand anderem geben, was nicht richtig wäre."

Lors de ses 80 ans, FRED ASTAIRE teste son habileté à un jeu appelé Pop que lui a offert sa famille. Fred venant d'apprendre que le magazine LIBERTY, une publication importante des années 1930 et 1940 qui recommençait à paraître, l'avait désigné comme l'acteur de la première moitié du siècle, il ne cessa de grommeler pendant tout son anniversaire en se plaignant de devoir assister au dîner que les éditeurs voulaient organiser en son honneur. Agacée, sa fille AVA lui dit finalement : « Papa, si tu ne veux pas y aller, n'y va pas. » Fred réfléchit un instant et répondit : « Ce serait impoli de ne pas m'y rendre. Et ils attribueront le prix à quelqu'un d'autre – ce qui serait une erreur. »

HENRY, SHIRLEE, PETER AND JANE FONDA, *Nate Cutler* 1980

MILTON BERLE, *Don Ornitz* 1965

PAUL NEWMAN AND ROBERT REDFORD, *Robert Fitzgerald* 1975

HENRY FONDA celebrates his 75th birthday and 50th anniversary in show business with wife SHIRLEE and children PETER and JANE. Each year on MILTON BERLE'S birthday, he charters a bus to take friends to Dodger's Stadium to watch the Dodgers play ball. Left to right: DEAN MARTIN, BERLE, DAVID JANSSEN, JACK BENNY, POLLY BERGEN. • PAUL NEWMAN plays the waiter for ROBERT REDFORD at Newman's 50th birthday party at Le Cave Henry IV in New York.

HENRY FONDA feiert seinen 75. Geburtstag und sein 50. Jahr im Showgeschäft, mit seiner Frau SHIRLEE und Kindern PETER und JANE. Jedes Jahr auf MILTON BERLES Geburtstag, mietet er einen Bus, um Freunde zu einem Baseballspiel ins Stadion der Dodgers zu fahren. Von links nach rechts: DEAN MARTIN, BERLE, DAVID JANSSEN, JACK BENNY, POLLY BERGEN. • PAUL NEWMAN spielt den Kellner für ROBERT REDFORD auf Newmans 50. Geburtstag im Le Cave Henry IV in New York.

HENRY FONDA célèbre son 75ᵉ anniversaire et ses 50 ans dans le show business avec son épouse SHIRLEE et ses enfants PETER et JANE. À chacun de ses anniversaires, MILTON BERLE loue un autocar et emmène ses amis au Dodger's Stadium assister à une partie de base-ball des Dodgers. On reconnaît, de gauche à droite : DEAN MARTIN, MILTON BERLE, DAVID JANSSEN, JACK BENNY et POLLY BERGEN. • PAUL NEWMAN joue les serveurs pour ROBERT REDFORD lors de la soirée des 50 ans de Newman à La Cave Henry IV de New York.

JOHN CARRADINE AND FAMILY, *Nate Cutler* 1974

JOHN CARRADINE celebrates his 68th birthday with the Carradine clan: his five sons, ROBERT, CHRISTOPHER, KEITH, BRUCE and DAVID, and David's significant other, BARBARA HERSHEY and their son, FREE.

JOHN CARRADINE feiert seinen 68. Geburstag mit dem Carradine-Clan: seinen fünf Söhnen, ROBERT, CHRISTOPHER, KEITH, BRUCE und DAVID, und mit Davids Partnerin BARBARA HERSHEY und ihrem gemeinsamen Sohn FREE.

JOHN CARRADINE fête son 68e anniversaire avec le clan Carradine : ses cinq fils – ROBERT, CHRISTOPHER, KEITH, BRUCE et DAVID – ainsi que BARBARA HERSHEY et son fils FREE, qu'elle a eu de David.

MARLENE DIETRICH AND MARIA RIVA, *Globe Archive* 1970

ALFRED AND ALMA HITCHCOCK, LARAINE DAY AND PATRICIA HITCHCOCK, *Nate Cutler* 1955

RAY WALSTON, TONY CURTIS, JACK AND FELICIA LEMMON, BILLY WILDER, KIM NOVAK, DEAN MARTIN, *Jack Harris* 1964

STEVE MARTIN AND CARL REINER, *Nate Cutler* 1980

A celebration in New York for MARLENE DIETRICH with daughter MARIA RIVA. • ALFRED HITCHCOCK can't resist getting a bit macabre at his 56th. • BILLY WILDER'S 58th on the set of KISS ME, STUPID. • CARL REINER gets some "help" from STEVE MARTIN.

Eine Feier für MARLENE DIETRICH, mit ihrer Tochter MARIA RIVA in New York. • ALFRED HITCHCOCK kann es nicht lassen, an seinem 56. Geburtstag etwas makaber zu werden. • BILLY WILDERS 58. bei den Dreharbeiten zu KÜSS MICH, DUMMKOPF (KISS ME, STUPID). • CARL REINER bekommt „Hilfe" von STEVE MARTIN.

Petite fête à New York pour MARLENE DIETRICH avec sa fille MARIA RIVA. • ALFRED HITCHCOCK ne peut résister à faire un peu d'humour macabre lors de son 56ᵉ anniversaire. • BILLY WILDER célèbre ses 58 ans sur le plateau de EMBRASSE-MOI, IDIOT (KISS ME, STUPID). • CARL REINER se fait « aider » par STEVE MARTIN.

ANTHONY AND FRANCESCO QUINN, *Nate Cutler* 1969

URSULA AND ROBERT TAYLOR, RONALD AND NANCY REAGAN, *Nate Cutler* 1964

CYBILL SHEPHERD, *Andrea Renault* 2000

EDGAR, FRANCES, CHRISTOPHERAND CANDICE BERGEN, *Nate Cutler* 1978

LIZA MINNELLI AND HARVEY KEITEL AT STUDIO 54, *Adam Scull* 1991

BROOKE SHIELDS, *Hy Simon* 1977

SONNY, CHER AND CHASTITY BONO, *John R. Hamilton* 1971

TOM JONES WITH JOAN RIVERS, SONNY BONO, JAMES DARREN,
DIONNE WARWICK, DEBBIE REYNOLDS AND LIBERACE, *Nate Cutler* 1974

JESSICA SIMPSON, *Tom Rodriguez* 2000

ANTHONY QUINN with son FRANCESCO on his 7th birthday. • The ROBERT TAYLORS help RONALD REAGAN celebrate at Chasen's. • CYBILL SHEPHERD'S 50th. • EDGAR BERGEN celebrates his 75th • ERROL FLYNN cast against type at daughter RORY'S birthday. • EDDIE CANTOR'S 62nd birthday cake was decorated with rolled up dollar bills instead of candles. • YVONNE DeCARLO gets in the spirit on son BRUCE'S 4th birthday. • JANE FONDA celebrates her 60th in Atlanta, Georgia.

ANTHONY QUINN mit seinem Sohn FRANCESCO an dessen 7. Geburtstag. • ROBERT TAYLOR und Frau feiern mit RONALD REAGAN im Chasen's. • CYBILL SHEPHERDS 50. Geburtstag. • EDGAR BERGEN feiert seinen 75. • EDDIE CANTORS Geburtstagskuchen zum 62. wurde mit aufgerollten Dollarscheinen anstatt mit Kerzen dekoriert. • YVONNE DeCARLO amüsiert sich auf dem Geburtstag ihres Sohnes BRUCE, der 4 Jahre alt wird. • JANE FONDA feiert ihren 60. in Atlanta, Georgia.

ANTHONY QUINN fête les 7 ans de son fils Francesco. • ROBERT TAYLOR et son épouse à l'anniversaire de Ronald Reagan au Chasen's. • Les 50 ans de CYBILL SHEPHERD. • EDGAR BERGEN célèbre son 75e anniversaire. • ERROL FLYNN en contre-emploi à l'anniversaire de sa fille Rory. • Le gâteau d'anniversaire des 62 ans de EDDIE CANTOR était décoré de dollars roulés à la place des bougies. • YVONNE DeCARLO fait la fête aux 4 ans de son fils Bruce. • JANE FONDA fête ses 60 ans à Atlanta (Georgie).

ERROL AND RORY FLYNN, *Larry Barbier Jr.* 1953

EDDIE AND IDA CANTOR, *Globe Archive* 1954

YVONNE DeCARLO AND SON BRUCE, *Nate Cutler* 1960

JANE FONDA, *John Barrett* 1997

CARL REINER and BEA LILLIE cozy up at Ross Hunter's party for the British comedienne. • SHELLEY WINTERS takes a fruit-filled rubber boat ride in Harold Robbin's pool. • GREGORY PECK is having a swell time at a "social" hosted by the matrons of the Wamsatta Club of New Bedford in honor of the MOBY DICK company filming in their area.

CARL REINER AND BEA LILLIE, *Nate Cutler* 1966

SHELLEY WINTERS, *Nate Cutler* 1973

CARL REINER und BEA LILLIE kommen sich auf Ross Hunters Party, zu Ehren der britischen Komikerin, näher. • SHELLEY WINTERS dreht in Harold Robbins Pool auf einem mit Früchten beladenen Gummiboot eine Runde. • GREGORY PECK amüsiert sich auf einem Treffen, das von den Damen des Wamsatta Club in New Bedford zu Ehren der Filmgesellschaft MOBY DICK, die in ihrer Gegend drehen, veranstaltet wird.

Gros baiser de CARL REINER à BEA LILLIE lors de la soirée donnée par Ross Hunter pour la comédienne britannique. • SHELLEY WINTERS rame dans la piscine de Harold Robbin. • GREGORY PECK lors de la soirée mondaine offerte par les matrones du Wamsatta Club de New Bedford en l'honneur des acteurs de MOBY DICK venus tourner dans leur région.

GREGORY AND VERONIQUE PECK, *Tom Caffrey* 1956

DOLORES GRAY, KATHRYN GRAYSON, HOWARD KEEL, ESTHER WILLIAMS
AND ANN MILLER, *Nate Cutler* 1950

HEDY LAMARR AND ROBERT STACK, *Nate Cutler* 1955

DEBBIE REYNOLDS AND LESLIE CARON, *Dave Sutton*1953

VIVIEN LEIGH AND LAURENCE OLIVIER, *Nate Cutler* 1949

BARBARA HALE, CLINT EASTWOOD, ANNE NEYLAND AND JOHN ERICSON,
Larry Barbier Jr. 1957

HELEN HAYES, JOAN CRAWFORD AND JUDY GARLAND, *Nate Cutler* 1953

MAURICE CHEVALIER AND SHIRLEY MACLAINE, *Nate Cutler* 1960

BARBRA STREISAND, DIANA AND ROSLYN KIND, *Nate Cutler* 1977

KEN MAYNARD, LEE MARVIN AND BETTY HUTTON, *Nate Cutler* 1970

WILL SMITH, *Lisa Rose* 1996

WILL SMITH is caked by fellow cast members at the final wrap party for the TV series FRESH PRINCE OF BEL AIR. • DEBBIE REYNOLDS is the surprise Santa at the annual Hollywood Women's Press Club Christmas party. • JON VOIGHT relaxes at a pizza and wine party. • DUSTIN HOFFMAN and KEIR DULLEA arm wrestle at the Variety Club's tribute to Jack Valenti in New York. • SALLY FIELD, then TV's Flying Nun, really goes flying as ALEJANDRO REY and DAVID SOUL toss her into the pool at Hacienda Cocoyoc in Mexico City. • ELEANOR PARKER gives ROBERT WAGNER a whiff of her new perfume. • Charades is the centerpiece of SUZANNE PLESHETTE and TROY DONAHUE'S home party with JAMES STACY coaxing answers out of CONNIE STEVENS, TROY and SUZANNE, and ARTE JOHNSON.

WILL SMITH wird auf der Abschlussparty für die Fernsehserie DER PRINZ VON BEL AIR (FRESH PRINCE OF BEL AIR) von Mitgliedern der Filmbesetzung mit Kuchen beschmissen. • DEBBIE REYNOLDS spielt auf der jährlichen Weihnachtsfeier des Frauenpresseclubs in Hollywood den Überraschungs-Nikolaus. • JON VOIGHT entspannt sich auf einer Party mit Pizza und Wein. • DUSTIN HOFFMAN und KEIR DULLEA beim Armdrücken auf der Party des Variety Clubs zu Ehren von Jack Valenti in New York. • SALLY FIELD, damals aus dem Fernsehen als fliegende Nonne bekannt, geht dieses Mal wirklich fliegen, als sie von ALEJANDRO REY und DAVID SOUL in den Pool auf der Hacienda Cocoyoc in Mexico City gestoßen wird. • ELEANOR PARKER gibt ROBERT WAGNER eine Kostprobe ihres neuen Parfums. • SUZANNE PLESHETTE und TROY DONAHUE schmeißen bei sich zu Hause eine Party. Weitere Gäste sind JAMES STACY, CONNIE STEVENS, TROY und SUZANNE und ARTE JOHNSON.

WILL SMITH se fait entartrer par ses partenaires lors de la soirée de fin de tournage de la série télé FRESH PRINCE OF BEL AIR. • DEBBIE REYNOLDS déguisée en Père Noël pour la soirée annuelle de l'Hollywood Women's Press Club. • JON VOIGHT se relâche un peu lors d'une soirée « vin et pizza ». • DUSTIN HOFFMAN et KEIR DULLEA font un bras de fer lors de la soirée d'hommage à Jack Valenti donnée au Variety Club de New York. • Projetée par ALEJANDRO REY et DAVID SOUL, SALLY FIELD, qui jouait alors dans la série télé THE FLYING NUN, s'envole au-dessus de la piscine de l'Hacienda Cocoyoc, à Mexico. • ELEANOR PARKER fait sentir son nouveau parfum à ROBERT WAGNER • JAMES STACY, CONNIE STEVENS, TROY et SUZANNE, et ARTE JOHNSON jouent aux charades lors de la soirée donnée par SUZANNE PLESHETTE et TROY DONAHUE.

DEBBIE REYNOLDS AND GREGORY PECK, *Nate Cutler* 1969

JON VOIGHT WITH HARRY AND CAROL NORTHRUP, *Ron Thal* 1970

DUSTIN HOFFMAN AND KEIR DULLEA, *Irv Steinberg* 1968

SALLY FIELD, ALEJANDRO REY AND DAVID SOUL, *Bill Greenslade* 1968

ELEANOR PARKER AND ROBERT WAGNER, *Nate Cutler* 1963

CONNIE STEVENS, TROY DONAHUE, SUZANNE PLESHETTE, ARTE JOHNSON
AND JAMES STACY, *Don Ornitz* 1964

Newlyweds TAYLOR and FISHER duet at their party for the Moiseyev Ballet company. • MICKEY ROONEY and RAY ANTHONY toot their horns while MARILYN MONROE joins on drums at the party to introduce Anthony's composition MARILYN.

TAYLOR und FISHER, frisch verheiratet, singen ein Duett auf ihrer Party für das Moiseyev Ballet. • MICKEY ROONEY und RAY ANTHONY spielen Trompete, während MARILYN MONROE sie auf dem Schlagzeug begleitet – bei einer Party, auf der Anthonys Komposition MARILYN vorgestellt wurde.

MICKEY ROONEY, MARILYN MONROE AND RAY ANTHONY, *Nate Cutler* 1953

DAN DAILEY, *Nate Cutler* 1969

EDDIE FISHER AND ELIZABETH TAYLOR, *Nate Cutler* 1961

SAMMY DAVIS JR., ROBERT MITCHUM, DEAN MARTIN, JAMES GARNER AND PAUL NEWMAN, *Nate Cutler* 1963

TAYLOR et FISHER, nouvellement mariés, font un duo lors de la soirée en l'honneur de la compagnie de ballet Moiseyev. • MICKEY ROONEY et RAY ANTHONY font sonner les trompettes tandis que MARILYN MONROE joue de la batterie lors de la soirée de présentation de MARILYN, une composition d'Anthony.

SHARE'S annual Boomtown party benefiting deprived children is the wettest bash in town, as STEVE McQUEEN demonstrates. • MADONNA models for designer Jean-Paul Gaultier at an AIDS benefit and raises the ante by lowering her top. • Inhibitions fade at the annual Cannes Film Festival. WOODY HARRELSON is tied up in knots and SHARON STONE performs a rousing number to raise money for AIDS research.

MADONNA, *Michael Ferguson* 1992

STEVE McQUEEN AND JOHN WAYNE, *Nate Cutler* 1970

WOODY HARRELSON, *Albert Ferreira* 1998

SHARON STONE, *Fitzroy Barrett* 1998

STEVE McQUEEN auf der Boomtown-Party der Organisation SHARE zu Gunsten benachteiligter Kinder. • MADONNA modelt auf einer AIDS-Gala für Jean-Paul Gaultier und erhöht die Spenden, indem sie ihren Oberkörper entblößt. • Hemmungslos: Auf dem Filmfestival in Cannes verrenkt sich WOODY HARRELSON und SHARON STONE gibt ein mitreißendes Konzert, um Geld für die AIDS-Forschung zu sammeln.

SHARE, une association de célébrités s'occupant des enfants déshérités, organise chaque année le Boomtown, une soirée qui a la réputation d'être la plus arrosée de toutes, comme en témoigne STEVE McQUEEN. • MADONNA, mannequin vedette de Jean-Paul Gaultier, a fait scandale en enlevant le haut lors d'une présentation au bénéfice de l'association AIDS. WOODY HARRELSON montre sa souplesse. • L'atmosphère du festival de Cannes permet aux vedettes de se débarrasser de leurs inhibitions, comme ici SHARON STONE.

DOLORES HART (AS SPUTNIK) AND VINCE EDWARDS, *Nate Cutler* 1960

JOHNNY WEISSMULLER, FRED MACMURRAY, JOHN WAYNE, FRED HALSEY, JEANNE CRAIN AND RED SKELTON, *Nate Cutler* 1955

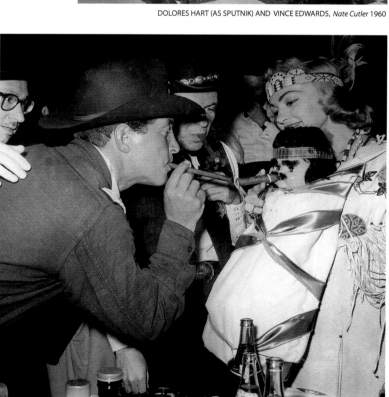

DEAN MARTIN, FRANK SINATRA AND EDIE ADAMS, *Nate Cutler* 1957

JANE WYMAN, *Nate Cutler* 1952

JULIET PROWSE AND FRANK SINATRA, *Nate Cutler* 1960

JERRY COLONNA AND LOU COSTELLO, *Nate Cutler* 1958

SID CAESAR AND LARRY HAGMAN, *Nate Cutler* 1980

HERMES PAN AND RITA HAYWORTH, *Nate Cutler* 1970

BURT AND NORMA LANCASTER, *Nate Cutler* 1959

VIRGINIA MAYO AND JUDY HOLLIDAY, *Nate Cutler* 1957

BARBRA STREISAND AND WILLIAM WYLER, *Nate Cutler* 1969

PEGGY LEE AND PATTI PAGE, *Nate Cutler* 1970

RAQUEL WELCH AND PATRICK CURTIS, *Nate Cutler* 1969

RICHARD BURTON, ELIZABETH TAYLOR AND ARISTOTLE ONASSIS, *Globe Archive* 1967

ROBERT AND MARY CUMMINGS, *Nate Cutler* 1964

POLLY BERGEN AND FREDDIE FIELDS, *Nate Cutler* 1969

BETTY GRABLE AND HARRY JAMES, *Nate Cutler* 1955

SALLY STRUTHERS AND SAMMY DAVIS JR., *Nate Cutler* 1973

CICELY TYSON AND PAUL WINFIELD, *Nate Cutler* 1972

JANE RUSSELL AND FRANKLYN PANGBORN, *Nate Cutler* 1971

DENICE DARCEL AND MARTHA RAYE, *Nate Cutler* 1955

SOPHIA LOREN AND JAYNE MANSFIELD, *Nate Cutler* 1958

EDIE ADAMS, JOHN GARY AND RUDOLF NUREYEV, *Nate Cutler* 1959

OMAR SHARIF AND CLAUDIA CARDINALE, *Nate Cutler* 1963

Peek-a-boo time. But to illustrate how important timing can be, our photographer's shot of LOREN meeting MANSFIELD was taken a split second after the now famous photo showing Loren registering both disbelief and fear that she might be struck by them.

Einen Blick erhaschen. Dieser Schnappschuss von LOREN und MANSFIELD zeigt, wie wichtig das Timing sein kann. Er wurde nur kurz nach dem heute berühmten Foto aufgenommen, auf dem Loren ungläubig und ängstlich die Dimensionen ihrer Nachbarin wahrnimmt.

Cache-cache. Le « timing » est très important en photojournalisme : la photo de LOREN rencontrant MANSFIELD fut prise quelques secondes après la photo devenue célèbre de Loren montrant son incrédulité et sa crainte d'avoir pu être découverte.

AUDREY HEPBURN AND HUBERT GIVENCHI, *Adam Scull* 1982

MIRA SORVINO AND GIORGIO ARMANI, *Albert Ferreira* 1998

DALE ROBERTSON AND DURANTE, *Nate Cutler* 1968

DURANTE AND JANE WYMAN, *Nate Cutler* 1968

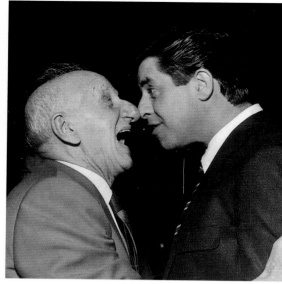

DURANTE AND JERRY LEWIS, *Nate Cutler* 1968

DURANTE AND PETER LAWFORD, *Nate Cutler* 1968

DURANTE AND DESI ARNAZ, *Nate Cutler* 1968

EDWARD G. ROBINSON AND DURANTE, *Nate Cutler* 1968

DURANTE AND KEN MURRAY, *Nate Cutler* 1968

MARILYN MAXWELL AND DURANTE, *Nate Cutler* 1968

DURANTE AND GEORGE RAFT, *Nate Cutler* 1970

JANE POWELL AND ERROL FLYNN, *Nate Cutler* 1957

GINGER ROGERS AND GROUCHO MARX, *Nate Cutler* 1958

GILDA RADNER AND GENE WILDER, *Adam Scull* 1985

JACK BENNY AND PHIL SILVERS, *Nate Cutler* 1957

LUCILLE BALL, JOE E. BROWN AND DONALD O'CONNOR, *Nate Cutler* 1964

One of Globe's favorite subjects, JIMMY DURANTE, known affectionately as The Schnoz, had a thing about rubbing noses. He was sure that coming into contact with his schnozola would confer good fortune on the rubbee. So guests in his company were invariably asked to perform the ritual. GEORGE RAFT goes one better – he plants a kiss on the Durante schnoz.

Next to an air kiss, giving a face a squeeze is the most popular expression of affection in Hollywood. Here are a few experts.

Eins von Globes beliebtesten Motiven, JIMMY DURANTE, der liebevoll The Schnoz (Die Nase) genannt wurde, hatte einen Tick fürs Nasereiben. Er war sich sicher, dass der Kontakt mit seiner Nase dem Reibenden Glück bringen würde. Somit wurden Gäste in seiner Begleitung ständig darum gebeten, dieses Ritual auszuführen. GEORGE RAFT geht noch einen Schritt weiter – er gibt Durante einen Kuss auf die Nase.

Neben zugeworfenen Handküssen, ist eine Berührung des Gesichts in Hollywood die beliebteste Art, Zuneigung zu bekunden.

JIMMY DURANTE, l'un des sujets favoris de Globe, était surnommé affectueusement le Schnozz (ce qui signifie gros nez ou pif en anglais) et aimait particulièrement ce qu'on appellerait le « baiser eskimo ». Persuadé que son nez portait bonheur, il proposait invariablement d'accomplir ce rituel aux personnes qu'il rencontrait. GEORGE RAFT va plus loin en embrassant carrément le pif de Durante.

Le petit baiser et le pincement du visage sont les deux expressions d'affection les plus populaires à Hollywood. Voici quelques experts dans cet art de la salutation amicale.

MAE WEST AND HER LEADING MEN, *Nate Cutler* 1978

BOB HOPE AND HIS LEADING LADIES, *Nate Cutler* 1966

REUNIONS: MAE WEST surrounded by four of her former leading men: PHILIP REED (KLONDIKE ANNIE), CARY GRANT (SHE DONE HIM WRONG), JACK LaRUE (the original stage production of DIAMOND LIL) and STEVE COCHRAN (the DIAMOND LIL revival). • BOB HOPE hosted a party for many of his leading ladies: LUCILLE BALL (four films including FANCY PANTS and SORROWFUL JONES), JOAN FONTAINE (CASANOVA'S BIG NIGHT), HEDY LAMARR (MY FAVORITE SPY), SIGNE HASSO (WHERE THERE'S LIFE), JOAN COLLINS (ROAD TO HONG KONG), DOROTHY LAMOUR (eight movies including all the ROAD films), VIRGINIA MAYO (THE PRINCESS AND THE PIRATE) and VERA MILES (BEAU JAMES). • HENRY FONDA and JANET GAYNOR reunite 38 years after costarring in THE FARMER TAKES A WIFE, Fonda's first film, at the opening of her art exhibition. • 46 years after they appeared opposite each other in CONSULTATION MARRIAGE, PAT O'BRIEN and MYRNA LOY at a party in honor of their movie reunion in THE END. The past and present costars sit in front of a blowup of that earlier film. • ETHEL WATERS and JULIE HARRIS 22 years after they costarred in THE MEMBER OF THE WEDDING. • MICKEY ROONEY and AVA GARDNER, once man and wife (she was the first of his nine wives, he the first of her three husbands) celebrate Rooney's stage hit SUGAR BABIES costarring ANN MILLER.

WIEDERVEREINIGUNGEN: MAE WEST wird von vier Filmpartnern eingerahmt: PHILIP REED (KLONDIKE ANNIE), CARY GRANT (SIE TAT IHM UNRECHT), JACK LaRUE (die originale Bühnenproduktion von DIAMOND LIL) und STEVE COCHRAN (das DIAMOND-LIL-Revival). • BOB HOPE gab für viele seiner Filmpartnerinnen eine Party: LUCILLE BALL (vier Filme inklusive HERZ IN DER HOSE und DER BESIEGTE GEIZHALZ), JOAN FONTAINE (DER SCHÜRZENJÄGER VON VENEDIG), HEDY LAMARR (SPIONE, LIEBE UND DIE FEUERWEHR), SIGNE HASSO (WHERE THERE'S LIFE), JOAN COLLINS (DER WEG NACH HONGKONG), DOROTHY LAMOUR (acht Filme, inklusive der ROAD-Filme, VIRGINIA MAYO (DAS KORSARENSCHIFF) und VERA MILES (SCHÖNE FRAUEN, HARTE DOLLARS). • HENRY FONDA und JANET GAYNOR trafen sich 38 Jahre nachdem sie Filmpartner in THE FARMER TAKES A WIFE waren, Fondas erstem Film, bei der Eröffnung ihrer Kunstausstellung wieder. • 46 Jahre nachdem sie sich in CONSULTATION MARRIAGE gegenüber gestanden haben, PAT O'BRIEN und MYRNA LOY auf einer Party zu Ehren ihrer Wiedervereinigung im Film (NOBODY IS PERFECT). Die früheren und jetzigen Filmpartner sitzen vor einem vergrößerten Bild des früheren Films. • ETHEL WATERS und JULIE HARRIS 22 Jahre nachdem sie in DAS MÄDCHEN FRANKIE die Hauptrollen gespielt hatten. • MICKEY ROONEY und AVA GARDNER, früher einmal Mann und Frau (sie war die Erste seiner neun Frauen, er der Erste ihrer drei Ehemänner) feiern Rooneys Bühnenhit SUGAR BABIES mit ANN MILLER in der Hauptrolle.

RÉUNIONS : MAE WEST entourée par quatre de ses anciens partenaires masculins : PHILIP REED (ANNIE DU KLONDIKE – KLONDIKE ANNIE), CARY GRANT (LADY LOU – SHE DONE HIM WRONG), JACK LaRUE (dans la production originale sur scène de DIAMOND LIL) et STEVE COCHRAN (le remake de DIAMOND LIL). • BOB HOPE a organisé une soirée pour quelques-unes de ses partenaires féminines : LUCILLE BALL (quatre films dont L'EXTRAVAGANT M. RUGGLES – FANCY PANTS et DES ENNUIS À LA PELLE – SORROWFUL JONES), JOAN FONTAINE (LA GRANDE NUIT DE CASANOVA – CASANOVA'S BIG NIGHT), HEDY LAMARR (ESPIONNE DE MON CŒUR – MY FAVORITE SPY), SIGNE HASSO (WHERE THERE'S LIFE), JOAN COLLINS (ASTRONAUTES MALGRÉ EUX – THE ROAD TO HONG KONG), DOROTHY LAMOUR (huit films, dont tous les films de EN ROUTE VERS … – ROAD, VIRGINIA MAYO (THE PRINCESS AND THE PIRATE) et VERA MILES (BEAU JAMES). • HENRY FONDA et JANET GAYNOR se retrouvent au vernissage de l'exposition de Janet 38 ans après avoir été partenaires dans THE FARMER TAKES A WIFE, le premier film de Fonda. • PAT O'BRIEN et MYRNA LOY réunis de nouveau, 46 ans après, sous l'affiche de leur premier film ensemble, CONSULTATION MARRIAGE, lors d'une soirée donnée en l'honneur de SUICIDEZ-MOI, DOCTEUR (THE END). • ETHEL WATERS et JULIE HARRIS se rencontrent 22 ans après avoir joué ensemble dans THE MEMBER OF THE WEDDING. • MICKEY ROONEY et AVA GARDNER, autrefois mariés (elle fut la première de ses neuf femmes et lui le premier de ses trois maris) célèbrent le succès au théâtre de Rooney dans SUGAR BABIES avec ANN MILLER.

HENRY FONDA AND JANET GAYNOR, *Nate Cutler* 1973

PAT O'BRIEN AND MYRNA LOY, *Nate Cutler* 1979

ETHEL WATERS AND JULIE HARRIS, *Nate Cutler* 1974

MICKEY ROONEY, AVA GARDNER AND ANN MILLER, *Nate Cutler* 1980

JAMES STEWART AND GINGER ROGERS, *Nino* 1990

ANNE BANCROFT, PATTY DUKE AND PATRICIA NEAL, *Sylvia Norris* 1988

SHIRLEY TEMPLE AND JANE WITHERS, *Bob Noble* 1976

CONNIE STEVENS, EDDIE FISHER AND DEBBIE REYNOLDS, *Bill Holz* 1968

JAMES STEWART and GINGER ROGERS, Oscar winners in 1940, reunite at the 1990 Oscar party at Stringfellows. • Reunion of the three stars of Broadway's THE MIRACLE WORKER, ANNE BANCROFT, PATTY DUKE and PATRICIA NEAL at the party for the publication of Patricia's autobiography. • SHIRLEY TEMPLE and JANE WITHERS, costars when they were children in the 30s, reunite at the Hollywood Women's Press Club's Golden Apple party. • EDDIE FISHER, with third wife CONNIE STEVENS and first wife DEBBIE REYNOLDS, at the Martin Luther King rally at the Hollywood Bowl.

JAMES STEWART und GINGER ROGERS, Oscar-Gewinner im Jahre 1940, sehen sich 1990 auf der Oscar-Party im Stringfellows wieder. • Das Wiedersehen der drei Stars des am Broadway aufgeführten Stückes LICHT IM DUNKEL (THE MIRACLE WORKER), ANNE BANCROFT, PATTY DUKE und PATRICIA NEAL, auf einer Party, die zur Veröffentlichung von Patricias Autobiographie gegeben wird. • SHIRLEY TEMPLE und JANE WITHERS, die schon als Kinder in den 30er Jahren Filmpartner waren, treffen sich auf der Golden Apple Party des Frauenpresseclubs in Hollywood wieder. • EDDIE FISHER, hier mit seiner dritten Frau CONNIE STEVENS und seiner ersten Frau DEBBIE REYNOLDS, bei der Martin-Luther-King-Versammlung am Hollywood Bowl.

JAMES STEWART et GINGER ROGERS, lauréats d'un Oscar en 1940, sont réunis à la soirée des Oscar de 1990 à Stringfellows. • Les trois vedettes de THE MIRACLE WORKER, une pièce jouée à Broadway – ANNE BANCROFT, PATTY DUKE et PATRICIA NEAL – se retrouvent à la soirée donnée pour la publication de l'autobiographie de Patricia. • SHIRLEY TEMPLE et JANE WITHERS, partenaires dans les années 1930 lorsqu'elles étaient enfants, se rencontrent à nouveau à une soirée du Hollywood Women's Press Club's Golden Apple. • EDDIE FISHER, avec sa troisième épouse CONNIE STEVENS et sa première femme DEBBIE REYNOLDS, lors du rassemblement en faveur de Martin Luther King au Hollywood Bowl.

JOAN CRAWFORD AND JACKIE COOPER, *Nate Cutler* 1959

Reunion? Check out page 114 of Cooper's autobiography.

Wiedervereinigung? Sehen Sie auf der Seite 114 in Coopers Autobiographie nach.

Réunion ? Voir page 114 l'autobiographie de Cooper.

DORIS DAY AND ROD TAYLOR, *Nate Cutler* 1965

GEORGE SEGAL, ELIZABETH TAYLOR AND RICHARD BURTON, *Sylvia Norris* 1965

JACQUELINE BISSET AND DEAN MARTIN, *Nate Cutler* 1969

DORIS DAY is about to lose her roll to ROD TAYLOR at the wrap party for THE GLASS BOTTOM BOAT. • GEORGE SEGAL, ELIZABETH TAYLOR and RICHARD BURTON at the Whisky-a-Go-Go. Watch her, George. • DEAN MARTIN helps himself to a few hors d'œuvres at the AIRPORT party. JACQUELINE BISSET helps him reconsider.

DORIS DAY verliert fast ihr Brötchen auf der Abschlussfeier zu den Dreharbeiten von SPION IN SPITZENHÖSCHEN (THE GLASS BOTTOM BOAT) an ROD TAYLOR. • GEORGE SEGAL, ELIZABETH TAYLOR und RICHARD BURTON im Whisky-a-Go-Go. Behalte sie gut im Auge, George. • DEAN MARTIN nimmt sich einige Hors d'œuvres auf der Party zum Film AIRPORT. JACQUELINE BISSET hilft ihm bei der Auswahl.

DORIS DAY se laisse piquer son petit pain par ROD TAYLOR lors de la soirée de fin de tournage de BLONDE DÉFIE F.B.I. (THE GLASS BOTTOM BOAT). • GEORGE SEGAL, ELIZABETH TAYLOR et RICHARD BURTON au Whisky-a-Go-Go. Surveille-la bien, George! • DEAN MARTIN veut se servir de hors-d'œuvre lors de la soirée de AIRPORT mais sa partenaire JACQUELINE BISSET le fait changer d'avis.

GUY MADISON AND TALLULAH BANKHEAD, *Nate Cutler* 1954

TALLULAH BANKHEAD AND TERRY MOORE, *Nate Cutler* 1954

TRUMAN CAPOTE AND GLORIA SWANSON, *Adam Scull* 1978

MICHAEL CAINE AND HEDDA HOPPER, *Nate Cutler* 1965

The irrepressible TALLULAH BANKHEAD plays both sides of the street at her welcome to Hollywood party. • TRUMAN CAPOTE and GLORIA SWANSON at Studio 54. • MICHAEL CAINE and HEDDA HOPPER at his Hollywood welcome party.

Die unbezähmbare TALLULAH BANKHEAD verdreht allen bei ihrer Ankunft in Hollywood den Kopf. • TRUMAN CAPOTE und GLORIA SWANSON im Studio 54. • MICHAEL CAINE und HEDDA HOPPER auf seiner Hollywood-Willkommensparty.

La pétulante TALLULAH BANKHEAD lors d'une soirée à Hollywood. • TRUMAN CAPOTE et GLORIA SWANSON au Studio 54. • MICHAEL CAINE et HEDDA HOPPER à la soirée organisée pour lui souhaiter la bienvenue à Hollywood.

CAPRICORN PARTY, *Nate Cutler* 1970

ANITA LOUISE was one of Hollywood's leading hostesses, well known for her astrological parties for friends born under a particular sign. Blowing out candles on the Capricorn cake are ARMY ARCHERD, LORETTA YOUNG, ANITA LOUISE, DAVID WOLPER, YOLANDA QUINN, LEE BOWMAN and JANE WYMAN. • TOM CRUISE and REBECCA DeMORNAY party at the Limelight in Atlanta. Their tablemate appeared with Rebecca in THE SLUGGER'S WIFE. • CHRISTIAN SLATER, with mother Mary Jo and brother Ryan, at the Pasadena Playhouse party for IT'S A WONDERFUL LIFE. An ironic title considering Slater went to jail the next day, ordered to do time for assault and drug abuse. • CARSON and McMAHON are gifted with early portraits for their 20th anniversary on NBC's TONIGHT SHOW. • LUCILLE BALL and DESI ARNAZ draw for door prizes at the annual Desilu company picnic.

ANITA LOUISE, eine der führenden Gastgeberinnen Hollywoods von astrologischen Partys, die sie für Freunde, die unter einem bestimmten Sternzeichen geboren waren, veranstaltet. Hier pusten ARMY ARCHERD, LORETTA YOUNG, ANITA LOUISE, DAVID WOLPER, YOLANDA QUINN, LEE BOWMAN und JANE WYMAN die Kerzen des Steinbock-Kuchens aus. • TOM CRUISE und REBECCA DeMORNAY im Limelight, Atlanta. Ihr Tischpartner spielte mit Rebecca im Film DIE FRAU DES PROFIS. • CHRISTIAN SLATER, mit Mutter Mary Jo und Bruder Ryan, auf der Pasadena Playhouse Party zum Film IST DAS LEBEN NICHT SCHÖN. Ein ironischer Titel, da Slater am nächsten Tag wegen tätlicher Beleidigung und Drogenmissbrauchs ins Gefängnis musste. • CARSON und McMAHON bekommen zu ihrem 20. Hochzeitstag in der NBC TONIGHT SHOW frühere Porträts geschenkt. • LUCILLE BALL und DESI ARNAZ nehmen an einer Tombola beim jährlichen Firmenpicknick von Desilu teil.

ANITA LOUISE était l'une des principales animatrices des nuits hollywoodiennes et était particulièrement connue pour organiser des soirées astrologiques réunissant tous ses amis nés sous le même signe. ARMY ARCHERD, LORETTA YOUNG, ANITA LOUISE, DAVID WOLPER, YOLANDA QUINN, LEE BOWMAN et JANE WYMAN soufflent ainsi les bougies du gâteau consacré au Capricorne. • TOM CRUISE et REBECCA DeMORNAY au Limelight d'Atlanta. Leur compagnon apparaissait avec Rebecca dans THE SLUGGER'S WIFE. • CHRISTIAN SLATER, avec sa mère Mary Jo et son frère Ryan, à la soirée pour LA VIE EST BELLE. Le titre est assez ironique car Slater fut mis en prison le lendemain pour agression et usage de drogue. • CARSON et McMAHON reçoivent leurs portraits jeunes pour les 20 ans du TONIGHT SHOW qu'ils animent à la NBC. • LUCILLE BALL et DESI ARNAZ tirent au sort les prix lors du pique-nique annuel de la compagnie Desilu.

REBECCA DeMORNAY AND TOM CRUISE, *Rick Diamond* 1985

CHARLES COBURN AND ROBERT STACK, *Nate Cutler* 1959

GROUCHO MARX AND RICHARD PRYOR, *Nate Cutler* 1966

GARY COOPER AND MARIA SCHELL, *Nate Cutler* 1958

CHRISTIAN SLATER, *Greg Vie* 1997

HUMPHREY BOGART AND LAUREN BACALL, *Nate Cutler* 1953

JOHNNY CARSON AND ED McMAHON, *Nate Cutler* 1978

LIZA MINNELLI AND SHIRLEY MACLAINE, *Nate Cutler* 1967

LUCILLE BALL AND DESI ARNAZ, *Larry Barbier Jr.* 1955

GRACE KELLY AND PRINCE RAINIER, *Ed Quinn* 1955

SIMONE SIGNORET AND MARILYN MONROE, *Nate Cutler* 1960

ANNA MAGNANI AND BETTE DAVIS, *FotoVedo* 1956

JOHNNY CARSON AND JACK BENNY, *Globe Archive* 1963

FIRST MEETINGS: This handshake marks the very first meeting of Hollywood queen GRACE KELLY and PRINCE RAINIER of Monaco. • SIMONE SIGNORET sizes up MARILYN MONROE (for good cause as it turned out) at the party to welcome Yves Montand, Signoret's husband and Monroe's leading man. • JOHNNY CARSON and JACK BENNY meet in Las Vegas. • Two of the world's most volatile actresses, ANNA MAGNANI and BETTE DAVIS meet in Rome at the party given for Davis' arrival in Italy.

ERSTE TREFFEN: Dieser Händedruck markiert das erste Treffen der Hollywood-Königin GRACE KELLY und PRINZ RAINIER von Monaco. • SIMONE SIGNORET zollt MARILYN MONROE öffentlichen Respekt (aus gutem Grund, wie sich herausstellte) auf einer Willkommensparty zu Ehren von Yves Montand, Signorets Ehemann und Monroes Filmpartner. • JOHNNY CARSON und JACK BENNY treffen sich in Las Vegas. • Zwei der impulsivsten Schauspielerinnen der Welt, ANNA MAGNANI und BETTE DAVIS, treffen sich in Rom auf der Party, die zu Ehren von Davis' Ankunft in Italien gegeben wird.

PREMIÈRES RENCONTRES : Cette poignée de main marque la toute première rencontre entre la reine de Hollywood GRACE KELLY et le PRINCE RAINIER de Monaco. • SIMONE SIGNORET jauge MARILYN MONROE (pour de bonnes raisons s'il faut en croire la suite) lors de la soirée organisée pour accueillir Yves Montand, mari de Signoret et partenaire de Monroe. • JOHNNY CARSON et JACK BENNY se rencontrent à Las Vegas. • Deux des actrices les plus explosives du monde, ANNA MAGNANI et BETTE DAVIS, se rencontrent à Rome lors de la soirée organisée pour l'arrivée de Davis en Italie.

WARREN BEATTY PARTY, *Nate Cutler* 1975

MODERN SCREEN PARTY, *Rick Strauss* 1958

TAB HUNTER PARTY, *Larry Barbier Jr.* 1957

RICARDO MONTALBAN AND DONNA REED, *Nate Cutler* 1964

WARREN BEATTY with guests OLIVE BERENDT, LEE GRANT, JACK NICHOLSON, JACK VALENTI and MICHELLE PHILLIPS. • Fan magazines often gave parties just for publication. This is a MODERN SCREEN party for young stars of the 50s: CAROL NUGENT and NICK ADAMS, TROY DONAHUE and MARIANNE GABA, FABRIZIO MIONI, CONNIE STEVENS and MARK DAMON, SAL MINEO, BRETT HALSEY and LUCIANNA PALUZZI, MOLLY BEE, DWAYNE HICKMAN, BRANDON DeWILDE and CAROL LYNLEY. • TAB HUNTER with guests LORI NELSON, JOHN and MILLIE ERICSON and BRETT HALSEY. • RICARDO MONTALBAN and DONNA REED back to back at Alan Ladd's luau.

WARREN BEATTY mit den Gästen OLIVE BERENDT, LEE GRANT, JACK NICHOLSON, JACK VALENTI und MICHELLE PHILLIPS. • Fanmagazine gaben oft Partys, um darüber berichten zu können. Dies ist eine MODERN-SCREEN-Party mit den jungen Stars der 50er: CAROL NUGENT and NICK ADAMS, TROY DONAHUE und MARIANNE GABA, FABRIZIO MIONI, CONNIE STEVENS und MARK DAMON, SAL MINEO, BRETT HALSEY und LUCIANNA PALUZZI, MOLLY BEE, DWAYNE HICKMAN, BRANDON DeWILDE und CAROL LYNLEY. • TAB HUNTER mit seinen Gästen LORI NELSON, JOHN und MILLIE ERICSON und BRETT HALSEY. • RICARDO MONTALBAN und DONNA REED Rücken an Rücken auf Alan Ladds Hawaiiparty.

WARREN BEATTY et ses hôtes OLIVE BERENDT, LEE GRANT, JACK NICHOLSON, JACK VALENTI et MICHELLE PHILLIPS. • Les fanzines organisaient souvent des soirées simplement pour avoir quelque chose à publier, comme cette réception donnée par MODERN SCREEN pour quelques stars des années 1950 : CAROL NUGENT et NICK ADAMS, TROY DONAHUE et MARIANNE GABA, FABRIZIO MIONI, CONNIE STEVENS et MARK DAMON, SAL MINEO, BRETT HALSEY et LUCIANNA PALUZZI, MOLLY BEE, DWAYNE HICKMAN, BRANDON DeWILDE et CAROL LYNLEY. • TAB HUNTER et ses invités LORI NELSON, JOHN et MILLIE ERICSON, BRETT HALSEY. • RICARDO MONTALBAN et DONNA REED dos à dos lors d'un pique-nique organisé par Alan Ladd.

RYAN O'NEAL with daughter TATUM, a few years away from her Oscar win, at the PEYTON PLACE beach party. • Pooped but happy, CAROL BURNETT at the end of her Beverly Hills "garage sale" which benefited the Jonas Salk Institute. • IAN McKELLEN and SUSAN SARANDON celebrate New Years Eve at Regine's. • MERYL STREEP and JOSEPH PAPP at the Public Theater celebration in New York. • MELANIE GRIFFITH and ANTONIO BANDERAS bring daughter Stella to the Planet Hollywood party in New York. • MATTHEW McCONAUGHEY parties in London.

RYAN O'NEAL auf der PEYTON PLACE Beach Party mit Tochter TATUM, Jahre vor ihrem Oscar-Gewinn. • Ausgepumpt aber glücklich: CAROL BURNETT nach ihrem Beverly-Hills-Trödelmarkt, der dem Jonas Salk Institute zu Gute kam. • IAN McKELLEN feiert mit SUSAN SARANDON Silvester bei Regine. • MERYL STREEP und JOSEPH PAPP auf der Public-Theater-Feier in New York. • MELANIE GRIFFITH und ANTONIO BANDE-RAS bringen Tochter Stella zur Planet Hollywood Party in New York. • MATTHEW McCONAUG-HEY feiert in London.

Lors de la soirée PEYTON PLACE, RYAN O'NEAL avec sa fille TATUM, quelques années avant qu'elle remporte un Oscar. • CAROL BURNETT à la fin du vide-grenier de Beverly Hills ; le produit de la vente fut offert au Jonas Salk Institute. • IAN McKELLEN et SUSAN SARANDON fêtent le nouvel an chez Regine. • MERYL STREEP et JOSEPH PAPP lors d'une fête au Public Theater de New York. • MELANIE GRIFFITH et ANTONIO BANDERAS avec leur fille Stella à la soirée du Planet Hollywood de New York. • MATTHEW Mc-CONAUGHEY fait la fête à Londres.

TATUM AND RYAN O'NEAL, *Gene Trindl* 1966

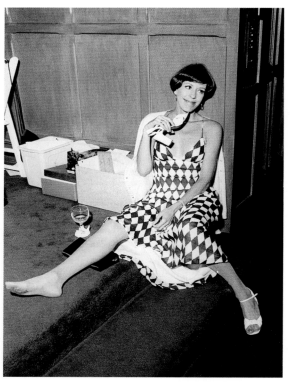

CAROL BURNETT, *John R. Hamilton* 1976

IAN McKELLEN AND SUSAN SARANDON, *Richard Corkery* 1987

MERYL STREEP AND JOSEPH PAPP, *Richard Corkery* 1982

MELANIE GRIFFITH AND ANTONIO BANDERAS, *Anders Krusberg* 1998

MATTHEW McCONAUGHEY, *Jeff Spicer* 1998

RED SKELTON, *Larry Barbier Jr.* 1960

LLOYD BRIDGES, HUGH O'BRIAN AND CAROLYN JONES, *Larry Barbier Jr.* 1960

JOHN BELUSHI, *DM/PT* 1980

JIM CARREY, *NBC* 1995

It's often said that stars will show up for the opening of a can of soup. An exaggeration of course but RED SKELTON did attend this opening of a billboard on the Sunset Strip advertising the Sahara Hotel in Las Vegas. The sign actually included a swimming pool. • BRIDGES, JONES and O'BRIAN cavort at the opening of their Whispering Waters hotel in Palm Springs. • JOHN BELUSHI and admirers at a record party. • JIM CARREY lets it all hang out at the 20th-birthday celebration of The Comedy Store in West Hollywood. The anniversary crowd included Comedy Store alumni RICHARD BELZER, BOB SAGET and PAULY SHORE, all of whom were on stage when Jim made this surprise appearance.

Es heißt, Stars würden auch beim Öffnen einer Dosensuppe auftauchen, wenn es Aufsehen erregt. Das ist übertrieben, aber RED SKELTON war bei der Eröffnungsfeier des Werbeschilds für das Sahara Hotel in Las Vegas auf dem Sunset Strip dabei. Das Schild verwies auch auf einen Swimmingpool. • BRIDGES, JONES und O'BRIAN bei der Eröffnung ihres Whispering Waters Hotels in Palm Springs. • JOHN BELUSHI und Fans bei einer Schallplatten-Party. • JIM CARREY lässt seinen Gefühlen auf der 20. Geburtstagsfeier des The Comedy Store in West Hollywood freien Lauf. Unter den Gästen waren die ehemaligen Mitglieder des Comedy Store RICHARD BELZER, BOB SAGET und PAULY SHORE. Alle waren auf der Bühne, als Jim seinen überraschenden Auftritt hatte.

On dit souvent que les stars aiment se donner en spectacle ne serait-ce que pour ouvrir une boîte de conserve. C'est naturellement exagéré même si RED SKELTON semble témoigner du contraire pour cette publicité, avec une vraie piscine, sur Sunset Strip pour le Sahara Hotel de Las Vegas. • BRIDGES, JONES et O'BRIAN gambadent pour l'inauguration à Palm Springs de leur hôtel Whispering Waters. • JOHN BELUSHI et des admiratrices lors d'une soirée d'enregistrement. • JIM CARREY a fait pis que pendre lors de la cérémonie du 20e anniversaire du Comedy Store de West Hollywood, où quelques anciens élèves comme RICHARD BELZER, BOB SAGET et PAULY SHORE étaient sur scène lorsqu'il fit son apparition surprise.

CLINT AND KYLE EASTWOOD, *Douglas Jones* 1971

HUTTON practices mime in a park. • WILLIAMS returns to The Improv where he got his start, to try out new material.

HUTTON übt Pantomime in einem Park. • WILLIAMS kehrt zum The Improv zurück, um neue Stücke zu testen.

HUTTON s'entraîne au mime dans un parc. • Pour tester ses sketches, WILLIAMS revient périodiquement au cabaret Improv.

TIMOTHY HUTTON, *John Partipilo* 1979

ROBIN WILLIAMS, *Steve Schatzberg* 1980

GEENA DAVIS, *Ralph Dominguez* 1984

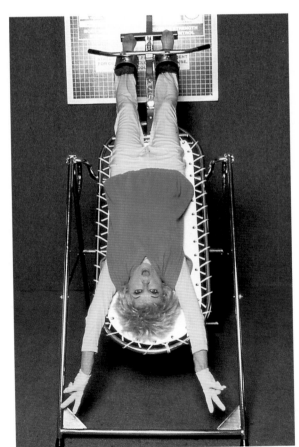

PHYLLIS DILLER, *Robert Landau* 1970

GEORGE RAFT, *Pictorial Press* 1962

GLENN CLOSE, *John Barrett* 1992

DILLER in gravity boots. • RAFT works the roulette table at his Colony Club in London. • GLENN CLOSE at a jam session with WOODY HARRELSON's band Mandy Moondog and the Three Cool Cats.

DILLER in Schwerkraft-Stiefeln. • RAFT bedient das Roulette in seinem Colony Club in London. • GLENN CLOSE bei einer Jam Session mit WOODY HARRELSONS Band Mandy Moondog and the Three Cool Cats.

DILLER en plein exercice. • RAFT se détend en travaillant à la roulette du Colony Club de Londres. • GLENN CLOSE lors d'une jam session avec l'orchestre de WOODY HARRELSON, Mandy Moondog and the Three Cool Cats.

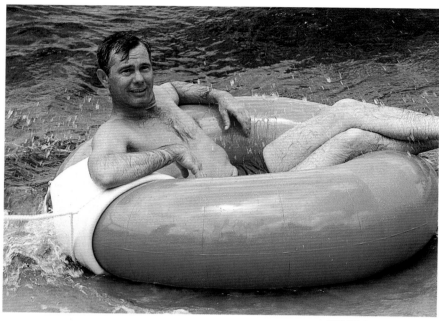

JOHNNY CARSON, *NBC* 1972

MARILYN MONROE AND JOHNNIE HYDE, *Nate Cutler* 1949

GEORGE SANDERS AND SAMUEL GOLDWYN, *Dick Miller* 1958

WILLIAM SHATNER AND DEFORREST KELLEY, *Bill Greenslade* 1967

MATT DILLON, *Hy Simon* 1982

CHER, *Hy Simon* 1979

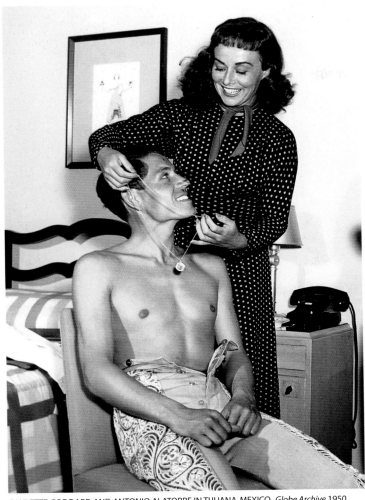

PAULETTE GODDARD AND ANTONIO ALATORRE IN TIJUANA, MEXICO, *Globe Archive* 1950

KEANU REEVES AT DOGSTAR REHEARSAL, *John Barrett* 1998

RIVER PHOENIX AT ROCK AGAINST FUR CONCERT, *Stephen Allen* 1987

DAVID JANSSEN AT THE AMBASSADOR HOTEL, *Larry Barbier Jr.* 1958

EDWARD BURNS, *Walter Weissman* 1999

EDWARD BURNS plays in the Artists and Writers softball game. • AL PACINO, PAUL NEWMAN and WOODY ALLEN play ball for the Actors Fund benefit games in New York. • GEORGE CLOONEY during a break on ONE FINE DAY. • GLENDA JACKSON and GEORGE SEGAL in London's Hyde Park. • EDWARD G. ROBINSON is thumbed off the field by LEO DUROCHER. • Bat girl MARILYN MONROE and player DALE ROBERTSON at a 20th Century-Fox studio game. • BOBBY DARIN changes in the locker room at Dodger Stadium. • BING CROSBY, at the time an owner of the Pittsburgh Pirates, with team manager HANS WAGNER, at Forbes Field.

EDWARD BURNS spielt Softball im Team der Künstler und Schriftsteller. • AL PACINO, PAUL NEWMAN und WOODY ALLEN spielen zu Gunsten des Actors Fund in New York Fußball. • GEORGE CLOONEY während einer Pause bei den Dreharbeiten zu TAGE WIE DIESER (ONE FINE DAY). • GLENDA JACKSON and GEORGE SEGAL in Londons Hyde Park. • EDWARD G. ROBINSON wird von LEO DUROCHER vom Spielfeld gewunken. • MARILYN MONROE mit Baseballschläger und Spieler DALE ROBERTSON im Spiel des 20th-Century-Fox-Studios. • BOBBY DARIN zieht sich im Umkleideraum des Dodgers Stadions um. • BING CROSBY, zu diesem Zeitpunkt Besitzer der Pittsburgh Pirates, hier mit Teammanager HANS WAGNER im Forbes Filed.

EDWARD BURNS joue au softball dans l'équipe Artists et Writers. • AL PACINO, PAUL NEWMAN et WOODY ALLEN participent à New York au tournoi de base-ball organisé au bénéfice de l'Actors Fund. • GEORGE CLOONEY pendant une pause de UN BEAU JOUR (ONE FINE DAY). • GLENDA JACKSON et GEORGE SEGAL dans Hyde Park à Londres. • EDWARD G. ROBINSON est sorti du terrain par LEO DUROCHER. • MARILYN MONROE en batteuse et DALE ROBERTSON en joueur lors d'un match de la 20th Century-Fox. • BOBBY DARIN se change dans les vestiaires du Dodger Stadium. • BING CROSBY, à l'époque propriétaire des Pittsburgh Pirates, avec l'entraîneur HANS WAGNER, à Forbes Field.

AL PACINO, *Michael Norcia* 1977

PAUL NEWMAN, *Jack Stager* 1974

WOODY ALLEN, *Robert Fitzgerald* 1974

GEORGE CLOONEY, *Alex Oliveira* 1996

GLENDA JACKSON AND GEORGE SEGAL, *Globe Archive* 1972

EDWARD G. ROBINSON AND LEO DUROCHER, *Neil Clemans* 1950

DALE ROBERTSON AND MARILYN MONROE, *Nate Cutler 1952*

BOBBY DARIN, *Nate Cutler* 1952

BING CROSBY AND HANS WAGNER, *Globe Archive* 1947

ALI MACGRAW, *Ralph Dominguez* 1980

JOHNNY MATHIS, *Nate Cutler* 1972

ALI MACGRAW exercises at the Jane Fonda Workout. • JOHNNY
MATHIS tries one of Wilt Chamberlain's shoes following a charity bas-
ketball game between Hollywood celebrities and the Harlem
Globetrotters. • JON VOIGHT and JIM BROWN during a charity basket-
ball game at UCLA's Pauley Pavillion.

ALI MACGRAW trainiert nach dem Jane Fonda Workout. • JOHNNY
MATHIS probiert nach einem Basketball-Wohltätigkeitsspiel zwischen
Hollywood-Stars und den Harlem Globetrotters einen von Wilt Cham-
berlains Schuhen an. • JON VOIGHT und JIM BROWN während einem
Basketball-Wohltätigkeitsspiel im UCLA Pauley Pavillion.

ALI MACGRAW à l'échauffement au Jane Fonda Workout. • JOHNNY
MATHIS montre l'une des chaussures de Wilt Chamberlain après un
match de basket de bienfaisance organisé entre des vedettes de Hollywood et les Harlem Globetrotters. • JON VOIGHT et JIM BROWN lors
d'un match de basket de bienfaisance au Pauley Pavillion de l'UCLA.

JON VOIGHT AND JIM BROWN, *Nate Cutler* 1975

TOM SELLECK plays volley ball in Honolulu. • AL JOLSON and MOLLY PICON – a day at the races at Belmont Park. • KATHARINE HEPBURN bikes home from A LION IN WINTER location in Bray, Ireland. • GEORGE SEGAL, on banjo, and CONRAD JANIS, trombone, formed the Beverly Hills Unlisted Jazz Band.

MOLLY PICON AND AL JOLSON, *Bert and Richard Morgan* 1946

TOM SELLECK, *Tim Ryan* 1981

KATHARINE HEPBURN, *Globe Archive* 1967

GEORGE SEGAL AND CONRAD JANIS, *Nate Cutler* 1979

TOM SELLECK spielt in Honolulu Volleyball. • AL JOLSON und MOLLY PICON – beim Rennen im Belmont Park. • KATHARINE HEPBURN fährt vom Drehort zu DER LÖWE IM WINTER in Bray, Irland, mit dem Fahrrad nach Hause. • GEORGE SEGAL am Banjo und CONRAD JANIS an der Posaune bildeten die Beverly Hills Unlisted Jazz Band.

TOM SELLECK à Honolulu. • AL JOLSON et MOLLY PICON à Belmont Park. • KATHARINE HEPBURN rentre chez elle à vélo depuis Bray où se tournait UN LION EN HIVER. • GEORGE SEGAL au banjo et CONRAD JANIS au trombone composaient le Beverly Hills Unlisted Jazz Band.

SEAN CONNERY, *Cesar Lucas* 1968

Before going into acting, SEAN CONNERY tried for a career as a professional soccer player and still keeps up with the sport. • LORENZO LAMAS practices martial arts at his home. • HECTOR ELIZONDO practises tai chi • JAMES CAAN learns karate from master Takayuki Kubota. • MICHAEL LANDON keeps in shape at UCLA.

HECTOR ELIZONDO, *Lynn McAfee* 1983

LORENZO LAMAS, *Steve Schatzberg* 1979

JAMES CAAN AND TAKAYUKI KUBOTA, *Nate Cutler* 1974

Bevor SEAN CONNERY Schauspieler wurde, versuchte er sich als Fußballprofi und blieb dem Sport verbunden. • LORENZO LAMAS übt Kampfsportarten bei sich zu Hause. • HECTOR ELIZONDO übt Tai-Chi. • JAMES CAAN lernt Karate von Meister Takayuki Kubota. • MICHAEL LANDON hält sich an der University of California in Los Angeles fit.

Ayant envisagé de devenir un joueur de football professionnel avant d'être acteur, SEAN CONNERY a continué de pratiquer. • LORENZO LAMAS s'entraîne aux arts martiaux à domicile. • HECTOR ELIZONDO fait du tai-chi • JAMES CAAN apprend le karaté avec le maître Takayuki Kubota. • MICHAEL LANDON conserve la forme sur le terrain de l'UCLA.

MICHAEL LANDON, *NBC* 1961

STELLA STEVENS is one of the first to try parasailing, flying 150 feet over the bay of Acapulco. • BURT LANCASTER coaches a harnessed ERNEST BORGNINE in acrobatics. The only thing Borgnine recalls about the session is that Lancaster kept calling him Lard Ass. • MACDONALD CAREY studied karate in 1961. Thirty years later he was still at it, with trainer Benny Urquidez. • MICKEY ROURKE, who had 26 amateur bouts as a teenager, began his professional career as a light-heavyweight, fighting under the name Marielito, in Fort Lauderdale. • When he became an actor, TONY DANZA quit professional boxing but returned to the ring for this fight with Max "Sonny" Hord in Madison Square Garden's Felt Forum.

STELLA STEVENS ist eine der Ersten, die das Gleitsegeln ausprobiert und ca. 45m über Acapulco schwebt. • BURT LANCASTER betreut ERNEST BORGNINE, der für diese akrobatischen Übungen angeseilt ist. Das Einzige, an das sich Borgnine bei dieser Übung erinnert ist, dass Lancaster ihn dauernd „Fettarsch" nannte. • 1961 lernte MACDONALD CAREY die Karatekunst. 30 Jahre später ist er immer noch mit Trainer Benny Urquidez dabei. • MICKEY ROURKE, der als Teenager 26 Amateurkämpfe bestritt, begann seine professionelle Karriere als Leicht-Schwergewichtler und kämpfte unter dem Namen Marielito in Fort Lauderdale. • Als TONY DANZA Schauspieler wurde, hörte er mit dem professionellen Boxen auf, kam aber für diesen Kampf mit Max „Sonny" Hord im Madison Square Garden Felt Forum in den Ring zurück.

STELLA STEVENS fut l'une des premières femmes à faire du parachute ascensionnel et à planer à env. 45 mètres au-dessus de la baie d'Acapulco. • BURT LANCASTER entraîne ERNEST BORGNINE à l'acrobatie. La seule chose dont se souvienne Borgnine est que Lancaster ne cessait de l'appeler « Lard Ass ». • MACDONALD CAREY a commencé d'apprendre le karaté en 1961 et a continué trente ans plus tard avec Benny Urquidez comme professeur. • MICKEY ROURKE, qui avait disputé 26 combats amateur lorsqu'il était adolescent, commença sa carrière professionnelle comme mi-lourd à Fort Lauderdale sous le nom de Marielito. • TONY DANZA quitta la boxe professionnelle lorsqu'il devint acteur mais remonta sur le ring pour ce combat contre Max « Sonny » Hord au Felt Forum de Madison Square Garden.

STELLA STEVENS, *Orlando* 1967

ERNEST BORGNINE, BURT LANCASTER, *Larry Barbier Jr./Chic Donchin* 1955

MACDONALD CAREY, *Ralph Poole* 1961

MACDONALD CAREY, *Robert Landau* 1991

MICKEY ROURKE, *John Barrett* 1991

TONY DANZA, *Dennis Barna* 1979

CHARLTON HESTON, *George Hurn* 1958

THE BEATLES IN MIAMI, *Photo Trends* 1965

CHARLTON HESTON in the surf on the coast of Italy. • THE BEATLES in the Florida surf. • JANE RUSSELL works out with WALTER SAXER. • Scuba diver (at least for a magazine cover) YVETTE MIMIEUX • ANTONIO SABATO JR. wind sails off Turkoise Island. • OMAR SHARIF plays football on the beach in Puerto Rico.

CHARLTON HESTON an der italienischen Küste. • THE BEATLES an der Küste Floridas. • JANE RUSSELL trainiert mit WALTER SAXER. • Taucherin YVETTE MIMIEUX (zumindest für das Titelfoto). • ANTONIO SABATO JR. segelt vor Turkoise Island. • OMAR SHARIF spielt am Strand von Puerto Rico Football.

YVETTE MIMIEUX, *Don Ornitz* 1960

JANE RUSSELL AND WALTER SAXER, *Larry Barbier Jr.* 1950

ANTONIO SABATO JR., *Lisa Rose* 1998

OMAR SHARIF, *Orlando* 1969

CHARLTON HESTON sur la côte italienne. • Les BEATLES en Floride. • JANE RUSSELL s'entraîne avec WALTER SAXER. • YVETTE MIMIEUX fait de la plongée (au moins pour la couverture d'un magazine). • ANTONIO SABATO JR. sur une planche à voile au large de l'île de Turkoise. • OMAR SHARIF joue au football américain sur la plage à Puerto Rico.

SYLVESTER STALLONE, *Neale Haynes* 1994

MATT DAMON, *Milan Ryba* 2000

KEVIN COSTNER, *Lisa Rose* 1998

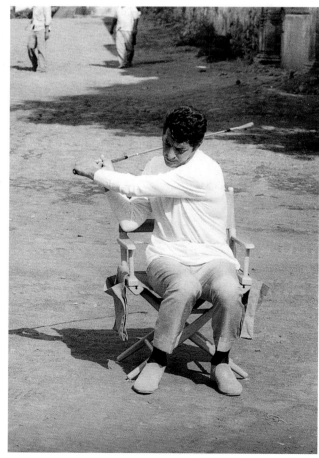

DEAN MARTIN, *Marty Mills* 1967

BOB HOPE, GERALD FORD, *Lynn McAfee* 1979

RICHARD NIXON AND JACKIE GLEASON, *Bob East* 1970

SYLVESTER STALLONE at the Foxhill Country Club, Surrey, England. • MATT DAMON at North Ranch Country Club in Thousand Oaks, California. • KEVIN COSTNER, at the Palm Desert Country Club. • DEAN MARTIN on the set of THE AMBUSHERS. • Former president GERALD FORD gets an eyeful of BOB HOPE's golf outfit at the Glen Campell Los Angeles Open in Pacific Palisades. • JACKIE GLEASON keeps President RICHARD NIXON from going into the lake along with his wayward golf ball.

SYLVESTER STALLONE im Foxhill Country Club, Surrey, England. • MATT DAMON im North Ranch Country Club in Thousand Oaks, California. • KEVIN COSTNER im Palm Desert Country Club. • DEAN MARTIN bei den Dreharbeiten zu WENN KILLER AUF DER LAUER LIEGEN (THE AMBUSHERS). • Der ehemalige Präsident GERALD FORD bestaunt das Golf-Outfit von BOB HOPE bei den Glen Campell Los Angeles Open in Pacific Palisades. • JACKIE GLEASON hält Präsident RICHARD NIXON davon ab, seinem eigensinnigen Golfball in den See zu folgen.

SYLVESTER STALLONE au Foxhill Country Club, dans le Surrey (Angleterre). • MATT DAMON au North Ranch Country Club de Thousand Oaks (Californie). • KEVIN COSTNER au Palm Desert Country Club. • DEAN MARTIN sur le plateau de MATT HELM TRAQUÉ (THE AMBUSHERS). • L'ancien président, GERALD FORD, jette un œil sur la tenue de golf de BOB HOPE lors de l'Open Glen Campell de Los Angeles à Pacific Palisades. • JACKIE GLEASON empêche le président RICHARD NIXON de suivre le même chemin que sa balle de golf.

RONALD REAGAN, *Gene Trindl* 1961

CARROLL BAKER, *Araldo Crollalanza* 1965

LEE MARVIN, *Larry Barbier Jr.* 1959

STEVE McQUEEN, *William Claxton* 1962

PAUL NEWMAN, *Winson Mulrow* 1967

RONALD REAGAN at his Santa Barbara ranch. • CARROLL BAKER and PAUL NEWMAN are avid go-karters. • LEE MARVIN was a novice motorcycle rider who was taught by friend Keenan Wynn for his role in THE WILD ONE. • STEVE McQUEEN once supported himself by competing in contests in the Long Island drag strip.

RONALD REAGAN auf seiner Ranch in Santa Barbara. • CARROLL BAKER und PAUL NEWMAN sind begeisterte Gokart-Fahrer. • LEE MARVIN war ein Anfänger auf dem Motorrad. Sein Freund Keenan Wynn gab ihm für seine Rolle im Film DER WILDE (THE WILD ONE) Unterricht. • STEVE McQUEEN verdiente sich einst seinen Lebensunterhalt als Rennfahrer auf dem Long Island Drag Strip.

RONALD REAGAN dans son ranch de Santa Barbara. • CARROLL BAKER et PAUL NEWMAN sont des passionnés de karting. • LEE MARVIN, qui ne connaissait pas grand chose à la moto, fut entraîné par son ami Keenan Wynn pour son rôle dans L'ÉQUIPÉE SAUVAGE (THE WILD ONE). • STEVE McQUEEN gagnait autrefois sa vie en faisant des compétitions sur la piste de Long Island.

ROBERT REDFORD, *William Claxton* 1965

ELVIS PRESLEY, *Wally Hill* 1956

ROD STEIGER, *Dick Miller* 1958

MADONNA, *Richard Pelham* 1990

DUSTIN HOFFMAN, *Bob Patterson* 1981

ROBERT REDFORD water skis on Lake Utah. • ELVIS PRESLEY in, not on, McKeller Lake in Memphis. • ROD STEIGER takes his morning run on the beach at Malibu. His companion is a neighbor's pet. • MADONNA jogs regularly no matter where she is – here in London. • DUSTIN HOFFMAN competes in the endurance test during the St. John's Hospital 10 Kilometer Run in Marina Del Rey.

ROBERT REDFORD fährt auf dem Lake Utah Wasserski. • ELVIS PRESLEY im, nicht auf dem McKeller Lake in Memphis. • ROD STEIGER wird beim morgendlichen Jogging am Strand von Malibu von einem Hund aus der Nachbarschaft begleitet. • MADONNA joggt regelmäßig, ganz egal, wo sie sich befindet. Hier ist sie in London. • DUSTIN HOFFMAN nimmt am Ausdauertest während des Zehn-Kilometer-Wettlaufes vom St. John's Hospital in Marina Del Rey teil.

ROBERT REDFORD fait du ski nautique sur le lac Utah. • ELVIS PRESLEY dans le lac McKeller de Memphis. • ROD STEIGER fait son jogging matinal sur la plage de Malibu avec le chien de son voisin. • MADONNA court régulièrement où qu'elle soit, comme ici à Londres. • DUSTIN HOFFMAN participe à la course d'endurance des 10 kilomètres du St. John's Hospital, à Marina Del Rey.

CARROLL O'CONNOR, *Nate Cutler* 1972

ED ASNER, *Bob Noble* 1977

NEVE CAMPBELL, *Lisa Rose* 1995

GINGER ROGERS, *Nate Cutler* 1952

DAVID NIVEN, *Giancolombo* 1963

BRAD PITT AND SHALENE McCALL, *Ralph Dominguez* 1991

TIM ROBBINS, *Walter Weissman* 1999

JAMES MASON, *Farabola* 1964

JULIA ROBERTS AND JASON PATRIC, *Albert Fereirra* 1991

ROBERT MITCHUM, *John R. Hamilton* 1966

SUZANNE PLESHETTE AND TROY DONAHUE, *Don Ornitz* 1964

PETER GRAVES, *J. Barry Herron* 1968

JULIA ROBERTS and JASON PATRIC discover you don't have to be alone to be alone. • ROBERT MITCHUM and the one that didn't get away. • SUZANNNE PLESHETTE and TROY DONAHUE fish at Santa Monica. • PETER GRAVES helps to lift his catch which will be tagged and returned to the sea during a whale hunting mission aboard the Marineland of the Pacific boat Geronimo.

JULIA ROBERTS und JASON PATRIC entdecken, dass man nicht alleine sein muss, um alleine zu sein. • ROBERT MITCHUM und der Fisch, der nicht entkam. • SUZANNNE PLESHETTE und TROY DONAHUE angeln in Santa Monica. • PETER GRAVES hilft beim Emporheben seines Fangs. Er wird während einer Walfangmission an Bord der Geronimo, einem Schiff des Marineland of Pacific, mit einem Etikett versehen und wieder freigelassen.

JULIA ROBERTS et JASON PATRIC se rendent compte qu'il ne faut pas nécessairement être seul pour se sentir seul. • ROBERT MITCHUM et un poisson qui n'en démord pas. • SUZANNNE PLESHETTE et TROY DONAHUE pêchent à Santa Monica. • Lors d'une mission de chasse à la baleine à bord du Geronimo, le navire du Marineland Pacifique, PETER GRAVES aide à soulever sa prise, qui sera ensuite marquée et remise à l'eau.

BURT REYNOLDS, *Globe Archive* 1958

WILLIAM HOLDEN, *Globe Archive* 1958

BURT REYNOLDS finds his own brand of adventure by hunting and tagging alligators in the Florida Everglades. • WILLIAM HOLDEN first encountered East Africa on safari in 1958 and fell in love with the country. Off and on he spent 25 years in Kenya and created a safari club on the slopes of Mt. Kenya which, in 1984, became the William Holden Wildlife Foundation, dedicated to bringing ecological awareness to new generations of African youth. A direct result has been the banning of hunting in Kenya.

BURT REYNOLDS findet seine Herausforderung beim Jagen und Etikettieren von Alligatoren in den Florida Everglades. • WILLIAM HOLDEN kam das erste Mal auf einer Safari nach Ostafrika und verliebte sich in das Land. 25 Jahre lang kam er hin und wieder nach Kenia und gründete einen Safariclub an den Abhängen des Mt. Kenya, der 1984 zur William Holden Wildlife Foundation wurde und die Grundzüge der Ökologie an die afrikanischen Jugend vermitteln will. Ein sofortiges Resultat war das Verbot der Jagd in Kenia.

BURT REYNOLDS aime l'aventure que sont la chasse et le maraquage des alligators aux Everglades (Floride). • WILLIAM HOLDEN se rendit pour la première fois en Afrique de l'Est lors d'un safari en 1958 et tomba amoureux de ce pays. Il s'y rendit régulièrement pendat 25 ans au Kenya et créa, sur les versants du Mont Kenya, un safari club qui devint en 1984 la William Holden Wildlife Foundation ayant pour but de faire prendre conscience à la jeunesse africaine de l'importance de l'écologie. L'un des premiers résultats fut l'interdiction de la chasse au Kenya.

No matter who or what or where Globe photographers shot, one call was heard from each and every editor hoping for that special, animated, fun picture that could make a layout irresistible or even get published as a "floater," the journalistic jargon for a photograph that could be run alone with little or no caption necessary for support. That call was:

Ganz egal, von wem oder was oder wo Globe-Fotografen ihre Bilder machten, eine Anfrage gab es von jedem Herausgeber, der sich ein besonderes, aussagekräftiges und witziges Foto wünschte. Es musste ein Foto sein, das die Aufmerksamkeit unwillkürlich auf sich zog, eines, das man sogar als „floater" (ein journalistischer Begriff für ein Foto, das man ohne Überschriften oder Erklärungen veröffentlichen kann) benutzen konnte. Diese Anfrage lautete:

Les rédactions des magazines ne demandaient aux photographes de Globe pas autre chose qu'une photo singulière, vivante ou drôle capable d'attirer l'œil sur la couverture de leur journal ou pouvant éventuellement être publiée en «floater», un terme de l'argot journalistique désignant une photographie publiable sans être accompagnée d'une légende. Peu importait en fait de qui, de quoi ou à quel endroit le photographe avait pris un cliché, le seul mot d'ordre était alors:

SHOW 'EM EATING
BEIM ESSEN
QU'ON LES VOIT MANGER

ANITA EKBERG, *Dick Miller* 1966

SHOW 'EM DANCING
BEIM TANZEN
QU'ON LES VOIT DANSER

SHOW 'EM KISSING
BEIM KÜSSEN
QU'ON LES VOIT S'EMBRASSER

TONY CURTIS AND JANET LEIGH, *Nate Cutler* 1951

ERNIE KOVACS AND EDIE ADAMS, *Nate Cutler* 19961

JOHNNY CARSON, *Don Ornitz* 1962

DORIS DAY, *Nate Cutler* 1970

STEVE McQUEEN, *William Claxton* 1962

ELIZABETH TAYLOR, *Nate Cutler* 1961

ROCK HUDSON, *Nate Cutler* 1959

SAL MINEO, *Globe Archive* 1960

MARCELLO MASTROIANNI, *Don Ornitz* 1962

SOPHIA LOREN, JAMES STEVENS, *Bill Kobrin* 1962

HARRY BELAFONTE, DIAHANN CARROLL, *Irv Steinberg* 1962

DANNY KAYE, *Giornalistica Fotovedo* 1955

GARY COLEMAN, *Ralph Dominguez* 1979

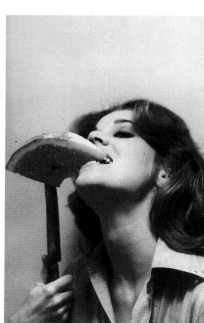

JANE FONDA, *Jack Stager* 1960

SID CAESAR AND ELLIOTT GOULD, *Judie Burstein* 1980

JOHN AND ROBERTA GARFIELD, *Nate Cutler* 1949

JOHN TRAVOLTA, *Robert Fitzgerald* 1976

MAMA CASS ELLIOTT, *Irv Steinberg* 1970

SHELLEY WINTERS AND FARLEY GRANGER, *Nate Cutler* 1951

FREDDIE PRINZE, *Rene Mendez* 1974

JACK KELLY AND JAMES GARNER, *Nate Cutler* 1959

LINDA BLAIR, *John R. Hamilton* 1974

JOYCE DEWITT AND PRISCILLA BARNES, *Ralph Dominguez* 1983

ESTHER WILLIAMS AND VIVIAN BLAINE, *Larry Barbier Jr.* 1951

KRIS KRISTOFFERSON AND BARBRA STREISAND, *Bill Greenslade* 1975

JANE RUSSELL AND ROBERT MITCHUM, *Globe Archive* 1951

VAN JOHNSON AND GREER GARSON, *Nate Cutler* 1954

JACK AND CYNTHIA LEMMON, *Nate Cutler* 1955

CHARLTON HESTON, *Larry Barbier Jr.* 1953

ANNA MARIA ALBERGHETTI, *Nate Cutler* 1960

TONY CURTIS AND MARILYN MONROE, *Nate Cutler* 1959

SHEREE NORTH AND LARRY PARKS, *Nate Cutler* 1956

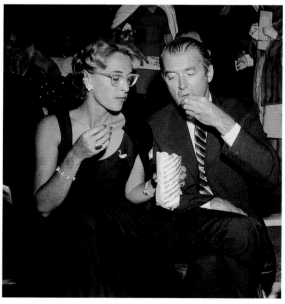

JAMES AND GLORIA STEWART, *Nate Cutler* 1956

KIM NOVAK AND FRANK SINATRA, *Nate Cutler* 1955

AUDREY HEPBURN AND PHIL SILVERS, *Nate Cutler* 1954

GINA LOLLOBRIGIDA AND ROCK HUDSON, *Nate Cutler* 1963

PIPER LAURIE, *Nate Cutler* 1953

GINA LOLLOBRIGIDA demonstrates the Italian way of eating grapes to her costar ROCK HUDSON at the STRANGE BED-FELLOWS party at Universal Studios. • Early in her career Universal Pictures put out the story that PIPER LAURIE was fond of eating flowers and that bit of fluff may have been one of the reasons she wasn't taken really seriously as an actress until the early 60s.

GINA LOLLOBRIGIDA zeigt ihrem Filmpartner ROCK HUDSON auf der Party für FREMDE BETTGESELLEN (STRANGE BEDFEL-LOWS) in den Universal Studios, die italienische Art, Trauben zu essen. • Am Anfang ihrer Karriere setzte Universal Pictures das Gerücht in die Welt, dass PIPER LAURIE gerne Blumen essen würde. Es kann an diesem Gerücht gelegen haben, dass man sie als Schauspielerin bis in die frühen 60er nicht richtig Ernst nahm.

GINA LOLLOBRIGIDA montre à son partenaire ROCK HUDSON comment les Italiens mangent le raisin lors de la soirée de ÉTRANGES COMPAGNONS DE LIT (STRANGE BEDFELLOWS) aux Universal Studios. • Universal Pictures ayant fait courir le bruit que PIPER LAURIE, alors à ses débuts, adorait manger des fleurs, ce «canard» pourrait être l'une des raisons pour lesquelles elle ne fut pas considérée sérieusement comme une actrice avant les années 1960.

TONY CURTIS, *Combi Press* 1960

GLENN FORD, *Combi Press* 1964

MEL FERRER, ELIZABETH TAYLOR, AUDREY HEPBURN AND EDDIE FISHER, *Sylvia Norris* 1961

BARBARA STANWYCK AND GILBERT ROLAND, *Nate Cutler* 1950

PETER FALK AND GOLDIE HAWN, *Nate Cutler* 1979

DEBBIE REYNOLDS AND MIKE TODD, *Nate Cutler* 1955

LAUREN BACALL AND FRANK SINATRA, *Nate Cutler* 1958

GENE TIERNEY AND ROCK HUDSON, *Nate Cutler* 1953

GLENN FORD AND HOPE LANGE, *Nate Cutler* 1961

ED BEGLEY AND NANCY CZAR, *Nate Cutler* 1966

NORMA SHEARER AND MARTY ARROUGE, *Nate Cutler* 1950

RICHARD DEAN ANDERSON AND MARCIA TAYLOR, *Nate Cutler* 1978

BUDDY EBSEN, *Steve Fritz* 1973

BETTE DAVIS, *Dick Miller* 1959

BUDDY EBSEN, who began his career as a dancer, performs at the Variety Arts Center. • BETTE DAVIS learns the can-can for a segment of WAGON TRAIN. The lady pulling out her hair is choreographer MIRIAM NELSON. • AMANDA BLAKE and her GUNSMOKE costar MILBURN STONE entertain at the Santa Fe Trail charity event in Dodge City. • DOROTHY DANDRIDGE works out with Swiss body culture expert WALTER SAXER.

BUDDY EBSEN, der seine Karriere als Tänzer begann, hier bei einer Vorstellung im Variety Arts Center. • BETTE DAVIS lernt Can-Can für eine Szene in dem Film WAGON TRAIN. Die Dame, die sich an den Kopf fasst, ist Choreografin MIRIAM NELSON. • AMANDA BLAKE und ihr Filmpartner MILBURN STONE in MÜNDUNGSFEUER (GUNSMOKE) sorgen bei der Santa-Fe-Trail-Wohltätigkeitsveranstaltung in Dodge City für Unterhaltung. • DOROTHY DANDRIDGE trainiert mit dem schweizerischen Körperkultur-Experten WALTER SAXER.

BUDDY EBSEN, qui débuta comme danseur, se donne en spectacle au Variety Arts Center. • BETTE DAVIS apprend le French cancan pour un épisode de la série télé WAGON TRAIN. La femme avec la main dans les cheveux est la chorégraphe MIRIAM NELSON. • AMANDA BLAKE et son partenaire MILBURN STONE dans LE TUEUR DU MONTANA (GUNSMOKE) font un numéro à l'occasion d'une vente de charité de la Santa Fe Trail à Dodge City. • DOROTHY DANDRIDGE s'entraîne avec le Suisse WALTER SAXER.

MILBURN STONE AND AMANDA BLAKE, *Larry Barbier Jr.* 1958

DOROTHY DANDRIDGE AND WALTER SAXER, *Dick Miller* 1958

GARDNER McKAY AND JOAN COLLINS, *Larry Barbier Jr.* 1959

INGRID BERGMAN, *Atlantic Press* 1960

RUDOLF NUREYEV, *Orlando* 1965

SAMMY DAVIS JR., *Nate Cutler* 1970

GROUCHO MARX AND DIANA ROSS, *Nate Cutler* 1966

ANN-MARGRET, *Globe Archive* 1964

CONNIE STEVENS, *Nate Cutler* 1962

STEVE McQUEEN, *Nate Cutler* 1967

EDDIE MURPHY, *John Barrett* 1983

ANN MILLER AND RED SKELTON, *Larry Barbier Jr.* 1949

LIZA MINNELLI AND TRUMAN CAPOTE, *Michael Norcia* 1978

GREGORY HINES AND DEBBIE ALLEN, *John Barrett* 1983

ANGELINA JOLIE AND PETA WILSON, *Lisa Rose* 1999

GENE HACKMAN, *Nate Cutler* 1972

MADONNA, *Ralph Dominguez* 1984

ANTHONY QUINN, *Peter Armatas* 1967

MADONNA at the AIDS Dance-a-thon. • ANTHONY QUINN dances Zorba style, complete with money on the floor, at Sirocco in New York.

MADONNA ist beim Tanzmarathon zu Gunsten der AIDS-Hilfe dabei. • ANTHONY QUINN tanzt im griechischen Zorba-Stil, ganz so wie es sich gehört mit Geld auf dem Fußboden, im Sirocco in New York.

MADONNA au Dance-a-thon (un marathon de danse) pour la lutte contre le Sida. • ANTHONY QUINN danse à la manière de Zorba le Grec au Sirocco de New York.

MICHAEL DOUGLAS AND HAYLEY MILLS, *Nate Cutler* 1962

MICHAEL DOUGLAS and HAYLEY MILLS dance at Michael's 17th birthday party.

MICHAEL DOUGLAS und HAYLES MILLS tanzen auf der Party anlässlich Michaels 17. Geburtstag.

MICHAEL DOUGLAS et HAYLEY MILLS dansent lors de la fête donnée à l'occasion du 17e anniversaire de Michael.

JESSICA LANGE AND BOB FOSSE, *Adam Scull* 1979

SHIRLEY MACLAINE, *Nate Cutler* 1965

JACK AND FELICIA LEMMON, *Nate Cutler* 1964

BEA ARTHUR, *Nate Cutler* 1976

CHER, *Ralph Dominguez* 1984

LAUREN BACALL, *Orlando* 1965

LANA TURNER AND STEVE CRANE, *Nate Cutler* 1948

BETTY FORD AND CESAR ROMERO, *Nate Cutler* 1976

LANA TURNER and second husband Steve Crane at Earl Carroll's. • First Lady BETTY FORD swoons for CESAR ROMERO, one of Hollywood's best dancers, at The Bistro. • MITZI GAYNOR and JACK BEAN, one of Hollywood's longest married couples. They celebrated their 46th anniversary in the year 2000.

LANA TURNER und ihr zweiter Ehemann Steve Crane bei Earl Carroll's. • First Lady BETTY FORD fällt aus Begeisterung für CESAR ROMERO, einem der besten Tänzer Hollywoods, fast in Ohnmacht. • MITZI GAYNOR und JACK BEAN, eines der am längsten verheirateten Paare Hollywoods, feierten im Jahr 2000 ihren 46. Hochzeitstag.

LANA TURNER et son second mari Steve Crane au Earl Carroll's. • Au Bistro, madame BETTY FORD tombe en pâmoison dans les bras de CESAR ROMERO, l'un des meilleurs danseurs de Hollywood. • MITZI GAYNOR et JACK BEAN, qui ont célébré leur 46ᵉ anniversaire de mariage en l'an 2000, forment le couple le plus longtemps marié de Hollywood.

MITZI GAYNOR AND JACK BEAN, *Nate Cutler* 1953

VINCENTE AND LIZA MINNELLI, *Nate Cutler* 1970

LIZA MINNELLI is embraced by her father VINCENTE MINNELLI on her opening night at the Cocoanut Grove.

LIZA MINNELLI wird von ihrem Vater VINCENTE MINNELLI bei ihrer Premiere im Cocoanut Grove umarmt.

LIZA MINNELLI est enlacée par son père VINCENTE MINNELLI lors de leur première au Cocoanut Grove.

NANCY REAGAN AND JOHN HUSTON, *Adam Scull* 1982

BILLY BARTY AND RUTA LEE, *Nate Cutler* 1976

Gentleman JOHN HUSTON pays tribute to NANCY REAGAN at the Rainbow Room in New York. • BILLY BARTY and RUTA LEE at the Thalian Ball.

Gentleman JOHN HUSTON verneigt sich vor NANCY REAGAN im Rainbow Room in New York. • BILLY BARTY und RUTA LEE auf dem Thalian-Ball.

Le gentleman JOHN HUSTON rend hommage à NANCY REAGAN au Rainbow Room à New York. • BILLY BARTY et RUTA LEE au Thalian Ball.

KIM NOVAK AND ZERO MOSTEL, *Nate Cutler* 1968

PETER LORRE AND SOPHIA LOREN, *Nate Cutler* 1965

PEGGY LEE AND CARY GRANT, *Nate Cutler* 1972

GWYNETH PALTROW AND BRAD PITT, *Sonia Moskowitz* 1997

GREER GARSON AND BUDDY FOGELSON, *Nate Cutler* 1952

LILLI PALMER AND REX HARRISON, *Nate Cutler* 1952

ANNE JEFFREYS AND ROBERT STERLING, *Nate Cutler* 1951

GENE KELLY AND RUBY KEELER, *Ralph Dominguez* 1991

JON PROVOST AND LASSIE, *Larry Barbier Jr.* 1960

JULIA ROBERTS AND CAMERON DIAZ, *Lisa Rose* 1997

KATHLEEN TURNER, *Adam Scull* 1984

JOHN TRAVOLTA AND KELLY PRESTON, *Michael Ferguson* 1990

KATE MOSS AND JOHNNY DEPP, *Rose Hartman* 1995

RYAN O'NEAL AND FARRAH FAWCETT, *Sylvia Norris* 1985

LAUREN BACALL AND HARRY GUARDINO, *Adam Scull* 1981

LOU COSTELLO AND YVONNE DECARLO, *Nate Cutler* 1955

HARRY BELAFONTE AND LENA HORNE, *Nate Cutler* 1968

JOAN CRAWFORD AND DANNY THOMAS, *Nate Cutler* 1955

PAUL AND MIRA SORVINO, *Fitzroy Barrett* 1996

PEGGY MOFFITT AND MADONNA, *Lisa Rose* 1998

ANGELINA JOLIE & BROTHER JAMES HAVEN, *Alec Michael* 2000

MICHAEL JETER AND SEAN BLUE, *Nina Prommer* 1998

DUSTIN HOFFMAN AND JOHN SCHLESINGER, *Adam Scull* 1985

JANE DARWELL AND CHARLIE RUGGLES, *Nate Cutler* 1967

JACKIE GLEASON, *William Read Woodfield* 1962

ANDY WILLIAMS AND CLAUDINE LONGET, *Nate Cutler* 1962

JUNE ALLYSON AND HUMPHREY BOGART, *Nate Cutler* 1953

SHIRLEY TEMPLE & SON CHARLES BLACK JR, *Dick Miller* 1958

GINGER ROGERS AND FRED ASTAIRE, *Nate Cutler* 1976

NOAH WYL AND GEORGE CLOONEY, *Lisa Rose* 1994

DEAN MARTIN AND ROSALIND RUSSELL, *Nate Cutler* 1959

SIMONE SIGNORET AND SIDNEY LUMET, *Adam Scull* 1979

MARY TYLER MOORE AND ED ASNER, *Nate Cutler* 1978

MILTON BERLE, *Nate Cutler* 1977

BING CROSBY, DOROTHY LAMOUR AND BOB HOPE, *Sylvia Norris* 1976

JULIE CHRISTIE AND ROD STEIGER, *John Cameola* 1965

DENNIS AND GERRY WEAVER, *Nate Cutler* 1962

BARBARA BARRIE AND E.G. MARSHALL, *Irv Steinberg* 1976

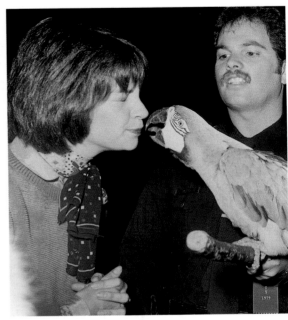

CINDY WILLIAMS, *Art Zelin* 1979

JASON ROBARDS JR. AND COLLEEN DEWHURST, *Adam Scull* 1981

BILLY WILDER AND GLENN CLOSE, *Dave Bennett* 1994

QUINCY JONES AND OPRAH WINFREY, *Lisa Rose* 1997

DONALD O'CONNOR, *Nate Cutler* 1955

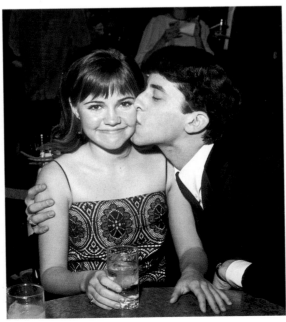

SALLY FIELD AND GARY LEWIS, *Nate Cutler* 1966

MERLE OBERON, NOEL COWARD AND JUDY GARLAND, *Nate Cutler* 1956

CAROL CHANNING AND MARY MARTIN, *Judie Burstein* 1988

DANNY KAYE AND LUCILLE BALL, *Nate Cutler* 1960

PAT O'BRIEN AND JEANETTE MACDONALD, *Nate Cutler* 1966

BETTY GRABLE AND DAN DAILEY, *Nate Cutler* 1955

MARILYN MONROE AND JOE DiMAGGIO, *Bob East* 1954

SHIRLEY MACLAINE AND DEBRA WINGER, *Richard Corkery* 1983

Examples of the ultimate Hollywood air kiss. CAROL CHANNING and MARY MARTIN at the opening of LEGENDS. • DANNY KAYE and LUCILLE BALL at CBS studio. • PAT O'BRIEN and JEANETTE MACDONALD at the Mocambo. • BETTY GRABLE and DAN DAILEY at Slapsy Maxie's. • MARILYN MONROE and JOE DiMAGGIO in Florida. • SHIRLEY MACLAINE and DEBRA WINGER in New York. • ELVIS and you.

Beispiele für herausragende Luftküsse in Hollywood: CAROL CHANNING und MARY MARTIN auf der Premiere von LEGENDS. • DANNY KAYE und LUCILLE BALL im CBS-Studio. • PAT O'BRIEN und JEANETTE MACDONALD im Mocambo. • BETTY GRABLE und DAN DAILEY bei Slapsy Maxie's. • MARILYN MONROE und JOE DiMAGGIO in Florida. • SHIRLEY MACLAINE und DEBRA WINGER in New York. • ELVIS und Sie.

Exemples des derniers baisers en vogue à Hollywood. CAROL CHANNING et MARY MARTIN à l'ouverture de LEGENDS. • DANNY KAYE et LUCILLE BALL au CBS studio. • PAT O'BRIEN et JEANETTE MACDONALD au Mocambo. • BETTY GRABLE et DAN DAILEY au Slapsy Maxie's. • MARILYN MONROE et JOE DiMAGGIO en Floride. • SHIRLEY MACLAINE et DEBRA WINGER à New York. • ELVIS et toi.

ELVIS PRESLEY, *Lloyd Dinkins 1977*

CARRIE FISHER AND HARRISON FORD IN NEW YORK, *Richard Corkery* 1984

SHUTTERBUGS

Even stars get the urge to get behind the camera. Some, like Roddy McDowall, Candice Bergen, Yul Brynner and Diane Keaton have earned professional status. But most snap away for their own personal scrapbooks, just like you and me.

HOBBY-FOTOGRAFEN

Selbst Stars bekommen den Drang, hinter der Kamera zu stehen. Einige, wie Roddy McDowall, Candice Bergen, Yul Brynner und Diane Keaton, sind sehr angesehen. Aber die meisten knipsen nur für ihre persönlichen Fotoalben, genau wie Sie und ich.

LES STARS PHOTOGRAPHES

Les stars ont parfois éprouvé le besoin de passer derrière une caméra ou un appareil photo. Si certains, comme Roddy McDowall, Candice Bergen, Yul Brynner ou Diane Keaton, sont même désormais considérés comme des professionnels, la plupart se contentent de prendre des photos uniquement pour leur album personnel, tout comme vous et moi.

YUL BRYNNER shoots cast members during a rehearsal for the stage revival of THE KING AND I.

YUL BRYNNER macht Fotos von den Darstellern während einer Probe für die Bühnenversion von DER KÖNIG UND ICH (THE KING AND I).

YUL BRYNNER prend en photo les membres de la troupe lors des répétitions pour la reprise au théâtre de LE ROI ET MOI (THE KING AND I).

YUL BRYNNER, *Michael Norcia* 1977

RODDY McDOWALL, *Winson Muldrow* 1964

RODDY McDOWALL selects photos for the first edition of his series of picture books DOUBLE EXPOSURE. • GINA LOLLOBRIGIDA, with son Milko, shoots frequently for French magazines • PETER SELLERS shoots wife BRITT EKLAND on the set of THE BOBO. • In 1979 DIANE KEATON published a book of photographs called RESERVATIONS. • CANDICE BERGEN shoots local women on the Taiwan location of THE SAND PEBBLES.

RODDY McDOWALL sucht Bilder für die erste Ausgabe seiner Bildbandserie DOUBLE EXPOSURE aus. • GINA LOLLOBRIGIDA, hier mit ihrem Sohn Milko, schießt regelmäßig für französische Zeitschriften Fotos. • PETER SELLERS fotografiert seine Frau BRITT EKLAND bei BOBO IST DER GRÖSSTE. • 1979 veröffentlichte DIANE KEATON einen Bildband mit dem Titel RESERVATIONS. • CANDICE BERGEN macht am Drehort zu KANONENBOOT AM YANGTSE-KIANG, der in Taiwan gedreht wird, Fotos von einheimischen Frauen.

GINA LOLLOBRIGIDA, *Fotovedo* 1959

PETER SELLERS AND BRITT EKLAND, *Globe Archive* 1966

CANDICE BERGEN, *Doris Nieh* 1965

DIANE KEATON, *John R. Hamilton* 1975

RODDY McDOWALL sélectionne ses photos pour la première édition de sa série de recueils DOUBLE EXPOSURE. • GINA LOLLOBRIGIDA, ici avec son fils Milko travaille pour des magazines français. • PETER SELLERS photographie BRITT EKLAND, son épouse, sur le plateau de THE BOBO. • DIANE KEATON a publié en 1979 un recueil de photos intitulé RESERVATIONS. • CANDICE BERGEN photographie des Taiwanaises pendant le tournage de LA CANONNIÈRE DU YANG-TSÉ.

LEE MARVIN, *Nate Cutler* 1964

MELINA MERCOURI, *Orlando* 1964

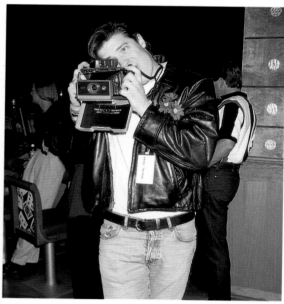

BRENDAN FRASER, *Fitzroy Barrett* 1995

DUSTIN HOFFMAN, *Fitzroy Barret* 1996

MATTHEW BRODERICK, *Hy Simon* 1985

RED SKELTON, *Nate Cutler* 1960

DREW BARRYMORE AND TOM GREEN, *Fitzroy Barrett* 2000

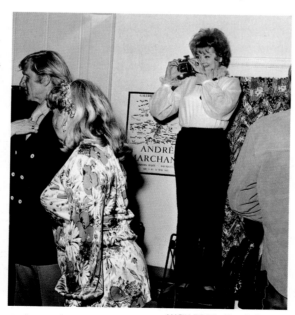

LUCILLE BALL, *Nate Cutler* 1971

URSULA ANDRESS AND JOHN DEREK, *John R. Hamilton* 1957

BOB CRANE, *Bill Kobrin* 1965

LEONARD NIMOY, *Bob Noble* 1976

A real photography nut, BOB CRANE takes a self portrait with his family. • LEONARD NIMOY converted a spare room into a photo lab.

BOB CRANE, ein begeisteter Fotograf, hier bei einem Selbstporträt mit Familie. • LEONARD NIMOY wandelte einen Abstellraum in ein Fotolabor um.

Vrai passionné de photographie, BOB CRANE fait son autoportrait en famille. • LEONARD NIMOY a transformé sa chambre d'ami en labo photo.

TONY CURTIS captures some high flying action on the set of DON'T MAKE WAVES. • PAUL NEWMAN and JOANNE WOODWARD play tourists in Israel. • BRIGITTE BARDOT and STEPHEN BOYD shoot each other on the set of SHALAKO. • SAL MINEO and JILL HAWORTH on a day off from filming EXODUS in Israel. • HARRY BELAFONTE on the location of BUCK AND THE PREACHER.

TONY CURTIS fängt einige heiße Actionszenen bei den Dreharbeiten zu DIE NACKTEN TATSACHEN (DON'T MAKE WAVES) ein. • PAUL NEWMAN und JOANNE WOODWARD spielen in Israel Touristen. • BRIGITTE BARDOT und STEPHEN BOYD fotografieren sich bei den Dreharbeiten zu SHALAKO gegenseitig. • Ein freier Tag für SAL MINEO und JILL HAWORTH bei den Dreharbeiten zu EXODUS, der in Israel gedreht wird. • HARRY BELAFONTE am Drehort zu DER WEG DER VERDAMMTEN (BUCK AND THE PREACHER).

TONY CURTIS saisit une cascade bien enlevée lors du tournage de COMMENT RÉUSSIR EN AMOUR SANS SE FATIGUER (DON'T MAKE WAVES). • PAUL NEWMAN et JOANNE WOODWARD jouent aux touristes en Israël. • BRIGITTE BARDOT et STEPHEN BOYD se photographient mutuellement dans les décors de SHALAKO. • Journée de repos pour SAL MINEO et JILL HAWORTH pendant le tournage de EXODUS en Israël. • HARRY BELAFONTE sur le tournage de BUCK ET SON COMPLICE (BUCK AND THE PREACHER).

TONY CURTIS, *Orlando* 1967

PAUL NEWMAN AND JOANNE WOODWARD, *Leo Fuchs* 1959

BRIGITTE BARDOT AND STEPHEN BOYD, *Herreros Rooney* 1968

JILL HAWORTH AND SAL MINEO, *Giancolombo News* 1959

SANDRA DEE AND ROCK HUDSON, *Leo Fuchs* 1961

HARRY BELAFONTE, *Sidney Baldwin* 1971

JACK LEMMON, *Tom Caffrey* 1968

RON HOWARD, *John R. Hamilton* 1975

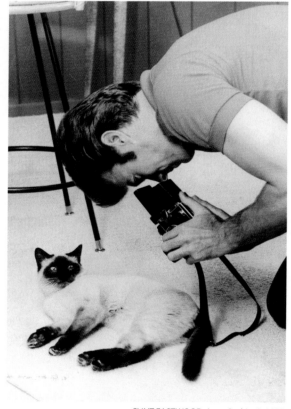

BARBARA HALE, BILL WILLIAMS AND CHILDREN, *Larry Barbier Jr.* 1954

CLINT EASTWOOD, *Larry Barbier Jr.* 1959

SAMMY DAVIS JR., *Globe Archive* 1965

JACK LEMMON shoots a frog prince. • RON HOWARD directs his pet spaniel. • BARBARA HALE snaps her family at Santa's Village: husband BILL WILLIAMS, children Laura and Bill Jr., later to be professionally known as WILLIAM KATT. • CLINT EASTWOOD photographs Sam, his Siamese. • SAMMY DAVIS JR. in the midst of all of his photographic equipment kept in the dressing room during the run of GOLDEN BOY on Broadway.

JACK LEMMON fotografiert einen Froschkönig. • RON HOWARD setzt seinen Cockerspaniel in Szene. • BARBARA HALE macht in Santa's Village Bilder von ihrer Familie: Ehemann BILL WILLIAMS, Kinder Laura und Bill Jr., später in der Filmwelt als WILLIAM KATT bekannt. • CLINT EASTWOOD fotografiert seine Siamkatze Sam. • SAMMY DAVIS JR. inmitten seiner Fotoausrüstung in der Umkleidekabine, während der Spielzeit von GOLDEN BOY auf dem Broadway.

JACK LEMMON photographie une grenouille. • RON HOWARD met en scène son épagneul. • BARBARA HALE et sa famille au village du père Noël: BILL WILLIAMS, son mari, et ses enfants Laura et Bill Jr., qui se rendra célèbre sous le nom de WILLIAM KATT. • CLINT EASTWOOD photographie Sam, son chat siamois. • SAMMY DAVIS JR. au milieu de tout son matériel photo dans sa loge de GOLDEN BOY à Broadway.

MARLON AND CHRISTIAN BRANDO, *Ralph Dominguez* 1990

THE COURT BEAT

Time was when courtroom coverage was limited to Hollywood divorce proceedings, custody battles and contract disputes. Appearances by celebrities on criminal charges were few and far between. Studios saw to that. If a misbehaving star was arrested, the first call was made not to a lawyer but to the studio head of publicity and before the media got knowledge of the incident, the star was safely out of their reach.

With the end of the studio contract system, actors who found themselves in trouble with the law usually had to fend for themselves. There was no publicity chief, no Howard Strickling or Harry Brand, to run interference for them. Today's personal publicists just don't carry the weight with the LAPD that these powerful studio men once did and with the media keeping an ever more watchful eye out for celebrity lawbreakers, the police station and courtroom became fertile territory. A new category of star coverage opened: the celebrity in handcuffs.

An interesting side note that illustrates both the changing times and changing attitudes of the press is the fact that criminal charges, regardless of the ultimate court rulings, used to mean professional death. Roscoe "Fatty" Arbuckle's career was ended by his involvement in the death of starlet Virginia Rapp even though he was never officially charged with a crime. Charlie Chaplin was acquitted in a paternity suit but public opinion was so negative that the majority of Americans agreed with an INS decree that his US visa be revoked. Errol Flynn was found not guilty of statutory rape but never regained the glossy stardom he enjoyed prior to the trial. It wasn't until Robert Mitchum, then an extremely popular up and coming star, was convicted of marijuana possession and served time in jail, that the tide turned. Rather than finding his career over, Mitchum emerged a bigger star than before.

From then on, notoriety seemed to add luster to thriving careers and resuscitate those on life support.

IM GERICHTSSAAL

Es gab eine Zeit, in der die Berichterstattung aus dem Gerichtssaal auf Scheidungsverfahren, Kämpfe um das Sorgerecht und Vertragskonflikte beschränkt war. Nur sehr selten mussten Stars wegen krimineller Vergehen vor Gericht erscheinen. Die Filmstudios kümmerten sich darum. Wenn ein Star, der sich daneben benommen hatte, von der Polizei verhaftet wurde, wurde zuerst der Publicity-Chef des Studios angerufen, nicht etwa ein Rechtsanwalt – und ehe die Medien überhaupt von dem Vorfall erfuhren, war der Star außer Reichweite.

Mit dem Ende des Filmstudio-Vertragssystems mussten sich die Schauspieler, die mit dem Gesetz in Konflikt gerieten waren, selbst verteidigen. Es gab keinen Pressechef, keinen Howard Strickling oder Harry Brand mehr, der sich für sie hätte einsetzen können. Die Agenten haben nicht mehr den Einfluss auf das Polizeipräsidium von Los Angeles, den diese mächtigen Größen aus dem Filmgeschäft einst hatten und dadurch, dass die Medien ein wachsames Auge auf die berühmten Straftäter werfen, werfen das Polizeipräsidium und der Gerichtssaal immer eine gute Story ab. Eine neue Rubrik der Star-Berichterstattung entstand: Prominente in Handschellen.

Eine interessante Randbemerkung, die sowohl die gesellschaftlichen Veränderungen als auch die Veränderung der Stellung der Presse illustriert, ist die Tatsache, dass — ganz gleich wie das endgültige Urteil lautete — Anklagen wegen krimineller Vergehen das berufliche Aus bedeuteten. Roscoe „Fatty" Arbuckles Karriere war mit seiner Verwicklung in den Tod des Starlets Virginia Rapp beendet, auch wenn er nie offiziell eines Verbrechens angeklagt wurde. Charlie Chaplin wurde in einer Vaterschaftsklage freigesprochen, aber die öffentliche Meinung über ihn war so negativ, dass die Mehrheit der Amerikaner einer Widerrufung seines Visum zugestimmt hätte. Errol Flynn wurde in einer Anklage wegen Unzucht mit Minderjährigen als nicht schuldig befunden, konnte aber nie an den Ruhm früherer Tage anknüpfen. Erst mit Robert Mitchum, der zu diesem Zeitpunkt ein extrem populärer und aufstrebender Star war, bahnte sich ein Wandel an. Der Star wurde wegen Besitzes von Marihuana festgenommen und saß eine Zeit lang im Gefängnis. Aber anstatt seine Karriere in Trümmern vorzufinden, wurde Mitchum zu einem größeren Star als zuvor.

Seit dieser Zeit schien ein schlechter Ruf glanzvolle Karrieren zu krönen und diejenigen anzufachen, die abzuklingen drohten.

AU TRIBUNAL

Il fut un temps où les seuls procès couverts par les photographes de Globe à Hollywood se limitaient aux procédures de divorce, aux conflits de garde d'enfants et aux différends contractuels. Il est vrai que les célébrités se trouvaient alors rarement impliquées dans des affaires pénales, les Studios veillant tout particulièrement à éviter ce genre de publicité. Si le comportement d'une star avait entraîné son arrestation par la police, elle ne passait pas son premier coup de téléphone à un avocat mais au chef du service publicité du studio et, avant même que les médias n'aient connaissance de l'incident, se trouvait déjà hors d'atteinte de leur curiosité.

Lorsque les acteurs acquièrent leur indépendance vis-à-vis des Studios, grâce à l'abandon du système des contrats, ceux qui eurent des problèmes avec la loi durent désormais se débrouiller seuls et sans l'intermédiation des chefs de publicité tels que Howard Strickling ou Harry Brand. Face à la police de Los Angeles (LAPD), les agents de publicité personnels des vedettes n'ont pas, de nos jours, autant de poids que ces puissants personnages des Studios. Le commissariat de police et le tribunal deviennent alors de fructueux territoires de chasse pour les journalistes qui, à l'affût vigilant des célébrités contrevenantes, développent un nouveau thème : la star menottée.

À l'époque, une inculpation pénale, quelque que soit d'ailleurs la décision ultime du tribunal, entraîne alors presque toujours la mort professionnelle de l'acteur concerné. Roscoe « Fatty » Arbuckle verra sa carrière ruinée malgré son acquittement d'une accusation d'homicide sur la personne de la starlette Virginia Rapp ; Charlie Chaplin est également relaxé dans un procès en paternité mais voit se dresser contre lui l'opinion publique américaine qui soutient unanimement un décret de l'INS révoquant son visa américain ; jugé non coupable de détournement de mineur, Errol Flynn ne retrouvera jamais la glorieuse célébrité dont il bénéficiait avant le procès. On assiste à un changement de mentalité du public et d'attitude de la presse lorsque Robert Mitchum, une star montante alors extrêmement populaire, est convaincu de possession de marijuana et fait un petit séjour en prison ; loin de voir sa carrière s'arrêter après cet « incident », Mitchum en sort au contraire une star encore plus adulée qu'auparavant.

Depuis ce jour, on a parfois l'impression qu'une mauvaise réputation ne fait qu'ajouter un certain lustre à des carrières florissantes et ranimer celles qui étaient déjà sur le déclin.

ROBERT DOWNEY JR., *Fitzroy Barrett* 1996

ROBERT DOWNEY JR. during his arraignment in Malibu court on drug possession charges. Downey was sentenced to a drug rehabilitation program but violated his probation and was subsequently incarcerated in a California correctional facility. • MARLON BRANDO lends support to son CHRISTIAN on trial for killing his sister's boyfriend. Christian was sentenced to 10 years in prison and released in 1996.

ROBERT DOWNEY JR. bei seiner Anklage wegen Drogenbesitzes im Gerichtssaal von Malibu. Downey wurde zu einem Rehabilitationsprogramm verurteilt, verstieß allerdings gegen seine Bewährungsauflagen und landete anschließend in einer kalifornischen Strafanstalt. • MARLON BRANDO steht seinem Sohn CHRISTIAN in der Gerichtsverhandlung bei. Letzterer wurde wegen Mordes am Freund seiner Schwester zu 10 Jahren Gefängnis verurteilt und 1996 entlassen.

ROBERT DOWNEY JR. au tribunal de Malibu pendant la lecture de l'acte d'accusation pour possession de drogue. Downey n'ayant pas suivi le programme de désintoxication auquel il avait été condamné, il fut alors incarcéré dans une maison de correction de Californie. • MARLON BRANDO vient soutenir son fils CHRISTIAN accusé du meurtre du petit ami de sa sœur. Condamné à 10 ans de prison, Christian fut libéré en 1996.

DEBBIE REYNOLDS exits the court after winning a divorce from Eddie Fisher. • RITA HAYWORTH dissolves her marriage to Orson Welles. The press was more interested in her knee-length mink coat than the proceedings. • The appearance of LANA TURNER in a Santa Monica court during the investigation into the murder of her lover, mobster Johnny Stampanato, by her daughter Cheryl Crane, was one of the first celebrity crime cases to be extensively covered by the press. Immediately after her examination on the stand, Lana is interviewed by newsman JIM BACON.
Following pages: Director JOHN LANDIS was found not guilty of manslaughter in the TWILIGHT ZONE set deaths of actor Vic Morrow and two Vietnamese child actors. • FRANK SINATRA, testifying before the Nevada Gaming Commission, lost his bid for

DEBBIE REYNOLDS verlässt nach der Scheidung von Eddie Fisher den Gerichtssaal. • RITA HAYWORTH löst ihre Ehe mit Orson Welles auf. Die Presse war mehr an ihrem knielangen Nerzmantel als an dem Gerichtsverfahren interessiert. • LANA TURNER im Gerichtssaal von Santa Monica während der Mordanklage gegen ihre Tochter Cheryl Crane. Diese hatte Lanas Liebhaber, Gangster Johnny Stampanato, umgebracht. Es war einer der ersten Kriminalfälle, in der ein Star verwickelt war, über den ausgiebig in der Presse berichtet wurde. Direkt nach dem Untersuchungsverfahren wurde Lana vom Journalisten JIM BACON interviewt.
Folgende Seiten: Filmregisseur JOHN LANDIS wurde vom Verdacht der fahrlässigen Tötung des Schauspielers Vic Morrow und zweier vietnamesischer Kinder, die dei den Dreharbeiten zu

DEBBIE REYNOLDS quitte le tribunal après avoir gagné son divorce contre Eddie Fisher. • RITA HAYWORTH fait dissoudre son mariage avec Orson Welles. La presse se montra plus intéressée par la longueur de son manteau de vison que par la procédure. • Le meurtre du truand Johnny Stampanato, l'amant de LANA TURNER, par sa fille Cheryl Crane fut l'une des premières affaires criminelles mettant en cause une célébrité à être largement couverte par la presse. Lana est interviewée par le journaliste JIM BACON immédiatement après son audition à la barre pendant l'enquête préliminaire au tribunal de Santa Monica.
Pages suivantes: Le metteur en scène JOHN LANDIS au cours de son procès pour homicide involontaire de l'acteur Vic Morrow et de deux petits Vietnamiens lors d'un accident survenu sur le

ownership of the Cal-Neva Lodge at Lake Tahoe. • FARRAH FAWCETT en route to testify against boyfriend James Orr, charged with beating her. • WOODY ALLEN during his child custody battle with Mia Farrow. • CHARLIE SHEEN, who has had more than a few fun-ins with the law, pleads no contest to battery charges. • More media space worldwide was devoted to the O.J. SIMPSON murder trial than any other in Los Angeles' history. Simpson was charged with the brutal murders of his estranged wife Nicole Brown Simpson and her friend Ron Goldman. In what many believe to be a major miscarriage of justice, Simpson was acquitted of the crimes.

UNHEIMLICHE SCHATTENLICHTER ums Leben kamen, freigesprochen. • FRANK SINATRA bei der Aussage vor der Nevada Gaming Commission, verlor seinen Antrag auf Besitz der Cal-Neva Lodge am Lake Tahoe. • FARRAH FAWCETT auf dem Weg ins Gericht, um gegen ihren Freund James Orr auszusagen, der sie geschlagen haben soll. • WOODY ALLEN bei seinem Sorgerechtstreit. • CHARLIE SHEEN, der sich nicht nur ein Mal mit dem Gesetz angelegt hatte, erhebt keinen Einspruch, als er wegen Körperverletzung verurteilt wird. • In der Geschichte Los Angeles schenkten die Medien keinem Fall mehr Aufmerksamkeit, als dem Mordprozess gegen O.J. Simpson. Er war wegen Mordes an seiner Frau Nicole Brown Simpson und ihrem Freund Ron Goldman angeklagt. In einem der umstrittensten Gerichtsurteile wurde Simpson freigesprochen.

tournage de LA QUATRIÈME DIMENSION (TWILIGHT ZONE). • L'offre d'achat de Cal-Neva Lodge à Lake Tahoe par FRANK SINATRA est rejetée . • FARRAH FAWCETT se rend au tribunal pour témoigner contre son ami James Orr, accusé de violences. • WOODY ALLEN lors de son procès contre Mia Farrow pour la garde de sa fille. • Accusé de voies de fait, CHARLIE SHEEN, qui a déjà eu de nombreux démêlés avec la justice, plaide coupable. • La presse du monde entier a consacré une plus grande place au procès pour meurtre de O.J. SIMPSON qu'à tout autre de l'histoire judiciaire de Los Angeles. Simpson était accusé du meurtre de son épouse Nicole Brown Simpson, dont il était séparé, et de son amant Ron Goldman. Pour beaucoup, l'acquittement de Simpson est une tragique erreur judiciaire.

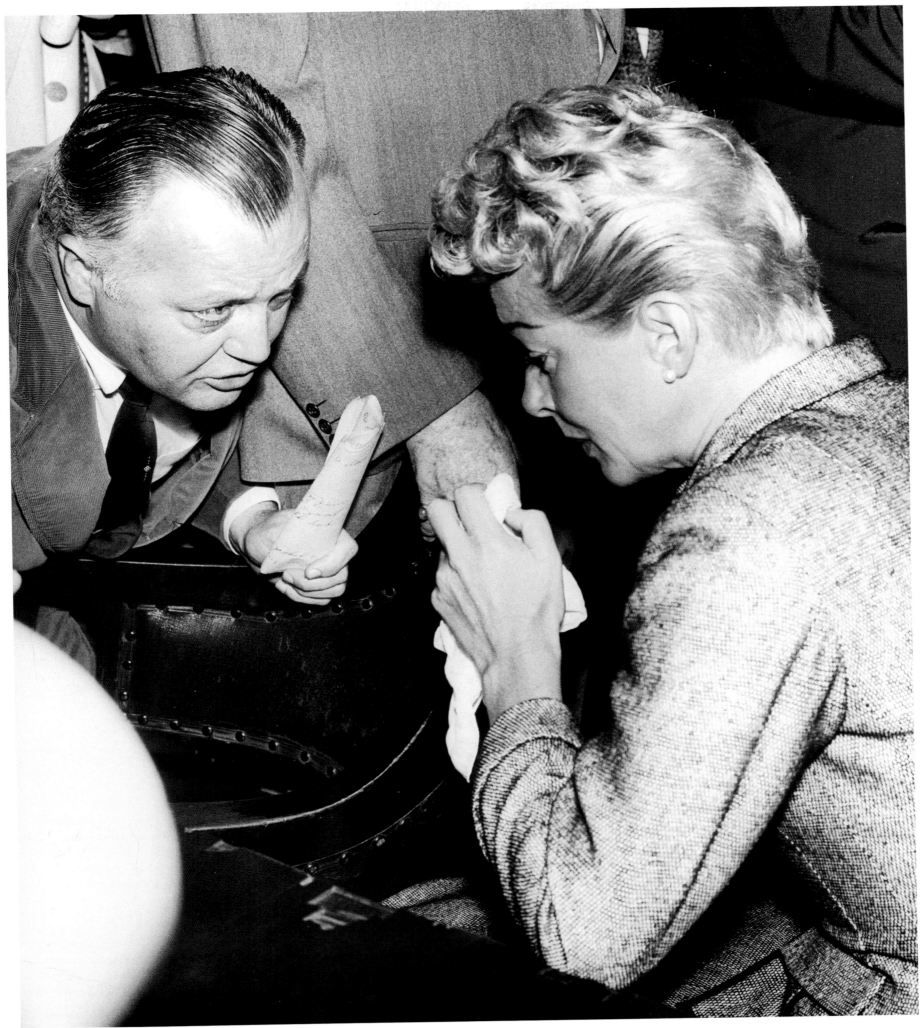

LANA TURNER AND JIM BACON, *Globe Archive* 1958

JOHN LANDIS, *Ralph Dominguez* 1987

FRANK SINATRA, *H. Herpolsheimer* 1984

FARRAH FAWCETT, *Milan Ryba* 1999

WOODY ALLEN, *Andrea Renault* 1993

TODD BRIDGES wurde zweier Vergehen angeklagt: Waffen- und Drogenbesitz. • TOMMY LEE in Handschellen, nachdem er der Körperverletzung an seiner Frau Pamela Anderson für schuldig befunden wurde. • JOHNNY DEPP bei seiner Verhaftung wegen Vandalismus in New York City. • SEAN „PUFFY" COMBS wird im Midtown South Police Precinct in New York wegen unerlaubten Waffenbesitzes festgehalten.

TODD BRIDGES is arraigned on two charges, one of carrying a firearm and one of drug possession. • TOMMY LEE is handcuffed after being found guilty of spousal abuse against wife Pamela Anderson. • JOHNNY DEPP is arrested in New York City for criminal destruction of property. • SEAN "PUFFY" COMBS is arrested for illegal gun possession at Midtown South Police Precinct in New York.

TODD BRIDGES est traduit devant la cour sous la double accusation de port d'arme et de possession de drogue. • On passe les menottes à TOMMY LEE après qu'il a été jugé coupable de violences conjugales envers son épouse Pamela Anderson. • JOHNNY DEPP lors de son arrestation à New York pour destruction criminelle des biens d'autrui. • SEAN « PUFFY » COMBS en état d'arrestation à la Midtown South Police Precinct de New York.

CHARLIE SHEEN, *Fitzroy Barrett* 1997

O.J. SIMPSON, *Lisa Rose* 1995

TODD BRIDGES, *Lisa Rose* 1993

TOMMY LEE, *Lisa Rose* 1998

JOHNNY DEPP, *Andrea Renault* 1994

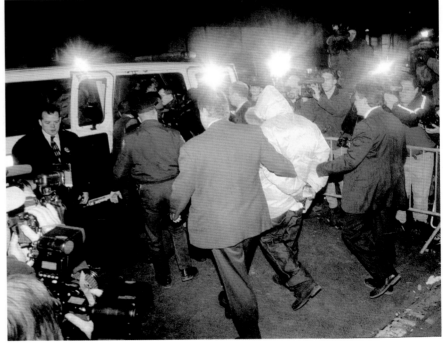

SEAN "PUFFY" COMBS, *Bruce Cotler* 1999

MARLENE DIETRICH AND MIKE TODD AT THE COPACABANA. *Globe Archive* 1955

DARYL HANNAH, *Ralph Dominguez* 1990

NITE LIFE

For years, Globe Photos produced a weekly feature for THE NEW YORK NEWS entitled HOLLYWOOD NITE LIFE. It was a page of candid photos of the stars at leisure in famous restaurants and nightclubs and at industry events such as premieres and play openings.

The public's fascination with Hollywood nightlife has remained unshakable for sixty years and shows no signs of waning. If anything, the demand has grown so strong that candid coverage represents the major billing for photo agencies and freelancers covering Hollywood today.

Nightlife photos were once found only in the opening sections of magazines, usually accompanying gossip columns. But in the 60s, this candid coverage made its way into the main body of the publications, illustrating features and supporting text, and even onto covers once reserved for portrait gallery art. The fan magazines were the first to use candid shots on their covers but today they can be found on the covers of most of our nationals as well.

Over the years, the venues have changed. The kind of photographer has changed as well as the kind of celebrity. Tonight's gang of paparazzi is no Nate Cutler. But then Roseanne Barr is not Deborah Kerr either.

As Globe's candid man, Cutler began covering nightlife during the Golden Era of the great restaurants and nightclubs. The stars frequented such eateries as Romanoff's, Chasen's, Perino's and LaRue. All are gone today. The popular spots in the 50s and 60s were Luau, Trader Vic's, Madame Wu's, La Scala, Dan Tana's and Au Petit Jean. All but Vic's and Tana's gave way to Le Dome, Ma Maison and Bistro of the 70s and 80s. Preston Sturges' Players, where the Rat Pack ate, became the Roxbury, the domain of the Brat Pack. It's now a Japanese restaurant. Drawing the lion's share of celebrities in the 90s were Nicky Blair's and Drai's. Today photographers regularly search out the stars at Spago, Morton's, Ivy and Mr. Chow.

The grand nightclubs like Cocoanut Grove, Trocadero and Mocambo faded as smaller clubs like Interlude and Crescendo, and coffee houses like Troubadour attracted the celebrity clientele. In 1967 Ciro's became Spectrum 2000. Today it's The Comedy Store. The famed Earl Carroll's ("Through these portals pass the most beautiful girls in the world") of the 40s was Moulin Rouge in the 50s, Aquarius in the 60s and Kaleidoscope in the 70s, where shirts and

NACHTLEBEN

Jahrelang produzierte Globe Photos für THE NEW YORK NEWS den Wochenbeitrag HOLLYWOOD NITE LIFE. Das waren Fotos, die Stars privat in Restaurants oder Nachtclubs zeigten, außerdem bei Film- und Theaterpremieren.

Die Faszination der Öffentlichkeit für Hollywoods Nachtleben ist seit 60 Jahren ungebrochen und hat nicht nachgelassen. Im Gegenteil: Die Nachfrage ist so gestiegen, dass Enthüllungsfotos mittlerweile zum Aushängeschild von Fotoagenturen und freien Fotografen in Hollywood geworden sind.

Früher platzierte man Fotos über das Nachtleben Hollywoods auf den Anfangsseiten eines Magazins, zumeist von Tratschkolumnen begleitet. In den 60ern wurden sie Teil der Titelgeschichten, sie illustrierten und unterstützten den Artikel und schmückten das Titelblatt, welches bis dahin den Porträts mit künstlerischem Anspruch vorbehalten war.

Die Schauplätze änderten sich. Genauso wie sich die Fotografen und Stars veränderten. Der heutige Paparazzo ist kein Nate Cutler. Aber wiederum ist Roseanne Barr auch keine Deborah Kerr.

Globes Mann, Nate Cutler, begann im Goldenen Zeitalter der berühmten Restaurants und Nachtclubs, das Nachtleben abzulichten. Die Stars besuchten Restaurants wie Romanoff's, Chasen's, Perino's und LaRue. Diese gibt es nicht mehr. Die Treffpunkte in den 50ern und 60ern waren Luau, Trader Vic's, Madame Wu's, La Scala, Dan Tana's und Au Petit Jean. Bis auf Vic's und Tana's machten sie in den 70er und 80er Platz für Le Dome, Ma Maison und Bistro. Preston Sturges' Players, in dem „The Rat Pack" (Frank Sinatra, Dean Martin, Sammy Davis Jr., Peter Lawford und Joey Bishop) zu essen pflegte, wurde zu Roxbury, Treffpunkt des „Brat Pack". Es ist jetzt ein japanisches Restaurant. Nicky Blair's und Drai's zogen in den 90ern den Löwenanteil der Stars an. Heutzutage suchen die Fotografen regelmäßig bei Spago, Morton's, Ivy und Mr. Chow nach ihnen.

Nachtclubs wie Cocoanut Grove, Trocadero und Mocambo verloren durch das Aufkommen kleinerer Clubs wie dem Interlude oder dem Crescendo und Kaffeehäusern wie dem Troubadour, die nun die Stars anlockten, an Anziehungskraft. 1967 wurde Ciro's zu Spectrum 2000. Heute ist es The Comedy Store. Das berühmte Earl Carroll's

VIE NOCTURNE

Pendant des années, Globe Photos a fourni les photos illustrant la rubrique hebdomadaire du NEW YORK NEWS, intitulée HOLLYWOOD NITE LIFE, grâce à laquelle les lecteurs pouvaient découvrir la vie mondaine menée par les vedettes dans des restaurants et des night-clubs réputés ou lors des premières de spectacles.

La fascination du public pour la vie nocturne à Hollywood ne s'est pas démentie depuis soixante ans et ne semble d'ailleurs montrer aucun signe de déclin. La demande du lectorat serait même si forte que la plupart des magazines publient aujourd'hui en couverture des photos autrefois réservées aux galeries de portraits.

Alors que les photos de la vie nocturne des stars étaient jusque là reléguées dans les premières pages des magazines, où elles accompagnaient les potins du chroniqueur, à partir des années 1960 elles commencèrent à avoir droit aux pages principales des revues pour illustrer des chroniques ou compléter un article, voire à occuper une couverture autrefois réservée à un portrait. Les fanzines, parmi les premiers à utiliser ce genre de photo, furent ensuite rapidement imités par la plupart des magazines américains.

Si les vedettes et le genre des photographes ont changé — les nouveaux paparazzi des nuits d'Hollywood ne sont sans doute pas des Nate Cutler, mais Roseanne Barr n'est pas non plus Deborah Kerr ! — le décor des rendez-vous du Tout-Hollywood n'a cessé de subir des transformations.

À l'âge d'or des grands restaurants et night-clubs de Hollywood, Cutler assura le reportage sur les stars fréquentant alors des restaurants comme Romanoff's, Chasen's, Perino's et LaRue, tous aujourd'hui disparus. Lieux à la mode dans les années 1950 et 1960, Luau, Trader Vic's, Madame Wu's, La Scala, Dan Tana's et Au Petit Jean ont (à l'exception de Vic's et de Tana's) tous cédé le devant de la scène en 1970-1980 à Ma Maison, Le Dome ou le Bistro. Le Preston Sturges' Players, où se réunissait la bande dite du « Rat Pack » (la « bande de rats » dans les années 60), est devenu le Roxbury, domaine réservé du « Brat Pack » (la « bande de sales mômes »), avant d'être transformé aujourd'hui en restaurant japonais. Si le Nicky Blair's et le Drai's accueillaient la plupart des célébrités des années 1990, les photographes vont désormais plutôt traquer les stars au Spago, chez Morton's, Ivy ou Mr. Chow.

Les grands night-clubs de Hollywood ont abandonné

JEAN SIMMONS, STEWART GRANGER AND DEBORAH KERR, *Nate Cutler* 1953

ROSEANNE BARR, *Milan Ryba* 2000

DEBORAH KERR at her most effusive and ROSEANNE BARR at her most sedate.

DEBORAH KERR so überschwenglich wie nie und ROSEANNE BARR so bedächtig wie selten.

DEBORAH KERR très excitée. ROSEANNE BARR plutôt calme.

shoes were not essential for admittance. Today the building houses the Nickelodeon Television Company.

In the 60s, dance palaces like the Palladium took a back seat to Whiskey-a-GoGo, Hollywood's first big discotheque. In the 70s, Whiskey's name clientele defected to the star-backed private clubs like The Factory and The Daisy. The Factory became Studio One, a gay disco, for several years and is now the home of Luna Park. The Daisy building houses several smart Rodeo Drive shops.

The 80s was the time of hot new clubs that all opened with a frenzy reminiscent of Manhattan's Studio 54 in its glory days and then disappeared with a speed matched only by the new publications of the decade. In the 90s photographers regularly covered celebrities at The House of Blues, Skybar, Sunset Room, Rainbow Room, and the Viper Room where young River Phoenix overdosed.

Globe's coverage of pub crawlers and their haunts changed too. For over thirty years, Cutler would be called daily by restaurant and nightclub press agents with names of celebrities on that evening's reservation list. He'd drop by the clubs, shoot the almost always gracious and well-groomed stars, tip his hat and say goodnight. Even when he was not invited inside, the stars would invariably stop at the entrance and give him the few moments he needed to shoot their pictures. Just professional courtesy – and good business too because the published photographs showed the celebrity in an attractive way. Nate saw to that. He would kill any shot that was unflattering.

Today there is little professional courtesy shown on either side of the camera. Coverage is still prearranged – the term currently in vogue is "photo op" (for opportunity) – but photogs have become inured to press agents who invite their presence and then shield the celebrated guests from their attentions. Like orphans in OLIVER TWIST, they are forced to shoot from positions less opportune than the favored electronic media. The gracious star has become an endangered species. Today's breed has a strong strain of rudeness and tease. And the press corps all too frequently resembles little more than a mob.

Confrontation is now the name of a fiercely competitive game. As celebrity journals continue to move into the void left by the venerable fan magazines, the market for paparazzo work, which extends from the tabloids through mainstream newspapers and magazines, continues to grow.

In keeping with the affectionate tone of this book, most of the photographs in Nite Life are not confrontational. Most – but not all.

(„Durch diese Tore gehen die schönsten Mädchen der Welt") der 40er wurde in den 50ern zum Moulin Rouge, in den 60ern zum Aquarius und in den 70ern zum Kaleidoscope, in dem für den Eintritt weder Hemd noch Schuhe notwendig waren. Heute beherbergt das Gebäude die Nickelodeon Television Company.

Tanzpaläste wie das Palladium wurden in den 60er Jahren von Whiskey-a-GoGo, Hollywoods erster großer Diskothek, verdrängt. Whiskeys Kundschaft wechselte in den 70ern zu privaten Clubs wie The Factory und The Daisy. The Factory wurde zu Studio One, einer Schwulendiskothek, und ist jetzt das Luna Park. Das The-Daisy-Gebäude beherbergt elegante Rodeo-Drive-Geschäfte .

Die 80er waren die Zeit der neuen Clubs, die mit einer Begeisterung öffneten, die an die Tage des Studio 54 in Manhattan erinnerte, um dann in einem Tempo zu verschwinden, das nur von den neuen Publikationen übertroffen wurde. In den 90ern waren die Stars im House of Blues, Skybar, Sunset Room, Rainbow Room, und im Viper Room, in dem sich River Phoenix eine Überdosis gab.

Globes Berichterstattung über die Kneipengänger und ihre Verfolger veränderte sich. Über 30 Jahre lang wurde Cutler täglich von Restaurant- und Nachtclub-Presseagenten angerufen, die die Namen der Stars preisgaben, die sich für den jeweiligen Abend angemeldet hatten. Cutler kam dann im Club vorbei, machte Fotos von den Stars, die fast immer anmutig und elegant aussahen, fasste sich an den Hut und wünschte eine gute Nacht. Wenn er nicht in den Club eingelassen wurde, blieben die Stars ausnahmslos am Eingang stehen und warteten, bis er seine Bilder gemacht hatte. Die veröffentlichten Fotos zeigten die Stars in einem angenehmen Licht. Nate vernichtete jedes Foto, das für einen Star unangenehm war.

Heutzutage gibt es auf beiden Seiten der Kamera wenig berufliche Höflichkeit. Berichterstattung wird im Voraus arrangiert – der Ausdruck heißt „photo op" (für opportunity – die Gelegenheit) – aber Fotografen haben sich an Presseagenten gewöhnt, die sie einladen, um dann die Stars vor ihnen abzuschirmen. Der anmutige Star ist zu einer bedrohten Spezie geworden. Heute sind die Stars oft grob und flegelhaft und die Presse ähnelt immer mehr einem Mob.

Konfrontation heißt das Spiel nun. Während die Regenbogenpresse zunehmend die Nische der ehrwürdigen Fanmagazine besetzt, wird der Markt für die Paparazzi größer, denn auch die Tagespresse und die Nachrichtenmagazine sind zu Abnehmern geworden.

Der freundliche Ton dieses Buches spiegelt sich auch in den Fotografien dieses Kapitels wider – in den meisten, nicht in allen.

leur clientèle de célébrités à des clubs plus intimes comme l'Interlude et le Crescendo ou à des cafés comme le Troubadour. Le célèbre Earl Carroll's (« Par cette porte passent les plus belles filles du monde ») des années 1940 a été successivement rebaptisé Moulin Rouge dans les années 1950, Aquarius en 1960 et Kaleidoscope vers 1970 ; c'est aujourd'hui le siège de la Nickelodeon Television Company.

Dans les années 1960, les dancings comme le Palladium ont été éclipsés par le Whiskey-a-GoGo, la première grande discothèque d'Hollywood, que sa clientèle a ensuite déserté dans les années 1970 pour se réunir dans les clubs privés tenus par des stars (The Factory, The Daisy etc.). The Factory est devenu le Studio One, une boîte gay, avant d'être occupé par le siège de Luna Park, tandis que l'immeuble du Daisy abrite des petites boutiques chics de Rodeo Drive.

Les années 1980 ont vu fleurir de tout nouveaux clubs s'inspirant joyeusement de la période glorieuse du Studio 54 de Manhattan qui disparurent ensuite très vite. Dans les années 1970, les photographes trouvèrent les stars au House of Blues, au Skybar, au Sunset Room, au Rainbow Room et au Viper Room.

La manière de travailler des photographes de Globe pour réaliser leurs reportages sur la vie nocturne de Hollywood a également évolué. Pendant plus de trente ans, les attachés de presse des restaurants et des night-clubs ont appelé presque chaque jour Nate Cutler pour lui donner le nom des célébrités ayant réservé pour la soirée. Ce dernier faisait alors un saut au club, photographiait des vedettes presque toujours aimables et disait bonne nuit en partant.

Cette époque de bonnes relations professionnelles, de part et d'autre de l'appareil, semble avoir vécu. Si le reportage est toujours pré-arrangé – le nouveau terme actuellement à la mode est « photo op » (pour opportunité) – les photographes ont appris à se garder des attachés de presse qui, après les avoir convoqués, semblent faire de leur mieux pour soustraire les vedettes à leurs attentions. À l'instar des orphelins de OLIVER TWIST, ils sont alors obligés de travailler dans des conditions plus difficiles que les télévisions, évidemment favorisées.

Il ne s'agit plus d'un jeu mais d'un véritable affrontement, férocement compétitif, entre les chasseurs et leurs proies. Le marché qui s'ouvre aux paparazzi ne cesse de croître tant le public est friand de la rubrique « people » des journaux, magazines ou tabloïds venus occuper le créneau abandonné par les vénérables fanzines.

Pour conserver le ton aimable et affectueux de cet ouvrage, la plupart des photographies de ce chapitre ne sont pas conflictuelles. La plupart – mais pas toutes !

GINGER ROGERS AND DON LOPER, *Globe Archive* 1955

JERRY LEWIS AND DEAN MARTIN, *Nate Cutler* 1956

MARION DAVIES, EVA GABOR AND MIKE CONNOLLY, *Nate Cutler* 1954

VAN JOHNSON AND THE HONEY BROTHERS, *Nate Cutler* 1953

On the Ciro's dance floor, GINGER ROGERS retrieves a bracelet she dropped and doesn't miss a beat. • MARTIN and LEWIS cut up at the Desert Inn. • MARION DAVIES, EVA GABOR and HOLLYWOOD REPORTER columnist MIKE CONNOLLY at the Mocambo. • VAN JOHNSON is literally dragged onstage at the Cocoanut Grove by the HONEY BROTHERS.

Auf der Tanzfläche bei Ciro's hebt GINGER ROGERS ein ihr heruntergefallenes Armband auf, ohne dabei den Rhythmus zu verlieren. • MARTIN und LEWIS haben viel Spaß am Desert Inn. • MARION DAVIES, EVA GABOR und HOLLYWOOD REPORTER-Kolumnist MIKE CONNOLLY im Mocambo. • VAN JOHNSON wird im Cocoanut Grove von den HONEY BROTHERS buchstäblich auf die Bühne gezerrt.

Sur la piste de danse du Ciro's, GINGER ROGERS récupère en mesure le bracelet qu'elle a perdu. • MARTIN et LEWIS font les pitres au Desert Inn. • MARION DAVIES, EVA GABOR et MIKE CONNOLLY, le chroniqueur d'HOLLYWOOD REPORTER, au Mocambo. • VAN JOHNSON est littéralement tiré sur la scène du Cocoanut Grove par les HONEY BROTHERS.

HENRY KISSINGER AND MARLO THOMAS, *Nate Cutler* 1971

PRESIDENT JOHN F. KENNEDY AND ANGIE DICKINSON, *Globe Archive* 1961

Some guys have it. Some don't. KENNEDY has everyone's attention, very especially ANGIE DICKINSON'S, and MARLO THOMAS is captivated by HENRY KISSINGER, but FRANCE NUYEN isn't exactly having the time of her life with Joseph McCarthy sidekick ROY COHN. • RITA HAYWORTH gets a light from Columbia Pictures top honcho HARRY COHN. • BETTE DAVIS seems to disagree with Warner Brothers chief JACK L. WARNER but didn't she always? • AVA GARDNER comes under the close scrutiny of her boss, LOUIS B. MAYER, at the premiere of SHOW BOAT. • CARROLL BAKER wishes Paramount chairman ADOLPH ZUKOR a happy 92nd birthday. • JENNIFER JONES captures an appreciative gaze from DAVID O. SELZNICK shortly after their marriage. • DORE SCHARY, who headed two studios (RKO and MGM) displays a talent for percussion that delights his MGM stars, DOLORES GRAY, CELESTE HOLM and ANNE FRANCIS. • 20th Century-Fox head DARRYL F. ZANUCK between wife VIRGINIA (right) and mistress BELLA DARVI at Ciro's.

ROY COHN AND FRANCE NUYEN, *Nate Cutler* 1965

HARRY COHN AND RITA HAYWORTH, *Nate Cutler* 1952

BETTE DAVIS AND JACK L. WARNER, *Nate Cutler* 1952

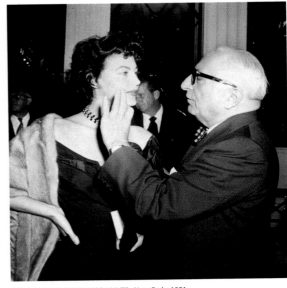

AVA GARDNER AND LOUIS B. MAYER, *Nate Cutler* 1951

CARROLL BAKER AND ADOLPH ZUKOR, *Nate Cutler* 1965

JENNIFER JONES AND DAVID O. SELZNICK, *Nate Cutler* 1950

DOLORES GRAY, CELESTE HOLM, DORE SCHARY AND ANNE FRANCIS, *Nate Cutler* 1955

BELLA DARVI, DARRYL F. AND VIRGINIA ZANUCK, *Nate Cutler* 1953

Manche haben's, andere nicht. KENNEDY hat die Aufmerksamkeit von allen, besonders die von ANGIE DICKINSON, MARLO THOMAS ist von HENRY KISSINGER fasziniert, aber FRANCE NUYEN hat nicht die beste Zeit mit Joseph McCarthy-Mitarbeiter ROY COHN. • RITA HAYWORTH bekommt von Columbia Pictures oberstem Boss HARRY COHN Feuer. • BETTE DAVIS scheint mit Warner Brothers Chef JACK L. WARNER eine Meinungsverschiedenheit zu haben, aber hatte sie die nicht immer? • AVA GARDNER wird von ihrem Boss LOUIS B. MAYER bei der Premiere von MISSISSIPPI-MELODIE (SHOW BOAT) begutachtet. • CARROLL BAKER gratuliert dem Paramount-Vorsitzendem ADOLPH ZUKOR zu seinem 92. Geburtstag. • DAVID O. SELZNICK wirft JENNIFER JONES kurz nach ihrer Hochzeit einen annerkennenden Blick zu. • DORE SCHARY, der zwei Studios leitete (RKO und MGM), zeigt Schlagzeugerqualitäten. Das erfreut seine MGM-Stars DOLORES GRAY, CELESTE HOLM und ANNE FRANCIS. • 20th-Century-Fox-Chef DARRYL F. ZANUCK zwischen Frau VIRGINIA (rechts) und Geliebter BELLA DARVI bei Ciro's.

Certains y parviennent, d'autres pas. KENNEDY bénéficie de l'attention de tous – notamment de ANGIE DICKINSON – et HENRY KISSINGER semble captiver MARLO THOMAS ; en revanche FRANCE NUYEN ne semble pas vraiment s'amuser en compagnie de ROY COHN, un collaborateur de Joseph McCarthy. • HARRY COHN, grand patron de Columbia Pictures, donne du feu à RITA HAYWORTH. • BETTE DAVIS ne semble pas d'accord – mais l'a-t-elle déjà été ? – avec JACK L. WARNER, le patron de la Warner Brothers. • AVA GARDNER subit l'inspection attentive de son patron, LOUIS B. MAYER, lors de la première de SHOW BOAT. • CARROLL BAKER souhaite un bon 92e anniversaire à ADOLPH ZUKOR, le président de la Paramount. • JENNIFER JONES sous le regard approbateur de DAVID O. SELZNICK, peu de temps après leur mariage. • DORE SCHARY, qui dirigeait deux studios (la RKO et MGM), montre un talent de batteur qui ravit ses vedettes de la MGM, DOLORES GRAY, CELESTE HOLM et ANNE FRANCIS. • DARRYL F. ZANUCK, le patron de la 20th Century-Fox, entre son épouse VIRGINIA (à droite) et sa maîtresse BELLA DARVI au Ciro's.

"PRINCE" MIKE ROMANOFF, HUMPHREY BOGART AT ROMANOFF'S, *Nate Cutler* 1951

ETHEL BARRYMORE AND ARLENE DAHL AT THE MOCAMBO, *Nate Cutler* 1954

MARCELLO MASTROIANNI, CARROLL BAKER AT THE BEVERLY HILTON, *Nate Cuter* 1958

SALLY STRUTHERS AT THE CIRCUS, *Nate Cutler* 1972

JAMES DEAN AND SAMMY DAVIS JR. AT CIRO'S, *Nate Cutler* 1955

ROBIN GIVENS AND BRAD PITT, *Judie Burstein* 1994

ROCK HUDSON AND ANN SHERIDAN AT AN ACTORS FUND BENEFIT, *Nate Cutler* 1957

ELSA MAXWELL AND GLORIA SWANSON AT THE MOCAMBO, *Nate Cutler* 1950

DEBRA PAGET AND MAMA WITH DEBBIE REYNOLDS, *Nate Cutler* 1953

WOODY ALLEN, *Oscar Abolofia* 1977

MARLON BRANDO, *Nate Cutler* 1955

For some 30 years WOODY ALLEN has been a sideman in Eddie Davis' New Orleans Jazz Band at Michael's Pub in New York every Monday night, including the Monday night he won the Oscar for best director. • MARLON BRANDO, an accomplished drummer since his days as a struggling actor, frequently played bongos at La Cubana in Los Angeles. • PETER O'TOOLE plays piano in a London pub.

30 Jahre lang spielte WOODY ALLEN jede Montagnacht in Eddie Davis' New Orleans Jazz Band im Michael's Pub in New York, inklusive der Montagnacht, in der er seinen Oscar als bester Filmregisseur gewann. • MARLON BRANDO, ein begnadeter Schlagzeuger seit seinen eher erfolglosen Tagen als Schauspieler, spielte gelegentlich Bongos im La Cubana in Los Angeles. • PETER O'TOOLE spielt in einer Londoner Kneipe Klavier.

WOODY ALLEN a joué tous les lundis soirs pendant près de 30 ans – et même la nuit où il a obtenu l'Oscar de la meilleure mise en scène – au Michael's Pub de New York dans l'orchestre de jazz New Orleans de Eddie Davis. • MARLON BRANDO, percussionniste accompli depuis ses tout débuts d'acteur, joue fréquemment des bongos au La Cubana de Los Angeles. • PETER O'TOOLE joue au piano dans un pub de Londres.

PETER O'TOOLE, *Pictorial Press* 1962

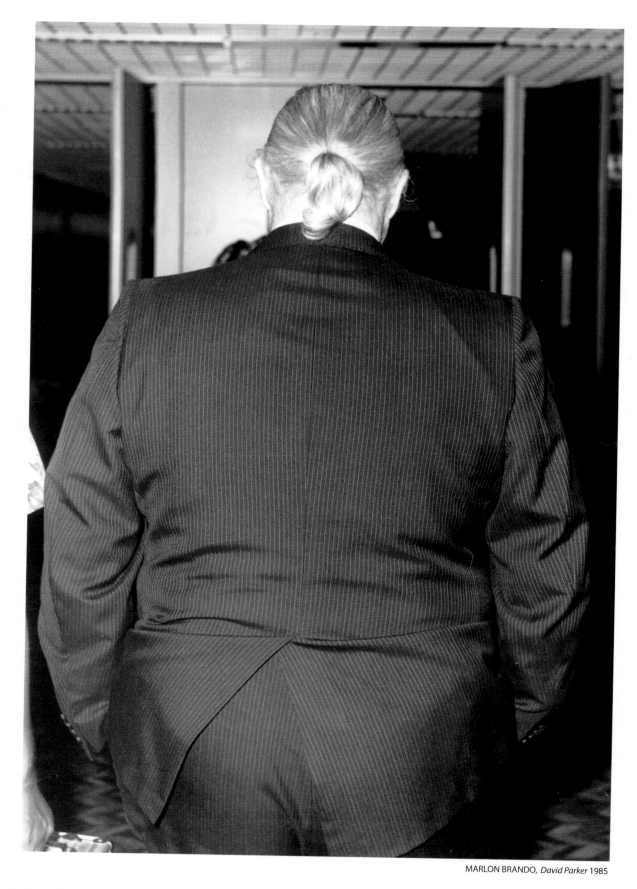

MARLON BRANDO, *David Parker* 1985

MARLON BRANDO at London's Heathrow Airport. • The lady herself said it:"By the time a woman is 50 she gets the face she deserves." INGRID BERGMAN, at the Ahmanson Theatre in Los Angeles, at age 54. • TRISH VAN DEVERE and GEORGE C. SCOTT

MARLON BRANDO am Londoner Flughafen Heathrow. • Sie selbst hat es gesagt:"Wenn eine Frau ihr 50. Lebensjahr erreicht, bekommt sie das Gesicht, das sie verdient." INGRID BERGMAN im Alter von 54 Jahren am Ahmanson Theater in Los Angeles.. • TRISH VAN

MARLON BRANDO au London's Heathrow Airport. • INGRID BERGMAN, photographiée ici à 54 ans au théâtre Ahmanson de Los Angeles, l'a déclaré elle-même : « C'est à 50 ans que la femme a le visage qu'elle mérite. » • TRISH VAN DEVERE et GEORGE C.

INGRID BERGMAN, *Nate Cutler* 1966

GEORGE C. SCOTT, TRISH VAN DEVERE AND CAMPBELL SCOTT, *Irv Steinberg* 1976

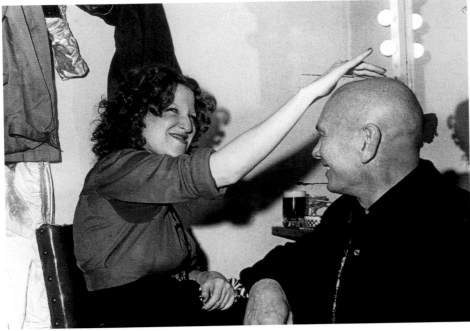

BETTE MIDLER AND YUL BRYNNER, *S.I.M.* 1975

CLAUDETTE COLBERT AND ROCK HUDSON, *Nate Cutler* 1961

with Scott's son CAMPBELL backstage on the opening night of their play SLY FOX on Broadway. • BETTE MIDLER welcomes YUL BRYNNER backstage at New York's Downstairs at the Upstairs. • Intermission at the Mark Taper Forum of the Los Angeles Music Center with CLAUDETTE COLBERT and ROCK HUDSON provides the opportunity of seeing the right side of Colbert's face which was never onscreen in any of her movies because she insisted her left profile was more attractive.

DEVERE und GEORGE C. SCOTT mit Scotts Sohn CAMPBELL bei der Broadway-Premiere ihres Stückes SLY FOX hinter der Bühne. • BETTE MIDLER begrüßt YUL BRYNNER hinter der Bühne im New Yorker Downstairs at the Upstairs. • Die Pause am Mark Taper Forum des Los Angeles Music Center mit CLAUDETTE COLBERT und ROCK HUDSON bietet die Gelegenheit Colberts Gesicht von der rechten Seite anzusehen, was in ihren Filmen sonst nie der Fall war, da die Schauspielerin ihr linkes Profil hübscher fand.

SCOTT avec CAMPBELL, le fils de Scott, en coulisses lors de la soirée d'inauguration de leur pièce, SLY FOX, à Broadway. • BETTE MIDLER accueille YUL BRYNNER en coulisses au Downstairs at the Upstairs à New York. • L'entracte au Mark Taper Forum du Los Angeles Music Center permet d'apprécier le côté droit du visage de CLAUDETTE COLBERT, accompagnée ici par ROCK HUDSON, que n'on l'a jamais vu dans aucun de ses films car elle trouvait bien plus beau son profil gauche.

MATTHEW BRODERICK, HELEN HUNT, *Michael Ferguson* 1988

LEONARDO DI CAPRIO AND GWYNETH PALTROW, *Rose Hartman* 1992

DEMI AND FREDDIE MOORE, *Nate Cutler* 1982

MELANIE GRIFFITH AND DON JOHNSON, *Nate Cutler* 1972

HEATHER LOCKLEAR AND TOM CRUISE, *Ralph Dominguez* 1980

ROB LOWE AND JODIE FOSTER, *Judie Burstein* 1984

At the Plaza Hotel in New York, photographer John Barrett was trying to shoot ERIC ROBERTS and JON VOIGHT but Roberts' little sister kept getting into the frame. Try as he might, Barrett couldn't cut her out of every shot. You might recognize her as JULIA ROBERTS.

Am Plaza Hotel in New York versuchte Fotograf John Barrett ein Bild von ERIC ROBERTS und JON VOIGHT zu schießen, aber Robert's kleine Schwester tauchte immer wieder im Blickfeld auf. Barrett konnte machen, was er wollte, er bekam sie einfach nicht aus dem Bild. Sie kennen sie vielleicht als JULIA ROBERTS.

Le photographe John Barrett essayait de photographier ERIC ROBERTS et JON VOIGHT au Plaza Hotel de New York mais sans parvenir à supprimer du cadre la petite sœur de Roberts, qui venait s'interposer volontairement dans le champ. Il s'agissait en fait de la future JULIA ROBERTS.

ERIC ROBERTS AND JON VOIGHT, *John Barrett* 1985

LIZA MINNELLI AND FRANK SINATRA, *Nate Cutler* 1959

LIZA MINNELLI is living every girl's dream at FRANK SINATRA'S opening at the Cocoanut Grove.

LIZA MINNELLI lebt den Traum eines jeden Mädchens auf FRANK SINATRAS Eröffnung im Cocoanut Grove.

LIZA MINNELLI vit le rêve de toutes les petites filles aux côtés de FRANK SINATRA, lors de l'inauguration de sa boîte, le Cocoanut Grove.

EDDIE MURPHY, *David Parker* 1989

EDDIE MURPHY and his battalion of bodyguards. • DANNY DE VITO and wife RHEA PERLMAN shoot craps at the gala for the John Tracy Clinic at the Playboy Club. • FRANK SINATRA and JOE E. LEWIS at the Desert Inn in Las Vegas. Sinatra portrayed Lewis in THE JOKER IS WILD. • HALSTON, BIANCA JAGGER, JACK HALEY JR. and LIZA MINNELLI at Studio 54. • LIZA dances up a storm at Studio 54.

EDDIE MURPHY und seine Horde von Leibwächtern. • DANNY DE VITO und Frau RHEA PERLMAN spielen Würfel bei der Gala für die John Tracy Clinic im Playboy Club. • FRANK SINATRA und JOE E. LEWIS im Desert Inn in Las Vegas. Sinatra spielt Lewis in SCHICKSALSMELODIE (THE JOKER IS WILD). • HALSTON, BIANCA JAGGER, JACK HALEY JR. und LIZA MINNELLI im Studio 54. • LIZA tanzt wie wild im Studio 54.

EDDIE MURPHY et son phalanstère de gardes du corps. • DANNY DE VITO lance les dés, sous les yeux de son épouse RHEA PERLMAN, lors du gala offert au Playboy Club en l'honneur de la John Tracy Clinic. • FRANK SINATRA et JOE E. LEWIS au Desert Inn à Las Vegas. Sinatra incarnait Lewis dans LE PANTIN BRISE (THE JOKER IS WILD). • HALSTON, BIANCA JAGGER, JACK HALEY JR. et LIZA MINNELLI au Studio 54. • LIZA danse comme une folle au Studio 54.

DANNY DE VITO AND RHEA PERLMAN, *Nate Cutler* 1979

FRANK SINATRA AND JOE E. LEWIS, *Nate Cutler* 1950

HALSTON, BIANCA JAGGER, JACK HALEY JR. AND LIZA MINNELLI, *Michael Norcia* 1979

LIZA MINNELLI, *Michael Norcia* 1980

The sensation of the 1967 Oscar ceremonies was INGER STEVENS in the new fashion called the mini. • SANDRA BULLOCK and BEN AFFLECK at the FORCES OF NATURE premiere. • CARROLL BAKER arrives at the premiere of THE CARPETBAGGERS by helicopter.

Der Minirock von INGER STEVENS, im Stil der neuen Mode, war die Sensation der Oscarverleihung 1967. • SANDRA BULLOCK und BEN AFFLECK bei der AUF DIE STÜRMISCHE ART Premiere. • CARROLL BAKER kommt im Hubschrauber zur Premiere von DIE UNERSÄTTLICHEN.

INGER STEVENS en robe mini, alors la nouvelle mode, fit sensation à la cérémonie de remise des Oscars en 1967. • SANDRA BULLOCK et BEN AFFLECK à la première de UN VENT DE FOLIE (FORCES OF NATURE). • CARROLL BAKER arrive en hélicoptère à la première de LES AMBITIEUX (THE CARPETBAGGERS).

INGER STEVENS AND RICHARD MCKENZIE, *Bill Holz* 1967

SANDRA BULLOCK AND BEN AFFLECK, *Fitzroy Barrett* 1999

CARROLL BAKER, *Nate Cutler* 1964

EDY WILLIAMS, JOHNNY GRANT AND RUSS MEYER, *Nate Cutler* 1968

ELIZABETH TAYLOR AND MONTGOMERY CLIFT, *Nate Cutler* 1951

HUMPHREY BOGART AND MARILYN MONROE, *Nate Cutler* 1953

While RUSS MEYER's back is turned, JOHNNY GRANT "interviews" EDY WILLIAMS (Mrs. Meyer) at the premiere of BEYOND THE VALLEY OF THE DOLLS. • ELIZABETH TAYLOR and MONTGOMERY CLIFT at the premiere of A PLACE IN THE SUN. • HUMPHREY BOGART and MARILYN MONROE at the premiere of HOW TO MARRY A MILLIONAIRE.

Während RUSS MEYER ihm den Rücken zudreht, interviewt JOHNNY GRANT EDY WILLIAMS (Mrs. Meyer) bei der Premiere von BEYOND THE VALLEY OF THE DOLLS. • ELIZABETH TAYLOR und MONTGOMERY CLIFT bei der Premiere von EIN PLATZ AN DER SONNE. • HUMPHREY BOGART und MARILYN MONROE bei der Premiere von WIE ANGELT MAN SICH EINEN MILLIONÄR.

Alors que RUSS MEYER a le dos tourné, JOHNNY GRANT « interviewe » EDY WILLIAMS (Mme Meyer) lors de la première de HOLLYWOOD VIXENS (BEYOND THE VALLEY OF THE DOLLS). • ELIZABETH TAYLOR et MONTGOMERY CLIFT à la première de UNE PLACE AU SOLEIL (A PLACE IN THE SUN). • HUMPHREY BOGART et MARILYN MONROE à la première de COMMENT ÉPOUSER UN MILLIONNAIRE (HOW TO MARRY A MILLIONAIRE).

GWYNETH PALTROW, *Andrea Renault* 1996

HELEN HUNT, *Greg Vie* 1992

MICHELLE PFEIFFER, *Ralph Dominguez* 1991

JULIA ROBERTS, *Ralph Dominguez* 1989

DIANE KEATON, *Milan Ryba* 1995

ROBERT DOWNEY JR., *Ralph Dominguez* 1991

CHARLTON AND LYDIA HESTON, *Nate Cutler* 1956

BRUCE WILLIS, *Albert Ferreira* 1997

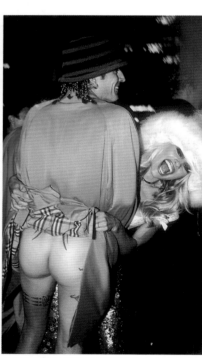

TOMMY LEE AND PAMELA ANDERSON, *Sonia Moskowitz* 1999

HELEN HUNT at the premiere of USED PEOPLE. • MICHELLE PFEIFFER at the Century Plaza Hotel. • JULIA ROBERTS at the Beverly Hilton. • DIANE KEATON at the premiere of FATHER OF THE BRIDE. • ROBERT DOWNEY JR. at the premiere of CHANCES ARE. • CHARLTON HESTON was the first (and last?) to wear Bermuda shorts at Ciro's. • BRUCE WILLIS at the Planet Hollywood opening in Myrtle Beach. • TOMMY LEE and PAMELA ANDERSON at the MTV Video Music Awards.

HELEN HUNT bei der Premiere von DIE HERBSTZEITLOSEN (USED PEOPLE). • MICHELLE PFEIFFER im Century Plaza Hotel. • JULIA ROBERTS im Beverly Hilton. • DIANE KEATON bei der Premiere von VATER DER BRAUT (FATHER OF THE BRIDE). • ROBERT DOWNEY JR. bei der Premiere von EIN HIMMLISCHER LIEBHABER (CHANCES ARE). • CHARLTON HESTON war der Erste (und Letzte?), der bei Ciro's Bermudashorts trug. • BRUCE WILLIS bei der Eröffnung von Planet Hollywood in Myrtle Beach. • TOMMY LEE und PAMELA ANDERSON bei den MTV Video Music Awards.

HELEN HUNT à la première de QUATRE NEW-YORKAISES (USED PEOPLE). • MICHELLE PFEIFFER au the Century Plaza Hotel. • JULIA ROBERTS au the Beverly Hilton . • DIANE KEATON à la première de LE PÈRE DE LA MARIÉE (FATHER OF THE BRIDE). • ROBERT DOWNEY JR. à la première de CHANCES ARE. • CHARLTON HESTON fut le premier (et le dernier ?) à porter un bermuda au Ciro's. • BRUCE WILLIS à l'ouverture du Planet Hollywood de Myrtle Beach. • TOMMY LEE et PAMELA ANDERSON aux MTV Video Music Awards.

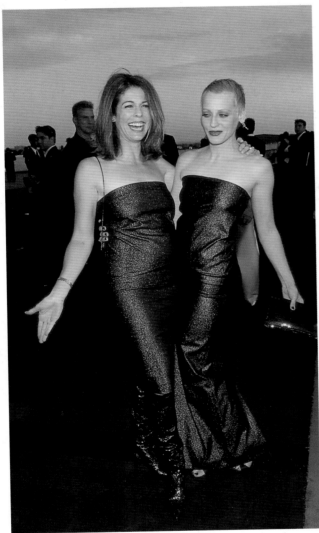

RITA WILSON AND LORI PETTY, *Fitzroy Barrett* 1997

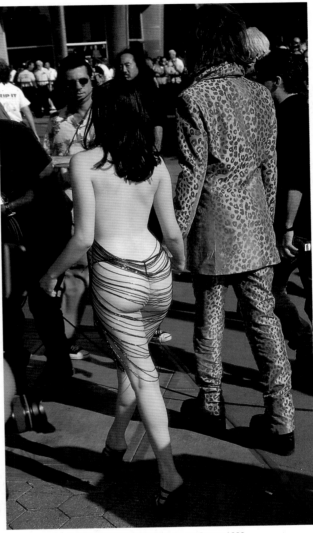

ROSE McGOWAN AND MARILYN MANSON, *Fitzroy Barrett* 1999

RITA WILSON and LORI PETTY show up in the same dress at AIDS PROJECT LOS ANGELES' Gucci Fashion Show. • ROSE McGOWAN doesn't have that problem at the MTV Video Awards at the Universal Amphitheatre.

RITA WILSON und LORI PETTY zeigen sich bei der Gucci-Modeschau AIDS PROJECT LOS ANGELES im selben Outfit. • ROSE McGO-WAN hat dieses Problem bei den MTV Video Awards im Universal Amphitheatre nicht.

RITA WILSON et LORI PETTY ont arboré la même robe au Gucci Fashion Show pour le AIDS PROJECT LOS ANGELES. • ROSE McGOWAN ne s'est pas posé le problème pour assister aux MTV Video Awards à l'Amphithéâtre Universal.

ZSA ZSA GABOR, ILONA MASSEY AND EVA GABOR, *Nate Cutler* 1949

ELIZABETH TAYLOR, MIKE TODD AND EDDIE FISHER, *Nate Cutler* 1956

JOAN CRAWFORD, JUDY GARLAND AND JANE WYMAN, *Nate Cutler* 1951

CHARLES LAUGHTON, EDNA BEST AND RONALD COLMAN, *Nate Cutler* 1952

THE THREE STOOGES, *Nate Cutler* 1950

PEGGY CASTLE AND RONALD REAGAN, *Nate Cutler* 1952

JACK AND FELICIA LEMMON WITH BUSTER KEATON, *Nate Cutler* 1960

BARBARA HELLER, ESTHER WILLIAMS, JEFF CHANDLER, *Nate Cutler* 1959

MATT DAMON, MINNIE DRIVER AND BEN AFFLECK, *Lisa Rose* 1997

MICHELLE PFEIFFER AND DAVID E. KELLEY, *Lisa Rose* 1998

JIM CARREY AND CAMERON DIAZ, *Fitzroy Barrett* 1999

GWYNETH PALTROW AND DAVID SCHWIMMER, *Albert Ferreira* 1996

KATHLEEN TURNER AND RICHARD CHAMBERLAIN, *Michael Ferguson* 1987

ROSALIND RUSSELL, *Peter J. George* 1956

OLIVIA DeHAVILLAND, *Globe Archive* 1971

SHARON STONE, *Lisa Rose* 1998

JEAN CLAUDE VAN DAMME, *Albert Ferreira* 1997

LEONARDO DI CAPRIO, *Henry McGee* 1999

KIM BASINGER, *Michael Ferguson* 1993

WINONA RYDER AND DAVID PRINER, *Michael Ferguson* 1994

BETTE MIDLER, *Ralph Dominguez* 1988

SEAN PENN, *Ralph Dominguez* 1989

As the media attitude toward celebrities moved from friendliness to aggression, so has the attitude of the celebrity toward the press occasionally turned from pleasant to surly.

Die Einstellung der Medien zu den Stars schlug mit der Zeit von Freundlichkeit in Aggression um. Daraufhin änderte sich die Einstellung der Prominenten zu der Presse von Wohlwollen in Verdrießlichkeit.

L'attitude des médias envers les célébrités passant d'amicale à agressive, celle des vedettes envers la presse devint plus revêche qu'agréable.

JOHN CAZALE AND MERYL STREEP, *Irv Steinberg* 1976

BARBRA STREISAND AND PETER BOGDANOVICH, *Nate Cutler* 1972

WARREN BEATTY AND JOAN COLLINS, *Nate Cutler* 1963

DIANA HYLAND AND JOHN TRAVOLTA, *Nate Cutler* 1976

ANJELICA HUSTON AND JACK NICHOLSON, *Nate Cutler* 1979

SPENCER AND LOUISE TRACY AT PERINO'S, *Nate Cutler* 1949

BING AND KATHRYN CROSBY AT THE OSCAR PRESENTATIONS, *Nate Cutler* 1955

CARROLL AND NANCY O'CONNOR AT THE ALGONQUIN IN NEW YORK, *Adam Scull* 1982

JOHN AND ESPERANZA WAYNE AT THE TROCADERO, *Nate Cutler* 1950

JAMES DEAN AND URSULA ANDRESS, *Nate Cutler* 1954

NATALIE WOOD AND WARREN BEATTY, *Nate Cutler* 1961

ERROL FLYNN AND LILI DAMITA, *Nate Cutler* 1943

ERROL FLYNN and LILI DAMITA celebrate their divorce at the Mocambo.　　ERROL FLYNN und LILI DAMITA feiern ihre Scheidung im Macambo.　　ERROL FLYNN et LILI DAMITA fêtent leur divorce au Mocambo.

CHARLES AND PATRICIA BOYER, *Nate Cutler* 1978

JEAN SIMMONS AND STEWART GRANGER, *Nate Cutler* 1952

ROSS AND LYDIA BRAZZI, *Nate Cutler* 1959

JANE WYMAN AND RONALD REAGAN, *Nate Cutler* 1950

JOHN HODIAK AND ANNE BAXTER, *Nate Cutler* 1952

ANGELA LANSBURY AND PETER SHAW, *Nate Cutler* 1952

BARBARA STANWYCK AND ROBERT TAYLOR, *Nate Cutler* 1950

FRANK SINATRA AND AVA GARDNER, *Nate Cutler* 1954

DINAH SHORE AND GEORGE MONTGOMERY, *Nate Cutler* 1950

TYRONE POWER AND LINDA CHRISTIAN, *Nate Cutler* 1950

FERNANDO LAMAS AND ARLENE DAHL, *Nate Cutler* 1954

EVELYN KEYES AND JOHN HUSTON, *Globe Archive* 1949

ELIZABETH TAYLOR AND EDDIE FISHER, *Nate Cutler* 1961

JOAN COLLINS AND ANTHONY NEWLEY, *Nate Cutler* 1969

ESTHER WILLIAMS AND BEN GAGE, *Nate Cuttler* 1958

PAUL NEWMAN AND JOANNE WOODWARD, *Adam Scull* 1985

At the dinner prior to the opening of TOSCA at the New York Metropolitan Opera House, PAUL NEWMAN and JOANNE WOODWARD were tucked away in a banquette when our photographer asked if he could take a photo. Paul nodded and asked, "What would you like us to do?" "How about – just look at each other?"

Beim Abendessen vor der Premiere der TOSCA im New Yorker Metropolitan Opera House waren PAUL NEWMAN und JOANNE WOODWARD gerade beim Bankett, als der Fotograf sie fragte, ob er ein Foto machen könnte. Paul nickte und fragte„„Was sollen wir denn machen?" „Wie wäre es damit, wenn Ihr Euch nur anseht?"

Alors que PAUL NEWMAN et JOANNE WOODWARD s'étaient mis dans un coin du restaurant où ils dînaient avant la première représentation de la TOSCA au New York Metropolitan Opera, notre photographe leur demanda s'il pouvait prendre une photo. Paul acquiesça en demandant : « Que voulez-vous qu'on fasse ? ». « Que diriez-vous… de simplement vous regarder ? »

For Apple Annie.

And for Nate Cutler – the best candid photographer who ever
worked the Hollywood beat. And more – he was a gentleman.

Dustin Hoffman 1989

I am grateful to the following for their assistance in compiling INSIDE HOLLYWOOD: Bernd Obermann, James Lee Wasson,
Joan Crosby, Jesse Morales, Danny Whelan, James Prideaux, Dale Olson, the Ray Whelans Senior and Junior, Mary Beth Whelan,
Robert Conway, Jonathan Green, Henry McGee, Sandy Pollack, Joanna Konefal, Marthe Smith of Time-Life, Angela Safronoff and
Blake Koh of Sotheby's and my talented and tireless designer, Gerald Behrendt. For being there with interest and support,
I thank Merv Kaufman and the community of the Abbey of Regina Laudis.

And for the proverbial service above and beyond, special thanks to Nina Prommer and Patricia DeNeut.

Dieses Buch widme ich Apple Annie.

Und Nate Cutler – dem besten Fotografen, der immer am Ort des Geschehens in Hollywood anzutreffen war.
Und darüber hinaus – war er ein Gentleman.

Ich bedanke mich bei folgenden Personen für ihre Hilfe bei der Zusammenstellung von INSIDE HOLLYWOOD:
Bernd Obermann, James Lee Wasson, Joan Crosby, Jesse Morales, Danny Whelan, James Prideaux, Dale Olson, Ray Whelan Senior
und Junior, Mary Beth, Whelan, Robert Conway, Jonathan Green, Henry McGee, Sandy Pollack, Joanna Konefal, Marthe Smith von
Time-Life, Angela Safronoff und Blake Koh von Sotheby's sowie meinem talentierten und unermüdlichen Designer Gerald Behrendt.
Ich danke Merv Kaufman und der Abtei Regina Laudis für ihr Interesse und ihre Unterstützung.

Außerdem für den sprichwörtlichen Einsatz drumherum, bedanke ich mich besonders bei Nina Prommer und Patricia DeNeut.

Je dédicace ce livre à Apple Annie.

Et à Nate Cutler – le meilleur photographe, qui se trouvait toujours là où il se passait quelque chose à Hollywood.
Par ailleurs, il était un gentleman.

Je remercie les personnes suivantes de m'avoir aidé à préparer INSIDE HOLLYWOOD : Bernd Obermann, James Lee Wasson,
Joan Crosby, Jesse Morales, Danny Whelan, James Prideaux, Dale Olson, Ray Whelan Senior et Junior, Mary Beth Whelan,
Robert Conway, Jonathan Green, Henry McGee, Sandy Pollack, Joanna Konefal, Marthe Smith de Time-Life, Angela Safronoff et
Blake Koh de Sotheby's ainsi que mon talentueux et infatigable graphiste Gerald Behrendt. Je remercie également Merv Kaufman
et la communauté de l'abbaye de Regina Laudis pour leur présence et leur soutien.

Et je remercie particulièrement Nina Prommer et Patricia DeNeut pour leur obligeance proverbiale.

Richard DeNeut

© 2000 Könemann Verlagsgesellschaft mbH
Bonner Str. 126, D–50968 Köln

For page 75 © Succession H. Matisse, VG Bild-Kunst, Bonn 2000

Publishing and art direction: Peter Feierabend
Project manager: Sally Bald
Project assistants: Lucile Bas, Sabine Gerber
Layout and typography: Gerald Behrendt
Translation into German: Nicole Barthel
Translation into French: Arnaud Dupin de Beyssat
Production: Oliver Benecke
Color separation: C.D.N. Pressing, Caselle di Sommacampagna, Italy
Printing and binding: Grafedit, Azzano, Italy

Printed in Italy

ISBN 3-8290-4831-9
10 9 8 7 6 5 4 3 2 1

ALL 8x10 DW BLEED